D1298914

American
Indians
of the
Southwest

970.49 D954 Rev.
Dutton, Bertha Pauline
American Indians of the
 Southwest   16.95

MID-CONTINENT PUBLIC LIBRARY

North Independence Branch
Highway 24 & Spring
Independence, MO 64050

NI

WITHDRAWN
FROM THE RECORDS OF THE
MID-CONTINENT PUBLIC LIBRARY

American Indians of the Southwest

Bertha P. Dutton

UNIVERSITY OF NEW MEXICO PRESS : *Albuquerque*

MID-CONTINENT PUBLIC LIBRARY

3 0000 115413167

MID-CONTINENT PUBLIC LIBRARY

North Independence Branch   NI
Highway 24 & Spring
Independence, MO 64050

Library of Congress Cataloging in Publication Data

Dutton, Bertha Pauline, 1903–
   American Indians of the Southwest.

   Rev., enl. ed. of: Indians of the American Southwest.
1975.
   Bibliography: p.
   Includes index.
   1. Indians of North America—Southwest, New.
   I. Title.
   E78.S7D79 1983   979'.00497   80–52274
   ISBN 0–8263–0703–5
   ISBN 0–8263–0704–3 (pbk.)

© 1983 by the University of New Mexico Press
All rights reserved
Seventh paperbound printing, 1994

This book
is respectfully dedicated
to
THE PEOPLE
the original inhabitants
who revered this land
and its creatures
and strived to save and protect them

Contents

Illustrations

Maps

Foreword

Syntheses of topics in anthropology are assuming greater importance as the literature reaches such proportions that only specialists in an area can be aware of the developing issues. In the Southwestern United States especially, the continuing zeal of the investigators has resulted in a body of data comparable to that of any other similarly defined region of the world. In turn, the wealth of information has served as a stimulus for greater efforts, since sophisticated problems can be formulated and research can be conducted in a laboratory-like atmosphere.

The attractiveness of the Southwest as a field for study has been based on many attributes. A large number of archaeological remains in a good state of preservation exist within regional accessibility. The many dating techniques applicable provide excellent time controls and have revealed a time depth of occupation in excess of eleven thousand years. There are links between the prehistoric populations and the modern descendants, links furnished by historical accounts beginning with the first European contacts in 1539. Today, the conservatism of many Southwestern Indians had led to a retention of a lifeway similar in basic aspects to that known from the historical records.

New hypotheses about the events that transpired throughout the time that the Southwest has been occupied continue to be developed, tested, and evaluated. From the research, a general picture is emerging. While sites of greater antiquity probably exist, the earliest remains now well dated appear to derive from peoples with a specialized hunting-oriented economy. With minor changes, the hunting-oriented pattern continued for at least three thousand years. However, a general trend toward a decrease in the effective moisture brought about changes in the economic base—the fauna—accompanied by an eastward withdrawal of the people. As that took place, there was an expansion of a pattern from the west and south that was based on an economic system oriented toward total environmental exploitation. The combination of varying cultural backgrounds represented, and the cultural flexibility to respond to the local resources in the different parts of the Southwest, resulted in the appearance of distinctive characteristic remains in the various districts.

It appears that the introduction of the idea of horticulture and of a primitive maize by at least 2500 B.C. had little immediate effect upon the tool inventory or the settlement patterns. In the following 2,200 years the basic lifeway remained the same; then, changes began to occur at an increasingly rapid rate. It would require an oversimplification to attempt to isolate the numerous factors involved, given the limitations of space and purpose of this statement. However, there are some circumstances that may have played a prominent role. Perhaps an early and major impetus for change existed in the appearance, and continued flow, of ideas and traits from Mesoamerica beginning about A.D. 300. The succeeding centuries witnessed an increase in horticultural practices, population growth, the formation of large social units, continued responses to local social and natural environments, and spatial identity of groups. The stress period brought about by changes in the environmental factors in the late A.D. 1200s and early 1300s was accompanied by dramatic demographic shifts; and, by the beginning of historic times, many regions that once held large populations were abandoned, only to be reoccupied in some cases by different peoples. Meanwhile, large increases in population occurred in regions such as the Río Grande drainage of northern New Mexico. Other dislocations of people, but to a lesser magnitude, continued throughout historic times as a result of incidents such as the Pueblo Rebellion of 1680, the spread of Navajo and Apache bands into many parts of the Southwest, and the movement of Yuman groups upstream along the Gila River. Thus, the Southwestern Indians today are the products of a long and complicated sequence of events.

Early investigators in the Southwest have viewed the gathering of descriptive data about present peoples and remains from the past as a justifiable goal. Throughout the late years of the nineteenth century and the early decades of the twentieth century, their efforts have resulted in the accumulation of vast amounts of information concerning many of the major archaeological remains and the surviving ethnic groups. Of equal importance is the fact that the basis for the research tools used at present in archaeological and ethnological investigations was established during that interval. The emphasis on cultural-historical reconstructions and descriptive works about present peoples brought about the recent desire to explain the processes of cultural change and stability that have operated over a long period of time. The models exist in the present inheritors of the past Southwestern traditions.

The appreciation of the culture of the Southwestern Indians today becomes a matter of reciprocal information between the archaeological past and the ethnological present. Today, there is a continuum of the processes that have led to regional distinctiveness, have been involved in the responses to local environments, have governed the conditions of culture contact and demographic movements, and have resulted in syncretism of cultural traits. But, the documentary record is far from achieving comprehensiveness.

In the present book, Dr. Bertha P. Dutton has provided a synthesis of the Southwestern Indian cultures today, based on a critical evaluation of the data tempered by long familiarity with the people. On the one hand, Dr. Dutton has provided detailed information to make the work a valuable source for both the specialist seeking information on a problem concerning Southwestern cultures and the nonspecialist who wishes a statement that will provide an integrated view of the peoples. On the other hand, there is in the book the means for the layman to appreciate the efforts of the Southwestern Indians to adjust to alien values and still retain a lifeway handed down for many generations.

ALFRED E. DITTERT, JR.

Preface

The objective is to make this book generally readable for students, teachers, and travelers who desire knowledge, understanding, and authoritative information regarding the Southwestern Indians; it is for those who wish to know the basic features of Indian life, but who do not, perhaps, have the time or specialized training to read extensively of these various peoples.

"The changing Indian" is much more than an often heard phrase these days. The *changing Indian* is a fact, an almost incomprehensible fact. And changes are occurring at such a rapid pace that whatever one writes may well be out of date before the words are printed. Thus it can be said that this publication is already outdated in certain respects. However, the latest census figures available (mainly 1980) afford a pivotal point, and the statements made regarding the Indian groups of the Southwest are comparable as of that time.

Throughout this work obvious changes are mentioned, and some of the more covert ones are noted. Although these may vary in kind and extent with the different Indian peoples, certain features in particular are undergoing alterations and transformations: education, living conditions locally and away from the home bases; labor opportunities, industries, economic exploitation, road works, soil treatments, dams and irrigation; health, welfare and social security; old ceremonies and new religions; and in some instances reappraisal of cultural values, appreciation of old mores, and intensification of self-esteem.

The writer has chosen diverse ways of presenting the information assembled; the material is too exhaustive for a book of this scope to be complete.

Emphasis has been given to certain aspects of one culture, outstanding facets of another; some of the main features of specific organizations have been portrayed, and the complex and far-reaching traits of the Southwestern societies indicated.

No attempt is made to give equal attention to each and every cultural group. Rather, the design is to show that all of the aboriginal peoples fitted themselves to their particular environment and strove to live harmoniously with nature. To all, the land was sacred. An eminent place was given to the mountains and hills, to the water sources and streams; to the plant and animal life; to the sky above and the celestial bodies seen traversing it, and to the clouds that brought summer rains and winter snows. The individual and the group were linked unconsciously with their surroundings, and thanks were rendered for the orderly progression of season after season and for the blessings received.

The very way of life itself gave rise to keen observations, philosophical thinking; myths, poetry, song, and drama, which treat of simple things or the majestic; grief and joy, lullabies and love, with diversity of melody and of text. Each of these merits studies by itself. Some of the poetic contributions of the Indians are included, and of non-Indians who have been inspired by them. Something of the philosophy, drama, and other manifestations of Southwestern Indian life will be found in the following pages.

Not infrequently, secondary sources are cited as well as original works. These may be available to readers who wish to pursue studies regarding the Indians; and many will refer to primary works not included with the references mentioned.

It is hoped that reading this book will aid in an appreciation of the first Americans and of their intelligent responses to the surroundings; of their developments and attainments; and then of their tenacious attempts to continue living according to their philosophy and judicious practices in the face of white colonization, conquest, and alternating procedures of the Europeans whose aggressiveness, missionizing and political ambitions, and material desires were so foreign to the Indian beliefs of proper conduct and rewards.

Simply recording brief facts of history and taking note of modern conditions—some of which evidence accretions and others diminutions—have made the consistency of pattern apparent and impressive: peoples came from Asia, slowly populated the Southwest (as well as all of the New World), adopted ways of life in keeping with the conditions at hand, and developed social organizations thus dictated, recognized the limits of their domain and the rights of others, and achieved their respective cultural patterns. Then came the outsiders.

Every conceivable means has been employed to overcome the indigenous peoples and their mores, to make them conform to the non-Indian's way of life. Through four and a half centuries, these efforts have met with relatively little success. Indians may be made to dress like Anglos, eat their foods, dwell in their types of structures, adopt their means of transportation, follow their

prescribed curriculums and business methods, undergo the missionizing en-
deavors of various sects, practice non-Indian forms of government, and the
like, but no individual or no aggregate body whatsoever can make the Indian
be different from what he *is*. He may change—if he sees fit—or he may mask
his feelings and appear to accept the Anglo customs; but the circumstances
which produced the people who came to be called American Indians and the
centuries that afforded them time to develop a racial identity and distinctive
social patterns made an immutable imprint.

Regardless of outside pressures the Indians have remained Indians, and they
always will. It appears inevitable that their resolute spirit will bear fruit,
now that their numbers are increasing; that their pride in the accomplish-
ments of their people has been intensified; and that they are beginning to
discern their existent capabilities and power, and their rights.

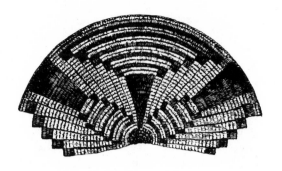

Note to the
New Edition

It always has been difficult if not impossible for non-Indians to gain insight into the lifeways of the American Indians. These are people with old, old Eastern origins (of the Mongoloid race in Asia). One of the better approaches is to learn something of their languages and converse with them directly. Having migrated to the Western Hemisphere from numerous regions in the East, at various periods of time, these people spoke a variety of tongues, from differing linguistic stocks that divided into families of languages with subdivisions and dialects.

The author, being influenced by past civilizations and concerned with those of our day, chose to become informed insofar as possible regarding Indians of the American Southwest. Advanced education under the aegis of learned instructors led to opportunities for witnessing Indian life in some of its actuality. Friendships were established with individual Indians in New Mexico and Arizona, primarily. Professional affiliation with agencies of those states made possible relevant research, traveling to particular areas, and excavations in ancient ruins. Writing and talking publicly about the opportunities which these pursuits afforded made it apparent that important changes are transpiring daily.

With no thought of presenting a complete accounting of the many groups of Indians here discussed, the chief purpose of this book is to share the writer's learnings with the readers. She hopes that they may review their knowledge of past occurrences and, perhaps, acquire certain new information concerning these people with whom we mingle—often casually.

During thousands of years the unoccupied Western Hemisphere gradually became populated by these original immigrants, from the Bering Strait to the southernmost tip of South America and from coast to coast. These first settlers were by no means savages; they were the possessers of ancient knowledge and varying types of social organization. They had long since recognized the universal laws of nature, of the universe; they were aware of basic facts which permitted them to adjust so as to "live in harmony with nature"— with the universe. So doing, they evolved social mechanisms—some simple, some highly complex and sophisticated—which satisfied their choices of environment and preferred manner of living.

Exacting laws and practices were followed. Each band or group lived within recognized territorial limits commensurate with the size and needs of each respective body or community. Within each domain, the Indians hunted and gathered foods required for their sustenance, and some at later periods engaged in horticulture. They obtained materials for necessary attire, and for shelter in keeping with the terrain and climate. With prayers, such things were sought; when attained, thanks were rendered to a deific Being—a Higher Power.

Thus it was when the Spaniards in the early 1500s forced their way into the Americas and contacted the Indians, with intent to conquer and missionize. From then on, conflicts have prevailed. Physical confrontations were obvious, but the major disruptions were covert—cultural and psychological. Indian attainments were shattered; their religious organization torn asunder.

Then, during the years that followed, a mixed aggregate of Europeans and subjects of Great Britain, bent on colonization, arrived on American shores. At first the Indians met all newcomers with friendly gestures. In return for the baubles given them by the immigrants, they presented maize, a variety of foodstuffs, tobacco and other products which the foreigners had not previously known.

With their predominantly Caucasian ancestry and multisource backgrounds, these peoples carried their Western philosophy into the New World. Whether conquerors or colonizers, they failed utterly to comprehend the Indian attitudes which had developed from their Eastern bases.

For the most part, we (all of *us*) who make up the non-Indian or non-Oriental population of this hemisphere did not, or do not, realize or fathom the cataclysm that the newcomers wrought. Hundreds of years afterward, ripples—though mainly undetected or unnoticed—continue to affect our lives. Fundamentally the Oriental perspective and the Occidental point of view are at the root of the conflicts. It is not simply a problem of traditional entities in this hemisphere; it is worldwide. This situation too often restrains understanding, each of the other, and tends to prohibit comingling harmoniously.

Perspectives among scientists, historians, and others are being altered, new mechanisms are being utilized, and methods of deriving data are improving constantly (for example, see *New Perspectives on the Pueblo Indians* and *Handbook of the Indians of North America*—especially Volumes 8, 9, and 10). To increase the value the present edition may offer, many new references are included.

These works cited in the bibliography will further illustrate some of the extent and variety of investigations now available. Accumulated, or accumulating, data are being analyzed. From them, new facts are being established, or they may give rise to further speculations. Where relevant, such added references are suggested as: (*Rel.* Doe 1850:123 ff.)

The descendants of the Asiatics, among them the Indians of the American Southwest (where the majority of the Indians dwell), have experienced widely varying treatment from the political organizations that have governed their destiny since the days of the Conquest. The Indians of the Southwest, within the last decade or two, have made tremendous strides forward. Of course not all groups advance at the same pace; in general, the larger entities seem to go ahead at a faster rate. With some groups, many tribal members hold university degrees, and are proving themselves capable administrators, well aware of the Indian problems. They are alert to opportunities for bettering their situation and are seeking to achieve ways to promote them. Most of the agencies and bodies of local officials have new, modern office and community buildings with up-to-date equipment, current information, and use of scientific techniques. They concentrate on hiring their own people first, and train them when feasible; otherwise they employ other Indians. In so doing they help hundreds; in other situations they aid even more Indian people. They encourage and help finance education, and promote improved housing. With increasing understanding on their part, and the cooperation of their non-Indian associates, the Indians of today are assuming more and more duties of living in the modern world. They appear equally as self-sufficient and adequate for running their own affairs now, as they did in the countless centuries before emigrants from Europe disturbed their lifeways.

These indigenes of the United States, abiding by the fate thrust upon them by Old World peoples, have continued their traditional ways through several hundred years, adjusting to circumstances foreign to them and changing insofar as required (or at least appearing to do so). In fact they live in parallel societies, in "two worlds," as it were. Having already portrayed an incredible history, and attained a seemingly unique position in the world, could these American Indians conceivably reach a stage in evolving their Eastern heritage to a point where it might actually coalesce with Western-acquired wisdom and abilities? Could they achieve a philosophy which would be universally acceptable?

Could the American Indians cause the inhabitants of the world to realize that *all* of the peoples on earth are human beings; that they must quit acts of terrorism and the destruction of each other's ways of life and their attainments? If the American Indians hold on tenaciously to principles followed by "the Old Ones," and carry them over into the times to come, they might possibly prove to be "the right people in the right place at the right time" to bring about universal harmony. Think about it!

BERTHA P. DUTTON
Santa Fe, 1982

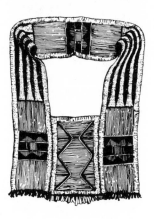

Acknowledgments

This book has been in progress for many years. Much of the basic research began in 1971, and was added to as cultural manifestations became accelerated and deviated from traditional ways ever more markedly. "The Changing Indian" has changed. By 1980 it had become obvious that although the old ways of the Indians were being carried into the present by the more traditional, the more conservative ones, their descendants—who were much more numerous than they—were advancing in channels being followed by the mainstream of citizens of the United States. They had to be portrayed, not only as in the past, but as Indians of the present.

In order to accomplish something toward such a portrayal, I acknowledge that which I owe to my mentors who taught me to *think*. I prize their charting of my pathways. To them and to my Indian friends and associates, those who have guided my research and writing, and have added to the knowledge and understanding of their cultures, I express a great debt. To my professional colleagues and those in related fields of endeavor I offer sincere thanks. A listing of the innumerable friends, institutions and their agencies, scientific organizations providing financial assistance, and others who have been helpful in a variety of ways, would fill pages of this book. My appreciation to them! To Dr. Caroline B. Olin, and Edith (Mrs. William D.) Powell, whose counsel and aid in editing my writing have been limitless, I convey deep gratitude.

For supplying source materials and miscellaneous data, I wish to thank staff members of the Navajo Nation, in their several offices, and the College of Ganado at Ganado, Arizona. The census officials of Arizona and New Mexico Commissions of Indian Affairs, of the Eight Northern Pueblos, the Southern Pueblos, the Jicarilla and Mescalero Apache groups, and the Zuñi Pueblo Council, have been most helpful in providing desired statistics from the 1980 census.

To the late Fermor S. Church, a co-author of certain of my writings, I offer homage. His extensive knowledge of the greater Southwest, gained in part through his engineering experience (degree therein from Harvard University), and his understanding of the southwestern peoples were invaluable. Our discussions of matters about which I was writing and the manner of presenting them added considerably to their significance. Some of the maps in this book were made from his original drawings.

As author of *American Indians of the Southwest*, I have drawn on many sources and have quoted material extensively. Permission to quote direct statements was sought, and outstanding cooperation received. Sincere appreciation is expressed to the following authors and publishers:

American Anthropologist, American Anthropological Association, Washington, D.C.
American Antiquity, Society for American Archaeology, Washington, D.C.
American Folklore Society, New York
Arizona Highways, Phoenix
The Arizona Republic, Phoenix
The Caxton Printers, Caldwell, Idaho
Columbia University Press, New York (through a daughter of William Whitman III, Mrs. Philip T. Cate, Santa Fe)
Diné Baa-Hane, Fort Defiance, Arizona
The Eight Northern Pueblos
Frontier Heritage Press, San Diego, California
Indian Tribal Series, Phoenix
Institute of American Indian Arts, Santa Fe
Museum of the American Indian, Heye Foundation, New York
Museum of New Mexico, Santa Fe
Museum of Northern Arizona, Flagstaff
The National Park Service
The New York Times
The Progressive, Madison, Wisconsin
Southwest Parks and Monuments Association, Globe, Arizona
Southwest Printers, Yuma, Arizona
Time: The Weekly Newsmagazine, New York
The University of Arizona (Department of Anthropology), Tucson
The University of Arizona (office for business affairs and treasurer), Tucson
The University of Chicago Press, Chicago
The University of New Mexico Press, Albuquerque
University of Oklahoma Press, Norman
University of Washington Press, Seattle

Uintah and Ouray Agency (office of the superintendent), Fort Duchesne, Utah
Ute Mountain Agency (office of the superintendent), Towaoc, Colorado
Robert W. Young and *The Gallup Independent*, Gallup, New Mexico

Specific citations are given with the references; therefore the full data appear in the bibliography. Photo credits accompany the specific illustrations. Most of the latter were prepared without charge for inclusion in this book.

Linguistic Notes

In pronouncing Indian and Spanish words, *a* is soft as in *father, e* as in *grey, i* as in *machine, o* as in *whole.* There are no silent vowels. The consonant *h* is silent; *ch* is sounded as in *church; j* is like *h* in *hay.* The first *l* of *ll* is lightly sounded and the second takes a *y* sound: therefore, *Jicarilla* is pronounced *Heek-ah-REEL-yah.*

As Professor George L. Trager, a recognized linguist who has worked on southwestern languages for many years, notes, "It is customary to refer to a people by the same form for singular and plural (as 'the Hopi,' 'a Hopi,' etc.)."

As for the spelling of the term Navajo, in this edition we use the Spanish *j,* a form favored by the federal government and by the Navajo Nation.

Maps

Major Indian Reservations of the Southwest

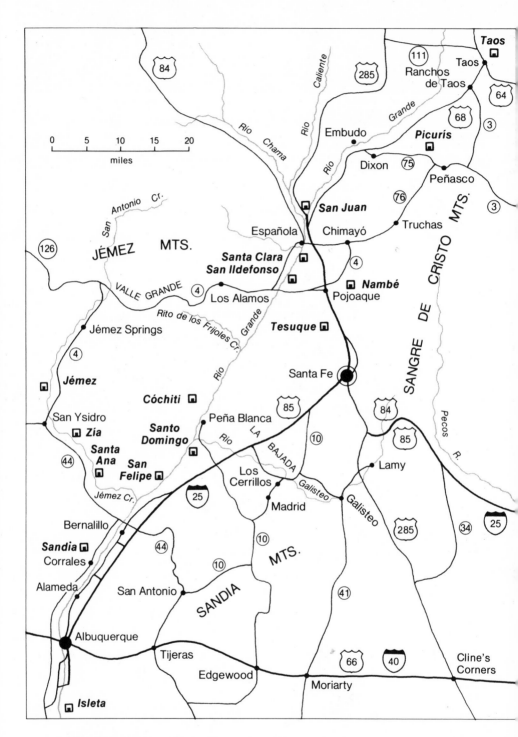

Northern Rio Grande Pueblos, New Mexico

Southern Utes and Colorado River Indians

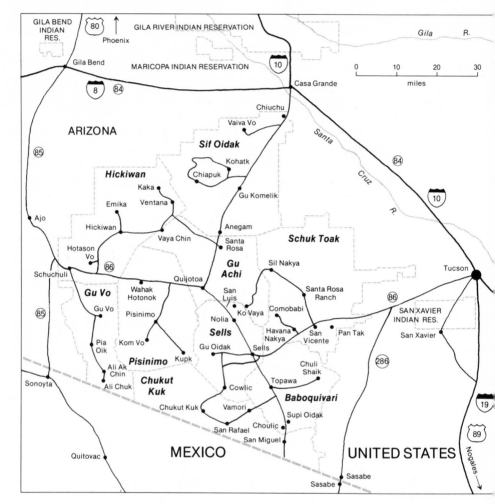

The Papago Indian Reservation, Southern Arizona

*American
Indians
of the
Southwest*

1
Who and Where

Physical Aspects of the American Indians

Those who study human beings from the point of view of their physical characteristics—the physical anthropologists, or somatologists (from *somato,* meaning body)—have come to recognize that the basic characteristics of the so-called American Indians show relatively little diversity. Their closest clear-cut resemblances are with the peoples of Mongoloid stock, the peoples of Asia. In pigmentation both are between the white, or Caucasoid, and the black, or Negroid races; they have straight, coarse, dark head hair, and sparse body hair; cheekbones agree in size and projection, as do the jutting jaws and face breadth. Both American Indians and Mongoloids have shovel-shaped incisor teeth and, at birth, display the Mongoloid spot—a blue spot above the rump, which fades within a short time; many also have the Mongoloid, or epicanthic, fold of the inner part of the upper eyelid. The eye color is dark brown.

Aside from these strikingly similar characteristics, the Indians display a number of more or less minor differences. Some are tall, others short, some are stocky and others thin; some have long heads, while the heads of others are round; lips may be thick or thin; and noses may be high and aquiline or low and concave. Such physical divergences are amply attested by variations among geographical and cultural areas, in both prehistoric and modern eras. "Seemingly . . . the Indian possesses a number of relatively fixed characteristics which are clearly Mongoloid and a number which are so variable in time and space that students often look to sources in other great racial divisions for an explanation . . ." while other students "express the opinion that the Mongoloid stock of Asia is sufficiently variable in itself to account for most of the diversity among American Indians" (Gabel 1949:9–10; Agogino and Kuntz 1971:24).

Starting thousands of years ago, peoples with these characteristics began migrating from Asia by one way or another. Many came into the American continent by way of the Bering Strait and worked their way southward from time to time, in small bands—some along the Pacific coast, others through intermountain corridors, and still others along the eastern slopes of the Rocky Mountains. Although they have lived in the Western Hemisphere for centuries and are inherently part of this land of mountains, forests, mesas, canyons, semiarid stretches, and deserts, their remote Asiatic ancestry must be held in mind.

The Land and the Aboriginal Inhabitants

The *Southwest* is an area with no specific limits or definite boundary, but for the purposes of culture studies, ancient and modern, it here includes all of New Mexico and Arizona, the southwest corner of Colorado, southern Utah, southwestern Nevada, and the California border of the Colorado River. The *Greater Southwest* adds the southern California Indians to the Pacific coast, western Texas, and dips down into northern Mexico on occasion (Strong 1927:1–5).

The first known inhabitants of the Greater Southwest are commonly designated as *Paleo-Indians,* the ancient ones who dwelt here from unknown millenia to around 6,000 B.C. (The earliest real date is 11,500 B.P., that is, before the present). The Paleo-Indians were highly specialized in their economy; as the environment changed and big game moved eastward, they withdrew eastward also as *Clovis, Folsom,* and other cultural groups. The big game Paleo-Indian tradition existed in the plains area until historical times.

Those who occupied the Greater Southwest from about 6,000 B.C. until approximately two thousand years ago are recognized as being of an archaic stage of culture, the *Desert Archaic,* or simply *Archaic* culture (6,000 B.C.– A.D. 1). Peoples from the western basins, the California desert regions, and northern Mexico moved into unpopulated areas of the Southwest as the big game hunters withdrew. On this culture horizon, which became the basis of modern populations, *maíz,* or "Indian corn," was received through northern Mexico (Galinat et al. 1970). This food, introduced probably between 2,500 and 3,000 B.C., made little difference in the habits or tools of the people for over two thousand years, however. It did not supply as much food as did hunting and gathering and it was only when it became a symbol that it assumed importance (Dittert 1958).

From A.D. 1–900 or 1,000 A.D., a period called the *Formative* becomes evident (Berman 1979). This lasts until the *Pueblo* period is recognized, bringing us up to Historical times. The modern Pueblo Indians in the Southwest are descendants of various prehistoric peoples who emerged from the Archaic and Formative inhabitants.

It is currently understood that four cultural entities can be identified for the Greater Southwest. A southern tradition has been named *Cochise* from its discovery in southeastern Arizona—*Cochise-Mogollon* (Sayles and Antevs 1941; Wheat 1955; Martin 1959 and 1979). This tradition plays an important role in Arizona and New Mexico especially. Best known is a northern tradition which entered the Southwest from the Great Basin-Intermontane region. This has been named the *Oshara*-Anasazi, which exhibits a cultural complex with traits distinct from those of the Southern aggregate (Irwin-Williams 1973, 1979:35–37).

From the vicinity of Phoenix, Arizona, southwestward is an extensive region wherein the third highly significant culture was determined, the *Hohokam* (Gummerman and Haury 1979). Following the Anasazi in its identification, the Hohokam excavations have revealed many manifestations of southern cultural ties. Lastly, evidence of a pottery-making people who developed a culture distinct from their contemporary prehistoric neighbors, the Anasazi, Hohokam, and Mogollon is becoming better understood. Being less spectacular, it is slower in becoming identifiable and its significance recognized. In a vast area between the Pacific coastal ranges and the Mogollon rim of Arizona, there dwelt a "rock-oriented" people, the *Hakataya* (Schroeder 1975, 1979b). An extensive trade relationship with the surrounding neighbors has been ascertained. From items exchanged between all of them, and their own ingenuity, it is indicated that the Hakatayan group evolved a liveable cultural pattern prior to the mid–1100s. They persisted into historical days.

During their years of wandering from the Old World to the New, and as they moved into chosen locations, it was necessary for the ancients to be highly observant of elemental and environmental features. Each day man had to derive his existence from the plant and animal world about him, and so these things were of the utmost significance. Thus it was that the Indian geared his life to the scene around him. The result was a culture that integrated the natural phenomena and biota of his world with mankind. Among all factors, universal interplay was ever present; man dwelt in a world of mysticism and symbolism.

A formative type of religion prevailed over wide expanses. It may be detected in eras when the Desert Culture peoples occupied the lands from coastal southern California across New Mexico and into Texas, from southwestern Nevada, southern Utah and Colorado, and over northern Mexico. All, or nearly all, of the Indians who inhabited these regions eventually became horticulturists. Horticulture prescribes a semisedentary mode of life, and then a sedentary existence. It requires specific implements and procedures for handling them, and these provide the foundation for rites and ceremonies which grow out of continuing cycles of behavior and growth.

The people were held together by simple relationships based on family organization exclusively; and it is deduced that this was by recognition of the bilateral family, wherein both father and mother influenced controls. Two or more families tended to live in proximity to one another, and they habitually wintered together. Children of unrelated families married one another. The family groups had leaders, headmen who were wise and honored.

Area Defined

The *Four Corners Region* is that area radiating from the common boundary point shared by the states of Colorado, Utah, Arizona, and New Mexico, the *Four Corners*—the only place in the nation where four states adjoin one another. In the nearer reaches four groups of Indians dwell. Based on the languages spoken, including a variety of dialects, they are designated as *Ute, Jicarilla Apache, Navajo,* and *Pueblo* Indians. Somewhat farther distant from the Four Corners are other Indian peoples known as the *Mescalero Apache* of south-central New Mexico and other Apache assemblages in southeastern Arizona, commonly called the Western Apaches; Pimans (*Pima* and *Papago*) and the Cahitan *Yaqui* in south-central Arizona; Yumans, representing upland and river divisions (*Havasupai, Hualapai,* and *Yavapai; Cocopah, Maricopa, Mohave,* and *Yuma,* respectively), in the central and western parts of that state; and the Ute-related *Paiute* and *Chemehuevi* who dwell in southern and southwestern Utah and along the western border of Arizona, respectively.

Development of Socio-Religious Patterns

The original inhabitants of this vast new land could not *see* their deity. Consequently, an intermediary, a *seeable* personage to intervene between deity and mankind, had to be conjured, and so the headman, or "chief," who played more the part of a father and spiritual guide than actual ruler, assumed that role. With some peoples the office became that of priest.

It would seem that a universal being was generally recognized—a great, sacred omnipotence, one deity yet held as expressing male and female unification or differing manifestations. In general, the omnipotent was believed to occupy a sphere high above that of man—just as most earthly beings view their relationship with deity. Thus, looking aloft, early peoples of the Greater Southwest—as in most of America—beheld the sun; it seemed to appear in the east with each morning's dawn, move in an orderly way across the heavens, and disappear from sight in the west. The fact that one could not look directly into the sun, because of its shining brilliance, added to its celestial mystery.

Among horticultural peoples, the chief or a priest directed the formalities that domestication demands; he introduced calendrical observances which, by the very nature of things, gave eminence to the sun. The earth, though equally important, is here, always at hand; the Indian lives *in* it or *on* it, and *from* it. But the sun comes and goes and alters its pathway observably from north to south, and then reverses its movement; it is something with which man must reckon. The moon divides the year into time periods and is thus a factor to be considered, almost as the earth which gives sustenance.

Such simple origins gave rise to priesthoods among the sedentary peoples, and to cults and attendant procedures, formalization, and all that follows. To make religion understandable to the people, a priest assumed the part of a sort of director-general of all deific manifestations. Just as a biologic family develops, the priesthood accommodated a growing ceremonial organization. The sun, with most peoples, came to be envisioned as the Sun Father of those dwelling on the earth, over which he spread his light and warmth. This led to a recognition of the complementary worldly sphere as the Earth Mother.

In the nature of a parable, a miraculous union of Sun Father and Earth Mother was portrayed as bringing forth offspring. This was primarily in the guise of twin boys commonly visible as the morning and evening stars. These celestial ones function as twin war gods, an Elder Brother and a Younger Brother, whose earthly representatives are war priests, chiefs, or war captains. On occasion the twain coalesce into one being; again they appear as a boy and a girl. As ceremonialism grew, the deific family was enlarged, and an increasing body or priesthood provided officials to represent the supernatural ones, each with specific duties and positions.

With the recitation of folk history, which is a vital part of all ceremonials, different manifestations of personages occur, resulting in multiplicity of characters. This led to the erroneous assumption by some students or researchers that the Indians had many gods, even idols, whereas these personages are actually visual aids in bringing knowledge and understanding of a supreme deity into the all-encompassing life of the people. They serve in maintaining discipline and in teaching the complex interrelationships of family and societal groups. The deific ones are portrayed bestowing their powers on earthly ones—the priests and their assistants, or whatever their designations.

According to the priestly teachings of the sedentary Indians, the first commandment of the omnipotent commonly was to build "a temple" in which he might be revered and given homage. Thus the family groups erected a ceremonial chamber, which was entered originally through a hatchway in the roof—so arranged as to permit light from the sun to shine within.

From the original bilateral family, increasing population brought lineages, or unilateral kinship groups, into being, wherein all members of a group were united through descent from a common ancestor. Among the majority of early dwellers in the Greater Southwest, this ancestor was recognized in the paternal line. With family and social growth, dichotomy commonly occurred, that is, the division of a group into two segments, which are usually designated as *moieties* (*rel.* Dozier 1970a:208). Membership in a moiety also followed the patrilineal line. With these developments, formation of small villages took place, and houseowning was a male prerogative. The people came to be controlled by hierarchal priesthoods, in which each official was subordinate to the one above him. The ceremonial chamber was built in the center of a village, contiguous to the dwelling of the priest.

In addition to the ceremonial house and the priest in charge, a third item was of utmost significance—the ark, as it were—a sacred bundle or fetish. Actually, the wrapping, or mat, of the fetish bundle is said to be its most important feature. Contents of the bundle are those things which the priest considers efficacious in the performance of his rites. They may include quartz crystals which reflect and divert the rays of the sun, turtle shell rattles and seashells felt to be potent in bringing rain, eagle feathers as representative of the messengers that carry man's word to his deity above, cone-shaped pipes the smoke of which is considered as cloud producing, rock concretions, and other peculiarly shaped objects bestowed with magical attributes, and so on.

The fetish bundle is always in the care of the priest or an equivalent officer, and is regarded as the "heart of the house." Its possession is passed on to a successor in the paternal line. Such paraphernalia, the ceremonies, and the sacred chamber or a holy place are considered as being owned by societies but controlled by their respective priests, or by the head religious dignitary. According to Indian philosophy, the fetish has been with them since the time of their coming forth onto this earth—from the Place of Emergence, which is known by its proper term in each linguistic group.

Although nomadic and seminomadic peoples have been influenced by those who followed sedentary patterns of life, they tend to have more flexible systems of religion, with officers other than priests and without a structure in which their practices are centered.

DIRECTION (Papago)

I was directed by my grandfather
To the East,
   so I might have the power of the bear;
To the South,
   so I might have the courage of the eagle;
To the West,
   so I might have the wisdom of the owl;
To the North,
   so I might have the craftiness of the fox;
To the Earth,
   so I might receive her fruit;
To the Sky,
   so I might lead a life of innocence.

By Alonzo Lopez

From *The Writers' Reader,* 1962–1966.
Institute of American Indian Arts,
Santa Fe, N.M.

2
The Pueblo Peoples

Brief History

As the Spanish explorers during the sixteenth century pushed northward from Mexico, following ancient trails across desert wastes, over high mountain ranges and along flowing streams, the majority of indigenous peoples whom they encountered were those who had developed a sedentary life. When the Spaniards saw Indians living in compact, many-chambered, flat-roofed structures built around plazas, or squares, and from one to several stories in height with entering passageways, they were reminded of the villages of their homeland, hence they called each settlement a *pueblo,* and the "village dwellers" en masse were called "Pueblo Indians"—as opposed to nomadic or seminomadic peoples, or those on *rancherias.*

Through the centuries these Indians had developed cultures based on hunting and gathering, to which horticulture was added in time. Stored food supplies provided for periods when products were not growing, and thus made it unnecessary for social units to move in search of food. With some 25 percent of their yearly food supply provided by horticulture, they were able to maintain increasingly larger groups and to attain a complex society. There became an orderly way of life, with attention given to pertinent arts and crafts. Each pueblo or ranchería was established in relation to permanent springs or running water, and also to a close area having a considerable range of elevational gradients, within a short horizontal distance which offered the maximum gathering potential. Near the villages were fertile gardens and fields where men and women shared their labors.

With the Spanish government taking formal possession of the Southwestern regions, Spanish saint names were given to the settlements. The Pueblo country was divided into districts and a Catholic priest was assigned to each. The Indians were required to take oaths of obedience and pay homage to the Catholic church and the Spanish crown.

At the pueblo of *Oke-oweenye* the Spaniards established the first capital of New Mexico in 1598, which they called *San Juan de Los Caballeros*. The next year, the Indian site of *Yunque-Yungue* on the west bank of the Río Grande, directly across from the initial settlement, was chosen for the Spanish location, and this they called *San Gabriel*. It served as the capital until 1610, when the seat of government was moved to an old pueblo site which had been occupied centuries before, *La Villa Real de Santa Fe,* along the Río Santa Fe.

Becoming antagonistic toward the Spaniards who encroached upon their lands and forcibly altered their ways of life, the Pueblo peoples finally united in revolt and, in 1680, drove the invaders from New Mexico. The name "New Mexico" as now applied appears to have been used for the northern province from 1582; the territory thus designated reached to the Pacific Ocean (Bloom 1940:106; *Carta Contenante . . . la Florida*). Twelve years of freedom from oppression were enjoyed until the Spaniards returned in 1692, under General Don Diego de Vargas and reconquered the northland.

Spanish rule continued until the Mexican Revolution of 1821, after which the Indians were declared citizens on equal basis with non-Indians. Life under Mexican authority, otherwise, was little changed for the Pueblos. Then the war between the United States of America and Mexico was fought, ending with the Treaty of Guadalupe Hidalgo which was signed in 1848. Mexico gave up all claim to territory east of the Río Grande and ceded New Mexico and upper California to the United States in return for payment of fifteen million dollars and other stipulations. Articles of the treaty provided for recognition and protection by the United States of Indian rights previously established under Spanish and Mexican rule.

Thereafter, title to Pueblo lands and those of the other Indian peoples were in question for decades. Settlers from the East intruded upon Indian holdings in increasing numbers. In 1849 the Bureau of Indian Affairs (which had been created in the War Department in 1824) was placed under the newly established U.S. Department of the Interior, and the first Indian agent in New Mexico Territory was appointed.

According to a treaty signed on 30 December 1853—the Gadsden Purchase—the United States paid Mexico ten million dollars for all of the territory along the present southern boundary of this country, from the Río Grande to the Colorado River. Then, on 1 August 1861, all of New Mexico south of the 34th parallel was organized as the Territory of Arizona, with the boundary later to be changed as it is today. Six months before, formation of the

Territory of Colorado reduced New Mexico in size, its northeastern section being included in Colorado.

Few of the pueblos could produce Spanish documents pertaining to their grants. The surveyor general of the federal government took Indian testimonials in 1856 as to the holdings of some of the pueblos. Certain surveys were made in 1858, and a greater number the following year; these were confirmed by the Supreme Court and patents were issued to most of the pueblos in 1864, while others were not forthcoming until years later. About a half-dozen pueblos have less land today than they had according to the original patents, some have about the same, and the majority have received additional acres through various governmental actions and purchases.

New Mexico was admitted to the Union as a state in January of 1912. Twelve years later, Congress declared all Indians born in the United States to be citizens. However, the constitution of New Mexico excluded "Indians not taxed" from the franchise. Not until 1948 was legislative action taken which made Indians citizens of the state as well as of the nation, and thus entitled to vote. Arizona became a state of the Union approximately a month later than New Mexico; it had similar laws regarding the Indian residents, and took corresponding legislative action to give them the franchise at the same time as did New Mexico.

The "Privileged People" Myth

Indians are not the privileged citizens that many people erroneously believe them to be. One fact widely misunderstood pertains to the relationship between Indians and the federal government. Let it be recorded here that:

The Federal Government makes no payments to a person merely because he is an Indian. Payments made to a person of Indian blood may represent income from his property collected for him by an agent of the United States. Other payments may result from compensation for losses incurred when lands are required in connection with Federal projects. Payments may represent the Indian's pro rata share of property belonging to the tribe of which he is a member. In each instance, money available for payments belongs either to the tribe or an individual and is held in trust by the U.S. Government. Therefore, Government checks are issued in making payments to individuals and to tribes. (Papago Indian Agency 1970:4)

Cultural Characteristics

The Pueblos follow a communal pattern. Society is concerned with the group as a whole. Until recent times an individual got no recognition for his personal achievements; no ancient vessel or other work of art ever bore the name of its maker.

Living in this great uncrowded region, with day following night in orderly fashion, season after season, and where cataclysmic events were exceedingly rare, the Indian had two wonderful culture-forming assets—space and time;

space so that he could see things clearly, and time so that he could think and consider all matters carefully. The Indian had no system of writing; he could not jot down notes, and thus he had to remember everything and pass his knowledge on orally. Time and space and memory resulted in sound philosophy, which is reflected in all phases of the cultures that were developed in this area. No need to hurry or to make quick decisions. When some innovation occurred, it was thoroughly examined and discussed, and then rejected or accepted according to the unanimous decision of the group concerned. Changes, if made, were made slowly and for logical reasons.

The Indian, particularly the Pueblo, is restrained and affable, exceedingly polite. He wants to give you, or at least appear to give you, what you want. If one sees an Indian woman with a piece of pottery or a basket, or something else, and asks: "Did you make it?" the answer is likely to be yes, because she senses that is the answer desired. Should one question: "Who made that vessel?" the answer might be: "my mother," or "my daughter," or "I did."

It should always be remembered that any Indian group, or even an Indian family, is now in a transitional stage. They are torn between their own ancient standards and those that are being urged or thrust upon them by those of non-Indian culture.

Pueblo children have an active part in the social organization, in the family from the time of birth. A child sees and is a part of everything that goes on at home or in the plaza. From this constant participation, the manners of his people are learned early and completely. The association of a young child with those a few years older, "brings the individual at a very early age into the youth-controlled, socially accepted milieu of his own generation" (*see* Hawley and Senter 1946:142–143). Pueblo Indians think that a baby should be kept happy, for "when it grows up it will have many troubles." If a baby cries, it is given attention—picked up and entertained—not punished. If a baby cries for food, it is fed. When children are scolded, it is done quietly with low, controlled voice. Whipping is a form of punishment used when other measures have failed, but it is done in the privacy of the family only (excepting some ceremonial occasions).

Indian children are given and assume responsibilities at an early age; gradually they learn and participate in all phases of life which they will follow as adults. The boys are miniatures of their fathers, the girls of their mothers. Not until they take on more and more of the non-Indian cultures are the Indians confronted with problems of so-called juvenile delinquency.

Sexual standards among the Indians are different from ours, and may well be more realistic than those which we have long endeavored to maintain. Living in close association with other members of a family, children grow up knowing as much about sex matters as any other aspect of their culture. Premarital sexual experiments are common. They are not secret, but usually take place in the common sleeping room of parents and brothers and sisters. Pueblo adolescents usually were given sexual instructions by certain elders, so that girls and young boys suffered few of the stresses and strains of clandestine affairs to which non-Indian youth are subjected.

Traditionally, if a child is born out of wedlock, no stigma is attached to that child. The girl's parents usually raise it, and it takes a normal place in society. It is clear that Indian youth have not suffered the physiological disturbances and often psychotic results that befall the youngsters of our society, one that has often failed to recognize adolescence as a distinct period when one is neither child nor adult.

The Pueblo Indians practice monogamy, whether they be married according to Indian customs or the ever-increasing civil and church ceremonies. Postmarital sexual infidelity is disapproved but is not uncommon. An erring wife, if caught, is usually punished by her husband, though a pueblo official may be sought for this purpose. Extramarital sexual relations are not uncommon either. Divorce, as well as marriage, is characteristically a family affair with the Indians. Among the Río Grande Pueblos divorce appears relatively rare; among the Zuñi it is more common.

Until modern patterns of life resulted in unbalancing the Indian economy and cultural mores and particularly in recent years of drought, wartime hardships, expanding economic, health and welfare programs, no Indian group failed to provide for its own orphans, old people, the ill and handicapped; and the group enforced punishments for infractions of its laws.

Most of the Pueblos, though they do not like death any more than we do, accept it for what it is, the end of man's material existence. It is the spirit which counts, and the spirit continues. A body is ceremonially prepared after death, dressed in traditional attire, and supplied with food, drink, and items of industry for use in the next world. Burial occurs as soon after death as possible, usually before nightfall of the same day as cessation of life. In its grave or cranny in the rocks, the body is watched for four nights, to keep away prowling dogs, coyotes, or other molesters. By then, the spirit, it is believed, has reached the spirit world, and what happens to the earthly remains is of naught. Body orientation in burial is important among some Indians, while others appear to disregard the position of the corpse.

The Pueblos, like all other Indians, have taboos, avoidance practices, and other customs that they hold significant (see Bulow 1972). Their reluctance to being photographed is not just a whim; it is a social matter with deep roots, and is related to sympathetic, or imitative, magic. If one has your likeness, he may exercise controls over you—usually to your detriment.

Gossip, criticism, and ridicule are major means of social control among the Indians. These factors tend to keep an individual from deviating from the norm of his culture. Indians are keenly sensitive to being singled out for public disapproval, laughter, or ostracism. They refrain from wrongdoing on the basis of such censure. Even where Christian training has spread to the Indians, the concept of postmortem reward or punishment has made little impression. Rather, they expect imminent and observable justice. For instance, if one does wrong, illness may befall his village or family group, a disastrous flood may destroy his property and crops, or severe drought may lay waste his season's efforts. It is much safer to observe the rules.

Indians feel that silence is part of the concentration that compels results. Speech, therefore, is restricted or taboo in certain ritual circumstances. The Pueblos have a profound conviction about the reasonableness of secretiveness. As long as one remains silent "his power is still in him" (Parsons 1939–1:433).

Even unto the present, some Indians regard long hair as "the badge of an Indian." It is considered by a man a necessary concomitant of his ceremonial life. As one Indian man put it: "When they cut [my hair], my heart hurt." Some were reluctant to have their hair cut, fearing they might be mistaken for Spanish Americans, to whom they consider themselves superior. One of the most severe blows to many an Indian's status came when the armed services insisted on cutting the hair of adult Indian men. According to their mores, the kerchief is acceptable for Indian men to wear; hats are considered improper. Blanket wearing, like long hair, is another symbol of status. Moccasins are proper, whereas shoes are not. But with the demands of today we see all these less and less regarded. Conflicts result as acculturation progresses.

General Appearance

Understandably, the Pueblo Indians are not a homogeneous group of people. They reflect differing physical strains and admixtures. In general, they hold an intermediate position, not being of greatest stature or the smallest. They differ in head form and other respects, and fall close to the Indian mean. In the New Mexico pueblos, where the principal foodstuffs were cereals, a tendency to stockiness is observable, especially among the women whose lives center in the household. The Hopi (HOH-pee), who are the pueblo dwellers of Arizona, commonly are of small stature, due in part doubtless to their rigorous environment and basically strenuous life.

Usually the Pueblo peoples wear attire appropriate for homekeeping and farmer-stockmen activities. On festive occasions they have special clothing, either traditional or modern.

Location and Population

Pueblo Indians live in metropolitan centers like Albuquerque, Santa Fe, Taos and Gallup as well as in their pueblos along the Rio Grande and in Zuñi, southwest of Gallup. One also may see Pueblo men, women, and children displaying their handicrafts in such public places as bus stations, airports, restaurants, hotels or motels, or museums; or they may have *ramadas*—temporary shelters—set up along the highways. In Arizona, the Hopi are much in evidence in the towns of Holbrook, Winslow, and Flagstaff.

As a matter of convenience, the pueblo dwellers of the Río Grande drainage are commonly spoken of as the Eastern Pueblos, while those of Zuñi and the Hopi villages are called the Western Pueblos. On occasion, Acoma and Laguna are included with the western peoples.

Traces of the Pueblo past—scattered fragments of pottery, rock chips and worked stones, mounds of earth and rock, and crumbling walls that mark former villages—may be found on every hand. Great and small deserted dwellings and ceremonial structures falling into ruin, silent and impressive, also abound. One never escapes the consciousness of the centuries that these people have lived a vivid and constructive life upon this land.

The Pueblo Indians do not constitute a tribe as that word is understood by anthropologists and related researchers. Usually with them the term means something of this nature: "A tribe is a social group of a simple kind, the members of which speak a common dialect, have a single government, and act together for common purposes such as warfare" (or *see* Hoebel 1958:661). A characteristic feature of a tribe is that it is a closed society—a group of individuals who have adjusted their interests sufficiently to cooperate in satisfying their various needs (Eggan 1950:4). Its laws and morals apply to its members and not to outsiders. Each Pueblo group functions as an entity, each an independent lot of farming, house-building people, alike in some features and dissimilar in others.

New Mexico's Pueblo Indians in 1980 totaled approximately 33,000. The number is slowly but consistently growing. At the same time, the Hopi numbered a few more than 8,250. *(See* pages 255–57 for population of the pueblos and reservations.)

Languages

The Pueblos, and all other Indians, may best be considered with a view to the languages they speak. (Linguists for the most part follow the J. W. Powell classification of Indian languages. Here, the author adheres to this system of grouping Southwestern languages. [*See* Powell 1891:3–142 and Swadish 1967]) For instance, the people of Taos (rhymes with *house*), Picurís (pee-kuhr-EES), Sandía (Sahn-DEE-ah), and Isleta (ees-LAY-tah) speak dialects of the *Tiwa* (TEE-wah) language.

On the reservations of San Juan (sahn HUAhn), Santa Clara (SAHN-ta KLAH-rah), San Ildefonso (sahn eel-day-FOHN-so), Pojoaque (poh-HWA-kay), Nambé (nahm-BAY), and Tesuque (tay-SOO-kay), the *Tewa* (TAY-wah) language is spoken. Tewa is also the language used at Hano in the Hopi country of northeastern Arizona, where some Pueblo Indians from the Río Grande valley migrated in about 1700. Jémez (HAY-mez) is the only pueblo in which the *Towa* (TOH-wah) language is now used. Tiwa, Tewa, and Towa are related tongues that derive from a common linguistic family, the Tanoan, the parent stock being known as Azteco-Tanoan.

The language of Zuñi, the westernmost pueblo in New Mexico, belongs to the Zunian family, which appears to derive from the Penutian stock. If true, Zunian and Tanoan may be very distantly related.

Keres (KAY-rays) is spoken with dialectic differences in the other pueblos of New Mexico—in Cóchiti (KOH-chee-tee), Santo Domingo (SAHN-toh doh-MEEN-go), and San Felipe (sahn fay-LEE-pay) along the banks of the Río Grande; in Santa Ana (sahn-TAHN-ah) and Zía (Tsee-ah) on the Río Jémez; and in the Laguna (lah-GOO-nah) and Acoma (AH-koh-mah) villages, roughly fifty miles west of Albuquerque. In general, linguists feel that Keres is quite distinct from any of the more inclusive language families of North America. Evidence indicates that the Keresans have been in the Southwest for a long, long time—as they say, "since time immemorial."

Excluding those who live in the pueblo of Hano, the Hopi Indians speak a single language, with several dialects, grouped under the Uto-Aztecan family tree, of which nine branches have been identified as stemming from a Proto-Uto-Aztecan parent language spoken about five thousand years ago (Miller and Booth 1972; *rel.* Hale and Harris 1979: 170 ff.; Dozier 1954:302).

Social Organization

Viewing the map of the northern Río Grande Pueblos (New Mexico) on page xxx, it is seen that loose geographic unity exists among the various linguistic groups. The northern Tiwa villages seem far removed from those of their kindred in Sandía and Isleta; considerable distance separated the eastern Keres from those of the western pueblos, Laguna and Acoma, and the dwellers in Hopiland are still further distant. What then makes these Indians seem to be one people and gives them the appearance of being a cultural unit? The answer undoubtedly is found in their attitude toward life as a whole, their religion in fact.

With the Southwestern Indians in general, and with the Pueblos in particular, religion transcends and permeates all else. It is the very core of their existence, day by day. All aspects of Pueblo life—the arts, crafts, industries, social structure, and religion—are inextricably interwoven, thoroughly integrated. From the simple tenet that *man must so live as to be in harmony with nature* ("nature's basic rhythm"), the Pueblo Indians developed a rich dramatic art—poetry, legendry, song, and dance; by these means religion is given outward expression.

Sacred rites are performed in their fields prior to the planting, and appropriate ceremonies are conducted throughout the seasons—prayers for germination, growth, and maturation of the crops, and then thanks are given for prayers "answered and unanswered," as one old Indian has told it. Their hunts are ceremonially ordered and conducted, as are their salt gathering missions and other practices. Many of the designs on their pottery and other works of art are derived from motifs connected with their ceremonial life. Through religion all else is given significance; the lean or bountiful years are attributed to faulty or improper observance of religious retreats and rituals. No understanding of Pueblo life apart from its religious beliefs and procedures is possible (*rel.* Ortiz 1972b:135–161).

Basically, each of the Pueblo communities is a closely united and highly systematized organization. Similar social patterns may be observed among the pueblos, yet great differences exist in regard to emphases upon certain organizations and practices. Some are meeting current stresses which the modern world puts on them by relaxing certain of their customs; others hold fast to their age-old strictures. Let it be kept in mind that the Pueblos are broadly alike, yet distinct. The people mingle, but hold apart. They do not favor marriage outside one's own village; while it may not be forbidden absolutely, it is often made difficult. The ceremonial dances are similar, but variations may be observed that are important. Physical differences exist. Taos, for example, was the buffer pueblo on the north, receiving the brunt of raids by hunting tribes from the Great Plains, and its people exhibit a mixture of blood. Foreign elements show in traditions, societal practices, ceremonies, and in stature, wearing apparel, hairstyle, and adornments.

Authority between the ecclesiastical leaders and those who serve in secular offices is sharply defined in each Pueblo group.

The Canes of Office

In the New Mexican pueblos, in accordance with a decree of the King of Spain in 1620, the secular officers' titles follow Spanish designations. In general these are a governor (*adelantado*), two lieutenant governors, *alguacil* (sheriff), and *fiscales* (men who serve as church assistants—deriving from the office of prosecutor). These take office during the first week of January—usually on the first—and serve for one year, except at Isleta, Nambé, San Ildefonso, and Zuñi where the term of office is currently two years. Metal-topped canes inscribed with the Spanish cross became the badges of authority for the secular officers.

When Mexico won independence from Spain, sovereignty was successfully established and new staffs, silver-thimbled, were presented to the pueblos; the governors were authorized and commissioned to function in line with their long custom, having two canes each in symbolic support of the office. Ten years after the Gadsden purchase, President Abraham Lincoln was persuaded to reward the Indians for their neutrality during the Civil War. He therefore ordered black ebony canes, silver crowned and inscribed with his signature, "A. Lincoln," for each of the then nineteen pueblos, extending the continuing authority and commission of the governors. Thus, in 1863, a third cane symbolizing the office under the new sovereignty came into possession of the pueblos in New Mexico (Barton 1953; Faris n.d.; Kubicek 1968).

The Spanish canes and the Lincoln canes bearing the name of a pueblo, the year, and the name of President Lincoln, are in evidence at any ceremony or gathering of the Pueblo Indians in any season of the year. Some of the pueblos have handed their Mexican canes over to the lieutenant governors; it appears that one or two of the villages have lost their Mexican canes and acknowledge having only two—the Spanish and Lincoln canes, as they are usually designated.

In 1883, Picurís lost the silver crown and ferule from its Lincoln cane. The stick was taken to an Indian Agent for replacement. Unfortunately, a heavier crown with paneled floral decoration was mounted, and an error was made in the date, showing the year as 1862. Pojoaque people lost the silver crown from their cane, having only the ebony stick left. But today, it is said that Pojoaque has a silver-headed, engraved cane (Hayes 1971). Some of the canes are battered, but for the most part they are kept in fine condition. The respect for the pueblo canes is no less than is the congressman's respect for the mace in the U.S. House of Representatives.

In 1960, silver medals showing the profiles of Lincoln and President Dwight D. Eisenhower side by side, surrounded by the wording, "Republican Centennial, 1863–1960," were struck, fashioned into pendants, and strung on ribbons of red, white, and blue. Each pueblo governor was presented with one of these. They, with beribboned canes, serve as impressive symbols of office.

Twenty years later, when the Pueblo peoples of New Mexico were holding extensive events in commemoration of the Pueblo Revolt of 9 August 1680—their Tri-Centennial—still another cane was created. Although the canes were intended for presentation to the New Mexico Pueblo Indians on the appropriate anniversary date, a series of delays postponed the ceremony to 16 March 1981.

In the kiva-style rotunda of the state capitol, Governor Bruce King made a gift of small cherry wood canes with crowns of highly polished white bronze to sixteen of the nineteen Pueblo governors (three were absent). Each cane bore the Zía sun symbol, the date of 9 August 1981, and Governor King's signature. A cane was presented also to each of the Athapascan groups: the Jicarilla and Mescalero Apache, and the Navajo Nation. *(See* the *Albuquerque Journal,* 14 March 1981; Dooling, A. *The Santa Fe Reporter,* 23 April 1981.)

The Tanoans

The Tanoan domain formerly extended widely from south to north and west to east. Tanoan social organization is characterized by strong dual organization, or dichotomy. In the northern Río Grande region, where the Tanoans now dwell, the two divisions—complementary ceremonial groups—are referred to generally as those of the north and south peoples, respectively, or as the summer people and the winter people. These divisions have been identified as moieties (*see* Ortiz 1969:57–59, 73, 84, 108; *see also* Fox, J. R. 1967).

Tiwa (Tigua) Indians

Of the Tanoan subfamilies, the Tiwa apparently were the initial Pueblo Indians to have entered the northern Río Grande. In prehistoric times Tiwa pueblos dotted the Río Grande valley from northern Mexico to the region of modern Albuquerque. *(Rel.* Ford et al. 1972:30, 36–37.)

Usually overlooked in works on the Indians of the Southwest is a dwindling Tiwa group near University Park at Las Cruces, New Mexico. Commonly known as *Tortugas* (tor-TU-gahs), the official name of this village is Guadalupe Indian Village. It is controlled by an Indian corporation, *Los Indígenes de Nuestra Señora de Guadalupe.* An elaborate celebration commemorates the patron saint's day on 12 December, with activities the day preceding and that following the major event. The colorful ceremonies, influenced by long association with the Catholic church, include ritualistic singing, candlelight procession, pilgrimage to the summit of Tortugas Mountain, and dancing in front of the village church—all conducted under strict rules passed down by generations of Tiwa Indians, even though Hispanic influences are evident too. The number of those who may be counted as Indians today is unknown.

Although the Indians of the Southwest have the franchise after a hiatus of many years, and Indian people are taking their place in the legislative bodies, it is worth noting that, during the 1927 session of the New Mexico legislature, one of the Tiwa men of the Tortugas group served as representative from Doña Ana county. He was a diligent committee worker, and was frequently called to preside over the House of Representatives, a position which he filled with skill and dignity.

Throughout historical times, the other Tiwa have occupied two locations. A northern group, of which the pueblos of Taos and Picurís remain, is separated by some 75 miles from their southern kinsmen who dwell to the north and south of Albuquerque, in Sandía and Isleta. Indians of the latter pueblos can readily converse with one another, as can those of Taos and Picurís; and the people of Sandía and Isleta can understand the dialects of Taos and Picurís, but the reverse is not true—Sandía and Isleta are understood by the northern Tiwa with difficulty. This suggests that the division occurred long ago and that the more isolated northern people have maintained the original character of their speech to a greater degree than have the others.

In addition to the Tortugas, whose settlement is actually about forty miles north of El Paso, Texas, another group of Tiwa Indians is still dwelling at El Paso—the Tigua, to use an older spelling. These are descendants of survivors of those Tiwa who fled down the Río Grande to escape the Pueblo Revolt of 1680. They came from as far north as Sandía and Isleta pueblos. It is said that a small number from Isleta were forced to go with the Spaniards who were fleeing for their lives. With other Indians who joined them along the way, they trudged the long way with only their most prized possessions— foremost, their canes of authority. They traveled to Ysleta del Sur, about twelve miles south of El Paso, where farms were established along the Río Grande.

With them, they carried their knowledge of the Tiwa traditions and life ways of yore. In their southern location they built a compact pueblo with their homes surrounding a rectangular plaza (see Fewkes 1902:61). A mission was constructed by the Catholics, not far away. It became the center of both the Catholics and the Christianized Indians. In the early 1900s, the Tiwa settlement, or el barrio de los Indios, was moved closer to the mission. This evidences the symbiotic relationship between the two peoples.

The fact that the Tigua and other Tiwa-speaking Indians who had accompanied them on the southward journey had carried their official canes with them—five of them, it seems—indicates that the male members were largely of the highest order in their respective pueblos. Five such important individuals among the small number that arrived at Ysleta would have been sufficient to rework the social fabric of the closely-knit pueblo which was established in the new setting. The home of a tribal officer became incorporated with the tribal building of the "tusla," túlag of the Southern Tiwa tongue. This specialized chamber, today, would probably be called a "kiva." It was there that the ceremonial paraphernalia was kept: the tribal drum, dance rattles, masks (see Houser 1979:336).

A sacred drum—another symbol of office—used during special dances, is carried by the war chief, or war captain. The drum in current use is reported to have been inherited from the Piro grandfather of a present-day drummer. The drum is covered with buffalo skin, and has a moon painted with a face on one side, and eight stars representing the sun on the other. The honored custodian of this drum is half Piro and half Tiwa. (In re Piros, see Schroeder 1979c:236–237.)

According to a recent report by Brewer (1981), the up-river Pueblos "virtually disowned the Tiguas because they did not fight the Spaniards in the revolt." As a consequence, to this day they have not been allowed "membership in the Pueblo Conference." When President Abraham Lincoln "granted lands to Indian tribes for reservations in the 1860s," the Tiguas were skipped because Texas was then a part of the Confederacy (Turner 1978).

Following Brewer further, "In 1871, the Texas Legislature allowed the local government to give public lands to settlers, and Anglo settlers forced the tribe off the land." These Tiwa practically faded into oblivion. They mixed with the Mexican-American people of the area, and suffered extreme poverty; they lived without water and utilities in adobe houses which were falling down. Many were ashamed to admit their Indian heritage. Children dropped out of school because they had no shoes. "In 1962 the average Tigua had three years of formal education," so stated Brewer.

At that time, a local lawyer heard of these destitute Indians, who were facing foreclosure of homes, "for failure to pay [El Paso] city taxes." In behalf of the Tigua, he set about trying to obtain governmental assistance for them.

In 1967, Texas recognized their tribal status and the Tigua Indian Reservation was established. The following year, the federal government "granted recognition and turned the care of the Indians over to the Texas Indian Commission."

With receipt of approximately eleven million dollars from the state, Brewer reported that "during the past thirteen years, the tribe has built a modern 114-unit housing complex on land granted" for their reservation at Ysleta—as the site is commonly called. Then in addition the Indians built a museum and an arts and crafts center, harmonizing up-to-date facilities with features of their unforgotten traditional lifeways. From these developments, the Tigua soon gained attention of the public; they were in a position to provide jobs for the tribal members and thus assure them revenue.

Consequently, this sorely treated group of American indigenes, who trekked down the Rio Grande three hundred years ago, carrying only their most prized possessions on their backs, have at last been released from bondage. Once again a group of Southwestern Indians can hold their heads aloft and walk proudly.

According to an Associated Press release in the *Albuquerque Journal* of 26 June 1981, the population for the Tigua was then 673 (cf. Houser 1979:341). This appeared with a primary announcement of the death of their spiritual leader, the cacique. Working closely with the cacique is the war chief. On the occasion of the death of this respected 81-year old official, the war chief was slated to succeed him as a cacique, after a four-day mourning period. His selection was made "by adult male members of the tribe, and is traditionally, but not necessarily, chosen on the basis of ancestry." Another war chief would be chosen.

In the dual system of the Tanoans each division has, or had in the past, its own priest, or *cacique*. (The term *cacique* [kah-SEE-kay], is a Haitian word that was used extensively by early chroniclers to designate the priest-chiefs; it was incorporated into the Spanish language with this significance, and was added to the Indian vocabulary.) The cacique of the north, or of the summer people, has control during the summer, and that of the south, or winter people, during the winter. The cacique is the head of all pueblo organization; he holds office for life and has a staff as a badge of authority. The cacique, the kiva chiefs, and their appointees or selectees to the secular offices, constitute a hierarchical form of government. *(See Lange in re cacique 1959:589.)*

At Taos and Picurís, six round ceremonial chambers are utilized. These are subterranean or semisubterranean rooms, built apart from the dwellings. Such a chamber is generally referred to as a *kiva* (KEE-vah), this being the Hopi name of a sacred ceremonial, assembly, and lounging chamber, characteristic of ancient and modern Pueblo settlements. "Kiva" embraces circular and rectangular structures of a specialized nature, whether they be built below ground or above, detached or among the houses. At Taos, each kiva is surrounded by a palisade of tall poles. Visitors are advised to keep a respectful distance from these. Paternal kiva membership is the pattern, but at Taos the choice of kiva is now optional, though the tendency persists for a father to "give" his child to his kiva or kiva cluster. The males are also the house owners. (*Rel.* Bodine 1979:255–267; Brown 1979:268–277; Dozier 1970a.)

In addition to its six kivas situated in the north and south segments of the pueblo—with a "chief" in charge of each—Taos has a seventh chamber of similar form which lies outside the village wall; it is sometimes described as "disused." Actually, it is used for retreats and prayers. Its original association was with a scalp society, or warrior cult, under the direction of the war chiefs. Picurís also has its structure designated as a scalp house, which undoubtedly has similar associations. Curing and healing were functions of the warrior society.

Formerly, if not at present, each Tiwa pueblo, as Taos today, had a race track as part of the village plan. Such tracks extend in an east-west direction, representing the courses of the sun and moon. Footraces are part of ceremonial ritual, being run to give power to travel to those celestial bodies. They represent contests between the north division of the pueblo and the south division. In the form of relay races, runners represent the north and south kiva groups, respectively; starting in the east, as the rising sun, they run to the west, touch another runner who races eastward, and so on until the winner is proclaimed.

Among the southern Tiwa the pattern regarding ceremonial structures is not so apparent. Inasmuch as deep subterranean chambers are known to have been in the region as long as a thousand years ago, it seems possible that the original kiva system may have been like that of Taos and Picurís. But Isleta and Sandía were in the main path of the Spanish *conquistadores,* and for over four and a quarter centuries they have been subjected to cultural disarrangements. The pueblos have been deserted, reoccupied after intervals of time, perhaps relocated, and admixtures of peoples have inhabited them. (*See* Brandt 1979:344 ff.)

The modern situation includes two rectangular ceremonial chambers built within the house blocks which are arranged about a central plaza. Isleta, largest of the pueblos in this group, has two rectangular kivas built among the dwellings and, in addition, a large circular chamber built almost wholly above ground and detached from other structures. It is a prominent feature of the architecture and is known as an "outside house." This is said to be used for maskless ceremonial dances, for painting the clowns, and for race ritual; it was primarily the place where scalps of enemies were kept.

At Isleta the divisions of the dual organization were known by the terms "Black Eye" and "Red Eye," respectively; everyone in the pueblo belongs to one or the other. Officers of the Red Eye (*Shúre*), or summer division, and the Black Eye (*Shifun*), or winter division, are prominent in the irrigation rituals and in certain maskless katsina dances; they direct the clowning, hunting, and ballplaying, and other group activities. (*See* Ellis, F. 1979a:356 ff.)

In general, *katsinas,* or supernatural beings, are *not* impersonated by masked dancers among the Tiwa, although the small kiva groups make offerings to those personages.

Everyone belongs also to one of seven "corn groups" that hold winter and summer ceremonies for the sun; these signify seasonal transfer of official duties. An Isletan belongs to his mother's corn group. The corn chief, who may be referred to as "Corn Father" or "Corn Mother," serves as an intermediary with the curers, or expediter of deceased ones. The corn fathers and their helpers operate as a priesthood. The moon is regarded as "our mother moon," and stars are considered to be sons of the divine parents.

Isleta shows resemblances to both the Keres and Tewa systems. It has a cult of the dead, believing that weather and crop spirits dwell in the mountains. Their supernatural beings, like the katsinas of other pueblos, are impersonated in dances, but no masks are worn.

It is said that the office of cacique no longer exists at Isleta. Ritual matters are supervised by the war captain.

In 1947, this pueblo was the second in New Mexico to adopt a constitution to govern itself. In 1970 the document was replaced by a new constitution. All enrolled members of at least twenty-one years of age have the franchise. The top vote getter becomes the governor, the second is declared president, and the third highest, vice-president. A council is appointed, four members being named by the governor, and three each by the president and vice-president. The president is executive officer of the council, and the governor is chief executive of the pueblo. None of the elected officials receives a salary *(see* Ellis, F. ibid.).

The pueblo of Sandía has two rectangular ceremonial chambers built into house blocks. Here the division into turquois people and squash people exists; one cacique holds office. He serves for life as the head of his people. The present middle-aged cacique succeeded a venerable man who had been named in the 1940s. The choice of naming a cacique is traditionally rotated among the clans [moieties?]. The cacique appoints all secular officers annually. Directly under the cacique, according to custom, is an executive officer, the war chief, who also serves for life; he controls the nonsecular activities, supervising the keeping of rituals and the holding of dances. The governor works through the war chief in reporting on affairs of the pueblo—all business dealings. Five or six fiscales assist the governor in carrying out the dictates of the council, which is composed of former governors and war chiefs. *(Rel.* Brandt ibid.)

Sandía has been affected by influences of many peoples; perhaps as a result of this, the pueblo is said to have several matrilineal clans, "the number varying as some die out" (Hume 1970b). Corn groups like those of Isleta are evidenced.

With the Tanoan peoples, clan organization is generally nonexistent, or is weakly represented—possibly indicating its adoption from neighboring Indian groups. A clan is recognized as a social group comprising a number of households, the heads of which claim descent from a common ancestor. *(Rel.* Dozier 1970b:162–176.)

Tewa Indians

Each of the Tewa villages in the upper Río Grande drainage is made up of small, loosely connected clusters of dwellings; their arrangement is irregular, with rooms generally offset, but they adhere to north-south and east-west axial lines. With growth, and possibly from long association with the Spanish Americans—who customarily built their communities around plazas, and frequently enclosed sections within walls—the pueblo clusters came to assume plaza form, at least to a degree. In some instances, squares surrounded by structures are in evidence; in other cases the so-called plazas are only a matter of loose application of the word. Certain it is that little or nothing comparable to the compact buildings and courts of the prehistoric peoples of the Four Corners region, or of the Hopi pueblos of today, exists in the Río Grande Tewa villages.

The Tewa people live in five pueblos, all to the north of Santa Fe; in addition, some one-hundred-odd individuals of Pojoaque affiliation hold title to the Pojoaque reservation, and reside there or nearby. In each of these pueblos, dichotomy is of prime importance. Formerly, and to some extent today, a cacique presides over each division; Nambé, for example, has not had a cacique for several years *(see* Speirs 1979:317). The summer cacique is in charge of the south people, while the winter cacique is in charge of the north people. Their office is for life.

The seasons are not evenly divided. Summer is considered to begin in February or March and to extend to November; winter lasts from November to February or March. Thus it appears that with the Tewa and Tiwa, and probably with all Tanoans originally, it is not the solstices that are of foremost importance in establishing the ceremonial calendar, but the seasonal transfer. The cacique of the south group gives the people to the cacique of the north group in November, and the latter gives the people to the former in the spring. The winter solstice ceremonial is observed in January, while the summer solstice is celebrated in June. The cacique of the summer people and his counterpart are equal in influence.

Membership in the dual organizations is patrilineal, but the affiliation may be changed. A woman may join the division, or moiety, of her husband on marriage, or may remain as she is; the husband can transfer to another group, though with difficulty. It is the custom for each moiety to have a specialized, rectangular chamber built in the respective house blocks. The summer people are associated with the squash chamber, and the winter people with the turquois chamber.

In varying degrees the old ceremonial groups and moiety organizations of the Tewa pueblos are now broken down and their former distinct functions are mingled and confused. Traditionally, initiation into a moiety took place in a "big kiva" (*see* Hawley 1950:289). Today, San Ildefonso and Tesuque each have two moiety houses; the former also has a large circular chamber. In Santa Clara and Nambé the houses of the moiety chiefs are used in lieu of separate moiety rooms.

At Santa Clara the government is run under a constitution adopted in December, 1935, making this pueblo the first in New Mexico to adopt a constitution. This action was instrumental in healing a factional dispute that began in the late 1800s, when the then conservative ones of Santa Clara "were opposed to the acceptance of federal programs designed to upgrade the living conditions of the pueblo."

"The constitution effectively divided the secular from the religious, allowing the conservatives to concentrate on retention of the old religion and the young people to concentrate on the secular government" (Hume 1970b). The governing officials number six: governor, lieutenant governor, secretary, treasurer, sheriff, and interpreter. These are elected annually. The governor receives a nominal salary, and all officers receive expense allowances when on pueblo business.

It is said that the constitution divides the pueblo into four groups, two subgroups in each of the moieties, the summer and winter. Each of these groups can nominate candidates for any of the elective positions, and the candidates then run in a general election. Those eighteen years old have the franchise in regular elections, but on constitutional amendments the age limit is twenty-one.

Santa Clara's council is comprised of the elected officials plus two representatives from each of the pueblo's subdivisions. They have their own law and order setup, with a tribal judge whose decisions may be appealed to the pueblo council.

As is traditional with the Tewa, Santa Clara has a cacique at the head of its ecclesiastical organization. The position is for life.

Among the Tewa the extended family is emphasized, on both the father's and mother's sides. These large family groups often assemble in the home of some leader-member to discuss important matters. Clans, if they ever existed, have no significance today—although the term has frequently been used in speaking of various groups or societies. The simple family consists of a man and his wife and their unmarried offspring, or a widow or widower with children.

A LULLABY OF NAMBÉ

Go to sleep,
Go to sleep,
Lest something come,

To take away
My little one.
So you must sleep,
My little one

From *Songs of the Tewa,* by H.J. Spinden
© 1933 by H.J. Spinden (Spinden 1933).

Heads of families, except old men and women, are responsible to the pueblo officials for such services as may be demanded of them. They may be called to clean the irrigation ditches, sweep the plaza before dances and feast day observances, and to perform ceremonial duties.

Patrilineal descent is the rule. House ownership is male, for the most part; and a tendency to build houses within a man's moiety seems evident. Originally, this created the basic architectural pattern.

At San Ildefonso, a pueblo numbering approximately 475 in 1980, the outward evidence of past ceremonial organization is still manifest. The pueblo has two rectangular chambers, that of the winter people built in the northernmost house block, and that of the summer people detached and in the southwestern part of the village. The large circular structure, built mostly above ground with an opening toward the southeast, appears prominently in the southern part of the pueblo. Entrance is by means of a stairway—formerly a ladder—leading to the top of the structure, where a hatchway gives access to the interior. The old ladder symbolized ascent from the underworld to a higher plane, or to an eminence. This chamber is said to be the oldest building in the pueblo; and it "belongs" to all of the people. It is used as a dance place. As at Isleta, this circular building is designated as the "outside house."

In certain of the pueblos, the war chiefs are also called "outside chiefs," and it appears that the outside house at San Ildefonso related to affairs of the warrior cult. The warrior society is no longer extant in the pueblo, although the paraphernalia is said to have been preserved. There is now a fine museum.

Until some years ago, the remains of a small, one-room building were observable on top of a low hill near the sacred spring of the west, of San Ildefonso. This was the chamber to which the old priest retired for his retreat.

- The late William Whitman reported that the religious hierarchy at San Ildefonso is based on paternalism, and he stated that: "The Cacique is not a priest in the sense that he is an impersonation of godhead. He is 'father and mother' of the people, mortal as his children, whom in his wisdom he leads and directs. . . . To insure divine blessing it is believed that propitiation must be made not only by the priests (headmen) but by the group as a whole, and that through the efforts of the group, led and supplemented by those of the priests, the forces of nature are compelled to act in accordance with the needs of the people" (Whitman 1947:118).

San Juan has two rectangular kivas built in the house blocks. The reader is referred to the extensive work of Alfonso Ortíz, himself an Indian, who dwelt in that pueblo with his family and has had unusual opportunity to study San Juan in detail (Ortíz 1969, 1979a:278–295). Santa Clara (Arnon and Hill 1979:298–302) has two similar chambers, but detached from the dwelling structures. Tesuque has rectangular kivas built in the house blocks, and probably utilized two at a time; the pattern has become confused due to recent demolitions and rebuilding. At Nambé one finds only a large, circular structure in evidence. Archaeological excavations there exposed a small underground kiva, the floor of which was six feet below the present surface. It was twelve feet in diameter; it had vertical walls, the adobe plaster of which curved slightly at the floor level. The chamber was dated around A.D. 1400. The excavator observed that: "Small underground kivas used in prehistoric times as ceremonial chambers of religious societies, were replaced in most of the Río Grande pueblos by aboveground houses built for that purpose, or even by adaptation of one room in the house of the leader of the society" (Ellis 1964:38).

The Tewa of Hopiland are mentioned later.

SONG OF THE SKY LOOM (Tewa)

Oh our Mother the Earth, oh our Father the Sky,
Your children are we, and with tired backs
We bring you the gifts that you love.
Then weave for us a garment of brightness;
May the warp be the white light of morning,
May the weft be the red light of evening,
May the fringes be the falling rain,
May the border be the standing rainbow.
Thus weave for us a garment of brightness
That we may walk fittingly where birds sing,
That we may walk fittingly where grass is green,
Oh our Mother the Earth, oh our Father the Sky!

From *Songs of the Tewa* by H.J. Spinden
© 1933 by H.J. Spinden.

Towa Indians

The pueblo of Jémez is the remaining member of a third Tanoan subfamily, the Towa *(see* Eggan, 1979:235; Sando 1979:418–437). It is located on Jémez Creek, or the Río Jémez, west of Santa Fe in the mountains of the Jémez Range. Seventeen survivors from the Pecos pueblo moved to Jémez in 1838, and descendants of Pecos parents and the Jémez people are presently enumerated together. Being located quite apart from the Tiwa and Tewa peoples, but close to non-Tanoan villagers, Jémez displays many characteristics which are attributable to the Keresans.

There are two large rectangular kivas, but the dual organization has broken down, although summer and winter people are recognized; no moiety houses exist. Society houses occur in the regular house blocks. The Jémez developed clans, with descent reckoned through the maternal line. One has to marry outside the clan. Clans play but a minor part in the economic and ceremonial life of Jémez. Weakness of the clan system probably reflects a borrowed trait, or a marginal occurrence. House owning rests with the males for the most part.

One cacique serves for life; he possesses a "Mother" fetish. The cacique is assisted by two men who are probably relatable to the war chiefs of old. Foremost duty of the cacique is to watch the sun, that is, to determine the arrival of summer and winter and set dates for ceremonies accordingly. Races of the kick-stick type are held on a north-south track.

Caves in the mountains, sacred eminences, springs, shrines, and features not often recognized by non-Indians, are scattered throughout the lands surrounding the pueblo of Jémez. The religion of the people is strongly tied to the Mother Earth, and change in the environment, said a Jémez spokesman, "would cause the whole religious cycle to be broken." The Indians have been threatened by a proposed geothermal plant, west of Los Alamos. This certainly could break the cycle of Pueblo religious customs.

Despite protestations of the Jémez and other pueblos intervening before the New Mexico Public Service Commission, drilling rigs were brought into the area, fences erected, and security guards posted. The Indians could no longer "go up there in the right frame of mind." One questioned: "How do you replace religious significance?" He added: "There is no mitigation for this. We cannot have this technology bring the destruction of our religion. The only mitigation is no plant at all."

A unanimous decision of the commission ruled that state law prohibits them from considering testimony given in regard to environmental, socioeconomic, psychological problems, and religious issues, when a proposed plant will produce less than 300 megawatts of power (see Seagrave 1980a:B16; 1980b:E12; anonymous 1980). The contenders admit that the planned plant far exceeds any power necessary for local consumption; it is intended for uses far from New Mexico.

The project, a joint effort of the Public Service Company, U.S. Department of Energy, and Union Geothermal Company, had an estimated cost of $126–134 million. Under pressures generated by *their* combined forces, the cultural concepts and lifeways of another indigenous people seemed destined to be unheeded and largely destroyed. However, the operations were suspended early in 1982.

The Keresans

The origin of the Keresan people is unknown. One linguist subdivides them into four groups: Acoma and Laguna, Zía and Santa Ana, San Felipe and Santo Domingo, and Cóchiti. He says that Acoma and Laguna, usually considered as the western Keres, "have had a history of linguistic development independent to a certain degree of the other dialects" (Davis 1959:78), that is, of the eastern Keres (rel. Hale and Harris 1979:171). Acoma and Laguna also have distinct histories extending into prehistoric times (Davis 1959:83). [Dr. A. E. Dittert, Jr., recognizes these two peoples as distinct in central western New Mexico for at least 4,500 years.] Some evidence of a closeness between the language of Zía and the western Keres has been detected (Spencer 1940; Hewett and Dutton 1945:19). And viewing the maps it is seen that the eastern and western villages share a continuity of terrain. Keres people have demonstrated a preference for locating their pueblos atop eminences, usually lofty sandstone mesas above the valley lands. Trails led directly between the two regions; and pueblo ruins now existing may have been occupied by Keres people.

Archaeological investigations indicate that those who now occupy the Keres districts have been there for a very long time. Like the Tanoans, their former territory well may have been more widespread.

One belief, although remote, is that the Keresan language may be of Hokan-Siouan affiliation, suggesting that the Keres represent an intrusion of peoples who pushed into the Southwest around 4,500 years ago—thus being descendants from Archaic peoples (Sapir 1929; Dittert 1959; Eddy 1965:24) who came from a southerly direction and merged with northerly ones. Such a position and history of the Keres would be in harmony with the finding of Strong (1927:57), who believed that certain peoples, including a Yuman-speaking enclave, pushed themselves into what had previously been a continuous Azteco-Tanoan domain (Strong 1927:57).

Regardless of their origin and regional developments, the Keres display cultural features that differ in varying aspects from those of the Tanoans. Acoma was established at or near its present location as early as A.D. 900, and its occupation has been continuous since 1075 (Dittert 1959). Its structures are built in parallel rows of terraced house blocks, tending in an east-west direction; all face toward the south. Among the dwellings, seven rectangular ceremonial chambers are situated on the ground floor. The head kiva differs from the other six in having a floor vault over which a plank is placed, acting as a resonator when used as a foot drum.

Contrary to Tanoan organization, with the Keres peoples clans are, or were, of foremost importance (see Dozier 1970b:150–151; Garcia-Mason 1979). Each Acoma Indian is born into his mother's clan. These clans are exogamous; that is, one must marry outside his clan, and so the chief function of the clan is to regulate marriage. Descent is reckoned in the maternal line, and houses are property of the women. The economic unit is the household. Although the part that clans play in ceremonies and general pueblo procedures may now be minor, in olden times the clan heads owned fetishes, settled disputes between members, went into a series of summer retreats for rain, assisted the medicine societies—particularly during the winter solstice observance—and conducted ceremonies relating to supernatural ones associated with the clans.

Only one cacique holds office at Acoma, and he represents and cares for the whole pueblo, reflecting lack of dichotomy, or dual organization. The cacique is the highest religious officer and the political head of the pueblo; his most important ceremonial function is to watch the sun and determine the solstices; he sets the date for practically all ceremonies. Here, as with the Azteco-Tanoans, the sun is recognized as representative of a supreme deity.

Laguna was without ceremonial chambers for many years. Formerly, two rectangular ones were built aboveground, one on the east side of the village and the other at the west end. The east kiva was the repository for all of the paraphernalia belonging to the warrior society, which performed the scalp dance. The west kiva housed all ritualistic property of the katsina cult. Children joined the kiva of the father, and wives that of the husband (*Rel.* Ellis, F. H. 1979b:448.)

A few years ago, a new chamber was constructed at Laguna, in the southwest part of the pueblo, and this is being called a kiva. It is said to be "all modern."

At Laguna, one cacique was chosen for life; he spent his time in prayer and sacrificed for the welfare of his people. The cacique was assisted by war chiefs, representing twin war gods; they were concerned with warfare, hunting, and guarding the people and the rituals. They were aided by chiefs' helpers.

Laguna followed a matrilineal-matrilocal pattern of organization, with exogamous clans bearing totemic names; they had ceremonial, judiciary, and economic functions. For many years, two groups—one conservative and the other progressive—have been observable at Laguna.

A degree of unanimity is found in the organization of the eastern Keres Pueblos, but their social pattern differs considerably from that of the western peoples, and from the Tanoans with whom they are in proximity. As a rule, the Keres did not live east of the Río Grande. Generally speaking, their settlements were on the west side of the stream, and their domain extended no farther than the eastern mountains which border the Río Grande valley, that is, the Sandía range and the Ortíz-San Pedro mountain group.

Today, five pueblos are extant among the eastern Keres: Cóchiti, Santo Domingo, San Felipe, Santa Ana with outlying settlements, and Zía. (*Rel.* sources for the pueblos named are: Lange 1959, 1979a:366–378, and 379–389; Strong, P. T. 1979:390–397, and 398–406; Hoebel 1979:407–417.) Whether large or small, each pueblo has two round ceremonial structures built aboveground and apart from the dwellings. One of these is associated with summer (squash or pumpkin) people and the other with winter (turquois) people. Each kiva group is associated with particular clans, and with certain medicine societies—thus involving a triple organization.

The spiritual leader, the cacique, in the larger pueblos is appointed by the war chief for life; he has to be a member of a particular society (Flint), and he is associated with a "clown" group. In no instance is the clan organization strong. It follows matrilineal descent for the most part, clan exogamy, and matrilocal residence. In the pueblo of Zía, however, clans display patrilineal descent; matrilocal residence may be followed for a while, then the groom builds a new home for occupancy.

Because of the prominent two-kiva system, relating to seasonal divisions made manifest by the occurrence of the winter and summer solstices, and in view of the ceremonies relating to each season, a general dichotomy in the social organization prevails. This has been identified as a moiety system by some investigators. Keresan society is better considered as clan-based, although the clans now function but weakly. Then, realizing the seasonal divisions and accepting the probability of influences from the strong Tanoan dichotomy system, it is possible to visualize an original Keresan pattern quite diverse from that of their neighbors. The Keres evidence a complicated social structure, embracing clans, kiva groups, and medicine societies. Under the control of its single cacique, each Keres pueblo in the east has two circular ceremonial chambers built apart from the dwellings, while in the west these are rectangular, built among the house blocks, and may number two or more. All are aboveground structures.

The Zunian People

Archaeological and linguistic evidence indicate that Zuñi-speaking people have been in their present location for some eight hundred years, or more. And it appears likely that Indians traveled between Mexico and the regions to the north for centuries; no boundary existed until the time of the Gadsden Purchase. In the 1530s, verbal accounts concerning Indians of the unexplored lands of the Greater Southwest reached the ears of the Spanish conquerors in Mexico. By 1535 they had heard of many-storied houses built of stone and adobe, in which the Indians dwelt. Don Antonio de Mendoza, the Spanish viceroy, soon became interested in the opportunity of adding new territory and expected riches to the empire of Charles V, and of Christianizing the Indians. Accordingly, a Franciscan friar, Marcos de Niza, was sent forth at the head of an exploring party, in the spring of 1539.

Among a group of Piman Indians—the Sobaipura (so-BAI-pu-rah) who occupied the Río San Pedro and the Gila valleys until about the end of the eighteenth century (Di Peso et al. 1953)—Fray Marcos met the first Zuñi Indian of whom specific mention is known. The old Indian told the friar of the pueblos of his homeland and of neighboring peoples. He was the original informant concerning Hawikuh, or *Ahacua,* which he described as the largest of the Zuñi pueblos.

Fray Marcos sent a member of his party, a black man named Estevan (es-TAY-vahn) de Dorantes, ahead with a few companions to scout the way to Zuñi and to pacify the Indians. Estevan is credited with having had a gift for dealing with strangers, but his reception among the Zuñi was anything but friendly. The Indians refused his entrance to Hawikuh; they stripped him of his possessions, sent him forth, then fell upon and killed him. Some of the party escaped and took word back to the friar, who retreated to Mexico. Another explorer, Francisco Vasquez de Coronado, entered Zuñiland the following year (1540). *(Rel.* Woodbury 1979b:467–473.)

Aside from the Estevan incident, the Zuñi, like the Pueblo Indians of the Río Grande, were friendly toward the Spaniards when they first entered the region. Other explorers and missionaries came and went; some of the latter were admired and respected by the Zuñi, others stirred resentment which caused their dispatch. The Zuñi took part in the Pueblo Rebellion of 1680, although they were less involved than were the Río Grande pueblos, who were closer to the scene of the uprising. When de Vargas effected his reconquest in 1692, he found the Zuñi withdrawn to the eminence called *Towayalane,* or Corn Mountain. Shortly thereafter, they began the building of their present pueblo, including the old site of Halona on the Zuñi River *(rel.* Ladd 1979a: 482).

Currently, most of the Zuñi people live in that pueblo; a few have permanent dwellings in nearby settlements. The lands of Zuñi were not recognized by executive order of the U.S. government until 1877. The boundaries then established were amended by Presidential order in 1883 and again in 1885. The reservation now covers some 408,404 acres to the southwest of Gallup, New Mexico. Zuñi is one of the most populous of the pueblo groups, numbering around 7,200 Indians. Nonresident Indians increase the population by several hundred, making about 8,000 in all *(see* Eggan and Pandey 1979:479).

Traces of a dichotomous organization have been detected at Zuñi, with recognition of north people and south people, or summer and winter people. The summer cacique is considered to be speaker to the sun, and the winter cacique, rain priest of the north. Clans are of considerable significance, although as such they have no social or political functions. *(Rel.* Ladd 1979a:485.) They number about thirteen, are totemically named, each being composed of one or more unnamed lineages; they are exogamous. Both the mother's and father's lineages are important; their social and ceremonial duties are differentiated sharply. Formerly, the clans were grouped into phratries, that is, major groups including a number of clans, which were associated with the six directions—

the cardinal points, zenith, and nadir. The economic unit is the household, normally composed of an extended family based on matrilocal residence—occupying a series of adjoining rooms which are owned by the women, since descent is matrilineal.

It has been noted that an individual is "fitted into an intricate and closely knit social organization." Also, "The elementary family, so important elsewhere, is merged into the household group, and the specific roles of relatives are affected by their position in the social structure. A Zuñi is born into a certain household, which determines his clan affiliation and kinship status, and, in part, his future ceremonial roles" (Eggan 1950:191). Ritual activities are primarily in the hands of the father's household, while economic activities are primarily in the hands of the mother's household and lineage. *(Rel.* Tedlock 1979.)

Zuñi has an elaborate ceremonial organization centering in six kiva groups (one for each direction), associated with medicine societies and an extensive esoteric cult (*kóko*) and priesthoods—all of which cut across clan and household groupings. The kivas, like those of the western Keres and the Tanoans, are rectangular and aboveground; some are built in the house units, others are detached. Sacred fetishes are in the care of the women and their brothers. On ritual occasions the men return to their natal household to carry out important ceremonial duties. Medicine societies are not tied in with the kiva system *(see* Ladd 1979a:482–487).

The Zuñi people, perhaps more than most of the Río Grande Pueblo groups, have maintained their social organization insofar as has been possible in the face of inevitable change. In recent years, isolation of the pueblo has ceased. Improved roads and pavement, modern vehicles, public utilities, development of resources, and government projects of varied types, have brought the Zuñi into cultural ferment, slowly but surely. Education has been available on the reservation since 1882, first through the primary grades only, then through high school since 1956; in 1980, Zuñi achieved its own school district. Those who have been graduated from high school usually continue in commercial or vocational schools and/or in colleges.

Alert officials at Zuñi became aware of a federal law of 1834 which had never been used, but which allowed Indians to administer their own reservations with the approval of the Secretary of the Interior. The Zuñi Tribal Council held a ratification election on a proposed constitution to replace custom laws which had been followed for centuries. All registered tribal members over twenty-one were allowed to vote, and they favored the change to home rule. Currently, eighteen-year-old Zuñi people are allowed to vote.

Formal agreement by which the Zuñi took over direction of the federal agency on the reservation was signed on 23 May 1970. This agreement was the culmination of a comprehensive development plan that had been worked on for a period of years. The plan contained forty-three programs, with the major goals of increasing individual income, enhancing educational opportunities, and improving living conditions. The agreement is described as being flexible; it could be canceled by either of the signing parties on 180 days written notice if it did not work out. By taking this impressive action, the council was presented the first Interior Department Indian Leadership Award for its initiative. This agreement marked an important step in the Zuñi taking effective control of their own affairs.

The Hopi Groups

The Hopi, the pueblo dwellers of Arizona, have occupied their domain for thousands of years (see Brew 1979:514; Adams and Hull 1980:11–27). The designation *Hopi* is abbreviated from *Hopituh Shi-nu-mu,* which means "the peaceful people." For the most part, their villages are perched atop three high, barren mesas located northwestward from Keams Canyon, where an Englishman, Thomas V. Keam, started a trading post in 1878. In that advantageous business he came to possess splendid collections of Hopi pottery and of other categories of Hopi arts and crafts (see Wade and McChesney 1980, 1981; Wade 1980:55–61.) The federal government established offices at Keam's Canyon in 1887. Keam's holdings being purchased and made part of the headquarters. From there, the mesas were called "First Mesa," "Second Mesa," and "Third Mesa," going from east to west. This was just opposite to the order in which the Hopi themselves regarded their highland sites.

In ancient times the location of the Hopi settlements on the three southern prongs of Black Mesa served as a natural protection from enemies. The dissected highland, some sixty miles in diameter, is drained by streams that carry sand and silt southward to the lower plain. There the prevailing southwest winds separate the soil materials and blow the sands back to form large dunes. These absorb the water and lessen the runoff when rains fall. Permanent springs thus result.

The villages on these mesas, like those of the Río Grande pueblos, have an intricately interwoven social structure (see Frigout 1979; Hieb 1979:577–580). They did not have a tribal government of any kind (see Connelly, J. C. 1979b:539ff.; 1980:51–63). Each village has its own organization and each individual has his own particular place in the operation of his community (see Dozier 1966b). The clan system is basic; it is matrilineal and matrilocal, resulting in blocks of houses built adjacent to the home of the matriarch. The clan is stronger among the Hopi than elsewhere among the Pueblos; and a strong clan system correlates with a weak political system (Eggan 1950: 117–118). It has been stated that to a casual visitor in a Hopi village, "its government is so lacking in form as to seem almost nonexistent." (James 1956:107.) Nothing of a dichotomous organization is to be seen. The household is the economic unit; labor is judiciously divided between the men and women. Each major clan has a fetish which is kept in the clan house and is presided over by the woman considered to be the clan mother.

Women own the houses, food, seed for the next year's planting, the springs and cisterns, and the small irrigated gardens that they work. The men do the herding, hunting, and farming away from the village. They gather and haul the fuel, and theirs are the duties of spinning, weaving (*see* Tanner and Tanner 1980:70), and moccasin making—all of which are becoming less and less evident today. Married men live in the household of the wife, but they continue association with their mothers' and sisters' homes—their "real homes"— and participate in ceremonial activities of the family clans.

The Spaniards visited Hopiland, or old Tusayan, under Don Pedro de Tovar, a lieutenant of Coronado, and occupied a village believed to have been the now ruined *Kawaiokuh* (kah-WAI-oh-kuh), from which the Indians had fled at the approach of the small party of armed invaders (*rel.* Dockstader 1979b: 524). The first contact between the Spaniards and Hopi followed—a friendly encounter apparently, for the Indians brought gifts and Tovar assembled his men in a camp near the pueblo. There, the Spaniards learned of a great river flowing in a deep canyon—the Colorado River of present days—and Don García de Cárdenas was ordered to search for the mighty stream, which has always played a major part in Hopi mythology. For forty years the Hopi were not again visited by the Spaniards.

In 1583, Antonio de Espejo and a few soldiers passed through the Hopi towns. They spent several days in *Awatobi* (ah-WAH-toh-bee), now in ruin a few miles east of Walpi (WAHL-pee), and in other villages. The Indians were cordial and gave the Spaniards many presents before Espejo continued on, seeking gold (but finding silver). Juan de Oñate visited Tusayan in 1598 and in 1604. From 1629 until 1680, Franciscan missionaries tried to convert the Hopi to Christianity. Missions were established at Oraibi (oh-RAI-bee), Shungopovi (shung-OH-poh-vee), and Awatobi (Montgomery, Smith and Brew 1949; Smith, W. 1952, 1971, and 1980:29–37). The period was one of great unrest among all of the Pueblo peoples: their priests resented the Spaniards' interference with the native religious ways; they chafed under the enforced labor demanded of them; and they deplored the ravishing of their women. Distrust and unfriendliness toward the intruders grew and intensified.

Like the Río Grande Pueblos, those of Tusayan were ripe for rebellion, and they joined in the uprising of 1680. They killed four friars and demolished the churches and outlying *visitas*. De Vargas, in 1692, was in Tusayan and gained some submission from the Indians; Oraibi did not give obeisance, for de Vargas did not visit that village. The Spanish reconquest meant little to the Hopi. Their isolation and the aridity of the region did not attract Spanish colonists. From those days, nearly three centuries ago, Spanish influence has faded into history.

Settlements have been moved. Shungopovi people went atop the second, or "Middle Mesa," and built a new pueblo in 1680; and those of Walpi moved to the tip of First Mesa after 1700. Following the Pueblo Rebellion, Tano Indians (Tewa from near Abiquiu in New Mexico), who wanted to escape the vengeance of the Spaniards who they feared would return to their pueblos, were invited to establish a village at Hano (HAH-noh)—as THAN-noh was pronounced in the western region—and serve as guards at the top of the trail (see Dozier 1966b:17–19; Stanislawski 1979:587). Hano and Sitchumovi (seet-CHEW-moh-vee), which was built in the 1700s as an overflow from Walpi, make the First Mesa structures appear almost continuous.

A new pueblo, Shipaulovi (shee-PAUL-oh-vee), was founded in its present location on Second Mesa, and Mishongnovi (mee-SHONG-noh-vee) was moved to the end of the mesa from a lower site near the Corn Rock shrine (originally two imposing sandstone pillars; now one has fallen).

A farming settlement was set up along Moencopi Wash in the western part of Hopiland by Chief Tuba, in 1870, and Upper and Lower Moencopi (MOH-en-koh-pee) came into being. A short distance from there, a government agency established by Mormon missionaries and named for Chief Tuba, or *Toovi,* from Oraibi, has become Tuba City. The Mormons hoped to produce woolen textiles on a large scale and founded a woolen mill there in 1879—a venture which was short-lived. The Mormons believe the American Indians to be descendants of the "lost tribes of Israel," so they feel obliged to treat them in a friendly manner. Their efforts to convert the Hopi have been but mildly successful.

Old Oraibi has occupied the same locale since about 1100; it vies with Acoma as being the oldest continuously inhabited village in the nation. It was one of the largest of the Hopi towns until 1906, when dissension brought about the founding of Hotevila (now more commonly spelled Hote-villa, but pronounced hoh-tah-VILL-ah), then Bacabi (BAH-kah-bee) in 1907, and New Oraibi (1910) on Third Mesa (cf. Coze 1971:4).

During the first quarter of the nineteenth century, Americans were visiting the Hopi country in steadily increasing numbers—explorers and trappers, soldiers and surveyors, traders and missionaries, government agents, and others. In 1853, the villages were ravaged by smallpox, an introduction of the white man. Lieutenant A. W. Whipple of the Topographical Engineers reported that at one pueblo he found "only the chief and one other man remained of all the able-bodied men of the town." The living dragged the bodies to the edge of the mesa and threw them over the cliffs. This cut the Hopi population drastically, as did another epidemic around 1892.

Hopiland was part of the U.S.A. for about twenty years before an agent was assigned to take over supervision of these Indians, in 1869. A year later a Protestant group established a mission school at Keams Canyon; like other attempts to convert the Hopi the results were negative. Their age-old religion provided security for the Hopi and their way of life—the "Hopi Way"—satisfied their needs (see Owings 1980:1, see also Sekaquaptewa 1980:7).

A Mennonite preacher, H. R. Voth, without approval of the Oraibi people (but with the consent of government officials) built a stone church on the mesa near the pueblo in 1901. It stood as an "offensive eyesore" until it was struck by lightning and gutted by fire in 1942 (James 1956:30). The ruin may be seen as one passes along the roadway a short distance from the pueblo.

When conditions became more settled, some individuals began moving to ranches on the lowlands, generally south of the mesas; others went to places such as Keams Canyon, where many work for various governmental divisions in numerous capacities, or to Polacca built below First Mesa, to Moencopi or Tuba City. Perhaps 1,200 work in more distant communities—Holbrook, Winslow, Flagstaff, and Grand Canyon or elsewhere. But most of these wage earners will be back in their hereditary homes on the mesas for the seasonal ceremonies. In these modern times, many ceremonials are scheduled for weekends, so the increasing number of off-reservation workers can return and take part. (Rel. Clemmer 1979.)

Among the Hopi Indians today are many qualified carpenters, painters, masons, mechanics, and other laborers who can secure work in non-Indian communities with no difficulty. The Hopi are shrewed businessmen. Many have proven to be adept machine operators and skilled forest firefighters. Those men who stay at home care for their sandy fields which they dry-farm, or on which they practice flood irrigation, wresting their livelihood from a harsh, though beautiful, environment. Considerable income is derived from the carving of figurines, watercolor painting, basketry, jewelry, and, to a decreasing degree, from weaving traditional textiles. The average annual income per family is estimated to be around $3,000. The women tend their fertile garden plots; some fashion beautiful pottery, others weave belts or make baskets. They are famous for *piki*, a tissue-paper-thin breadstuff made of cornmeal and baked on a red-hot rock slab. Several layers are rolled together while still warm. The rolls become crisp when cool; they are tasty and highly nutritious (*see* Connelly, C. 1980:28–32).

The Hopi Indians are very concerned about education. All their educational facilities have been upgraded in recent years. These include a dormitory housing boarding school students, and new classrooms at Keams Canyon. At Polacca, new facilities were built. A consolidated school at Second Mesa, and facilities at Hote-villa, have been in use for some twenty years. Formerly, children were educated through the tenth grade; then the ninth and tenth grades were abolished, and Hopi children were sent to off-reservation boarding schools or to high schools elsewhere.

Long unfulfilled plans for a high school on the Hopi reservation are yet but plans, although a site south of Piñon has been set aside for a high school and, perhaps, a community college. School attendance is good. Many Hopi students are enrolled in various colleges, particularly Ganado. Many seek work off the reservation and make their way among the non-Indian society.

Development of paved Highway 264, with hard-topped tributary roads leading to the north and south through Hopiland, has had severe effects upon the Hopi, both in the increased number of visitors who intrude upon their quiet way of life, and in the larger number of their younger generation who are drawn away from their hereditary world and culture. On 15 January 1971 a Hopi Culture Center built along traditional pueblo lines by a modern architect was opened by the Hopi Tribe. It contains deluxe hotel units, and has a restaurant and conference room. A museum and crafts shops are included in the complex, on Second Mesa.

As one walks by the house blocks or enters the small plazas of the Hopi pueblos, rectangular structures detached from the dwellings add striking features to the architecture. Tall, slender poles, two in number, stand high above the flat-roofed chambers—the kivas.

At Hano, established on First Mesa by Tewa from the Río Grande, clanship affiliations of the kivas are obscure. All villagers belong to one of the two kivas, but when the winter solstice ceremony is observed, part of a clan may go into one kiva and part into the other. Since the Tewa migrated with a patrilineal moiety system to join the matrilineal clanship organization of their hosts, the non–Tewa-speaking Hopi, this may well account for the variances found. When the Tewa were invited to live at Hano, they gave heed to their town chief's counsel and came as the summer moiety—not as any clan.

In other villages, the social organization follows its basic Hopi pattern. The main village, Walpi (now stabilized by the National Park Service, and approached by a paved road), has four unattached kivas and one built into a house block. The middle pueblo, Sitchumovi, has two kivas back to back in a plaza.

On Second Mesa, where three pueblos were built at their present sites in the 1680–1700 period, all of the kivas are detached; Shungopavi has five, Shipaulovi three, and Mishongnovi four. Of the Third Mesa group, old Oraibi has had a long history of rectangular kivas built apart from the houses; but since the total population is now less than 150, the ceremonial organization has suffered decline. Hotevilla, Bacabi, and the outlying farming community of Moencopi have detached kivas in active use.

A respected friend of the Hopi recorded that the nearest they came to having a legislative body was the meeting of the chiefs—"Chiefs' Talk"—held annually at the end of the *Soyala* ceremony, or winter solstice. The chiefs of the ceremonial societies constitute an assembly, with the village chief as headman. The latter selects his successor from among the sons of his brothers and sisters (*see* James 1956:105).

The time-consuming deliberations of the Hopi elders continually frustrated government officials, who wanted quick responses to their proposals and propositions. Eventually, they devised a "tribal council" comprised of a progressive faction and imposed it on the more conservative ones, thus achieving a body with which dealings could be carried on, whether the "old ones" approved or not. (*See* Connelly, J. C. 1980:61–62; 1979b:539.) When a constitution and by-laws were submitted for ratification by the Hopi, on 24 October 1936, they were adopted by a vote of 651 for and 104 against. In this election only some 30 percent of those entitled to vote cast their ballots (*Hopi Reservation* leaflet no. 5).

This "tribal council" is made up of members who must be twenty-five years of age, speak their own language, and have lived on the Hopi reservation for two years. Representation is based on village population. After certification by the respective village leaders, the representatives are certified by the outgoing council annually on December first. The council elects a chairman and vice-chairman from among its members; it appoints a secretary and treasurer who may or may not be council members, two interpreters and a sergeant-at-arms who are not members.

From early times, land limits and boundaries have grown to be a problem for the Hopi. After many centuries, the Hopi lands gradually came to be completely surrounded by the Navajo, whose presence became recognizable after A.D. 1500. Some 2,428,000 acres were federally acknowledged in 1882 as the Hopi reservation. This caused unsolved disputes between the two groups of Indians. Attempting to improve the situation, the government ruled in 1937 that the Hopi should have exclusive use of only 631,174 acres and should share the remaining acreage with the Navajo. In 1962, a decision of the Arizona District Court confirmed this ruling and it was upheld by the U.S. Supreme Court a few years later. The remaining acreage (nearly 1,800,000) was held between the two groups "in joint, equal and undivided shares." So the conflict continues (*See* p. 86 ff.).

In April, 1970, the Hopi filed a brief in federal court seeking to drive the Navajo off this shared area and to allow the Hopi living within their reservation, but outside the excluded land, to share grazing rights and leases on trading posts with the Navajo. The Indian Claims Commission meeting in Washington at the end of June, 1970, ruled that the Hopi should have been paid, by the 1937 land rates, for the 1.8 million acres taken from them and that they should have been paid, by 1882 land rates, for an estimated 5 million acres in aboriginal claims. Further hearings and more years of waiting are in store—specific acreages to be determined and values fixed, or other arrangements made.

A very important feature of social organization among the Pueblo peoples is curing; this is under the control of medicine societies operating within an esoteric cult generally known as katsina. The early Spaniards recorded this as *catzina* (Hackett 1937, III:131ff.; *see* Dockstader 1954:148, 1979a:7–15), which would be their rendering of the Keres "K'AH-tseen-ah" or of the Hopi "cot-SEE-nah." In written literature, the word is given diverse spellings such as katzina, katchina, kachina, cachina, katcina, kacina, and other pronunciations approximating the native language concerned.

Remember that none of the New World peoples had a written language of their own [unless some of the Mesoamerican glyph systems prove to relate to true written tongues]; so the spellings of Indian words followed systems of the recorders—some simply personal, others in accord with recognized phonetic or orthographic systems. It is likely that this gave rise to certain of the debased usages of today, for readers frequently do not give attention to the fine print or explanatory notes. For instance, Dr. Bunzel in her reports on Zuñi uses *katcina;* she gives a "table of sounds" in which "c" has the value of "sh" and would be heard as "kátshina," with accent on the first syllable (Bunzel 1932a:471).

Beliefs concerning the katsinas are similar, pueblo to pueblo. These supernatural beings are represented in various ways, all of which are associated in the Indian mind. First, they are *spiritual guises* of an anthropomorphic nature. Again they are masked, painted, and properly *costumed individuals* who appear in the village plazas and kivas as impersonators of the spiritual ones enacting esoteric rites and ceremonies. In another guise, they are *wooden figurines*— small representations of the life-size beings—by means of which Indian children become familiar with the katsinas as part of their religious training and culture history. *(Rel.* Connelly, J. C. 1980:60–62; 1979b:539–553 in re katsina cult.)

When the katsina cult functions fully, every man, woman, and child of a pueblo is supposed to be initiated into it, and every man takes an active, lifelong part in its ceremonies *(rel.* Bahti, M. 1980:2–7; Washburn 1980c: 39–49; Wright, B. 1979:17–21). Men only impersonate the male and female katsinas. Primarily, the katsinas are recognized as benevolent beings who dwell in the mountains, springs, and lakes, and who are the bringers of blessings, particularly rain, crops, and wellbeing. Some katsinas, however, are ogres or demons with disciplinary functions.

Throughout the millennia of man's struggle for existence in the semiarid Southwest, the dominating factor has been rain. Inasmuch as the Pueblo Indians are farmers, their ceremonies are primarily for rain. The building or decorating of a kiva is said to be a prayer for rain or crops. And the feeling is that the correct performance of numerous ritualistic acts brings the desired results. Thus the katsinas, the spirit rainmakers, truly symbolize the climatic drive or weather control of Southwestern man past and present.

Upon death, it is believed, a Pueblo person becomes a katsina; he may appear henceforth as a cloud—that is, as a masked personator. A boy belongs to the kiva of his father, into which he is initiated; girls also may be initiated, but they do not wear masks or belong to the kiva groups. Although the cacique is not a curer, or "medicine man," he has authority over the curers and the kiva chiefs. The duties of the cacique keep him somewhat aloof from the people; on the other hand, the war chief is the most important officer, visibly, but he is virtually under the authority of the cacique. Thus, the katsina organization is under the direct control of a cacique and his assistants.

According to legend, in bygone days the katsinas used to come to the people when they were sad and lonely, and dance for them. They brought gifts to the people and taught them their arts and industries and how to hunt. After a time the people began to grow their own foodstuffs. When rain was needed the katsinas would come and dance in the fields; then the rains always came.

Pueblo versions vary slightly, but all agree that the people came to take the katsinas for granted. Respect and veneration for their benevolence were lost by some; others had violent fights with the supernatural ones. The katsinas left, refusing to return. However, they taught a few of the faithful young men some of their ceremonies and showed them how to make masks and costumes; as long as the earthly ones followed their instructions properly, as long as "their hearts were right," they were permitted to act as if they were katsinas, and the "real katsinas" would come and possess the persons of the masked dancers. Rain would follow. On this assurance the masked katsina dances are performed to this day.

Serving as a means of uniting man and spirit beings, the katsina masks are very sacred. In some instances they are privately owned, in others they are communal property; they may be kept in certain households along with other ceremonial paraphernalia, or kept in the kivas.

The katsina cult, then, exists for the purpose of impersonating the supernatural rainmakers, so that weather controls may be exercised with resultant moisture for the crops and pastures. The organization is composed of various groups, each managed by a medicine society. Initiations take place in the house of a medicine society. A great deal of accoutrement is necessary. When masked dances are presented the masks may be all alike, or specific combinations, or they may be of mixed character.

Many of the Spanish officials and zealous missionaries did all they could to destroy the aboriginal religious rites. In the Río Grande valley, where the Spanish influence became so strong, the masked ceremonies were forced underground, or away from foreign eyes, for the most part. Frequent changes among the governmental officials and agents of the Catholic church, with alternating policies and practices, resulted in the Indian's compounded confusion. Within a hundred years after the *entrada* of Coronado and with less than a half-century of colonization, the culture of the Indians had been irretrievably altered. After preceding administrations had rigidly suppressed the Indian religious observances, Governor Bernardo López de Mendizábal, who was exceedingly oppressive in most ways, not only gave permission for the performing of katsina dances, but commanded the Indians to enact them. Accordingly, from about 1660 on, these previously forbidden ceremonies were held in the Tewa and Tiwa pueblos, as well as among the Keres, and even in the plaza of Santa Fe! But that ceased long ago.

Among the western pueblos, where Spanish influence was less disruptive, masked dances continued to be performed much as they were in pre-Spanish times. Later "reformers" in the Southwest found the Indian rites offensive, "horrifying and unclean." But those who understood—some of those non-Indians who were intimate with the Indians and were allowed in the kivas—refuted such charges.

It must be remembered that values differ from one culture to another, and they alter from time to time. Actions that appear innocent to us may be considered extremely vulgar by those of another social group; and things appearing obscene to us may be inoffensive to others.

It is now a rare instance when an outsider is allowed to witness a katsina dance at one of the Río Grande pueblos; even Indians of other Pueblo groups are frequently kept from viewing such events. At Zuñi outsiders are permitted to view many of the masked dances. For instance, in the spectacular *Shalako*—a fertility and house-blessing ceremony—masked personators dance before large audiences of white people, as well as Indians, local and otherwise (*see* Gonzales 1969). And in the Hopiland villages restrictions are even less evident. There, some two hundred and fifty or more katsinas are known; the number is highly flexible for a variety of reasons (*see* Dockstader 1954:23ff; Wright, B. 1973, 1977; Hartmann 1978).

Studies that have been permitted in pueblos of the Río Grande region have revealed that Keres ceremonialism is highly complex. In common with most Southwestern Indians, the Keres hold that they emerged from the dark underworld (*see* Ellis, F. H. 1979b:440; Strong, P. T. 1979a:390–391; Lange, C. H. 1979b:383–384). They have a long myth which recites the facts of their life in the netherland. There they appointed priests, or organized societies, to take their places, and each deity, or group of spirits, taught their human successors how to perform the rituals that were essential to human welfare. Then came the emergence—the coming out of the people at *Shipop* (SHIP-op). It is said that after they emerged they made an extensive trip "around the world"—their world, bounded by certain mountain ranges with specific directional peaks, sacred springs, and related features.

Through the years the Pueblo Indians have been faced with a variety of situations which have altered their traditional beliefs regarding illnesses and curing. Slowly, they became influenced by the white doctors' knowledge of medicine and medical and surgical practices. In some pueblos, or in towns nearby, clinics were established, providing nursing assistance and professional consultations. In fewer instances, hospital facilities were provided. On availing themselves of these newer services, some Indians received sympathetic treatment and kindly attention to their needs; others fared less well, and many were the occasions of long or fruitless waits to secure aid. The Indians reacted accordingly.

In 1950, during the first session of the 83rd Congress, Public Law 568 was passed, transferring health services from the BIA and placing them under the U.S. Department of Health, Education and Welfare. This act was opposed by the Pueblo Indians at that time. They feared that the change would result in less understanding of their problems and requirements. As they came to comprehend the Public Health Service plans better, they became more hopeful. Soon, great improvements in health facilities for the Indians were initiated; and the trend has continued.

Countless surveys relating to Indian health conditions have been made, and many volumes have been written on the subject. Readers interested in learning more on this subect are referred to PHS publications and related sources.

Today, an increasing number of Pueblo Indians seek and receive modern medical and surgical treatment, just as do the majority of the population.

With the Keres, medicine societies as well as clans have been important (*see* Dozier 1970b:150).

Great attention is given to the combatting of disease. The small, secret medicine societies are composed of male members who have the knowledge of the initiated and possess mighty supernatural powers by virtue of that knowledge. Their ideology, paraphernalia, ritual, and ceremonies are grouped together under the term "medicine cult" (White 1935:120). The medicine societies deal only with sickness due to supernatural derivation. Benevolent and malevolent supernaturals being recognized, the latter call forth the services of the curers most frequently.

At Santo Domingo, largest of the eastern Keres pueblos, four major medicine societies are known: the Flint, *Cíkame,* Giant, and *Bóyakya (rel.* Lange, C. H. 1979b:386). These societies work together for the good of the pueblo, uniting their efforts in serious cases. Their power lies not in themselves but is believed to have been secured from supernatural animals. To gain power from these, and make use of it, the curers employ their extensive collections of fetishes and figurines, medicines and numerous efficacious items. Cures may be conducted at any time of the year. The curers wear prescribed attire. Although females may belong to medicine societies they do not know all the secrets. Several channels of attaining membership are recognized, voluntary or by compulsion. In addition to their curative functions, some of the religious societies also have important governmental controls.

The Keres have no moiety houses. Each medicine society has a chamber in which its initiations take place, solstice ceremonies are performed, and retreats held; each society has its headman who exercises some authority over his fellow members. These society chambers, or houses, built in the midst of the pueblo dwellings, are linked with the circular "big kivas" of the Keres system which are used for dances and ceremonies pertaining to the village as a whole. They function intimately in the katsina order, each kiva group being associated with particular clans and with two complementary divisions of anthropomorphic personages. These manlike spirits are recognized as sacred clowns called *Koshari* and *Kurena* (and by comparable terms in other Pueblo languages). The koshari societies do not practice curing; they are concerned with fertility and growth (cf. Dozier 1970b: 151).

The koshari are members of the Flint society which is associated with the turquois kiva—thus the winter people, while the kurena are members of the Cíkame society and function with the squash kiva—the summer people. The kiva heads organize the katsina dances, act as custodians of the masks, and supervise preparations for dances; they also select dancers for special parts such as those who enact the buffalo dance.

Santo Domingo has had four other curing societies of minor importance: Ant, Snake, *Kapina,* and *Beraka,* each with power to cure some ailment. Some of these societies occur in the other Keres pueblos, and similar organizations are found among other peoples.

The legendary belief is that Koshari came from his home in the east, near

the sunrise; and Kurena had a home close to Koshari, at a spring somewhat
to the south. Long ago, these beings also are said to have lived with the people; but, when they went back to stay in the east, arrangements were made
that ordinary men might represent them if properly initiated, costumed, and
otherwise prepared. When these personators function it is as if the "real"
koshari and kurena were present. Thus they serve as mediators between the
people of the earth and their ancient spirits. Those of the koshari organization whom we see are held to be the living embodiments of the spirits of the
ancient ones.

Differences in attire and accoutrement, body painting, and hairdress help
to distinguish the kurena from the koshari. The trunks, limbs, and faces of
the koshari are painted white with black horizontal stripes (or sometimes the
bodies are painted grey, sometimes with spots instead of stripes). Black circles surround the eyes and mouth. The hair is daubed with white clay and is
done up with cornhusks into "horns" on either side of the head. An old dark
rag serves as a breechclout, looped over a thong around the waist and from
which cow hooves may be suspended. At times rags are tied about the wrists,
knees, and neck. The feet are usually bare. Narrow strips of dried cornhusks
are symbolic of the koshari.

Bodies of the kurena are painted in vertical divisions—the right side orange, the left side white. Vertical stripes of orange and black are painted on
the face. The hair is worked into a single bunch on top of the head. Ragged
loincloth and arm and knee decorations are like those of the koshari. A blue
and red necklace made of cornstalk with beads may be worn. Feathers of the
desert sparrow serve as symbols of the kurena. But as Pueblo customs break
down, traditional features show certain changes. Members of the medicine
societies accompany the masked dancers in rites from which the public is
excluded. They also participate in some of the open ceremonies, such as corn
dances, where they dance in and out among the formal dancers. Men and
boys who dress like the koshari and kurena and act like them, but who are
not members of the societies, may dance, too, on such occasions. Frequently,
both the koshari and kurena function as clowns to the merriment of Indians
and visitors alike. Indian cultural mores provide for a balance of pleasurable
or amusing activities and grave or sedate pursuits. The serious duties of these
society members, however, are far more important. Each of these societies
goes into individual retreats before a dance is held. In September the kurena
society has a dance of its own, and in February the koshari has its dance;
obviously these pertain to seasonal changes.

On occasion, among the Keres peoples, certain other impersonators are
seen who are identifiable by knobby protuberances on their masks and accen-
tuated circles around the eyes and mouth—the commonly called "mudheads."
These relate to times when the Indians had not yet emerged from the dark
underworld. Each Pueblo group recognizing these characters explains their
origin as their migration myths are recited. The mudheads serve as messen-

gers of the people and their deities. The western Pueblos place greater emphasis on them. *Gomaiowish* of Acoma, for instance, equates with Kóyemshi of Zuñi. More will be said of these personages under the discussion of the secret orders at Zuñi.

In the past, each pueblo had a warrior society, whose members had killed an enemy and taken his scalp in a prescribed ritual manner. Even though such a society may now be defunct, masked warriors' dances or scalp dances may be performed. Patron deities of the war cult are the twin war gods (*Masewi* and *Oyoyewi* of the Keres). The koshari and kurena collaborate with the warriors' society in the scalp dance. Although created as clowns to amuse the people, they have other functions that are serious and far-reaching.

Another important organization is the hunters' society, in which membership is voluntary. It is composed of medicine men who manipulate supernatural power in order to control game, thus assuring plentiful animal food for mankind. Their power is believed to have been derived from the beasts of prey. The society has, or had, its own ceremonial house and considerable equipment. It has a prominent part in the communal rabbit hunts, and plays a role in the buffalo dance.

Among the Tewa peoples, as noted above, the large surface structure of circular form—serving an entire pueblo—is associated with the warrior cult. Ceremonial emphases originally were on war, not on rainmaking as is found among other Pueblos. Medicine societies were not part of the social organization, although curing was effected by officers of the warrior cult. The concept of katsinas apparently was lacking in the primary pattern. Later, esoteric organizations with powerful priesthoods, the katsina cult, clowning orders known as *kossa* and *kwirana,* and various ceremonial procedures—largely borrowed from the Keres—were added to Tewa practices (*see* Hill 1982:209–212).

Among the Tiwa, Isleta gave asylum to a conservative group of Laguna (Mesita) people aound 1879, inviting them to establish a colony at the western limit of the pueblo; this is called Oraibi—the same name as that of one of the Hopi pueblos. Two groups of medicine men, both curers and weather controllers, came to function at Isleta—the Town Fathers and the Laguna Fathers. A hunt chief is recognized, and a war chief who is more or less the executive for the town chief and his assisting bow chief.

Properly speaking, no katsina organization into which all of the youth are initiated exists at Isleta, but they have katsina chiefs, the headman being chief of the yellow corn group. Their supernaturals, like the katsinas of other pueblos, are impersonated in dances, but no masks are worn. What katsina organization prevails was introduced from Laguna. The medicine men derive their powers from animal spirits. Clowns, *k ápyo,* are associated with the katsinas and appear with their bodies painted in stripes, with spots, and contrasting colors: six represent each kiva and a young boy wearing small deer horns dances at the head of the line of dancers.

It has been stated above (page 21) that Taos and Picurís have chambers used by the warrior cult and scalp societies, and that curing was a function of the warrior society. The clowns are called *Chifunane* (Black Eyes), or commonly pronounced *Chifonetti;* their bodies are painted similarly to the koshari of the Keres groups.

At the Towa pueblo of Jémez, some twenty groups of a ceremonial nature exist, and they include two clown orders, each relating to a kiva; one, the *tabösh,* is associated with the squash kiva which has charge of the summer activities, and the other, *tsúnta tabösh,* is associated with the turquois kiva which has charge of winter ceremonies. Most of the pueblo men belong to one or the other of these groups; they are self-selective. Women also are members. The tsúnta tabösh is concerned with the sprouting of plants, and the tabösh with their maturing. The latter group represents the turquois people and the other, the ice people; they are said not to recognize themselves as summer and winter people. The chief of the tabösh retreats to the turquois kiva in November, and the tsúnta tabösh chief to the squash kiva in the spring. The tabösh have two fetishes, or "mothers," and the other order has one. The tabösh participate in dances in September and on 12 November, while the tsúnta tabösh come out only on 2 August—the feast day of the Pecos people who migrated to Jémez in 1838.

Jémez has no katsina organization, as such, but it has adopted the concept of katsinas from neighboring peoples and has related them to their secret ceremonies, manifest through masked dancers who personate the supernaturals. *(See* Dozier 1970b: 175 in re social organization, etc.) Jémez katsinas, recognized in pairs of male and female, are envisioned as cloud people, identified with their deceased ones; they bring rain for the growing crops.

A father to the katsinas is appointed by the cacique and is called "chief." He is entrusted with a corn ear fetish, or "mother," and he is in charge of ceremonial whipping. Wherever katsina organizations obtain, the principal initiatory rite is that of whipping by a katsina whipper. Girls as well as boys are whipped—a rite of exorcism to drive off evil spirits.

Ceremonial races of the kick-stick type are held at Jémez on a track oriented north-south.

Two medicine orders function in the pueblo, a fire society and an arrowhead society (Parsons 1925:49). They treat illness caused by supernaturals of bird, animal, and human form—the so-called "witches." They also engage in weather control. Each group has its chief and each member possesses a fetish, or "mother." The fire society may have women members. The chief of the arrowhead society has charge of the war god figurines. No warrior society now exists. The chief of an under-chief society is in charge of the scalps; this society holds a scalp dance, a function of the warrior's society elsewhere.

As has been noted, the Zuñi have an elaborate ceremonial organization. This includes a large number of esoteric societies, each of which is devoted to the veneration of special supernaturals or groups of supernaturals. Each society has a priesthood, a special meeting place, a body of secret ritual, permanent possession of fetish-derived power, and a calendrical cycle of ceremonies. According to Zuñi philosophy, the sun is the source of life and is duly honored at solstice observances. The most revered and most holy man in Zuñi is the sun priest who has charge of solstice ceremonies and is keeper of the calendar. He is held responsible for the welfare of the community; thus his duties are those of the so-called cacique in Tanoan and Keresan societies. The Zuñi calendar also includes lunar observations.

Utmost attention is given to a cult of rainmakers that comprises twelve priesthoods. Memberships in these is usually hereditary in the matrilineal family residing in the house in which the fetish of the group is kept. These fetishes are said to be the most sacred objects in Zuñi. Rather than presenting public ceremonies, the rain priesthoods observe retreats in the household of the fetishes; their rites are primarily concerned with weather control—securing rain for the growing corn.

A significant feature of Zuñi ceremonial organization is its emphasis on ancestors, resulting in an ancestor cult. Every Zuñi participates in their veneration, and "they are involved in every ceremony. They guide, protect, and nourish human life," being identified with clouds and rain. It is said that while priests and medicine men pray to special groups of ancestors, the ordinary Zuñi prays to ancestors in general (Eggan 1950:203; 1979:232; Ladd 1979a:482 ff.).

The katsina, or kóko, cult is pueblowide, including every adult male, but normally not the women. Upon death, one goes to join the katsinas, but "only those intimately associated with the cult can be sure of joining them after death." Chief concern of the katsina priests is with fertility, rather than with rain.

Zuñi has a strong cult of the beast gods under management of twelve curing societies, in which both men and women may hold membership. This cult centers around the animals of prey "who live in the east, control long life, and are the givers of medicine and magical power." Each society practices general medicine and specializes in certain diseases or afflictions.

The cult of the war gods is in the hands of the bow priesthood, whose members are those who have killed an enemy. It is in the charge of an elder and younger bow priest, who represent the twin war gods, sons of the Sun Father. This priesthood serves as the executive arm of the religious hierarchy. In recent years, the warrior society has deteriorated. Membership has come to be limited; some have said the society no longer existed, and others that it did.

In the recent past, certain members, or surviving relatives who possessed the fetishes and other ceremonial gear, have sold these surreptitiously. Collectors paid well to obtain such rare paraphernalia of a passing culture trait. The opportunity to secure like benefits inspired clever artisans (Indian and non-Indian) to produce similar fetishes—fashioned of antler and embellished with feathers, beads, and other symbolic features—and ceremonial pottery, especially old jars covered over with tiny flakes of turquois, and to which fetishes and feathers may be tied with leather thongs. The antiqued specimens show traces of pollen or sacred meal, and readily pass as authentic. About two decades ago some of these spurious items began appearing in the hands of dealers who commonly kept them under cover. It was a while before the quantity available aroused suspicions as to their authenticity.

At the end of January 1970, press notices made it known that Owaleon, the "last of the old Zuñi war chiefs," had died. His age was estimated to be 106 years. A son is quoted: "Now all the memories of his Indian prayer are disappeared forever . . . none of the new war chiefs visited him after he was sick." And the son remarked, "He wanted to be buried at the new cemetery because he believed in God, not in the old way" (Anonymous 1970f). Although he actually was buried in the old cemetery, this remark reflects cultural changes which have occurred among the Southwestern Indian peoples during the past century, particularly the last sixty years. A warrior society continues to be recognized at Zuñi, but the "new war chiefs" have a different role than did the old ones.

The Zuñi run ceremonial races that are contests between the elder and younger war gods; these are of the kick-stick type, comparable to the Keres races. Clan races also may be held, or ceremonial races by kiva groups.

It appears that the social organization of Zuñi is the most complex to be found in the Southwest.

According to their mythology, the twin sons of the Sun Father guided the Zuñi from the undermost world to this world. Here they organized four esoteric fraternities. The people traveled about for many years. Then the rain priest sent forth two of his children, a youth and a maiden, to search out a good place and build their village. The two ascended a mountain where the maiden stayed to rest while her brother looked over the country. When he returned his sister was asleep; she appeared so beautiful that he desired her. His act of passion enraged the girl, but their unnatural union resulted in the birth of ten children, that very night. It is said that thenceforth "they talked a changed language, but there was no change in appearance." The first born was normal in all respects, but the others lacked the seeds of generation, and thus were infertile. As evidence of this abnormality, their seeds are contained within knobs growing on their heads; from the puckered mouth flows unintelligible talk. "Silly were they, yet wise as the gods and high priests."

Realizing that it was not well for him and his sister to be alone, the youth hurried to make things ready for the coming of their people. He created two rivers and a lake with a village in its depths. When the people reached the river—said to be the Little Colorado of today—many were afraid; strange happenings occurred. Following their leaders came the women with little children on their backs. As they became crazed and terrified, many of the children dropped into the water and instantly became aquatic creatures—tortoises, water snakes, frogs, tadpoles, other vertebrates, amphibians, and reptiles. Those transformed ones went from the river to the lake village, the home of the kóko, or rain people who have died; there they "were restored to normal condition" and immediately attained maturity.

The rain priest's son who had sired the "nine lastborn children" and his offspring became mudheads, or Kóyemshi—old dance men; the mother became the mother of the gods—old dance woman, *kómokatsi*. After creation of the gods, Father Koyemshi decided they must not appear outside of their dance house unmasked. The head of one of the esoteric fraternities, the *Néwekwe*, copied the mask of Father Koyemshi, and others of that fraternity copied the remaining nine masks. The masks are made of cotton cloth of dun color, with a piece of black cloth at the base; under the latter, packets of seeds of the native crops are concealed. A black kilt and brown moccasins are worn; fawnskin pouches hang from the right shoulder. Each Kóyemshi differs slightly from the others in appearance and conduct. They became the attendants of the kóko—sages and interpreters of their ancient dance dramas.

Whereas the Hopi are known far and wide for their katsina dances and their snake dances, Zuñi is famous for its Shalako ceremonial held annually in late November or early December. This is a re-enactment of the creation and migration of the Zuñi people to their "middle-place," or *Héptina*, from their sacred lake village. The Shalako—giant-sized messengers of the rain gods—come to bless the houses constructed in their honor (a maximum of eight may be built—one for each of the six Shalako, one for the mudheads, or koyemshi, and one for the Council of the Gods) and to offer prayers that the Zuñi may enjoy fertility, long life, prosperity and happiness. Every member of the pueblo is committed to honoring the Shalako by aiding his clan and kiva relatives; this is done by contributing labor and material goods.

The religious enactments are under control of caciques of the six kivas which represent the cardinal directions, the zenith and nadir. Each kiva has a spectacular group of dancers—the Kóko, or so-called katsinas—in magnificent attire. The Shalako ceremonial closes the Zuñi year. Their New Year comes near the time of the winter solstice, usually the first part of January. Then the cycle of religious activities begins, and the initial preparations for the Shalako are made; the personators of the dance characters are selected, and households accept responsibility for building new houses or remodeling old ones wherein the Shalako will be entertained. The year-long duties of the personators are assumed; these consist of religious activities, usually held in private, through which the long chants are learned and their presentation practiced.

Date of the Shalako is determined in the fall, and announcement is made that the return of the gods will occur in forty-nine days.

DEATH IN THE WOODS (Keres)

> Corn swaying in the rhythm of the wind—
>   Graceful ballerinas,
>   Emerging at the edge of the forest.
> All dip and dance;

Wind tunnels through long silken hair.
Golden teeth-seeds.
Trees chatter nervously
    Awakening sky in fright,
    Pointing at Woodman.
A mighty thud! Blow leaves deep scar;
    He strikes again . . .
Corn mourns golden tears,
    Rows, praying for fallen brother.
Jay mocks the greedy beast
    Who has doomed majestic brother,
    His life home.
Wind tosses leaves aside as
    Woodman tramps on his way,
    Ax dripping oak's blood.
The forest, damp and silent,
    Mourning for lost Oak.
And now remains but a
Chirp of a lonely cricket and
Silhouette of Woodman,
Diminishing,
        beyond the
            saddened hill
            as the far
            sun sinks.

By Harold Bird, Laguna-Santo Domingo

From: *The Writer's Reader*, Fall, 1966.
The Institute of American Indian Arts,
Santa Fe, N.M.

On Shalako day, about midafternoon, activities which visitors may witness
are begun. The little fire god and his ceremonial father come from the south
and cross the Zuñi river; they are followed by a retinue of splendidly adorned
personages. After their retirement, intervals occur during which the ceremonies are covert, but the great drama continues throughout the night, with all
participants appearing in the pueblo and certain ones dancing in the Shalako
houses. As sunrise comes, activities cease and a few hours are spent in resting. Then rites are resumed. Around midday, the Shalako and their assistants
come forth for a culminating spectacular which is performed on the south
side of the river—the six giant figures, like great birds, engaging in a ceremonial relay race.

One who had observed many Shalako ceremonies prepared a small publication which should be read by everyone attending this unique and centuries-old
enactment (Gonzales 1969).

The Hopi have been influenced by contacts with the Río Grande Pueblos
for centuries and they have borrowed extensively from the the Zuñi. They

have a strong katsina organization in operation. New katsinas are introduced from time to time, some coming from other pueblos and some from non-Pueblo peoples such as the Havasupai, Apache, and Navajo. The Spaniards brought the horse, cow, sheep, and domesticated fowl to the Southwest, and these came to be represented by katsinas; more recently other representations—even Mickey Mouse—have been portrayed.

We are told that if a first performance by the personator of a new katsina is followed by good weather, rain, and fertile crops, he is adopted and becomes an integral part of regular performances. If such an introduction appears to cause bad weather, drought, and loss of crops, rarely does he come again. The older katsinas are generally held to have superior power, more prestige, and greater dancing skill, but *Húmis* (often wrongly called *Niman*)—regarded as originating at Jémez—is held in extreme reverence and is a most popular katsina.

It is said that few katsinas "function as clan ancestors: the names by which some of the ancient kachinas are known are the same as clan names, and living clan members claim that the kachina of the same name as their clan is also their clan 'ancient,' or ancestor (*Wöye*)." Usually the *wöye* masks are kept in the custody of their respective clan mothers, who see to their safe-keeping, and ritually feed them regularly.

> The totemic aspect is present, but very few of the kachinas that are traditionally regarded as the most ancient have any marked totemic character—most of the apparently totemic kachinas seem of more recent origin, and some are of recognizably alien provenience, either alien-Indian or White. (Dockstader 1954:14)

Only a few of the katsina ceremonies are given on set dates. After the opening of the katsina season in November, with enactment of the emergence from the underworld, any individual katsina or groups of katsinas may be selected for presentation. If the village chief gives permission for a ceremony, word goes out as to date, place, and katsinas to be impersonated. Series of night dances in the kivas are performed freely between the time of Soyala in December and the beginning of *Powamû* in February. The latter is the major ritual of the katsina cult in Hopiland; it is a nine-day ceremony. One of the chief features is the promotion of fertility and germination in the approaching season. Growth of beans is forced in kiva rites by Powamû members, and dramatic performances portray Hopi mythology.

Young people are initiated and learn the many aspects of the katsina mysteries. Then come curing rites, "for Powamû is regarded as having strong medicine for the cure of rheumatism" (Stephen 1936:156). While curing is ostensibly secret among the New Mexico Pueblos, it is under little specific prohibition among the Hopi. Rainmaking receives greater emphasis than does curing. Powamû, or bean dances, are presented and the horned water serpent ceremony, or *Pálulukoñ,* is performed with night dances in the kivas. These two ceremonies are closely connected, the main elements of both being similar. It is early April by the time all of the activities involved are terminated. The weather then permits daylong katsina dances in the village plazas.

After costume preparing and rehearsals, which take place in the kivas, the public ceremony is ready for presentation. On the day announced, "the performers, painted and costumed, proceed to one of several shrines outside the village, where they ritually don their masks. In the regular dance pattern, there may be from thirty to forty performers all costumed alike. These are usually accompanied by six masked *kachinmanas* (kachina maidens), or female kachinas, who are thought of as sweethearts, or sometimes sisters, of the kachinas. These *manas* are usually men dressed as women. As the sun rises, they start for the village where they are met by the *kachina-amu*, usually an old man not in costume, who has the function of encouraging the dancers, guiding them, and offering to them the prayers of the villagers" (Dockstader 1954:18; *see also* Wright, B. 1973; 1979:17–21).

A significant feature of the masked dances at the Hopi villages, as well as at Zuñi (and seemingly in the Río Grande pueblos), is the processional order of the participants. In certain instances the same individual takes a given part each time a ceremony is performed; he is followed by a particular personator, and so on down the line. In the Hopi observances the old, uncostumed man, or "father," usually leads the dancers in single file into the plaza (*kísonvi*) along a path he has prepared by sprinkling sacred cornmeal on the ground. The meal symbolizes feeding of the dancers; during the dancing the father sprinkles meal on the participants' shoulders and thus feeds them strength. The dancers are led to the south side of the plaza where they line up facing the east. The leader of the dance group is in the center of the line. He shakes his rattle and starts the singing. The other dancers join in, one by one taking up the song and rhythm. Each comes in on cue down to either end, where the poorer singers and novices are placed.

When the songs have been sung once, the father leads the dancers to the east side of the plaza where they face toward the north; the songs are repeated. Next, the line is led to the north, where the participants, facing west, sing the songs again. Then the dancers leave the plaza and go to a secluded part of the mesa, where they remove their masks, smoke, eat, and rest; they also have a short rehearsal of the next set of songs. They return to the village and present another round of singing and dancing. Such a ceremony continues from dawn until sundown. During the midday break, women of the proper clan bring food to the participants. The family of the dance sponsor has the major responsibility for providing this food.

This usual procedure differs from another type of dance performance, which is more akin to the Río Grande pattern. In it, all the dancers are costumed alike; the dancers do not sing, but are accompanied by a chorus of a dozen or more singers—usually older men.

Gifts from the katsina personators or other villagers are commonly brought into the plaza. Then, at the end of the third songset, the dancers distribute them. A bow and arrow for boys and a carved figurine for girls are traditional; now, gifts may include foodstuffs, store goods, and a variety of items.

Other participants in these dances include a number of mudheads (Coze 1952:18–29), similar to those of Zuñi; in Hopiland they are called *Táchukti*. Individuals may elect to give an impromptu show, or several organized clown groups may take part. They hold privileged positions in the katsina observances and, in their vari-faceted manifestations of jester-great hunter-medicine man, they are immune from taboos.

Still another katsina performance involves individual dancers who may enter a village singly, in pairs, or in small bands. These are the "character actors," some of whom have distinctive actions or calls which give rise to their names; others are known for their unique costuming. They may come almost any time during the katsina season, even while regular katsinas are performing, or in mixed katsina dances.

As the summer solstice approaches, the dance season draws to a close, and the final act of the katsina drama commences. Whereas at Soyala the badger clan ushers in the katsina ceremonies, the katsina clan has charge of the ceremonial departure of the katsinas, when they "go home" to their legendary dwellings. This, the Niman ceremony, usually occurs in July. At this time, impressive dances are given in the villages.

The people of Hano (Tewa) have adopted the katsina cult and a number of the ritualistic activities from the Hopi, but they have not borrowed the major Hopi ceremonies. They do not have men's societies. Katsina dances, games, races, and other observances—including competitive events like those of the Río Grande Tewa—are frequently held by kiva groups. It seems probable that kiva membership is associated with katsina initiations or with the winter solstice ceremonies. A Tewa clown organization exists; and great emphasis is placed on curing. All religious matters are in the hands of a hierarchy headed by the village chief. A war chief is responsible for guarding the pueblo against enemies and witches, and for settling internal quarrels. *(Rel.* Washburn 1980c:39–49.)

Open Ceremonials

To newcomers in the Southwest, the promise of Indian dances is often a strong lure. The term "dance" as used here has little of the meaning of dances of modern western society, or of esthetic and interpretive dances. The Pueblo Indian (as does his racial kindred) feels he is an important part of nature, that all parts of the universe are interrelated, and that he and the universe must be kept in balance. If this equilibrium is upset by selfish or hostile attitudes, disaster will result. Each considers it his duty to perform ceremonies to help the seasons follow one another in proper succession, to promote fertility of plants and animals, to encourage rain, and to insure hunting success. All this is voiced in his prayers and dramatized in his dances—rhythm of movement and of color summoned to express in utmost beauty the vibrant faith of a people in the deific order of his world and in the way his ancient ones devised for keeping man in harmony with the universe.

Numerous Indian dances are given which visitors are permitted to witness. Some are purely social dances, performed for the pleasure of dancing and having an enjoyable time. To these, non-Indian people and other Indians are welcome. Many of the dances occur on fixed dates, each year *(see* pages 251–54). Some of these are the culminating performances of rites which have been going on secretly for days in a pueblo—purification rites, retreats, prayers, and sacred enactments *(rel.* Kealiinohomoku 1978:28).

It is well to keep in mind that centuries of communal life have taught personal restraint. Consequently, the fact that visitors are admitted to certain dances does not mean, necessarily, that their presence is desired. (On occasion, non-Indian neighbors of the Pueblos, commonly operators of trading stores, erect "WELCOME" signs and direct traffic by their places of business, en route to a pueblo that is holding dances.) The Indians may not resent the presence of outsiders, but, remembering that the ceremonies being enacted have been going on for centuries—long before Europeans came to the New World—we can hardly feel that our being there is a truly welcome addition. We should feel honor bound not to abuse our privilege.

Some pueblos allow the use of cameras—*if these are carried under permit from the governor,* and usually *after payment of a fee.* Other pueblos are deeply opposed to picture taking, and permits for cameras are rarely granted. Anyone taking a camera or tape recorder into a pueblo should go at once to the governor or his representative and make sure of the existing conditions. Sketching and note taking are also forbidden unless special permission is granted.

Visitors sometimes commit offenses unintentionally, such as getting in the way of dancers, walking across the dance plaza, or standing or sitting in places that cut off the view of the pueblo residents, even to crowding them from their own premises. Others are shamefully rude, making unkind comments about the Indians or the ceremonies they are performing (as if the Indians do not understand English perfectly well), talking loudly, complaining because "nothing is happening," walking into homes where they are not invited, and utterly disregarding the fact that they are attending a ceremony which may be as sacred as any held elsewhere, in church or temple or synagogue. The Golden Rule should be observed in an Indian pueblo as well as—or perhaps even more than—any other place.

Participation in ceremonials is a communal duty and privilege of all the Pueblo people. Individuals are trained to take part in the dances from early childhood. Some of the most colorful and attractive dances are performed by children exclusively, as for example, Christmastime and Eastertime ceremonies at the pueblo of Santo Domingo.

Every item of the dance attire has a special significance–the things worn, body decoration, and accoutrement carried. Spruce or fir twigs held in the hands, or which adorn the body, symbolize longevity and everlasting life. Gourd and tortoise shell rattles imitate the swish of summer rain on the growing crops. Feathers and tufts of down or cotton are cloud and sky symbols. Before he can take part in a dance, each performer has to wash his hair as a rite of purification. Both men and women dance with their hair hanging loosely, the beautiful black tresses often falling below the waist. Crests of varicolored feathers worn on the men's heads are symbolic of the glowing zenith. The women's headdresses—fashioned from thin boards, or tablets (*tablitas*)—are decorated with carved-out or painted figures indicating the sky arch, cloud terraces, sun and moon, and other motifs of a sacred nature. Colors here, as with many aspects of Pueblo and other Indian cultures, have significance such as turquois of the sky, yellow of pollen, green of vegetation, red of life, and black of death, with recognized connotations.

The men wear moccasins ornamented with black and white skunk fur, to repel evil spirits from the feet of the dancers. In the summer ceremonials, the women's feet are traditionally bare, and they are scarcely lifted from the earth—thus representing the closeness of womankind to Mother Earth, and betokening fertility.

Men's kilts and sashes are decorated with sacred symbols in colored embroidery or brocade. Weaving has been a traditional art of the men. The white braided girdles with long flowing tassels represent falling rain, and are often referred to as "rain sashes." The brocaded sashes show a conventionalization of the katsina mask, Broad Face. This design is not embroidered but woven in the weft. These sashes are made by the Hopi men (or, nowadays, by students in the Indian schools or participating in projects which have been initiated in recent times) by whom they are sold or traded to other Indian groups, where they are widely used in dances. Many textile designs have lost their original significance or have been altered in their details, but this particular decoration is always essentially the same in design and colors. The zigzags indicate teeth, and the central diamonds represent eyes. On each side of the eyes are figures called "angular marks." In the black bands, the vertical white lines are called "face marks." (*See* Tanner and Tanner 1980:75, Fig. 56.)

From a man's waist, in the center of the back, a fox skin hangs. This is worn by many dancers, especially, by most of the dancing katsinas. It is considered to be a relic of the earliest days of man, for the katsinas "were transformed while mankind was still tailed and horned" (Bunzel 1932b:870). Often a string of shells is worn over the left shoulder crossing to the right hip; and several necklaces of shells, silver, or coral and turquois beads may adorn a dancer. Above the elbows may be painted rawhide armbands, and at the knees, turtle shell rattles (now commonly replaced with clusters of harness bells) and hanks of colored yarn.

The women usually wear a one-piece dress called a *manta,* secured at the right shoulder leaving the left shoulder bare, or exposing a cotton undergarment of bright color. Silver and turquois pins or buttons serve as decorations on the sides of the mantas. The waist is encircled by a woven belt of red and green or black. Around the neck are numerous necklaces, and on hands and arms many rings and bracelets.

These are the principal costume features of the summertime dances; the same items may be used in varying assemblages in yearround ceremonies. Through them all forms of life are represented: animals, birds, and shells of the sea; vegetation of all kinds; all the elements and features of the universe.

Each pueblo has a fixed date for a ceremonial, or fiesta, in the Río Grande groups, honoring its patron saint as introduced by the Spaniards. In prehispanic times, the Pueblos had certain set or relatively definite dates for ritual observances. The Spanish priests found it advantageous to select the name of an appropriate saint for such ceremonies, hoping gradually to accomplish a transfer from veneration of a sacred personage of the Indians to reverence for a Catholic patron. In part, they were successful. In one way or another, saints' names were applied to specific villages, with accompanying feast day observances.

Through the years, a blending of Indian and Christian ceremony came to be observable. Perhaps Mass is held early in the morning in the Catholic church of a pueblo, with Indians in the choir and congregation taking part in the service—with apparently the same reverence and fervor that they bring to their own, aboriginal ceremonials. After Mass, an image of the patron saint may be carried into the plaza and placed under an arbor of boughs (ramada), in front of which the Indians later dance. The Indian cosmography includes many supernatural beings, so the people seem able to acknowledge the Christian God while holding to their own faith. Throughout the dancing Indians may be seen going into the ramada, or improvised shrine, and dropping on their knees before the image of the saint.

Corn Dances

Probably the so-called corn dances, or tablita dances, are seen most frequently. For centuries corn has been the main staple of the Pueblo Indians. It has become more than nutritional, taking on a symbolic character. The corn fetish is most sacred. Corn is exchanged as a sign of friendship. The public performances that we witness occur at the culmination of purification rites which take place in the kiva; these last from one to five days. The corn dances relate to the germination, growth, maturation, and harvesting of the crop and, therefore, are held throughout the summer months. All summer ceremonials are concerned with rain. The corn ceremonies may be very spectacular and onlookers are often deeply moved, even though comprehending only a fraction of their significance.

A typical corn dance, like that at Santo Domingo, may begin with historical pageantry. First, one sees the koshari emerging from the turquois kiva. These ghostly figures encircle both divisions of the pueblo, thus symbolically throwing the protection of the ancestral spirits around all the people. They will perhaps meet the kurena who have come out of the squash kiva, and an excited conference takes place. Runners are sent out in the cardinal directions. They disappear into the kivas or rooms of nearby houses. The spirited parley continues.

After a time the runner from the east returns, and the excited throng crowds round him to receive his message. Animated speeches are made, accompanied by dramatic gestures. The runner from the west comes back, and the same performance is repeated. These are the runners who having been sent to the frontiers, have brought back word about the enemies—Apache, Comanche, Navajo, Ute—prone to make raids upon the Pueblo crops. Then from the north and south, runners arrive with liquids of which all partake—a rite of purification before warriors set forth to meet the enemy. One then sees a dramatization which may be interpreted as preparation for battle. After its conclusion, the participants file back into the kivas, and the historical portion of the ceremony ends.

Where the two-kiva system prevails, a great standard, a long ceremonial wand, will be observed on the roof of each kiva. By watching these, it is possible to know when dancing in the plaza is about to begin. When a wand is brought down, elaborately costumed figures, equal numbers of men and women, alternating, come forth from the kiva. The summer people usually emerge first. They form into two rows and enter the plaza, following a rain priest who carries the great wand. They are accompanied by a drummer beating a large double-headed drum and a male chorus that provide the song and rhythm for the dance.

The wand is highly symbolic. At the top of a pole some fifteen feet in length is a bunch of brilliantly colored feathers, traditionally those of the macaw. Just below this cluster are bunches of parrot and woodpecker feathers tied on with strands of colored beads and ocean shells. Near the top, a fox skin, bespeaking the long ago, is suspended. An embroidered banner—decorated with clouds, rain, and related symbols—is fastened lengthwise along the pole; it is trimmed at intervals with eagle feathers which float out from the one edge of the banner, and a cluster of small medicine pouches. This wand represents all life in nature. The rain priest stands alongside the dancers and waves the throbbing sacred emblem over them throughout the ceremony. During the course of the day, all of the participants are supposed to pass under the wand as an act of purification.

In a complete presentation of a corn dance, the group from each kiva dances four times, and at the end of the day, the two groups join in a final grand spectacle.

Animal Dances

During winter months, the most important ceremonies include hunting or animal dances, variously called buffalo, deer, antelope, or game animals dance. These are dramatizations of the supposed relationship between the Indians and the larger game animals which, during the centuries, furnished their principal wintertime food. Dancers dress to represent bison (buffalo), deer, antelope, elk, and sometimes mountain sheep. They wear headdresses and horns or antlers which make the likeness to the various animals even more realistic. They carry slender sticks in the hands and by leaning forward on these as they dance, increase the likeness.

In a buffalo dance, the leader is dressed as a hunter and several other hunters may participate. The animal dancers are usually in two lines, with a woman, or two, between them. In December, the woman wears a sun symbol on her back and she is called the buffalo mother (or buffalo woman); but in January, she wears a feathered headdress, and is then called the wild turkey. The buffalo mother is the symbolic mother of the larger animal life of the region. At dawn, she goes out to look for game, and leads the animals to the village. The coming in of these animals from hills surrounding a pueblo and the pantomime which follows is one of the most spectacular dramas that one is ever likely to see. Small evergreen trees may be planted in the plaza, suggestive of the forest. Participants in the ceremony enter their kiva after all are gathered in the plaza. They come out and dance four times during the forenoon, and four times in the afternoon. The dancers are accompanied by a drummer and male chorus whose leader wears a Plains Indian costume; for it was to the great plains that the Pueblos had to go for the largest of all the game animals, the bison. The final event of the day is the enactment of a hunt. In the end, the game is "killed," and the limp bodies are carried from the plaza. The other animal dances are performed along these lines.

Eagle Dance

The eagle dance as we see it today is a fragment of a ceremony which was formerly common to all the pueblos. It is performed in the early spring and is likely to be repeated throughout the year. The eagle has direct communication with the sky powers and is highly venerated. It is not uncommon, even now, to see a specimen of the Golden or American Eagle kept in captivity in a pueblo, where it is treated with every mark of respect. The eagle dance is a dramatization of the relationship believed to exist between man and the eagle and deific powers. Two young men are costumed as eagles, one a male and the other female; in the course of the dance, they imitate almost every movement of these great birds. One sees them in the act of soaring, hovering over the fields, circling, perching on high places, resting on the ground, and going through mating gestures. Although the costume may vary from pueblo to pueblo, the basic features are the same.

Each dancer's body is painted realistically; he wears a kilt, usually decorated with an undulating serpent design. On the head, is a close fitting headdress covered with feathers; the eyes are indicated, and at the front, is a long, curved beak—in all, a very good representation of an eagle's head; over the shoulders and attached to the arms, are great feathered wings and a feathered tail is attached to the belt in the back. Being such a spectacular display of artistry, this dance is a favorite with the public and is frequently performed at public exhibitions.

Basket Dance

One of the most beautiful and significant of all the seasonal dances of the Pueblos is the basket dance, which takes its name from the use of the food baskets in the ceremony. The baskets in the dance symbolize their normal contents—not only the food which preserves the life of the people, but the seeds that are planted in the ground and which must be fructified in due time; the fruits or grain that the earth yields in response to the efforts of the people; the meal which is produced when the harvest of corn is ground; and finally, the loaves of bread ready for sustenance of the Pueblo groups. The invocations for fertility which occur in a basket dance embrace not only the food plant life, but the human race, which must multiply and transmit the gift of life from generation to generation. A complete series of the scenes presented in this ceremonial would constitute an epitome of woman's life, her consecration to childbearing and the sustaining of the life of the pueblo. All participants are costumed spectacularly—men and women—and the basketry display is outstanding (see Hill 1982:259–262).

Miscellaneous Dances

In most of the pueblos, Christmas, New Year, and Easter are definite dance dates. Generally, the Indians dance on these holidays, and on the three following days. A few other dances occur on fixed dates as will be seen from the calendar on page 251–54, but the dates of most ceremonials are optional and variable with the Indians. Among the dances commonly performed are the snowbird, bow and arrow, feather, butterfly, turtle, horse, crow, basket, hoop, sun, cloud, Comanche, Kiowa, Navajo, dog, pine or evergreen, and war and peace dances. Comanche and Kiowa dances were adopted from the Plains Indians. The idea of frightfulness in connection with the Comanche has been intensified by the enormous feathered headdress—which was never a part of Pueblo costume—as well as by the action of the performance. In the typical war dance, formerly performed in preparation for battle, the body is painted black. Nothing is more significant than this painting of the body: when the Indian painted himself from head to foot, it meant war. This was the supreme symbol of anger and deadly intent. Many of the so-called war dances are in reality peace dances, enacted in religious spirit to celebrate the close of hostilities.

ON CORN (Tiwa)

The green corn stands
in the field
close to Mother Earth
earth worms sacrificing
themselves to hungry birds

Look at their golden
tassels like hair
hanging, touching
earth, close
to moist soil
and getting ripe

I danced for the gods
She danced for me
I prayed for rain
She prayed for me

Singing to the sun-
She sang of me

I dreamed not of her
But of animals
She dreamed of me. . . .

By Joseph Concha, Taos

From *The Writers' Reader,* Fall, 1970.
Institute of American Indian Arts,
Santa Fe, N.M.

Snake Dance

Other than the katsina dances, the best known of the Hopi dances are the
snake dances. These are among the most involved of enactments. They take
place in late August, in one or more of the villages. Many days of preparation
are required before the public dance is presented on the final day: at Hote-
villa or Shipaulovi and Shungopavi in even-numbered years, and at Walpi and
Mishongnovi in odd-numbered years *(see* Wright 1979:17–21).

As part of the preparation, men and boys of the snake and antelope fraternities enter their kivas. They emerge, painted and costumed, and spread out
on the desert flatlands; equipped with snake whips, they gather snakes over a
period of four days from each of the directions. Day after day, rites are performed in and outside of the kivas and other sacred places. Then comes the
day of the great spectacle that has long attracted the local citizenry and visitors from all points of the compass. (At the end of summer 1971, the village

chief at Mishongnovi, Second Mesa, made a firm announcement that the Snake Dance there would be closed to the public. Acting without proper authority, the tribal council and the BIA at Keams Canyon attempted to override this statement of policy by issuing their own announcement that public attendance would be permitted. The village chief, upholding his decision, was able to keep the Snake Dance closed to outsiders. One should inquire before visiting.)

As the sun lowers in the afternoon, a single file of antelope priests enters the plaza, singing a solemn chant. After circling the plaza, they line up along one side to await the arrival of the snake priests. The atmosphere is tense and exciting by the time the latter enter the plaza, opposing the antelope priests. In the plaza center is a small bower made of cottonwood branches, the *kisi,* in which the snakes are kept. In front of it is a wooden drum—a heavy plank atop an excavation in the ground. This symbolizes the *sípapu,* or entrance to the underworld. The snake priests stomp on the drum "to notify the gods of the underworld that the ceremony is beginning."

As the two groups of spectacularly attired and painted priests face each other across the plaza, "the gourd dance rattles vibrate to emulate the sound of some giant rattlesnake, and a deep, sonorous chorus that now begins reminds one of some tremendous tempest approaching from the distance. As the song increases in volume, the lines of the priests sway back and forth and, at a climax in the song, break up. Thereupon, the snake men reform in groups of three, and these groups dance with a strange leaping motion entirely different from any of the steps so far used. From an observer, we learn that:

As these dancers pass the *kisi,* the first man of each trio reaches in among the boughs of cottonwood. The priest hidden within hands him a snake which he immediately places in his mouth, grasping it with his teeth and lips a few inches back of the reptile's head. The second man puts his arm over the shoulder of the one carrying the snake, and the third man walks behind. If the snake becomes unmanageable, the second priest distracts it by stroking it with his snake whip, or wand.

Each snake priest dances the circle with his snake four times, then he drops it to the ground and the third man of the trio, the gatherer, picks it up. If the supply permits, the first man will reach into the *kisi* for a second, a third, and even a fourth snake. The length of the performance is determined by the number of snakes that have been caught—as many as seventy or eighty—and the number of men participating. . . .

As the dance continues, a priest who preceded the dancers to the plaza continues to sprinkle corn meal on both dancers and snakes. At one point, several women, garbed in old-style Hopi costume, enter the plaza. They bear in front of them baskets containing finely ground corn meal, pinches of which they, too, sprinkle on both snakes and dancers. When all the snakes have been danced with and are being held by either the gatherers or the antelope men, the priest with the corn meal uses what is left of it to draw a circular design upon the ground. All the snakes are then tossed onto the design and the women scatter the rest of their fine meal upon the writhing mass. The Hopi spectators near the spot add their spittle to the sprinkling of corn meal—and woe betide any white visitor who happens to be too close!

There ensue a few minutes of confusion. Snakes dart in all directions, and the gatherers have a difficult time keeping them heaped upon the corn meal design. Occasionally an unusually swift one gets well away into the crowd, and the screams and laughter that follow serve well to direct the gatherer to it. Then the Snake men dash in, seize handfuls of the writhing reptiles, and rush out of the village and down the steep trails. . . .

Back in the village, the Antelope men circle the plaza a few times, stamp on the plank to tell the underworld that the ceremony is at an end, and then march back to the kiva. . . . After the Snake Dance, the entire village relaxes and for four days there are feasting and jollity. Games and races are frequent. . . . Most of the white visitors leave the village as soon as the Snake men have left to liberate the snakes. (James 1956; *see also* Forrest 1961).

Dramatic buffalo and mountain sheep dances—both very old observances—and a more modern butterfly dance are given in the Hopi villages; these are social in nature to a degree. All three are believed to have derived from the Río Grande Pueblos. Only the buffalo dance is given at a set time (*see* page 254). Many dances are scheduled but a few days prior to their occurrence.

We are told that most of the main Hopi ceremonials are performed twice a year, once as a minor (preparatory) form and then as a major presentation. "Winter in the upper world is summer in the underworld and reciprocal ceremonies are believed to take place—a major ceremony in the underworld is parallelled by a minor ceremony in the upper world and vice versa" (James 1956:183). Ceremonies may last from one to seventeen days, with much of the time spent in preparations.

REGRET (Keres)

I have made a name for myself.
Of this, I am ashamed.
I have failed to sprinkle cornmeal
To the Great One above.
Knowing the day is ending,
I pray to you,
You who have given
The beauty of Mother Earth.
I dare not ask anything more
. . . but forgiveness.
It was evil of me to fail you;
I regret that I have no excuse.
Sincerely, from my heart, I promise,
I will never fail you again.
Whatever the punishment may be
I will take,
But still . . . I am ashamed.

By Rosey García, Santo Domingo

From *The Writers' Reader*, Fall, 1966.
The Institute of American Indian Arts,
Santa Fe, N.M.

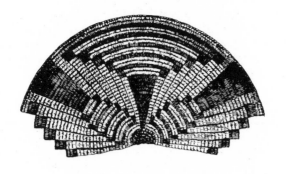

3
The Athabascans

The Interjacent Peoples: Early History

Long, long after the original, and successive, peoples began to inhabit the western hemisphere and scattered over the two continents, other migrants started to trek from Asia into the New World. Perhaps around three thousand years ago (Young 1968:3), family groups or small bands of people began coming from northernmost Asia via the Bering Strait. The major body, designated by linguists as the *Nadene,* includes subfamilies called Tlingit, Eyak, Haida, and Athabascan, the latter of which is by far the largest.

At one time, Nadene peoples occupied much of Alaska and wide expanses of northwestern Canada; eventually, they reached into northern Mexico. Some of them were skilled fishermen, others were great hunters, and all were food gatherers who followed their preferred game and favored foodstuffs along various routes. Today, small enclaves still remain along the Pacific coast as far south as California; of these latter, the Tolawa and Hupa are representatives. What caused certain groups to come into the Southwest, and why they selected the routes they traveled, have been matters of conjecture in large part. However they came, they considered themselves to be "The People," the *Dine'é.*

A form of chronological evidence known as the lexicostatistic dating method, or glottochronology, places the divergences of these Dine'é from the northern Athabascan groups some seven hundred to a thousand years ago. Computations fix the southern movements at a time about one thousand years past, and continuing for approximately four hundred years (which fits well with traditions). This method, then, indicates that the arrival of Athabascans in the Southwest took place in the mid-fourteenth century (*see* Hoijer 1956; 1963:1–29; 1971:3–6; 1974; Young, 1968:4), or slightly later.

Certain indications suggest that some of the Dine'é traveled through the intermontane region west of the Rocky Mountains (Willey 1966:232; Huscher 1942, 1943; Harrington 1940:523, 525, 527–529; Hale and Harris 1979: 171 ff.), but no evidence of this has been established. And archaeological findings of the last few years and historical references to a limited degree reveal that significant movements of Athabascans followed down the eastern slopes of the Rocky Mountains during the 1400s. Some of these migrants reached the southern limit of present day Colorado around 1500. Part of them edged eastward into southwestern Kansas, the panhandle of Oklahoma, and central-west Texas to become known as Kiowa-Apache. Certain of the bands continued southward, some centering in southwestern Texas as the Lipan Apache, others turned westward to occupy chosen locations in southwestern New Mexico and eastern Arizona. And those who were to become known as the Jicarilla Apache and the Navajo found their way westward through mountain passes which brought them into north-central New Mexico, into the upper reaches of the San Juan River.

The New Homeland

The region into which the Jicarilla Apache and the Navajo found their way had been occupied by small numbers of village-dwelling peoples from about A.D. 400–700; after 700 until 1050, the population had increased. These facts are recognizable by distinct phases of Pueblo occupation (*see* Eddy 1966). The district, then, like most of the Southwest, suffered long periods of drought during the late thirteenth century. It was not the first time this had happened. The significant fact which caused abandonment of pueblos and movements of people into more favorable areas was the shift from a summer dominant precipitation pattern to a winter pattern. Having occupied higher elevations where rainfall was sufficient for cultivation of crops, the change in precipitation with its shorter growing season caught the people living above what was an area of a sufficient growing season. They had either to revert to a Desert Culture economy—which meant the break up of large social units—or move. They moved (*see* Schoenwetter and Dittert 1968; Eddy 1974). The Athabascans, because of their basic hunting and gathering economy, were able to exist in small groups. It is possible that the earliest of them coming into the Colorado-New Mexico border locations from the east were wandering raiders who, discovering the abandoned pueblos and adjoining lands of the upper San Juan, deemed it expedient to move into the then promising region. Several investigators of Navajo history have determined that the earliest area of Navajo occupation in the Southwest is the traditional *Dinetah,* meaning "among-the-people" in the Navajo language; this is identifiable as an area centering in the Gobernador and Largo tributaries of the San Juan River, about seventy-five miles northwest of Santa Fe.

Cultural Characteristics

Through the preceding narration, it has become evident that the culture of the Pueblo Indians may receive additions which are grafted onto the basic social structure, and that losses may occur during time and from outside pressures or other contingencies; but change with regard to traditional mores, or lifeways, has been resisted resolutely. In the latter respect—change—adherence to a dual ceremonial organization dictated inflexibility; the Pueblos have held on with age-old tenacity. Major concern has been for an entire village or community, the *group as a whole,* with little thought for the individual, although changes in minor traits could take place.

In contrast, the Athapascan-speaking peoples have a culture system of completely opposite nature. With those of our special concern, the Navajo and his closely related cousins, the Apaches, who constitute a single ethnic group, sharing a common culture core (Steward 1955:37), it is the *individual* who is of primary importance.

Habitat and Social Organization

Fundamentally, each Athabascan band had its headman who selected a location for his people in an unoccupied district that provided good hunting and gathering opportunities. In the Southwest, they chose protected canyons and high plateaus, or mesas, with extensive grasslands and the timbered mountain fastnesses where game was plentiful. Constant streams were not so vital to these transient ones as they were to the sedentary peoples who dwelt in pueblos or other permanent communities. The Apaches and Navajo moved about at first, camping or living temporarily near good springs for the most part, or by small streams, ponds, or lakes. Residential shifting was seasonal in accordance with the climatic fluctuations that controlled food supply and forage.

From various lines of evidence, it is apparent that these newcomers followed a patrilineal system of descent, with patrilocal residence, and it is believed that they had "a shamanistic-individual religion preoccupied with curing," without priestly officers such as obtain among the Pueblo Indians (*see* Hester 1962:87), and without permanent religious structures.

As they passed along the eastern side of the Rocky Mountains, marginal to the Great Plains, the immigrants came into contact with Plains Indians (the Kiowa and others) who had culture traits unknown to the Athabascans. Being quick to see the advantages some of these features offered, they were promptly added to the meager trait list of the immigrants, who brought only the knowledge they could carry in their heads and things they could carry on their backs and perhaps the backs of dogs.

Among the possible additions to their original culture may have been conical dwellings of forked-stick construction or crude rock shelters and cylindrical pottery with roundly pointed bottoms—a Woodland type. The immigrants could have become familiar with agriculture from the Plains peoples (see Willey 1966:232). These items and knowledge, apparently, the Dine'é brought into the Southwest, with a new type of weapon, the sinew-backed bow which was a far more formidable instrument than the simple wooden bow long used by the Pueblos.

Origins of Band Names

Accounts of the Spaniards, who entered the Southwest not long after the arrival of the Athabascans, make little reference to people who may have been of that subfamily. Chroniclers of the expedition of Coronado (1540–1542) made slight mention of Indians who can be so identified; but the Espejo expedition of 1582 encountered a band near San Mateo (Mount Taylor), New Mexico, which was probably ancestral to the Cañoncito Navajo of present times (Brugge 1969).

The term "Apache" appears in 1598, identifying Indians of the Texas and New Mexico plains. The Spaniards appear to have met members of the southern bands first. To differentiate one group from another, they noted particular characteristics or locations. Those who gathered an agave species, *mescal,* for food were called "Apache de Mescalero," the Mescalero Apache. The ones that occupied the Chiricahua mountain strongholds became the Chiricahua Apache; and those farther north were designated as "Querechos," and later as the Gila, San Carlos, White Mountain, Tonto, Cibecue, and so on, utilizing regional terms. Because some of those who took up locations in the north made fine basketry containers which served purposes of small gourds, or *jicarillas,* with which the Spaniards were familiar, they were called "Apache de Jicarilla." And others who were found cultivating crops became "Apache de Návaju." This term is believed to have derived from the Tewa word *Návahu'u,* or "the arroyo with the cultivated fields" (see Schroeder 1963:6, 11; Gunnerson 1979:162–169; Schaafsma, C. F. 1978:58).

FIRST SNOWFALL *(Navajo)*

> The snow has come at last;
> Coming down in soft flakes,
> Caressing my face with tenderness
> As if it were telling me,
> "You are the first I've touched."
> And, as I walk along,
> The snowflakes seem to sing
> A song that has never been heard,

A song that has never been sung—
Unheard!
Unsung!
Except in my heart.

By Tommy Smith

Winner of the Second Prize,
Scottsdale National Indian Arts
Exhibition, 1964.

From *The Writers' Reader,* 1962–1966.
Institute of American Indian Arts,
Santa Fe, N. M.

The Navajo Indians

According to their legends, the Navajo came to this earth through a progression of underworlds. The number of worlds may vary. In some versions these are recognized as numbering twelve, which are grouped by fours into three layers, or "rooms," known as the Black World, the Red World, and the Blue World, respectively (*see* Young 1968:2; Yazzie 1971). Again, four underworlds are recognized, the world in which we dwell, the sky immediately above, and one still higher—Land-beyond-the-sky (*see* Reichard 1963:14ff.).

It is believed that not only did The People originate in underworlds, but so did the land itself and all forms of water, the animals, all vegetation and other features. All were brought to the surface by supernatural beings. The place of emergence, *Xajiinai,* is considered to be a hole in La Plata Mountains of southwestern Colorado. The Navajo origin myth is long and detailed (*see* Matthews 1897:63–159; Schevill 1947:29–48; Moon 1970; Dutton and Olin 1978:I).

Once in this region—tradition sets the time six hundred to eight hundred years ago—The People wandered about. As they say, "many groups joined the original people, to become the progenitors of the earliest clans." By accretion the groups grew, some coming "from the ancient pueblos; some from people who spoke a language similar to Navaho . . . ; and, at a later date, Mexicans and Utes" (Young 1968:2; Schaafsma 1978:61–64).

Brief History

The Beginnings of Change

Archaeologically, two phases of culture appear to be distinguishable in the Dinetah domain. The earlier one—as yet not clearly defined, due to a paucity of datable remains—brought the immigrants into contact with eastern

Pueblo peoples. One of the results was that the Navajo, the interjacent ones, recognizing the Pueblo culture to be more advanced than their own, began to adopt practices which were advantageous to them. Modifying their hunting-gathering mode of life, they acquired horticultural knowledge and began raising corn, or maize. In time, farming brought about a semisedentary residence pattern.

Prior to the coming of the Spaniards, Pueblo peoples occupied river valleys from Old Mexico to northern New Mexico. Don Juan de Oñate brought the first Spanish colonists to settle in northern New Mexico in 1598, after which time comments were made about Apache or Apachean peoples. Certain historical documents speak of them as raiders who, following attacks, were traced back by the Spaniards to their homes, where they were found to be growing corn—which suggests that these were Navajo (rel. Goodman 1982).

Fray Zárata Salmerón first referred to the Navajo as a specific Apachean group, in 1626. By the third decade of the seventeenth century, the Navajo had became a large and powerful people, spreading from the Chama to the Little Colorado River, in eastern Arizona. Various bands had their recognized headmen; and it would seem that war and peace chiefs were distinguished. The Benavides report of 1630 refers to Apache and Navajo chiefs, as well as those of the Pueblos, without giving their names—as was common in the Spanish accounts.

The People were dwelling in earth-covered houses and were growing crops: corn, beans, squash, and other Southwestern products. They also gathered wild foods and hunted widely. And they engaged in extensive trade with other Indians and the Spanish settlers. They were holding large gatherings where dances were performed.

As the Spaniards increased in numbers, they edged into the desirable Pueblo holdings and demanded more and more of the Indians. Frequently, they attacked the pueblos, capturing or killing the people, or burning their structures. Prisoners were impressed into servitude or were sold as far south as Mexico. Undoubtedly, the Pueblos, resentful of the growing Spanish pressures and domination, encouraged attacks on them by the Apache-Navajo. At any rate, strife mounted and reprisals increased. Fray Alonso de Benavides, in 1630, published an account of conditions of the period (see Young 1968: 12–16; Forrestal 1954:44–52). He established contact with the Navajo and endeavored to achieve peace between the diverse peoples and to introduce Christianity to the Indians—both without much success.

It was recorded that in 1653 a Spanish punitive expedition surprised some Navajo holding a native ceremonial. Although no pictographs or petroglyphs on the cliff walls or in caverns have been identified for the earlier archaeological period, it is possible that impermanent art portrayals (dry paintings?) may have been made in connection with ceremonials. The historical records also suggest that, by the mid-seventeenth century, the Spaniards had asserted themselves to such a degree as to cause the Navajo as well as the Pueblo Indians, to go underground, as it were, with their ceremonial practices.

After the Pueblo Revolt of 1680 and the reconquest of 1692, many of the pueblos were abandoned, and the Indians therefrom were pushed northward toward the San Juan, which brought them into significant contact with the Navajo. In some areas, the two peoples mingled. As a consequence, "In the space of a few years the Navaho adopted the Puebloan styles of architecture, manufacturing techniques, and religious paraphernalia, plus many elements of non-material culture such as clans, matrilineal descent, matrilocal residence, the origin myth, and ritual" (Hester 1962:91). But with these changes, the preferred residence of the Navajo continued to be the *hogan,* a house type traceable to the Asian World.

Immediately after 1696, sites of the upper San Juan consisted of open clusters of hogans and masonry *pueblitos,* or small pueblos, of three or four rooms, indicating that Pueblo refugees were living as isolated family units. Like settlements did not appear in the Gobernador and Largo canyons until some twenty years later, showing that the Navajo and the Pueblo refugees were moving southward.

Huge masonry compounds and pueblitos were built in the Gobernador, in defensive locations on high rock pinnacles. Some of the buildings were in the form of towers equipped with loopholes. Certain sites contained as many as forty rooms. It has been noted that the "only peculiarly Navaho architectural features were the hogans and sweat lodges inside the masonry compounds" (Schaafsma, P. 1966:4).

Archaeologists have called the period dating from 1696 to 1775, the *Gobernador phase.* By the terminal date, Ute, Comanche, and Spanish enemies had brought such pressure to bear on the Navajo that they had completely abandoned the eastern Dinetah—the area east of Blanco Canyon. For the Gobernador, data are much more numerous than for the pre-1696 phase. The economic pattern included hunting and gathering of wild plants, with some herding and dry farming. Water was controlled by storage behind sand dikes in a few instances. By 1706, herds of sheep, goats, horses, and cattle were kept—all Spanish introductions. Corrals and horsegear have been found in archaeological excavations. And pecked and painted depictions of people are portrayed on the cliffs—some as blackrobed friars on horseback, some wearing fringed attire of Plains Indians, and others with mantalike garments of the Pueblos; with these are *yé'ii* figures (Holy People), eagles, corn plants, bison, and a variety of symbols.

During the earliest part of the eighteenth century, the Pueblo culture dominated the San Juan basin; the Navajo had adopted it in full force. However, in the last half of the century, Pueblo traits were modified or simplified; and by the end of the period, with abandonment of the upper San Juan-Gobernador-Largo and Chama districts, the refugees had been absorbed by the Navajo (*see* Schaafsma, P. 1966:9; Schaafsma, C. H. 1975; 1978).

Pueblo and Navajo ceremonial paraphernalia have been excavated from the same caches, giving credence to the belief that much modern Navajo ceremonialism is derived from early Pueblo contacts. Pueblo influences—including sandpaintings, metate and firepit styles, and weaving at least in part—altered the basic Navajo culture, and within a few centuries, distinguished it from that of the Apaches who were less in contact with the Pueblo peoples.

Not the least of the changes was in the spoken language. At the time of the entrada of Coronado, the Athabascan groups spoke closely related, if not essentially similar tongues. Linguists have calculated that the Navajo and Chiricahua Apache were close relatives and historically very friendly, and that their languages became distinctive one from the other during a period of only 149 years (Hoijer et al. 1963; but *see* Schroeder 1963:17). The Navajo, by the same calculation, are separated by 279 years from the San Carlos and Jicarilla Apaches, and by 335 years from the Lipan Apache (*see* Young 1968:4).

Shifts of Location

The folklore of the Navajo traces their movements from the original locations in the upper San Juan region, down through the Gobernador, Largo and Blanco, into Chaco Canyon and to the Big Bead Mesa districts some thirty or forty years later; there, Navajo ceremonial art appears to be relatively scarce. Farther to the west, where Canyon de Chelly in northeastern Arizona was settled by Navajo people before the earlier sites in New Mexico were abandoned, some of the initial art forms seem to have proliferated, while others are absent. Tree-ring dates for archaeological remains have been found to show later occupation going from east to west.

In one instance, however, investigations at an archaeological site at the base of Mariana Mesa, some ten miles north of Quemado in west-central New Mexico, are said to have yielded "the earliest tree-ring date yet obtained from a Navajo forked-pole hogan—1387." Fifteen additional tree-ring dates supporting the antiquity of this site were also obtained (Navajo Tribal Museum 1968). [For a full report on Mariana Mesa sites, *see* McGimsey 1980.] Perhaps this late fourteenth century dwelling was inhabited by migrant Athabascan people who entered the Southwest by an intermontane route, rather than by the common trails leading into north-central New Mexico.

In general, each Navajo community had certain individuals known as men of wealth, with influence, ceremonial knowledge, and good judgment. These usually were referred to as *naat'áani,* or headmen, peace leaders who always knew the Blessingway, which is intended to gain the good will of Navajo supernaturals and to bring good fortune; it is not primarily curative (*see* Van Valkenburgh 1945:71–72; Shepardson 1963:78).

Intruders

Numerous accounts have been written of the Navajo and Apache during the years following their entrance into the Southwest and the decades that saw them fighting against many odds, including other Indian peoples and, especially, the non-Indians who came in ever-increasing numbers—the Spaniards and then the Anglo-Americans. References to pertinent publications are given in the bibliography of this book.

Juan Bautista de Anza, who served as governor of New Mexico from 1778–1789, initiated a plan whereby Navajo headmen were called "captains" or "generals" in the Spanish army. At that time, a prominent Navajo known as Antonio el Pinto was recognized as a general. He received gifts regularly from the Spaniards and was influential in maintaining peaceful conditions until the time of his death in 1793. This type of bribery was carried on after Mexican rule prevailed.

Early years of the nineteenth century were filled with strife, with short periods of peace. The first treaty that defined a boundary between the Spaniards and the Navajo was agreed upon in 1819. The population center was then in Canyon de Chelly, from which westward movements were made into the canyon and valley lands of Chinle, Black Mesa, Navajo Mountain, Klagetoh, and Steamboat Canyon. (See Brugge and Correll 1971.)

Mexican control extended from 1821 to 1846. From the time of the arrival of General S. W. Kearny with the U.S. Army, in the latter year, the Americans made intermittent attempts to achieve peace with the Navajo, who were warring and raiding. Through the mid-nineteenth century, a few Navajo chiefs are identified by name—Zarcillos Largos, for example. Antonio Sandoval, a "medicine man," is mentioned as leader of the Cebolleta Navajo, and Narbono, the renowned chief and a man of great wisdom, comes to our attention. When a treaty was signed by Colonel A. W. Doniphan and the Navajo on 22 November 1846, these three were signers for their people, as were Caballada Mucha, Alexandro, Kiatanito, José Largo, Segundo, Pedro José Manuelito, Tapia, Archulette, and Juanico and Savoiette García (Young 1968:33–34).

Treaties were proposed, some made (always with communication difficulties) and shortly broken. By 1849, Anglos were crossing the Southwest in the rush for gold in California. It was common practice for them to abuse and take advantage of the Indians—Navajo, Pueblos, and others alike. Increasing encroachment of the Anglo-Americans on lands that the Navajo considered to be their own added to misunderstandings and mounting violence. It is recorded that by 1858 the Navajo lived "scattered over a wide area, from the Jémez Mountains to the Hopi Country and from the San Juan River to the region south of the Little Colorado" (Young 1968:38; see Harrington 1940:514, fig. 32).

Forts and garrisons established by the U.S. to control Navajo uprisings were left unmanned, in general, following the outbreak of the Civil War of 1861. The Navajo and Apaches were quick to take advantage of the situation and soon were the scourge of the countryside. A few army troops did engage in war against them rather ineffectually. Then Colonel Christopher (Kit) Carson, of Taos, was called to lead a campaign that was destined to bring the turmoil to an end. On 20 July 1863, he and his troops, joined by a band of Ute Indians, reached Fort Defiance, Arizona, to fulfill the ruthless policy formulated by General James Carleton who, in the first place, proposed to resettle the Navajo and Apaches. On a reservation created at Fort Sumner, New Mexico, they were to become farmers like the Pueblos. All captives who surrendered voluntarily would be taken there and all male Navajo who resisted were to be shot. Their livestock and food supplies were to be destroyed—and they were.

Days of Captivity

As under Spanish oppression, the Navajo scattered into isolated canyons, attempting to avoid Carleton's attacks. From November, 1863, nevertheless, captives were rounded up and forced to go to Fort Sumner, or *Bosque Redondo,* on the "Long Walk." By December, 1864, 8,354 Navajo and 405 Mescalero Apache were confined there. The next year, it was reported that 6,447 Navajo were concentrated at Fort Sumner. It was estimated that 1,200 had escaped captivity and remained in Navajoland (*see* Young 1968:41). Chiefs Manuelito and Barboncito eluded Kit Carson's roundup and refused to surrender to the army. They and other chiefs held out in their isolated locations.

The Carleton experiment was a horrible failure. Crops that the Navajo and Apache were forced to plant produced a disheartening yield. Confinement, and crowded and unnatural conditions resulted not only in discontent and disease, but in a great number of deaths among the Indians. The enormity of Carleton's despotic regime was finally recognized and he was relieved of his command in the fall of 1866. The following January, custody of the Navajo was returned to the BIA.

On 1 June 1868, a treaty was concluded and on 12 August of that year, it was signed, establishing a 3.5 million acre reservation for the Navajo within their old domain. Signers of the document were W. T. Sherman and S. F. Tappan of the Indian Peace Commission, and twelve Navajo chiefs: Barboncito, Armijo, Delgado, Manuelito, Largo, Herrero, Chiquito, Muerto de Hombre (Biwos), Hombro, Narbono, Narbono Segundo, and Ganado Mucho. All signed with X marks (*see* Link 1968).

Though this was but a small portion of their former holdings, the Navajo were jubilant. Many tribulations, however, had to be met and endured before the return to their homeland was actually accomplished. Old Fort Fauntleroy, renamed Fort Wingate, was reactivated in 1868 and served for a time as an agency for the returning Navajo. Then the agency was moved to Fort Defiance.

Political Reorganization: The Tribal Council

As late as 1922, no political body that could be considered as tribal existed among the Navajo. Chapters where initiated in 1927 on a community level, where two types of leaders were recognized: formal and informal. The informal leaders, in some communities at least, were influential men who to a certain extent continued the traditional naat'áani system (*see* Young 1961:371ff.; Hill 1940). Showing something of the counterbalance, or dichotomy, of Navajo social organization was the fact that war leaders were recognized also—men who always knew the Warway.

Formal leaders came to hold elective offices in the chapters and/or agencies of broader authority. Chapter officers are a president, vice-president, and secretary; a Council delegate, et al.

The Navajo population was increasing significantly and the people's relations with the rest of the nation were growing more and more complex. Need for an entity that could serve the interests of all the Navajo people became critical. A Business Council, on which three influential Navajo served, was established. Its first meeting was held on 7 July 1923. One of the three was Henry Chee Dodge, who had served as Navajo interpreter for some years. Intelligent, educated, and with great leadership abilities, he "became the ladder along which the Navajo people tortuously made their way out of the early post-treaty period into the modern age" (Young 1968:50). Chee Dodge was leader of the Navajo for over seventy years. Organization of the Business Council was only a step toward a workable arrangement. Gradual developments continued. Fifteen years later, a tribal council was formed; and this led to organization of the Navajo Tribal Council in 1938. By 1950, this was well established and "the tribe was fast becoming a political entity" (Young 1968:63).

After a Century

Now more than a century has passed and successive generations of Navajo have come into being since the days at Fort Sumner. Only a few of the old ones lived to witness the Centennial observances which were prominently featured during 1968. Varieties of activities were held, including a re-enactment of the Long Walk to Bosque Redondo; and a series of publications was issued. In these, one finds a wealth of information concerning the Navajo of the past and of today (*see* bibliography and publications of the Navajo Tribe and BIA).

As one views modern maps, the Navajo domain is generally located as the region bounded on the northeast by the Continental Divide, on the southeast by the Río Puerco, on the south by the San José and Puerco rivers, on the west by the Little Colorado and Colorado rivers, and on the north by the San Juan River. [In accord with a decision rendered by the United States Board of Geographical Names between 1 July 1936 and 30 June 1937, it should be understood that the Puerco River "rises in township 16N, range 13W, McKinley County, New Mexico, and flows west and southwest to join the Little Colorado in Navajo County, Arizona. Henceforth (the Board stated) this stream will be known as the *Puerco River* and not the Río Puerco or Río Puerco of the west" (Southwestern Monuments 1937).] The entire area, broadly speaking, is an almost level plateau, averaging some 5,500 feet in elevation. In places, however, mountains rise to a height of more than 10,000 feet, and deep, sheer-walled canyons cut into the plateau. This results in spectacular landscape, with isolated mesas and buttes, desert wastes, arroyos that are usually dry channels—but which, in seconds, may become raging torrents that gouge out the earth and cause erosional destruction. The topography is matched by great contrasts in climate. Winters are cold and summers are hot; and, always, insufficient moisture renders the country marginal insofar as agricultural pursuits are concerned. Only the arroyos and limited areas on which water can be utilized by gravity flow are suitable for farming . . . unless modern irrigation techniques are employed. And these are slow in coming to Navajoland. Steps have been taken by the BIA and the tribe to train the Navajo in modern farming methods and animal care, and the tribe has appropriated hundreds of thousands of dollars for the training program.

The Navajo Nation

Land holdings of the Navajo have increased periodically and substantially since the days of their return from Fort Sumner. But never have the increases kept abreast of the growing needs of the people. The main reservation embraces 16,000,000 acres, or about 25,000 square miles, reaching out from the Four Corners to include northeastern Arizona, northwestern New Mexico, and southwestern Utah, in order of acreage. Much of the land is desert and semidesert, sandy or rocky and of little productive value. In some districts, 240 acres are necessary for the pasturage of one sheep for a year. The farmlands acreage is being increased annually, particularly on irrigated areas. A total of 34,783 acres was planted in spring and fall, 1980. The Cameron Farm Project sowed alfalfa and pasture, and planted trees and vegetables. Wells, pumping apparatus, water lines and improved roads were readied—the latter designated for 1981 paving (rel. Goodman 1982:3–50).

The Navajo want to remain as members of living communities. Covered by twenty-five census county divisions in the three states, the 1980 count estimated 148,832 in mid-May 1980. The total Navajo Nation population, including some 13,850 non-Navajo residents, is about 162,682 (Navajo Nation, 1980 Annual Progress Report).

With completion of a dam on the San Juan River and diversion canals in prospect, 110,000 acres of irrigable land became available. As the water and land are developed, large enterprises are destined to follow. The Navajo Nation is determined that it will get full benefit of its resources: lands, water, minerals, timber, and all else (Ibid. iv and ff.). Some 36,000 acres have been dry-farmed for decades.

Until the present time, the Navajo never settled in communities that could be called villages or towns. They lived in desirable locations scattered over the entire reservation. Following the matrilineal pattern, a Navajo grandmother is the center of the family. The children belong to her and are members of her clan. Because it is taboo for a Navajo man to look at his mother-in-law, or to talk with her, a woman and her husband do not live with the wife's mother. Instead, they erect a home nearby, so that the woman and her children can frequent the maternal abode. Thus, one may find several generations dwelling together or in proximity: grandmother, mother, daughter, and grandchildren. It is usual for the dwelling, the crops, and the livestock to be cared for by the mother and her children, so these are owned by the woman. Pottery making is woman's work (see Brugge 1963; Kent, S. 1981).

Inasmuch as property ownership among the Navajo is individual, a woman disposes of the rugs she weaves, and of her crops and stock; she spends her money however she chooses. A man does likewise with his silver jewelry, with the wages he earns, and with the income from his stock raising or farming. It is the man who represents the family in public and at ceremonials.

Visit Navajoland

To see the Navajo properly, one must go into their own country—far afield, and often over dirt roads. Road construction and maintenance were long neglected on the vast, thinly populated expanses. Today, however, hundreds of miles of black-top highways have been, and are being, built on the main reservation, and even more of graveled roadways.

The typical Navajo dwelling, the hogan, is usually round or hexagonal, sometimes octagonal, constructed of logs and mud, or sometimes of rocks, with a central air vent in the ceiling (see Richards 1970:8–9). Rarely are more than two or three together, and a traveler is likely to pass by without seeing them in daytime—so well do they blend with the natural setting in the evening, one is surprised at the number of fires whose flickering light gives evidence of the Navajo dwelling or camp near at hand. (See McAllister 1980.)

Near the hogan or under the shelter of a brush-covered ramada, Navajo women may be seen weaving rugs on an upright loom, which was adopted from the Pueblo Indians. Textile belts are woven on a loom made from a forked branch of a juniper tree, or on a board frame erected on a slight diagonal in front of the seated weaver. Small children will be playing nearby, or perhaps helping to card the wool. The older children and the husband are usually away, herding sheep or on an errand to the trading post. This picture is not so easily found today as the pattern of life is ever changing by acculturation. The Navajo rug is becoming a relatively scarce article, and weavers are decreasing in number.

Away from their homeland, Navajo Indians are seen at Pueblo ceremonies, especially at Jémez, Laguna, Zuñi, and in the Hopi villages. They come to trade and barter, to sell rugs and jewelry, and to take home agricultural products and other Pueblo items. While Navajo are seen on the streets of Cuba, Santa Fe, or Albuquerque, their numbers increase as one goes westward. In

Farmington, Gallup, Flagstaff, and other towns nearby they make up a considerable segment of the population. Part of the year, they are conspicuous in the southern Colorado towns where they go to work in the beet fields or engage in other work. In Window Rock and other places on the Navajo reservation, such as Shiprock, Chinle, Tuba City, Kayenta, Ganado, Fort Defiance, and Crownpoint, they are naturally predominant. It may be noted that these communities have a hospital or health center, schools, and various facilities. Consideration is being given to moving the administrative center, the "Navajo capital," to a more advantageous location—perhaps Chinle or Shiprock.

Physical Appearance and Attire

The Navajo tend to be taller than the Pueblo Indians, and most of them are slender. They have long, somewhat raw-boned faces and a number of the men have mustaches. Back of the heads are flattened by cradleboards on which infants are carried. A typical Navajo woman might be described as having small arms, hands and feet, with thin legs; long face, nose and chin; and thick lips. The slanted, oriental eye is fairly common among women and children. Their particular style of walking and their manner of making gestures are identifying characteristics of Navajo people.

A few old Navajo men still may wear the attire of earlier days, at least in part. But in the main, clothing, like that of other Indian men, has come to be that of the western stereotype: blue denim pants worn with an ornamental belt, cowboy boots or heavy shoes; colorful shirts and kerchiefs, large felt or straw hats, or maybe a bright headband, coat or leather jacket. Particularly on special occasions, silver and turquois jewelry is worn. If the occasion demands, dress clothing, including tuxedos, may be worn.

The female attire has shown less change through the years. Until recently, most women and girls wore garments reflecting the style of the 1860s, when the Navajo women began to wear long, full skirts of calico or some other colorful material, and velveteen blouses—these from patterns that were supplied during the Fort Sumner days. In their homeland, Navajo traditional moccasins of deerskin and cowhide are still in evidence to some degree.

The Pendleton blanket, or one of similar manufacture or appearance, is a favorite of older men and women, worn about the shoulders or folded over an arm. These attractive, machine-made products often have been admired by newcomers to the Southwest as *Indian blankets,* which, indeed, they have become—by adoption only. (The Pendleton Woolen Mills of Portland, Oregon, long ago sent designers to the Southwest where they spent a great deal of time with the Navajo. They learned the symbolism and Navajo preferences. "Using this knowledge they then designed blankets in the Indian concept and in the colors and patternings the Indians most desired" [Eklund 1969]. The Pueblos and other Indian peoples have distinct preferences, also, as to designs and colors.)

More and more, Navajo people abandon their distinctive clothing for the styles of their non-Indian neighbors. At one time, professional dress designers adapted the old, full-skirted garments and bedecked blouses of the Navajo women into gay frocks that they marketed as *squaw* or *fiesta* dresses which found favor among the young Navajo women and tourist alike. Today, skirts may be long or at knee length. Many variations and combinations are seen, reflecting traditional and counter-culture influences.

The universal badge of distinction among the Navajo is the silver and turquois jewelry—rings, bracelets, necklaces, earrings, buttons and pins, hatbands, and even shoe buckles. But don't let this display of wealth deceive you. It may indicate something of the wearer's own prosperity, but most likely—especially if worn at a ceremonial or public gathering—it represents his borrowings from family and friends or from a nearby trading post operator. A Navajo frequently arranges to remove valuable belongings from pawn with a trader for display at special functions.

Contemporary Life

Herdsman versus Farmer

Differences between the Navajo and the Pueblos are deeper than clothing, stature, or spoken tongue. The heritage of each is quite disparate. The Pueblo is a house-dweller and horticulturist, first and last; the Navajo is a herdsman basically and for that reason follows a shifting pattern of life. Kluckhohn stressed the fact that the Navajo has never been a nomad (*see* Kluckhohn and Leighton 1974:38–39). Although the Navajo practice agriculture to some extent today, and engage in livestock raising, these sources of income are significantly augmented by miscellaneous revenues from other resources, such as timber (of which there are over 472,700 acres of commercial value), oil, gas, vanadium, uranium, coal, sand, and gravel. The Navajo tribe is in big business, totaling in the millions, which requires employment of skilled attorneys, businessmen, and officials. Per capita personal income may average above $800, and the Navajo median family income between $3,000 and $4,000 (*see Navajo Nation* 1980 APR, pp. 3–6).

Education

After decades during which the Navajo saw little reason to send their youngsters to the white man's schools, or to schools following the Anglo curriculum, the Navajo have come to realize that the young should be trained to cope with modern demands. Consequently the tribe and individuals as well exert their influence toward having adequate schooling for the young; and also they promote adult education. Great emphasis is placed on education.

The overall Navajo education norm has reached the 6.5 grade year. In 1979–1980 some 55,300 pupils—kindergarten through high school—were enrolled in schools on and near the reservation; 2,300 Navajo seniors were graduated. Students were enrolled in not less than 150 colleges in thirty states. Years ago, the Navajo Tribe set up a multimillion dollar trust fund for scholarships for qualified Navajo high school graduates to attend colleges or universities of their choice. Since then several institutions have come to offer scholarships. During 1980 a total of 1,979 Navajo were the recipients of scholarships.

Many of the pupils in remote schools are picked up by bus and travel distances as much as fifteen miles. A study drafted by University of New Mexico professors disclosed that sixteen new elementary schools and eight new high school facilities are needed on the reservation. When they enter school, a great number of children speak only their native tongue, Navajo.

The Navajo say that the Comprehensive Employment Training Act (CETA) has had a profound effect on the Navajo labor force since the early 1970s. It provided Navajo workers with a substantial number of jobs and increased their skills required for employment in agriculture and mining, concentrating on semi-skilled and skilled classifications. An ONEO program directed attention to development of skills for grassroot Navajo workers, primarily for rural and countryside areas. Many of the young Navajo go on to vocational colleges or special schools.

Navajo Community College opened in January, 1969, in borrowed quarters at Many Farms, Arizona: this was the only college established on an Indian reservation or to be sponsored by Indian people. Its success and growth resulted in the planning of a beautiful campus for the college, situated in the ponderosa forests north of Fort Defiance, near Tsaile Lake, on 1,200 acres of land provided by the tribal council. Loans totaling $2,530,000 were approved by the U.S. Department of Housing and Urban Development for use in constructing the college, and a number of significant grants were made by foundations and commercial organizations for its operation. The new site of the college was dedicated on 13 April 1971, with some two thousand people attending the ceremonies. The plans were conceived to reflect Navajo culture in design and construction.

Most commanding of the structures is that of the Ned A. Hatathli Culture Center, thoughtfully conceived and built symbolically as a museum for the assembling, preserving, and exhibiting of Navajo manifestations of their lifeways from dimly historical times to the present. In this magnificent museum, many myths, legends, and practices of the past and present—such as records inscribed on great red rocks and sandpaintings from sacred ceremonials, as well as artifacts—can be preserved and exhibited. Whether they desire it or not (and some do, while others resist changes) the Navajo find that their mores are being forced to merge more and more with the streams of an engulfing Greater American culture. This museum can be a bulwark, a unique and enduring monument to the Navajo way of life.

Of importance, also, to the Navajo is the College of Ganado, established by the Presbyterians about thirty miles west of Window Rock in the heart of the Navajo Nation. There many Navajo are the classmates of the Hopi, other Indians, and non-Indians.

Incidentally, visitors to Window Rock will find the Tribal Museum in changed quarters, next to the Motor Inn (which the tribe has taken over) on Highway 264. It opened at this location on 13 July 1980. Closed for the winter, it reopened in May, 1981 with new exhibits.

Modern Government

To this day, the Navajo continue their organization based on regulations promulgated by the Secretary of Interior. Modifications are made as occasion demands "by the governing body itself, with the consent and approval of the Secretary, rather than an institution based on a constitutional framework approved by the people it represents" (Young 1968:61). The governing body is composed of a chairman, vice-chairman, and seventy-four delegates elected on a land management district basis. Elections are held every four years; campaigning becomes active at these times. Voters, both men and women over twenty-one years of age, must register; voting is done by secret ballot. Women can and do serve on the tribal council. The term is four years. All officers are sworn in by a district judge from Arizona or New Mexico.

Council meetings are held in the Council House at Window Rock, a structure built in octagonal shape like a huge hogan. Each member of the council has a desk with his or her name on it. Meetings are conducted entirely by the Navajo; Indian Service personnel are available for consultation but do not participate unless requested. A number of committees serve, such as the advisory committee (which is comparable to the Cabinet of the federal government), and smaller bodies, each attending to specific duties. A trained and uniformed Navajo police force is selected by the advisory committee. Surrounding the council chamber is a complex of administration buildings in which offices and necessary facilities are housed.

In 1969, the advisory committee, serving as the executive arm of the tribal council, directed the council "and all departments, divisions, agencies, enterprises, and entities of the Navajo Tribe to use the phrase 'Navajo Nation' in describing the lands and people of the Navajo Tribe." Furthermore, the advisory committee directed that "all resolutions of the Tribal Government be certified as being duly enacted at Window Rock, Navajo Nation (Arizona)." Perhaps in way of explanation, it was stated: "The Treaty of 1868 recognized the Navajo People as a sovereign nation and spelled 'Navajo' with a 'j'."

A tribal parks commission was created in 1957, and it has become very active. One of its important duties is to protect the hundreds of prehistoric ruins that are located within the confines of the Navajo reservation. These are considered to be among the tribe's irreplaceable assets, and great efforts are made to protect them from vandalism and "pot hunting." A reward has

been posted for information that will lead to the arrest and conviction of anyone illegally excavating in the ruins. Violators can be fined or sentenced to
not more than ninety days in prison, or both.

Parks and visitor centers have been developed, guided tours have been organized, tourist accommodations developed over the vast reservation, and arts
and crafts promoted. Annual fairs are held, as well as the many scheduled
and unscheduled ceremonials, sings, rodeos, rug auctions, and other events.

Industry and Commerce

With a labor force approaching 50,000—and many individuals without
employment—the Navajo Nation is seeking new and continuing industries.
It encourages investment by outside capital to develop the extensive natural
and human resources of the reservation. Most known metals, minerals, and
other raw materials for today's industrial needs are said to be within reasonable access to the reservation: coal, oil, gold, silver, copper, vanadium, uranium, cement, limestone, clay, gypsum, puzzolan, and bentonite. Considerable
progress has been made in the development of certain resources, and an ap-
preciable income has been realized from leases, bonuses, royalties, and annual rentals from oil, natural gas, and other mineral resources. From these
monies, Navajo-owned businesses have been financed, and land and buildings provided for new industries.

Major Navajo growth centers have been planned at Window Rock/Fort
Defiance, Navajo, Chinle/Many Farms, Shiprock, Kayenta, Crownpoint, and
Tuba City. In October, 1980, Tuba City received an EDA grant of $1.4
million for a large shopping center (see Navajo Times, 2 October 1980). Secondary centers include Leupp, Ganado, Tsaile, Tohatchi, Ojo Amarillo, and
Dilcon. Thus wide development of the reservation should lead to its economic
betterment.

Already, Fort Defiance has an industrial park, where a large modern structure was financed and built by the Navajo and leased to General Dynamics, a
multimillion dollar operation of technically skilled Navajo. The park is a
50-acre site six miles north of Window Rock, with some 30,000 Indians and
around 3,000 non-Indians dwelling within a 25-mile radius. The town of
Fort Defiance has a population of approximately 4,000.

In 1960, the Navajo established the Navajo Tribal Utility (NTUA) with
headquarters in Fort Defiance. A generating plant established there supplies
electricity, gas, water, and sewer service to the people and installations on
the reservation. Electric power lines have been strung across the terrain, and
underground pipe lines for water, oil, and gas crisscross the land.

Vast timberlands are being utilized for simple sawmill operations to a sophisticated lumbering industry. First was a lumber camp at Sawmill, Arizona, which came to produce around twenty million board feet of lumber
annually. Then, the tribal council appropriated eleven million dollars for new

sawmill operations in the Chuska Mountains along the Arizona-New Mexico border. Wisely, the council appointed four Navajo men with five longtime western lumbermen to its board of directors, and hired an expert manager for the sawmill.

Architects and city planners designed Navajo, New Mexico, about twenty miles north of Window Rock—a complete assemblage of residences, utilities, schools, churches, and commercial and community facilities. Construction was begun in 1962, and the mill was dedicated on 6 September. Soon Navajo pine lumber with its distinctive *Horned Moon* trademark entered the market, where it has earned a reputation for high quality and dependable delivery. It is marketed in more than twenty-five states.

Millions of dollars have directly entered the Navajo economy, and additional millions indirectly. The Navajo Forest Products Industries (NFPI) developed a large asset value with adequate reserves for working capital, replacement of worn and obsolescent equipment, and plant expansion. Thousands of Navajo have been given employment at the two sites. In addition, forest roads have been built, totaling thousands of miles. The production of lumber is accompanied by the utmost utilization of wastes, resulting in wood products for nationwide distribution.

In the mid-1950s, forward-looking companies concerned with the development of fuel components and power began to prospect in promising locations on the Navajo reservation. El Paso Natural Gas Company of El Paso, Texas, leased 40,287 acres in the Burnham area, some fifty miles south of Farmington, New Mexico, with a view to possible strip-mining operations. Explorations revealed a potential of 824.5 million tons of strippable coal in the whole area.

The Utah Construction & Mining Company (now Utah International, Inc.) headquartered in San Francisco, leased a twenty-five mile long strip of Navajo coal land and got a 50,000-acre-foot water allotment on the San Juan River from the New Mexico State Engineer. Currently, at Fruitland, New Mexico, huge draglines, one of which weighs four million pounds, strip away dirt and rock to a depth of as much as 120 feet to expose a low grade coal seam. This is then blasted before shoveling and hauling the coal to the Fruitland power plant. In 1970, this mine was expected to produce around 8.5 million tons of coal per year—more than any other mine in the world at that time. At an agreed rate of fifteen cents a ton, the revenue—royalty and lease rentals—to the Navajo tribe was estimated at $1.3 million (*see* Montgomery 1970b; 1970d). Presently these rates are a matter of contention.

The Navajo employed in the mine and generating plant receive limited economic benefit from this industrial undertaking, and from several similar or related projects. But the tremendous amounts of water required for cooling the generating plants arouse the deep concern of far-seeing conservationists who realize that the mining of the water may have detrimental results of increasing significance. Smoke, fly ash, and chemicals have filled the air and were deposited over a wide area annually. Strictures to control pollution had to be determined and enforced.

A related multimillion dollar coal mining project under lease involves the Navajo and Hopi Indians, covering Black Mesa (the Navajo "female mountain") south of Kayenta and extending southwestward to the Hopi villages. There, the Peabody Coal Company of St. Louis, Missouri, arranged to operate on a 64,858 acre area where it is estimated that some 16 billion tons of coal occur at two main levels. Some 350 to 400 million tons of coal appear to be economically feasible for strip mining. The project furnishes fuel for power generating plants at Mohave Station in southern Nevada and at Page, Arizona, on the Navajo reservation. Page originated in the 1950s as the construction camp for the building of the Glen Canyon Dam. The generating plant there is Arizona's largest source of electricity.

Huge draglines remove the ground cover of grass and piñon trees, and great shovels lift the thirty to forty feet of overburden and gouge out giant bites of coal. Water is being mined from sources built up during millions of years, from a depth of 2,000 feet or more below the top of Black Mesa. The water pours into a pipe eighteen inches in diameter and is mixed with an equal part of finely pulverized coal for transportation along a 273-mile slurry line to the Mohave plant. This is expected to move 117 million tons of coal over a thirty-five-year period. This pumping of water is calculated by certain water experts to result in the lowering of the watertable around Kayenta by one hundred feet. Water required for the thirty-five years' pumping is calculated to be 33,000 acre feet a year. It is purchased from the Navajo tribe at $5 per acre foot. An eighty-mile electric railroad, costing $40 million, is designed to deliver the coal from Black Mesa to the plant at Page (Montgomery 1970d).

Peabody's 1967 contract called for an annual rental of $1 an acre the first five years of the lease and $2 an acre thereafter for the life of the lease on the 64,858 acre plot of mesaland (Montgomery 1970c:A5).

All aspects of these monumental undertakings were expected to provide millions of dollars of income for the outside companies and subsidiaries, sizeable salaries for a small number of Indians, and lesser sums for others involved. It has been estimated that in the period 1963–1970, some $4 million in tribal funds were expended in efforts to bring new industries to the reservation.

Other companies followed Peabody as coal became an increasingly needed source of energy. A labor code was put into effect. Since 1973, the Office of Navajo Labor Relations has been enforcing Navajo labor preferences "by requiring mine operators to sign letters of agreement and to comply with Office guidelines. These specify the minimum percentage of Navajo craftsmen to be employed in each job category, wages, hiring, promotion and termination procedures." In 1978, reservation energy companies employed 4,000 people, 2,382 of them Navajo. "The coal companies have the best record for compliance, while the power plants have the worst" (Ruffing 1979:16).

The Ruffing study observes that:

The Navajo Nation not only receives minimal returns from its minerals, but also pays most of the economic, environmental and social costs of their development. In 1978 approximately one million acres were leased for oil, gas, coal and uranium activities. While the companies compensate for damages, they do not compensate surface users on an annual basis for their loss of livelihood. The Navajo Nation also permits energy producers to use 65,000 acre feet of water from the Colorado River System and the ground water systems at virtually no cost. The Navajo Tribal Utility Authority currently charges $360 per acre foot for treated and delivered water. If energy producers were allowed a $110 per acre foot credit for pumping their own water, they would still owe the Navajo Nation $16,250,000 (another very rough estimate).

Ruffing finds that the Navajo have great need of a well advised mineral policy. She says:

The Navajo Nation still possesses approximately 80 million barrels of oil, 20 million MCF of natural gas, 2.5 million tons of strippable coal, and 75 million pounds of U_3O_8 (Armstrong, W. D., 1976. Navajo Minerals Department, 1966–1985, Office of Minerals Development, Navajo Tribe). Despite such mineral wealth the Navajo people are subject to a degree of poverty unequalled by any other minority group in the U.S. Such poverty is the result of under-development of the Navajo economy. The major cause of its under-development is the fact that large corporations siphon off Navajo mineral wealth.
During 1977 the Navajo Nation produced 9.2 million barrels of oil, 5.2 million MCF of natural gas, 9.2 million MCF of gasoline, 7 million gallons of liquid products, 18 million tons of coal, and 502,573 pounds of U_3O_8 earning approximately $16.5 million in royalties which was only 8.5% of total corporate sales of $192.6 million.

The Navajo captured such a small portion because of the low royalty provision in its mineral leases—either a unit royalty of $0.15 per ton, or a percentage royalty—5 percent of selling price (Ruffing 1979:3).
The study finds that:

Mineral revenues must be committed to industry, agriculture, and supporting infrastructure for the benefit and use of future generations. And it states that "The Navajo Nation can increase its mineral revenues while minimizing environmental and social costs if it controls mineral development through a consistent and coherent mineral policy."

It is inevitable that the landscape of Navajoland is being altered, although present contracts call for restoration of the land to some degree. The natural beauty will be changed forever, as will be the centuries-old lifeways of the aboriginal inhabitants of the region. Federal laws require that strip-mined land be reclaimed. That which is being reclaimed is said, by the companies' own admission, to still be in an "experimental stage." Recent studies estimate the cost of reclamation to be between $1,840 and $5,040 an acre or $0.12 to $0.26 a ton mined (USBM 1976:7—rough estimate). The Ruffing study states that "The Navajo Environmental Protection Commission (NEPC) has found energy companies' performance under federal laws so unsatisfactory that it designed its own time-phased reclamation plan." The cost of such regulation and subsequent monitoring is borne by the Tribe (1979:4, *rel.* Reno 1981).

For more than a decade, the clustering of business establishments has been slowly appearing on the reservation. Early in 1969, a supermarket chain, FedMart Corporation, opened a large shopping center in Window Rock, an innovation bringing with it a much-needed filling station. There, too, was a laundromat and a coffee shop. Then a bank added its financial services. Now there is a mall with a theater and other occupants. Nearby, Colonel Sanders' Kentucky Fried Chicken provided welcome food for the hungry traveler and passing Navajo. Motels and other enterprises came into being.

And with expansion of businesses, new housing projects kept pace. Some homes are privately financed. Hundreds of low rent housing units have been erected under the Navajo Housing Authority; and mutual help units are constructed, with families achieving equity through participation in the building. Several thousand Navajo have taken part in a home improvement program, adding needed space, a new roof, or completing sanitary facilities.

It is one thing to live in a remote hogan—when a floor becomes uneven more earth may be carried from outside to level worn spots. When timbers disintegrate, others can be felled and fitted in as needed, and chinked with mud plaster. (Where rock hogans prevail, they also can be repaired with earth, rocks, and logs at hand.) But living in a frame house with separate, rectangular rooms presents different contingencies. Furniture has to be acquired to accommodate four or five people. Beds must be provided, replacing pallets; tables, perhaps, instead of sitting on the floor and eating from vessels placed before a gathered family group; sanitary facilities and running water substituted for water hauling and "going outside."

In such new neighborhoods, built in the pattern of clustered houses along paved streets, children run and play in restricted, mainly unplanted, treeless yards; and indeed they play roughly. Indoors, their vigor is tough on the often flimsy furniture, the hard wall plaster, screen doors or glass window panes. Confinement, in contrast to wide open spaces which surround the traditional hogans, soon takes its toll on HUD-built homes. Upkeep has commonly been neglected and funds difficult to obtain.

More and more families have come to centers where industrial, commercial, and educational opportunities have concentrated. Take, as an example, Chinle, at the entrance of the majestic Canyon de Chelly and Canyon del Muerto. The 110 rental units developed there evidenced wear and tear within a short period of time. Just recently, in 1980, Washington awarded $3,424,780 for upgrading. In the *Navajo Times,* published at Window Rock, 18 September 1980 (which has a Navajo for its general manager and editor), it was reported that "to do this 110 families will have to be relocated so construction work can begin." The HUD director announced, "We plan to upgrade the roads, re-do the plumbing, electrical work, renovate the bathrooms, kitchens and practically re-build the entire house." A two-year project was estimated, involving the relocation of 550 residents. To accomplish such a project and qualify for the grant, said the director, "We had to have more than 100 housing units in order to qualify." Chinle was the only specific project that had more than 100 units. Fortunately, the Chinle endeavor is to include construction of a recreation center near the rental units.

Elsewhere in the same newspaper, it was stated that a grant of $3,080,000 had been awarded to the Navajo Housing Authority (NHA) to weatherize 710 housing units. That project is expected to get under way also in Chinle; it will include Fort Defiance (now with over 100 units), Window Rock, and more distant areas: Tuba City and Kayenta, Arizona; Church Rock near Gallup and Navajo, New Mexico, public rental units. Most of these were built in the late 1960s and early 70s, and were never insulated. The director noted that, "Unlike other housing units on the reservation, these units are public rental and NHA has to pay the utilities." Last year, they paid $1,125,800 "just for utilities alone," and it cost about $78.97 per month to heat these 710 units.

During April, 1971, the community of Piñon scored a first on the reservation with the opening and blessing of a retail enterprise called the Dine-Bi-Naa-Yei Cooperative. It is a dues-paying member of the Arizona Grocers Association. Open six days a week in the remodeled old arts and crafts building of the Piñon chapter house, it is operated solely by and primarily for the Navajo people of Piñon, located on reservation Route 4 between Second Mesa and Chinle. Members pay a small fee. Expectations were that the enterprise would be grossing about one thousand dollars a day. Federal funds, those of the Navajo, and of others were utilized in this undertaking.

In June of 1971, the Navajo took a historic step toward more independence from the federal government with the signing of an agreement to take over the federal commodity food program on their reservation.

Many of the younger Navajo and government officials want innovations to come to the reservation, and their views are coming to prevail in tribal elections. Jobs, changes in traditional concepts, and urbanization become increasingly important factors. A BIA official has said "if the economy can be stepped up, we can see sizeable towns develop." And he remarked that the Navajo are "very rapidly urbanizing and modernizing" (Graves 1970:24 August).

At the same time, economic growth on the reservation is viewed with concern by the "traditional" Navajo who want to continue living as they have in the past. The opposing points of view result in conflicts. This is not a new trait in Navajo culture, but certain conflicts result in mental illnesses which old practices no longer control. Although youthful suicides are all but unheard of among many Indian groups, such as the Pueblos, the Navajo now have an exceptionally high rate of suicide (see Levy 1965; Levy et al. 1969: 124–147). Speaking of this, Dr. Karl Menninger has said, "Where one commits suicide, scores are in despair." Alcoholism is widespread.

The poem on page 127 gives a Navajo's arresting commentary on progress versus Indian tradition.

Off-Reservation Employment

An increasing number of Navajo take off-reservation employment each year. This may be seasonal, with the Navajo working for a few months and then returning home to spend the remaining months with his family; with the development of industries on or near the reservation, jobs become longer lasting. In addition, an ever-growing number are leaving the reservation and settling in industrial areas. For these, employment is relatively permanent. Many thousands now live in Los Angeles, San Francisco, Oakland, Denver, Chicago, Dallas, and other cities. Such resettlement has been successful only when the Navajo has had sufficient education, hand skills, and understanding of non-Indian culture.

During times of war or other national stresses, the Navajo—both men and women—have made fine records in the armed forces, and in supporting industries. Today they are well represented in most branches of the armed services.

Hopi-Navajo Land Disputes

Through the years, Navajo and Hopi dissatisfaction over the lands supposedly shared between them has increased. Each has become more and more vocal about the matter, and press notices on the subject appear frequently. Since early 1970, the news media have carried extensive accounts of Navajo claims and Hopi briefs presented to the federal Indian Claims Commission (a body established by Congress in 1946 to adjudicate and settle, once and for all, Indian claims against the United States "for unconscionable acts in previous years that had injured or unjustly deprived Indian tribes of lands and resources" (see Young 1968:75). After hearing pro and con arguments, the commission finally laid down boundary lines involving about thirty million acres, and ruled that the Navajo should have been compensated therefor in the 1968 treaty. Still the disputes continued and intensified. (Rel. Clemmer 1979:533–538.)

The Hopi have age-old traditions pertaining to the land they have occupied since prehistoric times. To them, their domain abounds with sacred places that exist both in actuality and in myths and legends. Their roots indeed are there. Noted as a peaceful people whose social system, historically, embraced care of the old and widowed, ill and orphaned, those unfortunate in times of drought, famine, or flash flood, the agricultural Hopi were ill-prepared to fend off the migratory Navajo—a people with a different heritage and culture. These late-comers unobtrusively and slowly encroached, here and there, along the unfenced limits of the Hopi lands, a practice that was initiated in about 1750.

Because of recurring jurisdictional disputes since 1882, Congress passed legislation in July, 1958, that resulted in the appointment of a special three-judge federal court, which met in Prescott, Arizona, to decide the respective rights of the two tribes concerning 2,472,095 acres in question. Then, it was reported:

> In the landmark case of Healing vs. Jones, which was heard from Sept. 26 to Oct. 22, 1960, the court determined that the Hopis have exclusive right to the surface and subsurface land within District 6, as defined in 1943, and the Hopis and Navajo have "joint, undivided and equal rights" in both the surface and subsurface land as defined by the 1882 Executive Order, except for District 6.

The Court held that it did not have jurisdiction to partition the joint-use area, which in turn led to continuing disagreements over the next decade. The Navajo Tribe appealed the Healing vs. Jones decision to the Supreme Court, but that ruling was affirmed by the high court in 1963. Despite the joint-use decree, however, the Navajo exercised almost exclusive control over 1.8 million acres. (Phil Niklaus, *Albuquerque Journal,* 21 July 1974.) Some 8,800 Navajo continued to dwell on Hopi land. Through intervening years, officials of the two tribes hoped and felt that their problems—which basically stemmed from competition for resources in the disputed areas—could be settled without outside interference. At a seminar on Human Relationships the Hopi Chairman issued the statement: "If we can sit down and work out our problems, we can say that we can accomplish anything that needs to be worked out." And the Navajo Tribal Chairman said: "I hope we can get rid of the attorneys and Congress in this case and let the two tribes sit down together to resolve the question." (Jim Largo, *Albuquerque Journal,* 15 May 1957.) This reflects Indian philosophy, wherein it has been a traditional practice to discuss and talk out problems until such time as they are settled.

When the Court drew up lines for the partitioned area, in 1977, some 5,000 Navajo found that they had no right to stay at their long-held homesites, and about 50 Hopi faced relocation. Practically everyone involved was unhappy, except a few of the younger Indians. The Navajo offered to buy out the Hopi interests; they wanted to avoid relocation. The Hopi did not want to sell; they wanted their land. As one investigator reported:

> Relocation is a terrifying prospect for those who know only the life of land, livestock, and extended family; whose world view has been shaped by Navajo myth and the Navajo language; who find even the small towns on the reservation bewildering.
> A comprehensive relocation plan is being developed by a special federal commission. Congress approved $37 million in relocation benefits in 1974, but the commission is now saying $250 million may be (and certainly, at the current rate of inflation) necessary to complete relocation successfully.
> Through direct contact with the land dispute area, the relocation commission has come to understand what Congress could not—that while the Navajo reservation sprawls for 25,000 square miles, it does not contain room for relocatees to move with their sheep. Most of the reservation is poorly vegetated, and every inch of it is jeal-

ously guarded as part of some family's customary herding area. On a reservation where per capita income is about $1,000 and unemployment hovers around 40 percent, few Navajos can afford to make room for relocatees. . . . Two Indian tribes haggling over a chunk of high desert off in a corner of the Southwest weren't of much concern to legislators in those days of Watergate. (Kammer 1980:173–191)

In 1980, Congress continued its attempts. With an Act for Navajo and Hopi Relocation Amendments, the new legislation did not alter the basic program set in 1974, which even some Congressmen consider "harsh and inhumane." It has been pointed out that:

The new legislation raises a number of questions for the federal relocation commission, which now has the responsibility for allocating and administering the new land and for determining who gets left estates. . . . [It] will put a strain on the [Navajo] tribe's budget. In an economy move designed to avoid a veto . . . it requires the tribe to foot the bill for 150,000 of the 400,000 acres to be acquired for relocatees. (Kammer 1980:215)

Tribal officials are wondering how the tribe will be able to come up with the $20–$30 million that will be necessary to buy the land. They also complain that once again the Navajo are being made to pay for the mistakes of the federal government. The matter of life estates is of grave concern. As Kammer has put it simply:

Life estates do not translate smoothly in the Navajo language. . . . Indeed they come across offensively as "death estates." A life estate allows people to live out their lives on a piece of land. But Navajos believe it is wrong, even dangerous, to talk about dying, to anticipate your own death or the death of someone else. That is playing with the natural order of things. (Kammer 1980:213–216)

As one Navajo explained, "When you implant something in someone's mind, you cause it to happen." And so it is considered with life estates, "in essence what we'd have to say is, 'You're going to die.' " He says that the Navajo do not like to hear that kind of talk; they feel uncomfortable. Another man commented, "It is very disturbing to know that your livelihood and traditions on the land are going to end when you die. When there is going to be nothing you can leave for your children, nothing of the land where you were raised, for a Navajo that is very hard" (Ibid., p. 216).

Still another man said that the Navajo have a lot of faith in justice, "even though it's not being given to them, because a lot of the families sent men to fight in the service. Some of them died in foreign countries. Some of them came back with disabilities. They fought in good faith for their land, and now the families can't believe it was all in vain." Not only the Navajo feel that Congress has made a grave mistake, as shown by a non-Indian scientist who has remarked that Congress "was and is terribly uninformed" on the harmful effects of relocation. (Ibid., 219.) At the present, relocation is continuing (see Goodman 1982:97; rel. Kammer 1980).

Navajo Ceremonies

Among the Pueblo peoples, weather control—placing great emphasis on rainmaking—is fundamental in religious organization and ceremonial enactments under the control of priests. In contrast, Navajo religion centers in curing ceremonies directed by shamans following a system of imitative and sympathetic magic. All Navajo rituals are performed with certain aims in mind: restoring health, securing food, insuring survival. In the Navajo universe, two classes of personal forces are recognized, human beings and the Holy People, or supernatural beings—holy in that they are powerful and mysterious. The Navajo believes his universe functions according to certain set rules. If one learns these rules and lives in accordance with them, he will keep safe or be restored to safety. The Holy People have great powers over the people on earth; on the other hand, they may not only be supplicated and propitiated, but may be coerced as well.

The Navajo greatly fears death and everything connected with it. This intense feeling—which has many ceremonial expressions—stems from the fear of ghosts and witches of the afterworld. He fears the dead may return as ghosts to plague the living. Therefore, any dead person is a potential danger. Ghosts are believed to take the form of human beings, animals, birds, or whirlwinds, spots of fire, etc. They appear only after dark or at the approach of death. Ghosts may foreshadow general disaster as well as harm to an individual. When a Navajo sees a ghost or dreams of one, it is imperative that the proper ceremony be performed or the individual will surely die. If successful, such ceremonial cures are believed to have killed the witch, one way or another.

Disease and accidental injury are felt to result from attack by the Holy People, and may be traced to some transgression on the part of a victim. A cure must be effected by a specific chant (a song ceremonial, the songs of which are accompanied by the use of a rattle), and by making sacrificial appeasement to the offended Holy Person, or be engaging the mightier power of a higher divinity to remove the witchery and evil influence of an inferior one. Should a given ceremony fail to cure the sickness, it merely indicates that the offense has not been properly traced and the source must be further sought. Numerous chants may be performed until the patient recovers, or dies. Death is considered to be beyond human calculation. When death of a patient becomes certain, the official singer (*hataaɫii*), or "medicine man," who conducts a song ceremonial, withdraws before the inevitable.

Chants and Sandpaintings

In general, every chant has its own particular sandpaintings. These represent the divinities or some event connected with a divinity, as told in Navajo legends. More than five hundred different sandpaintings have been recorded, and fifty-eight or more distinct ceremonies, each with its own body of leg-

ends. Navajo mythology tells us that originally the drawings were made by
the gods, or yé'ii, themselves, and were stitched into some kind of fabric.
Actually, it would be more accurate to call these *dry paintings,* for pollen,
meal, and other vegetal material, as well as pulverized clay and certain minerals may be used in addition to sand; and occasionally, the paintings are
made on buckskin. Usually, the paintings are made on a background of clean
sand. The details of the patterns are handed down by memory from one singer
to another. Different colors are made by crushing rock, charcoal, or other
material into fine powders and mixing them with sand or dirt for easier handling.

Probably due to the influences of various Indian groups encountered during
Navajo migrations and selection of dwelling sites in the Southwest, their
"medicine men" devised befitting symbols. These related to *their* mythology,
songs, and dances. Since the Navajo did not erect permanent structures for
their holy places, their depictions were carved or painted on the cliff walls
or in caves of their new homelands. Many of these symbols pertain to ritualistic paraphernalia, to the fauna, vegetation, and personages recognizable in
the sandpaintings (*see* Olin and Hadlock, 1980:26–31; Schaafsma, P. 1966;
1980a:20–27; 1980b:301–333; Brugge and Frisbie 1982).

SONG OF THE TWO
WHO GO ABOUT TOGETHER

That which is good,
May it be made as offering to him [the Holy Spirit Boy]
May it be made as offering to him;
The young man who walks in the darkness,
May it be made as offering to him,
May it be made as offering to him;
The pretty black bead,
May it be made as offering to him,
May it be made as offering to him;
The pretty sparkling stone,
May it be made as offering to him,
May it be made as offering to him;
The pretty blue flower pollen,
May it be made as offering to him,
May it be made as offering to him;
The pretty corn pollen,
May it be made as offering to him,
May it be made as offering to him;
They will be exchanged for his mind, his voice;
May they be made as offering to him.
That which is good,
May it be made as offering to him,
May it be made as offering to him;
The young woman of the dusk,

May it be made as offering to her,
May it be made as offering to her;
The pretty white shell,
May it be made as offering to her,
May it be made as offering to her,
The pretty sparkling stone,
May it be made as offering to her,
May it be made as offering to her;
The pretty blue flower pollen,
May it be made as offering to her,
May it be made as offering to her;
The pretty corn pollen,
May it be made as offering to her,
May it be made as offering to her;
They will be exchanged for his voice, her mind;
May they be made as offering to her;
   That which is good,
May it be made as offering to her,
May it be made as offering to her.

From *Chants of the Creation Myth,* Vol. I,
Navajo Religion Series (1940:129–130).
Museum of Navajo Ceremonial Art,
Santa Fe, New Mexico

Each chant has certain songs, prayers, and herbal medicines which are held
to be particularly its own, and the appropriate sandpainting is made inside
the hogan where the ceremony is held, or out-of-doors on occasion. But regardless of which chant and paintings are being performed, the basic procedure is the same. Upon completion of the treatment, the patient leaves the
hogan, the painting is destroyed in the same order in which it was made, and
is deposited to the north of the hogan. *(See* McAllester and McAllester 1980.)

Navajo chants may be grouped according to their mythological associations,
rituals they have in common, and as they are addressed to the same or related
forces. The six main groups of song ceremonials are: *Blessingway* rites and
ceremonials; *War* ceremonials (obsolescent), *Gameway* (hunting) rites (obsolescent); and the three curing ceremonials, *Holyway* employed for the attrac-
tion of good, *Evilway* (Ghostway) for exorcism of evil, and *Lifeway* for curing
bodily injuries. One of the Holyway curing group, *Beautyway,* will likely be
given if snakes have been offended. If lightning or thunder must be appeased, a
Shootingway will be used. Where one has trouble from contact with bears, the
Mountain Topway is the proper treatment. Sometimes a Navajo contracts illness from a non-Navajo, and then he needs to have the *Enemyway* performed.
The Enemyway was formerly used in connection with war.

All Navajo rites are accompanied by social functions. One of the features
of the Enemyway is the so-called squaw dance. Originally, the intention of
this dance was to announce publicly the fact that the girls participating in

the ceremony, and who asked the young men to dance with them, were of marriageable age. The young men came to sing and to look over the girls. And crowds gathered to watch the procedure. Today, squaw dances are popular with Indian and non-Indian audiences alike. Groups of Navajo often perform them publicly; and non-Indian people frequently participate. Since the man has to give the girl a present—commonly money—before she will release him from dancing with her, an innocent "victim" may afford the audience much amusement before he "catches on"; and he may accumulate considerable indebtedness to the girl. The squaw dance goes on all night long.

The Blessingway places the Navajo in tune with the Holy People. It is performed in approval of a newly selected headman, for an expectant mother, for men going away in their country's service or upon their return. Blessingway songs are sung in the girls' puberty rites and in marriage ceremonies.

Navajo boys and girls are introduced to full participation in ceremonial life by a short initiation rite which is usually held on the next to last night of the Nightway. The initiation ceremony and the entire Nightway are popularly known as the *Yeibichei*. The name comes from the principal figures in the initiation ceremony, who represent *yé'ii* (supernaturals). The Nightway is one of the few Navajo chants that has an attending public dance.

Nightway (Yei Bichei)

The Nightway is a nine-day ceremonial, during which the patient is treated. It is a complex of ceremonies, having a name and an origin legend, carried out according to a certain ritual. Singing occurs for nine nights, sandpaintings are made on the last four days, and prayers and other symbolic offerings and rituals are tendered. On the ninth night comes the climax, a drama illustrating an elaborate myth. The Navajo ride in from far and near, make camp, build their fires, and arrange themselves for the night.

Necessary for the enactment of the Nightway are actors representing certain yé'ii: Talking God, Water Sprinkler, and preferably twelve dancers, representing male and female deities in equal numbers. Monster Slayer, Calling God, Black God, Fringed Mouth, and others may also appear. With these are the singer and the patient.

The dancers impersonating male divinities have their naked torsos, upper extremities, and thighs whitened. Each wears a mask, collar of spruce, loincloth of some showy material, dark wool stockings with red woven garters and moccasins, a silver concha belt with foxskin suspended in the rear, ear pendants, bracelets, and many necklaces of shell, turquois, silver, and coral. In the right hand, each carries a gourd rattle painted white and sometimes decorated with spruce twigs; in the left hand is a spruce twig wand. The casque-shaped mask is painted blue, with a horizontal yellow streak at the bottom crossed by four pairs of perpendicular black lines. A fringe of hair crosses the mask from side to side over the crown of the head. Small eye holes are outlined by red triangles. From the front of the mask, a snout projects; at its base, is a fringe of fur. Two eagle plumes and a bunch of owl feathers are affixed to the mask. *(Rel.* Koenig; Olin; Dutton and Olin; and Rodee 1982: 28–73.)

Dancers who impersonate female deities are usually small men or youths. Sometimes women take part; and when they do, they dress in ordinary female costume with which they wear a mask like that of the men. They carry no rattles, but have spruce boughs in each hand. They have no foxskin and wear no blanket; they dance a different step from that of the men. When men impersonate female deities, they sing in falsetto and wear an ornate kilt or scarf around the hips. Otherwise, they are dressed like the other dancers with whitened body, concha belt with fox skin hanging behind, dark wool stockings and moccasins, ear pendants, necklaces, and bracelets, but in each hand, they carry spruce boughs and their masks are different. The masks cover only the face and throat, and the hair flows free. The masks are nearly square, slightly rounded at the top, painted blue, but with white "ears" protruding at the sides; eye margins are black triangles, and black squares surround the mouth holes; from the bottom of a mask may hang a piece of red cloth, and at the top may be a fringe of short hair. At the center of the top is tied a piece of abalone shell with turkey, eagle, or woodpecker feathers behind it; beads, bits of shell, and other articles of adornment may be added.

The dancers are dressed and painted in the medicine hogan; then they go into an arbor across a cleared area in front of the hogan where they get their masks, wands, and rattles. The performance is in two parts: outside is dancing and singing; within the hogan is chanting, but no dancing.

The visitor will become conscious of soft singing, to the accompaniment of the swishing rhythm of rattles, coming from the hogan. After a time, the performers enter the dancing area. The singer leads the procession. He is followed by Talking God, then by the dancers in single file, and finally by Water Sprinkler. When all are in front of the hogan, the singer turns and faces the others, who halt. The patient, warned by a call, comes from the hogan. Patient and singer then walk along the line of dancers, from west to east. The singer takes meal from a basket carried by the patient and, as they pass each dancer, he sprinkles it on the right arm. Sometimes, the patient takes part in the sprinkling. Patient and singer then turn, sunwise, and retrace their steps to the front of the hogan and face the dancers. The dancers have taken up the sprinkling movements and continue them. Then, with shaking of rattles, and whooping, the dancing and singing get under way.

Water Sprinkler serves as clown. While the others are dancing, he engages in all sorts of capers, getting in their way, sometimes imitating Talking God, losing some item of attire and making a great to-do about it, dancing, and acting as buffoon in general.

Throughout the night, different acts are performed in an orderly and regular manner. The participants take short rest periods. It is said the most desirable number of repetitions of the dance is forty-eight, when four sets of dancers perform twelve times each. But many variations from the standard may be seen. After the dancers have finished their last song, singers inside the hogan chant the four Finishing Hymns; one or more assistants may aid the singer, sitting at his right. Those who are near the hogan may hear this singing, but few white people are privileged to witness the ceremony within a medicine lodge. As the last verse is sung, the singer overturns an inverted basket drum toward the west, making movements as though releasing winged insects from under the basket and driving them out through the smoke hole in the roof; he blows a breath after the invisible insects as they supposedly depart. During this song, an assistant to the singer has been applying meal to the lower jaw of the patient. Finally, an act of unraveling the drumstick is performed. While an assistant carries out this procedure, the singer gives final instructions to the patient. All are then free to depart. Certain taboos must be observed and definite rites followed. The patient must not go to sleep before sunset. The singer retires to the medicine hogan to sleep and must do so for four consecutive nights (Matthews 1902).

Mountain Topway

The Mountain Topway—commonly known as the Mountain Chant—is usually held over nine consecutive days. The first four days are not of particular interest to the general visitor. On the fifth day, in conjunction with the curative rites, the first sandpainting is made in the hogan. Other paintings are made on the three succeeding days. On the ninth day, preparation goes forward for the nighttime ceremonies—the making of plumed arrows, wands, trees, and so forth. The final night is the big spectacle. A great woodpile is surrounded by a huge corral with an opening to the east. It is made of evergreen branches. As this corral is being finished—just after sunset—the head singer stands at the entrance, singing and shaking his rattle. As night falls, the Navajo spectators enter the sacred enclosure, build their small fires near the confining wall and settle themselves to watch the night's performances.

When the great bonfire is roaring, a warning whistle is heard from the outer darkness. A dozen lithe, lean men come bounding into the corral. They wear only breechclouts and moccasins. Their bodies are painted white. They carry feather-tipped wands which they wave to the four directions as they move around the fire. The heat is terrific, but they circle it twice. Then, they plunge toward the flames, close enough to burn the plumes from the ends of their wands. The next feat is for each to restore the feathers to his wands.

Because of this startling spectacle at the beginning, this ceremony is frequently called the fire dance. A dozen or so dances may follow—each with its chorus of male singers. Acts such as arrow swallowing, growing of the yucca plant, feathers dancing in a basket, and other skillful legerdemain may be performed. Very elaborate costumes are worn.

The final act in this ceremony is another fire dance around the renewed fire. Before the dancers appear, strange sounds are heard in the distance—the blowing of horns and shrill calls. As the sounds come closer, perhaps ten men advance through the eastern entryway into the corral. They wear only narrow loincloths and moccasins, and their bodies are covered with white clay, giving them a ghostly appearance. Each man, except the leader, carries a long, thick bundle of shredded juniper bark in each hand; and one carries an extra bundle for the leader to use later. The leader carries four small fagots of flaming juniper bark. All dance around the great central fire four times, waving their bundles toward the fire. On the east side, they halt; the leader kindles one of the fagots, shouts loudly, and tosses it over the east wall of the corral. Then, they move around to the south, the west, and the north, where similar acts are performed. But before the leader throws the burning brand to the north, he lights the bark bundles of the other dancers.

The entire group begins to dance wildly about the roaring fire. They run hither and yon, the breeze fanning the brands into long brilliant streamers of flame, which play upon the bodies of the participants. As the bundles burn, glowing fragments drop off; these are tossed about or thrown upon the other dancers. Every time a brand is applied to the flesh of one of the performers, the trumpeting sound is heard. The juniper bundles are relighted from the central fire in case they cease to burn. When a brand finally is consumed, the dancer drops the ash and runs out of the corral. One by one, they all disappear (Mathews 1887).

The fire dies; dawn comes. Three more openings are broken in the corral wall. The Indians pick up their blankets and fire-blackened coffee pots, mount horses or pile into wagons or motor vehicles, and head for home. By the time the sun is well over the horizon, the cars are out of sight, but the horses and wagons are still drawing crooked lines across the countryside.

The fire dance is frequently performed alone at public exhibitions, such as at ceremonial events in Gallup, the Flagstaff Pow-wow, and similar exhibitions, where it makes a dramatic climax to an evening's program.

Most of the Navajo chants can be held at any time of the year, but the curing ceremonials are restricted to certain months. The Nightway and the Mountain Topway cannot be given until after the first killing frost; they are usually held in November and December. The Enemyway is generally performed after completion of the spring work and before the harvesting and marketing season arrives.

The Ramah Navajo (see pp. 99–101) do not hold some of the longer chants, such as the Nightway and Mountain Topway, but many of the shorter ceremonials are performed frequently. Local practitioners—who include singers, curers, prayer makers, diagnosticians, and witches—know about twenty different ceremonials. Around twenty adult men are classed as practitioners, but most of these are curers, who know only part of a ceremonial, as opposed to singers who know at least one ceremonial of five or more nights' duration.

(*See* Vogt 1951:17.) All who practice any form of divination are known as diagnosticians, "those who investigate to reveal" (Kluckhohn and Wyman 1940:15–16). A dozen or so of the Ramah men and women are, or were, diagnosticians.

Cost of ceremonials is borne by the patient or by his family. Today, that means as much as seven hundred dollars or more for a Yeibichei, and four hundred dollars for a squaw dance. A Yeibichei singer receives from seventy-five dollars to one hundred and fifty dollars in cash, plus one hundred dollars to two hundred dollars worth of goods, and small contributions from people going in to witness the sandpaintings. For a squaw dance, the singer may get twenty-five dollars for preparations and procedural instructions, plus a possible additional take from contributions during the ceremony. Those assisting the singer are also paid. Equipment such as baskets, herbs, deer skins, and the like, must be purchased. And, most important of all, those who attend the ceremonial must be fed. Thus, all Navajo ceremonials are expensive undertakings. *(Rel.* Aberle 1967.)

The Peyote Cult

During the difficult times that prevailed in the 1930s, the peyote cult gained a foothold among the Navajo and some of the other Southwestern Indians. Peyote, a hallucinogenic cactus, had been widely used among Mexican Indians in religious rites since prehistoric times. Spanish documents mention it early in the seventeenth century. Until the 1800s, peyote was eaten by Indian peoples privately to induce visions or as a trance-producing feature of group dancing. Then, toward the end of the nineteenth century, use of peyote became the core of a new ceremonial complex among the Indians of Oklahoma; it was highly developed by the Kiowa and spread to other Indians who used peyote in various rites.

In 1918, a number of the Indian peoples in Oklahoma incorporated a movement known as the Native American Church; peyote served as the means of spiritual communion between man and his diety—known to the Navajo as *pioniyo*. The Navajo, around 1940, began to practice the peyote cult with increasing vigor. They learned the peyote ceremony from the Ute Indians of southern Colorado, who are said to have used peyote for years.

In 1944, the name was changed to the "Native American Church of the United States," and in 1955, it was changed again, to the "Native American Church of North America," to include Canadian peyote groups (Anonymous 1970a:12).

For a long time, the use of peyote by the Navajo was "an underground phenomenon illegal by tribal law, the subject of fierce, though carefully hushed, controversy. Now, it is said to be surfacing as one of the Navajo's most significant cultural crutches in a troubled time. The cult displays a unique blending of traditional Navajo ceremonialism, fundamentalist Christian elements, and 'pan-Indian moral principles' " (Nabokov 1969:129); it appears to be meeting the deepest spiritual needs of a transitional people. Estimates of the practicing Navajo membership in the Four Corners region run from one-third to 80 percent.

The increase of peyotism seems due, largely, to the introduction of new and varied doctrines by missionaries of differing Christian denominations. In the majority of instances, the result was a partial Christianization, which left the Navajo (and other Indian groups) with a sense of insecurity regarding their traditional religion. One investigator, who made an in-depth survey at mission stations on the Navajo reservation, found that "a good deal of Christian mission work completely missed the idea that religion is involved in the whole life for any people who have come out of animism," as have the Navajo. It was noted that the Native American Church has positive values in its favor, for example, emphasis on family life and stress on fellowship. The investigator stated that, "Despite twenty-five years of work, and considerable expenditure, mission work for the church I was studying had made an unsatisfactory impact" (*see* Thrapp 1967:II:6).

Before the peyote cult reached the Navajo, nothing seemed to bridge the gap between the old ceremonial ways and the new patterns resulting from culture changes and the demands of the modern world. More and more, the ills which formerly called forth a singer to perform a Navajoway, or a curing ceremony, came to be met by Peyote Road rites.

A participant in a Navajo peyote ceremony has stated that peyote (*Lophophora williamsii*) when eaten, produces "relatively standard physiological effects, but markedly varying psychological ones, depending on the user's cultural background." He explains that:

Peyote's make-up of alkaloids—at least 15 at latest count, the most studied being mescaline—acts like a series of timed depth charges. First comes an unpleasant, stomach-unsettling sensation. Within a half-hour this dies, leaving a face starting to flush, pupils dilating, salivation increasing and a sense of exhilaration growing through the body, resembling the effect of swift intakes of pure oxygen. Then one moves into a period of withdrawal, of intense color awareness, of successions of hallucinations when eyes are closed, energies focused inward.

A few hours later, this levels off onto an intense plateau. Then whatever one is prompted to concentrate upon—here the cultural situation is a critical determinant—becomes uncannily luminous. During these hours, reflexes are heightened, occasional muscle twitching is common, time is overestimated, spacial perception is altered, hearing and sight yield intensified tones, ideas flow rapidly, but physical movement is awkward.

This final period . . . diminishes through the following day with no after-effects. . . . (Nabokov 1969:30)

The performance of rites of the Peyote Road is a dusk-to-dawn affair which is conducted by an officiating priest known as the Road Chief. He is assisted by three other principals: a Drummer Chief who does much of the drumming, the Cedar Chief who sprinkles powdered juniper ("cedar") on the fire during the meeting, and a Fire Chief. With "Indian sage," the Road Chief prepares an altar on the floor of a hogan, shredding the sage while the Fire Chief, who sits on the north side of the door, tends the fire built in the center of the chamber of uniformly split wood. The sticks are arranged in V-shape, and flames rise upward from the tip. Then, the Road Chief arranges a nest of sage pods in the middle of the altar which he has fashioned in a crescent of earth known as the Peyote Moon. A large peyote blossom is carefully placed in the sage bed, representing the Peyote Chief, symbol of the spirtual medium of the Peyote Road.

After the altar has been prepared, the participants take the sacramental food, munching on peyote buds that have been sliced and dried, or sipping brewed "tea" made therefrom. The final period of effectiveness is entered toward midnight. Then, the Road Chief readies a kettle drum, inside of which are a few soaked coals and water "to 'strengthen' the drumbeats." The religious services then begin—a night of ceremonial praying, smoking, and singing, of confessing and weeping, which continue until dawn. Then, a traditional blessing of the peyote breakfast occurs, followed by a final prayer.

Such ceremonies take place on Thanksgiving eve and the night before Christmas and the New Year, at Easter, the Fourth of July, and on Armed Forces Day.

Insignia of the peyote cult consist of a cardinal red tie and socks, silver "water bird" ornament, and a rectangular box made of "cedar" for ritual paraphernalia—feathered fans, drum, eagle bone whistle, gourd rattles with beaded handles, and a horsehair-tipped staff. As one travels through Navajoland, the decals he sees with the letters "N.A.C." and a spread-wing bird motif affixed to car or truck windows indicate membership in the Native American Church.

State and federal laws are in conflict and confusion regarding the legality of use of peyote. A bill permitting the use of peyote for bona fide religious purposes was passed by the New Mexico Legislature in 1956. Four years later, the state of Arizona decreed peyote use legal for NAC members, and a few other states have taken similar action; federal tolerance of its ritual use depends largely upon a Supreme Court ruling of 1961.

It is recorded that: "On October 9, 1967, the Navajo Tribal Council adopted a declaration of basic Navajo rights which cancelled all previous laws denying freedom of religion inconsistent with this declaration."

Title 17, subchapter 21, section 641, of the Navajo Tribal Code, in re "sale, use or possession" of peyote, states:

It shall be unlawful for any person to transport peyote into Navajo country or buy, sell, possess or use peyote in any form, and any person convicted of violating this provision shall be guilty of a misdemeanor punishable by a fine not to exceed $100 or imprisonment not to exceed nine months or both; provided that it shall not be unlawful for any member of the Native American Church to transport peyote into Navajo country, or buy, sell, possess or use peyote in any form, in connection with the religious practices, sacraments or services of the Native American Church. (Anonymous 1970a:12)

The Navajo, like all other Americans, have been beset by the barrage of capitalized initials that are poured continually into governmental nomenclature, the news media, and everyday speech. Much of the time, those outside a particular organization have little or no concept of what various initials may denote. Then, when the Navajo, or others, select initials to indicate certain committees, groups, agencies, operations, and the like in their *own* language, the uninitiated are indeed perplexed (Yes, the Navajo language has now been fully recorded, as set forth by Young [Young 1961:430–500; Young and Morgan 1980]).

One reading periodicals, viewing TV, or listening to radios which report happenings in the Southwest frequently sees or hears comments on DNA. These initials are seldom explained. And small wonder. They refer to *Dinebeiina Nahiilna be Agaditahe,* Navajo for the Office-of-Economic-Opportunity-financed "attorneys who contribute to the revitalization of the people" (Anonymous 1970g).

Off-Reservation Navajo Groups

Ramah Navajo

Not only visitors in the Southwest, but residents of New Mexico as well, are often surprised to learn that several groups of Navajo Indians have lands located away from the main reservation. The largest of these is the *Ramah Navajo,* numbering over 2,000, many of whom reside in the community. Their land lies southeast of Ramah, New Mexico—settled by Mormons—on State Highway 53, a few miles east of the pueblo of Zuñi. The Reservation is approximately eighteen by thirty miles in extent, with elevation averaging around 7,000 feet, but ranging up to 9,000 feet in the mountains, where good hunting is offered. Although there are deep canyons to the north, most of the region consists of broad valleys covered with grass or sagebrush bordered by ridges forested with piñon and juniper. Nearly five hundred different kinds of plants have been identified in the area, and the Navajo knew the names of all but three of these (*see* Vestal 1952).

Some of the Navajo and also a number of Apaches managed to escape from Fort Sumner during their exile. We are told that among the Navajo escapees were the parents of a man known as Many Beads, who went to live among the Chiricahua Apache. Many Beads had a son who was born among the Chiricahua and was but two years old when the Navajo captives began their trek back from captivity. Learning of this movement, the lad's parents also set forth for their old homeland. After a winter spent at Acoma, the family settled in the mountains near Fort Wingate. There they were joined by Many Beads, who accompanied them back to a place where they had dwelt formerly, at a spring near present Ramah (where Mormon missionaries in 1876 persuaded the Navajo to allow them to establish a small colony—which, in spite of a severe smallpox epidemic, was refounded in 1882 and has grown into a community of several hundred people). Another Navajo and his mother lived there likewise, and thus, we know of the two families in that locality about 1876; undoubtedly, others settled there, for the released captives strongly tended to return to their former homesites. The son of Many Beads became a patriarch of the community and longtime leader. (*See* Young 1968:43.)

The Ramah Navajo have a political structure with characteristics of a band, and, as such, have had a single headman. Through time, a number of factions have developed, following the conservative and progressive pattern of so many Indian groups. The former wish to continue their old ways, while the latter favor the ways of the white man. Of the total of 146,996 acres under control of the Ramah group, relatively few acres are farmed; more attention is given to the handling of livestock. In most ways, the ceremonial, political, and economic structures follow those of the other Navajo.

The people of the community constitute the Ramah Chapter, which has an elected delegate to the Navajo Tribal Council, at the "capital" of the Navajo nation. Other chapter officials include a president, vice-president, and secretary who, as in the majority of chapters, is a Navajo woman member; these are assisted by a Grazing Committee chairman and committee members.

Isolated, and generally unknown to the world at large, the Navajo of this group are enterprising and industrious. Back in the early 1970s, a public broadcasting station, KTDZ-FM was established twelve and a half miles southeast of Ramah, near the chapter house. It has been on the air since 24 April 1972, broadcasting both in Navajo and English to people living in Bread Springs, Oak Canyon, Fence Lake, Quemado, Tohatchi, Iyanbito, Ramah, and points in between.

> For the several hundred persons living in those sparsely settled communities and for residents of hogans in between, [the station] is their only means of community communication. . . . Some of the messages broadcast . . . would never be found on a commercial station but an important service is performed when you hear, 'Leonard José will be at the bus station at Gallup between 7:30 and 8:30 P.M. Someone please pick him up' and give him a ride to Fence Lake, Bread Springs or Ramah more than 40 miles away. (Eric McCrossen, *Albuquerque Journal*, 8 February 1973)

With several full-time staff members (students from afar engaged in work-study programs, students from local schools, and volunteers) and with grants and contributions, the station persists with support by the Ramah Chapter. Staff members go into the countryside with tape recorders to tape Navajo legends and songs for future broadcasts or they prepare programs for special features. They present helpful hints including news, cooking recipes, and many bits of information that link the people with the mainstream of culture.

For many years, the Ramah Navajo have been disturbed by the educational opportunities introduced for youngsters living on their reservation. The offerings from the white man's curriculums, as effected through the BIA, did not meet the needs of the Navajo as they lived and strived to develop in a changing world. Other than BIA schools. public schools in the town of Ramah and public and private schools at distant locations, with transportation necessities, provided changing conditions—most of them dissatisfying to the Navajo (see Blanchard 1971).

Ultimately, members of the tribe got together and organized the Ramah School Board, which was incorporated in February, 1970 and in the fall opened the first private Indian school controlled by an all-Indian board. The board began working toward an all-Indian administrative staff, responsible for the school's program. Negotiations by the BIA and by the N.M. State Department of Education with the Navajo brought about advanced facilities on the reservation, the Pine Hill School. This multimillion dollar complex was begun in 1979, and now affords education on the Ramah reservation from kindergarten through the twelfth grade (the high school is accredited by the North Central Association). Its program is built on bilingual training and cultural awareness in conjunction with usual academic requirements.

The Edward Elliott Foundation of New York helped fund the summer school, and officers of the foundation are deeply impressed by the efforts of the Navajo to control their own school.

The Puertocito (Alamo) Navajo

Next in size of the off-reservation groups is the *Puertocito Navajo,* a band that has been separated from the main body for some one hundred-odd years. This group developed in part from Navajo slaves who ran away from their Spanish masters living in Socorro. They congregated at Alamo, or "at Field's place," about thirty-five miles northwest of Magdalena, New Mexico; from this location, they are commonly called the "Alamo Navajo" (see Anonymous 1972). It is said that they were once part of the "enemy Navajo," and that they are called *Tsa Dei'alth,* or "stone chewers," for, when they fought, they got so angry that they chewed rocks. (See Harrington 1940:515–516.)

The few who settled in the Field locality intermarried with Chiricahua and Mescalero Apaches and with Mexicans; they were joined by Navajo from other areas, some of whom fled there to escape Kit Carson, and others who fled from Fort Sumner. Between 1912 and 1920, allotments were made to these Puertocito Navajo, and purchased lands were added to their holdings by the federal government and the Navajo tribe. Their semiarid domain now embraces some 56,670 acres, and their population is about 1,300. Some of the people herd sheep on the limited grass among piñon and juniper growth. A few weave or make jewelry; others are on welfare. The unemployment rate is high.

In 1941, a day school was built and opened for the Alamo youngsters.

Teachers did not like the isolation and student attendance was irregular; as a result, the school failed. A survey made in 1959 revealed the average adult education to be one and a half years. That year, a dormitory was opened at Magdalena so students could live there and attend the public schools. Some Alamo parents continue to send their children to the Magdalena school. The road is now paved all the way.

Although the dormitory plan continued, this arrangement met with increasing dissatisfaction with the majority of the Indians. They wanted their own school, locally situated. In 1970, the BIA initiated a community school at Alamo, but it did not thrive. In 1978, the Alamo Chapter took advantage of the Indian Self-Determination Act of 1975, which directs federal agencies to assist Indians in assuming control of the education of their children. The chapter sought "start-up" funds from the BIA for a community school. The Navajo Tribe provided $150,000 for the required feasibility study, and has since contributed other funds. Various problems arose and were met.

Early in September of 1979, four large, portable buildings were brought to the reservation and placed on a hilltop near the chapter house (where there was also a health clinic). In these buildings, after a century, the Indians had their school. A fifth building added later provided offices and sanitary facilities for the grades two through eight, while close by, the BIA initially gave instruction to the kindergarten and first grade.

The Alamo Community School, with director and a curriculum director, opened on 1 October 1979, staffed in part by Navajo instructors and bilingual tutors, under the direction of an all-Navajo school board. The student body is bussed to school. The youngsters number about 250 (of 400 school-age children), and the teaching staff totaled nineteen. The atmosphere is said to be "easy and friendly." Students advance at their own pace, for few of them can read at their grade level.

For the 1979–1980 fiscal year the school had an operating budget of $414,230. "Distribution of school funds by the BIA is similar to that under the New Mexico school funding formula. The basic per-student allocation this year is $1,600, plus add-ons for various ages and special needs" (Virginia Johnson, *Albuquerque Journal*, 6 January 1980).

The opening of the reservation school had a counter effect on the Magdalena school system, which suffered a loss of students and of its dollar resources. A great reduction would occur if the Alamo board's plans for a high school, next, materialize. An envisioned complex would cost many millions of dollars.

Until the early 1960s, almost everyone lived in log-built hogans. Then a house-building project was initiated and now most of the Navajo families have moved into new homes. Each faces the east, as do traditional hogans. In 1967, a Rural Electrification Administration power line was brought to the reservation, enabling the people to have modern appliances for the first time. The main water source, Alamo Springs, was improved and the beginnings of a running water system was begun (see American Association on Indian Affairs Newsletter No. 99, 1979).

The political structure follows that of the main reservation (see Euler 1961) at Window Rock about seventy miles distant.

The Cañoncito Navajo

A third group, which lives some twenty-five miles west from Albuquerque, a few miles north of Interstate Highway I-40, is known as the Dine'é Ana'i, or "enemy Navajo." They derive from Navajo who had moved southwestward into the Cebolleta Mountains under Spanish pressure during the eighteenth century, and they remained there when the main body of Navajo moved to the west. Then, as those who had been confined at Fort Sumner trekked back toward their homeland, Chief Delgadito separated about four hundred people from the seven thousand who left Fort Sumner on 15 June 1868—fifteen days after the Treaty of 1868 was signed. These returned to their old territory in the Cebolleta region. Later, remnants of Sandoval's Cebolleta band received allotments and other lands in what came to be known as the Cañoncito reservation (see Largo 1973:A6). Since those earlier days, other Navajo have married into the community. Today, they number around 1,500. Their land holdings total 76,813 acres. Frame houses have electricity and running water.

Cañoncito has an elementary school with kindergarten through the fifth grade. It has featured the Title I language arts program; special education is being developed. Many of the Cañoncito people are middle-aged or older. Under the Title VII program of nutrition for the elderly, more than half receive freshly cooked meals at their locally operated "Golden Age Center." During 1980, 165 meals were served daily. Four bus drivers provided the transportation. The program costs well over twenty thousand dollars per year. The aged Navajo are picked up in the morning and brought to the center where they work on crafts or have other activities until meal time at noon. After lunch, they are returned home. The drivers also deliver meals to those elderly unable to come to the center. (Reduced federal funds, here and elsewhere, may affect forthcoming programs.)

In 1969, the Cañoncito group initiated an annual rodeo. This is scheduled around the middle of July, and may follow a horse sale. The rodeo features bareback riding and bull riding, calf roping, team roping, and barrel racing. Winners of each event, based on average points, receive awards. Refreshments are sold.

Each of these off-reservation groups lives in accordance with the general pattern of Navajo culture, outgrowing their original way of life. They all engage in farming and stock raising. Several Cañoncito Indians are silversmiths, some of the women make fine fabric dolls with characteristic adornments, and they fashion attractive beaded ornaments. A limited number of baskets are made by the Ramah Navajo.

These groups are under the Eastern Navajo Agency, in District 16, with headquarters in Crownpoint. Their officers are those as indicated for the Ramah Chapter. The total population of these off-reservation groups is now found to be increasing with fair consistency at a rate of just over one percent annually.

The "Checkerboard Area"

In addition to the above off-reservation peoples, over 25,000 Navajo live in the so-called "checkerboard area." This extends eastward from the Navajo reservation to the Jicarilla Apache reservation, and south of that beyond the town of Cuba. Here the public domain (662,776) has been allotted so that each alternate square mile is Indian land, with non-Indian sections in between—hence the designation *checkerboard*. The normal allotment to an Indian is 160 acres. Built south of Huerfano Mesa near the Blanco Trading Post, just off Highway 44, a large, modern school complex called the Eastern Navajo School serves a wide area of the reservation.

GREAT WIDE BEAUTIFUL

that's how I describe the Apache land
on which I live.
You see, I'm an Apache
living around wonderful rivers, grass and cactus.
I will long remember the times I had
with my mother when we walked across fields
among the dancing flowers. With a mother around
every joy is here.
We went through places where long ago
my people once lived
and now it is deserted
with trees, weeds, growing here and there.
Mountains are on all sides blue, green mixed together,
which makes a pretty color. . . .
And before us was a river flowing
and alongside it were grasses, trees
dancing among the breeze: then. . . .
Slowly we started home in the direction
where the sun was setting.
This place which I call home is really my home
and I hope it always will be.

By Lenora Palmer (White Mountain Apache)

From *Art and Indian Children.*
Curriculum Bulletin No. 7, 1970.
Institute of American Indian Arts,
Santa Fe, N.M.

The Apache Indians

Brief History

The Apache peoples spread southward, as Athabascan bands, along the eastern side of the Rocky Mountains. Each local group had a headman, who led by reason of prestige and good example, and a headwoman, whose function was to council her people in the ways of living, and especially to organize food gathering parties among the women.

Our data on the Apaches have come mostly from documentary accounts written by non-Indians and from ethnological studies. It was said that the Apache dwellings were similar to the forked-stick hogan, and the people had many culture traits akin to those of the Navajo of the Gobernador Phase. In their migrations, they picked up numerous Plains Indian characteristics, such as the type of dwellings (tipi), articles of attire and hair styles, and perhaps, elementary knowledge of horticulture (see Gunnerson, D. A. 1974; Kessell 1979).

Formerly not a great deal has been known about the Apaches archaeologically, although the late Carl Lumholtz is said to have dug some sites in Chihuahua, Mexico, about the turn of the twentieth century (see Lister 1958 and Lumholtz 1902). Now, works have revealed that: "For two centuries or more, many Apaches were peaceful farmers, living in permanent villages on the eastern edge of the American Southwest and in the central and southern plains." In the Southwest, these Apaches "rapidly learned a new way of life that included dependence upon corn. They manufactured pottery, and constructed houses more permanent than the skin tepees [tipis] in which they had originally lived." Investigating along the eastern base of the Sangre de Cristo mountain range, near Cimarron and Las Vegas, New Mexico, in 1967, archaeologists made an exciting discovery; they uncovered a seven-room adobe dwelling that had been built around 1700 by the Jicarilla Apache, in Pueblo manner (see Gunnerson, J. H. 1960; 1969a and b; 1979).

The cultural material associated with the house structures indicated extensive trade with the Pueblos and western Texas peoples. The Apache went on extensive bison hunting expeditions. At another site, evidence was found of a type of dwelling not previously identified with the Apache—a circular pit about twelve feet in diameter and two feet deep, which had had a rock wall laid up around it and roofed over. Spanish contact materials were found there. A large site near Las Vegas exhibited more of the ringed construction. Some 250 rings of rocks appeared to have been used to hold down the bottoms of tipis. There, residence was less permanent, and this indicates a shifting from location on the valley floors to low terraces (reflecting a need for more protection from unfriendly peoples, such as the Comanche). Trade items in these villages appear to date in the nineteenth century (see Anonymous 1967; Gunnerson, J. H. 1979). (See also Noble 1981.)

In 1969 and 1970, investigations were made at the ruins of Pecos, for the pueblo had been an important trading center for Pueblo-Plains Indians in the late 1600s and early 1700s, and probably long before. Within the confines of the Pecos National Monument, nine areas were found that yielded Apache pottery. Other sites in the area have been discovered with further investigating (see Gunnerson and Gunnerson 1970).

The historical Apache were known as notable enemies whose hardihood was incredible. Meat was the favorite food, and where available, mescal was harvested and eaten in great quantities. When necessary, the Apache literally could "live off the land," eating berries, roots, seeds, cactus, or crawling animals (but never fish, or snakes—which they feared—or turkeys and dogs that ate them). They were extremely healthy before European diseases were introduced, and could go practically naked in zero weather.

Characteristically, the Apache has a splendid physique. Although individuals vary greatly, the people average above medium height. The well-formed head rests on a short muscular neck. The face is broad, with high cheekbones and strong nose. Apache men have rather sparse beards which they formerly plucked.

Little girls were given the same training as boys. Every day, they practiced with bow and arrows, slings and spears. They were taught to mount an unsaddled horse without help, and to ride expertly. At puberty, Apache youths were tested in all kinds of hardships by their elders. Girls went through extensive rites, which are described later.

The Apache men have high regard for their women; in days of old, particularly, they were respected, cherished, and protected. Chastity was rigidly enforced. Children were seldom spaced closer than four years. In times of warfare, wives were permitted to go on the warpath with husbands. With the Apache, scalping was not a custom; they abhorred mutilation. When death occurred, sympathy was not extended by words. A killing obliged the next of kin to seek revenge. Great store was set by promises, and a liar was despised by all. The Apache felt that "without respect no human relationship (was) of any value" (Ball 1970:29).

Essentially, the Apache were a mountain people, traveling from ridge to ridge, but they were at home equally in the parched semidesert wastes by which they were surrounded; they were hunting and fighting people. As one writer has said summarily:

They moved about freely, wintering on the Río Grande or farther south, ranging the buffalo plains in the summer, always following the sun and the food supply. They owned nothing and everything. They did as they pleased and bowed to no man. Their women were chaste. Their leaders kept their promises. They were mighty warriors who depended on success in raiding for wealth and honor. To their families they were kind and gentle, but they could be unbelievably cruel to their enemies—fierce and revengeful when they felt that they had been betrayed. (Sonnichsen 1958:4)

They became primarily tipi-dwellers. Those who lived in the forested dells in the mountains erected shelters fashioned of slender poles which were covered with brush and grass—the wickiup. Two general types of these were used: one built on a tipi frame, and the true dome-shaped *wickiup*. Each was built with a doorway toward the east. Adopting matrilineal descent, the Apache also took over matrilocal residence as a social pattern (*see* Kaut 1957:39; Gerald 1958:5–11). Band exogamy was not required, but marriages between kinsmen were forbidden. A girl's mother and other female relatives constructed a dwelling for a newly married couple, not far distant from the maternal abode. The mother-in-law taboo is observed, and cousins of the opposite sex are not supposed to talk directly; they should have some sort of a screen between, or at least have their backs to each other. Kinship is reckoned bilaterally.

Rather than shaking hands, or kissing, as is common in many cultures, Apaches embrace upon meeting one another. They are very modest, and highly respect the privacy of others.

The Chiricahua and Mescalero

The Chiricahua and Mescalero Apaches are closely related, and they formerly occupied adjacent areas. It is commonly said that the Chiricahua territory lay to the west of the Río Grande, centering around Ojo Caliente, or Warm Springs, the water of which seeps from the foot of a little hill on the west side of the San Mateo range, north of Monticello, New Mexico. From there, bands, numbering around one thousand persons in all, ranged through southwestern New Mexico and southeastern Arizona, and over the northern parts of Sonora and Chihuahua in Mexico. By the seventeenth century, they were strongly entrenched in those regions and fighting to retain them.

More details have been given to us by James Kaywaykla, an Apache who was born near Warm Springs and who died in 1963 at the age of about ninety years. Early writers included the Warm Springs Apaches as Chiricahua, but Kaywaykla has said that the Apaches themselves recognized four bands; of these, only the groups headed by Cochise and by Chihuahua were true Chiricahua.

In the words of Kaywaykla, "Juh was chief of the *Nednhi* Apaches, whose stronghold was in the Sierra Madre of Mexico (their "Blue Mountains"). Gerónimo was leader, but not chief of the *Bedonkohes,* whose territory was around the headwaters of the Gila. Though closely associated, we were distinct groups." The Warm Springs Apache in their own tongue were *Chihinne,* or "Red People," so called because of a band of red clay which was painted across their faces (Ball 1970:xiv).

The band was the political unit, with leader and followers. This system had no tribal chief, no council of leaders, and no device for decision making. The bands were not local groups; "they were not resource holding units, and exercised no control over a specific portion of land" (Basehart 1970:92). For another thing, bands "grew, lost members, disappeared, and new groups developed," resulting in "a continual but gradual redistribution of the population" (Basehart 1970:93). This was difficult for government officials to comprehend; they needed some fixed point of reference.

If a band was small, the members usually formed a single scattered encampment; larger bands might have several camps. The core of a band was a "relative group," primarily—but not necessarily—kinsmen.

The Apache women of these bands wore two-piece dresses made of calico; skirts were long and full, and long blouses were worn outside of the skirt belts. Each woman carried a knife, and some had ammunition belts and rifles. Apache girls had their hair arranged around two willow hoops, worn over the ears. Some of the older women dressed their hair in Plains Indian manner, parted in the middle, with two braids. The attire for warriors consisted of calico shirt, a muslin breechclout supported by a belt, one or more cartridge belts, moccasins, and a headband to keep their long hair out of the eyes. To distinguish themselves, the Warm Springs people wore a band of buckskin, colored yellow with sacred pollen of cattails, over the right shoulder and tied to the belt under the left arm. Buckskin shirts and beaded robes of the women were used for ceremonial attire. Blankets, too, were used. Some men wore large, loose deerskin coats in winter.

The moccasins had high tops that could be drawn up for warmth, or could be folded below the knee for protection against thorns and rock. Kaywaykla has said: "In those folds we carried our valuable possessions, valuable primarily in the sense of usefulness. Sometimes these included extra cowhide soles, for soles wore out quickly and had to be replaced. We carried the endthorns of a mescal plant with fiber attached for sewing the soles to the uppers. The soles were tanned with the hair left on, and they projected beyond the toes and terminated in a circular flap with a metal button sewed to the center. This piece turned back over the toes for additional protection. Because we frequently had to abandon our horses to scale cliffs, the moccasin was our most important article of dress" (Ball 1970: 17–18).

In Kaywaykla's youth, Victorio (who succeeded Mangas Coloradas, after Cuchillo Negro had been leader for a time) was their chief; among the notable leaders were Nana and Loco. Leaders were men of influence rather than wielders of power.

When the U.S. assumed sovereignty over New Mexico in 1848, the Mescalero utilized the country to the east of the Río Grande, extending from northern Mexico to the region south of Santa Fe; a branch dwelt on the plains in western Texas. Natziti was the head chief, a contemporary of Victorio. The Apaches all knew their territory intimately; they had no specially built strongholds but survived by ranging rapidly in and out of wild, rugged places. When they camped, they never stayed close to the edge of a water body, for "the water belonged to all creatures, not man alone." They selected a campsite in a grassy location or a wooded area and carried water from the source to the camp.

Horses were well cared for, never ridden to death. The Apache did not travel at night, nor did they fight during the nighttime unless forced to do so by soldiers or others.

Harassment and encroachment by the Spaniards, conflicts with the Comanche during the latter part of the eighteenth century, then Mexican domination and the American occupation of the mid-1800s with its increasing pressures and controls; such vicissitudes were more than these free souls could accept. Their original friendliness toward foreigners ceased. Striving to hold their ancestral lands, their lifeways, and their very lives brought forth the fierce emotions of the Apache. Naturally, they raided the newcomers' settlements and drove off their animals—especially horses, mules, and burros, which increased their mobility and speeded their getaway. They killed when it seemed necessary, and came to be the most dreaded warriors of the Southwest.

As the westward expansion of the white men heightened, the Apache were pushed from their holdings and the game upon which they depended was driven away. Having no place to go, they turned southward into Mexico, from where raids were made across the border. After the Mexican and U.S. governments combined efforts to quell the Apaches, the life of the aborigines became perilous.

In 1863, about four hundred Mescalero Apache were taken to the concentration camp, Bosque Redondo (Fort Sumner) on the Pecos River (*see* McNitt 1970). Colonel Carleton planned to put all of the Apaches there . . . and make farmers of them! When the Navajo, enemies of the Apaches, were rounded up and confined there, too, the situation became unendurable. Smallpox contracted by the Navajo from the soldiers contaminated the water being used by the Mescalero. Seeing the Navajo dying by the hundreds, the Mescalero took what they could carry and fled to one of their old campsites on the Bonito, above Fort Stanton—which had been established in 1855.

Victorio outwitted Colonel Carleton and kept his band from being sent to Bosque Redondo. By an Executive Order in 1870, the government promised him a permanent reservation for his Chihinne band at Warm Springs. The decimated group assembled there, and an adobe building was erected for their headquarters across the Cañada Alamosa from Warm Springs.

At the same time, Cochise, the Chiricahua chief, who had gathered his band near Warm Springs, was to have a reservation about his stronghold. Neither promise was kept. As a result, Cochise resumed raiding. In 1872, the Chiricahua were separated from the Mescalero by establishment of reservations for each group.

Because another Executive Order had come through, returning the Warm Springs (Chiricahua) reservation to the public domain, Victorio was commanded to move his people to a high mountain valley of the Tularosa River in westernmost New Mexico—an impossible place during the winter. Severe cold, starvation, and death among the Apache forced the government agent to let them return to Warm Springs for a short time. Other leaders, including Gerónimo, who was also a shaman, brought their bands to camp in the vicinity.

During 1877, Gerónimo had been joined by bands of Apaches from Mexico, and numerous raids were made in southern New Mexico and Arizona. Victorio received orders from the agent at San Carlos to come there and bring his people. For their compliance, all of the leaders were arrested. Gerónimo and seven other headmen were already there, chained in a corral. Victorio, Nana, and Loco were not confined.

San Carlos was considered to be "the worst place in all Apacheria" (Ball 1970:5). The Apaches were quartered at old Camp Goodwin, which had been abandoned by the cavalry because of many deaths from malaria. Summer temperatures allegedly got as high as 140°F. "There was no game, no food except the occasional meager and unfit stuff issued to them (by the Indian agent). The insects swarmed about them and almost devoured the babies" (Ball 1970:50).

During the summer, Victorio saw his people suffer and die. Finally, joined by Nana and Loco, plans for flight were carefully arranged; they evaded the cavalry for weeks, but were eventually captured and imprisoned. The Army fed them until November, 1877, and then returned them to Warm Springs (Ball 1970:52).

Then came Carleton's insidious orders—the orders of a man determined to exterminate the Apaches. Victorio was to take his people to San Carlos again . . . that horrible place! If they did not go, the orders stated, every man, woman, or child, found off the reservation was to be shot without being given a chance to surrender.

Nana, who was considered to be the "fiercest and most implacable of all Apaches" (Ball 1970:71), and his followers had no intention of returning to San Carlos. They could have joined Juh in Mexico, but it was decided that the most feasible thing at the time was to join the Mescalero, from whom permission was obtained. In December, 1878, Nana took his Warm Springs band to Blazer's Mill on the Tularosa River in south-central New Mexico, then the headquarters of the Mescalero Apache reservation. Sixty-three were there enrolled, received ration cards, and were issued rations. They were allowed to settle in the remote and rather inaccessible Rinconada Canyon— where Nana had previously (and secretly) sent most of his young men and horses. Brush arbors were built and covered with hides; wood, water, and game were abundant (Ball 1970:25–27).

Victorio, too, came to the Rinconada encampment—with a bounty on his head—for a warrant had been issued for his arrest. The arrival of soldiers at Blazer's caused him and his men to make their way to their sacred mountain in the San Andres, where they could not be captured.

Loco started to take his band to San Carlos on the Gila River. At the east end of Cook's Peak (north of Deming, New Mexico), they were attacked by U.S. cavalry and several Apache were killed before Loco could convince them that they were going to San Carlos voluntarily. When the soldiers were convinced, they escorted the Apache band toward the Gila. A snowstorm forced them to turn north to Fort Apache, and Loco's group was taken to Camp

Goodwin. Victorio learned of these developments, and was prepared to aid Loco, should he decide to flee to Mexico.

Nana decided to lead his people to Chihuahua by way of the Big Bend country in Texas; several other small bands joined in the dangerous journey. Victorio dashed from place to place, drawing the cavalry away from the traveling ones. It is said that Victorio took about four hundred people with him, seventy-five of them warriors; some were Mescalero and Lipan (Ball 1970:75). In 1880, they headed north again.

Gerónimo made peace with General George Crook in 1882, but this lasted only three years. Then the Apache were forced to assemble again, and raiding was resumed. In 1886, Gerónimo brought his people forth to surrender. As a result, he was imprisoned and sent to confinement in Florida, where the Chiricahua and all associated bands were transferred.

Later, a home for them was sought in Alabama; finally, they were taken to Fort Sill, Oklahoma, "to round out a term of twenty-seven years as prisoners of war. In 1913, they were released and given the choice of taking up residence on the Mescalero Indian Reservation in New Mexico (northeast of Alamogordo) or of accepting allotments of land in Oklahoma" (see Opler 1942: viii). Some one hundred took the allotments, but the majority of the Chiricahua joined the Mescalero. Henceforth, the development of these groups may best be considered as the Mescalero-Chiricahua; however, scholars have been able to gain specific data from Mescalero, Chiricahua, and related informants, and thus to establish their respective past history to some degree.

In their social organization, an extensive bilateral reckoning of kinship is found among the Apache (see Goodwin 1942). The Mescalero, for instance, did not require band exogamy, but marriages between kinsmen were forbidden; consequently, unions outside the band were most common. Marriages tended to be easily broken, especially during the early years of a union. Polygamy was allowed, but was rarely practiced. More usual was "serial monogamy," wherein "a married man might go to another area, perhaps on a raid, extend his residence there, and eventually marry again. The social network of an individual Mescalero was both extensive and flexible, permitting him to activate ties with a wide range of cognates and to initiate new affinal bonds to meet the demands of a specific situation" (Basehart 1967:284). Marriages with outsiders were frowned upon by the Mescalero—particularly when they resulted in the loss of a Mescalero to another group.

The ordinary house type of the Chiricahua was the domeshaped wickiup of brush. Mother-in-law avoidance was followed, as with the Navajo. Like the Navajo, too, the Chiricahua regarded birds, insects, and coyotes as once having been people; mankind, then, is but following in the footsteps of those who have gone before. No one account of the creation of human beings seems to have existed (see Opler 1942:1). Mythical personages are closely related to those of the Navajo; they bear similar names, but they have differing positions of importance in some instances.

If death were to occur in a dwelling, it was deserted; the name of the deceased was not spoken. Other death customs included hair cutting and wailing. If a funeral party were seen or a newly bereaved family encountered, a Chiricahua would avoid a meeting or join in the wailing for the dead. A successful war expedition was always followed by a victory dance.

The area east of Tularosa on U.S. Highway 70 became the Mescalero reservation, and today it covers some 460,000 acres. There the Apache have adjusted themselves to the life of their fellow Americans by becoming farmers, ranchers, loggers, machine operators, nurses, ministers, artists, carpenters, clerks, accountants, policemen, and firefighters. They were the first to offer the U.S. Forest Service a trained and organized unit of firefighters to help put down forest fires in the Southwest; they now go afar also.

Currently, attire is much like that of any western citizen. Most of the Apache men have adopted "western wear" for everyday: colorful shirts, denim pants, cowboy boots or shoes, and fitting accessories. Most Apache men have their hair cut, and they commonly shave. Some of the Apache women still wear a one-piece dress of Mother Hubbard style, or a loose hip-length blouse overhanging full skirt. Now, the tendency with the young is to wear non-Indian clothing. Mescalero deerskin moccasins are seldom worn except at ceremonial events. They are dyed yellow and made with the peculiar upturned toe and circular element which serves as protection against cactus spines and other prickly vegetation (*see* Dutton 1980).

In recent years, outlying Mescalero communities have been abandoned almost completely, the people concentrating in the Agency town, Mescalero, on Highway 70. Their houses, once scattered over the reservation, have been moved into the main settlement, and many new structures have been built. A federal charter declares the Mescalero a federal corporation. They operate under a constitution and by-laws, governed by the Mescalero Tribal Business Committee. Officers of the tribe are a president, vice-president, treasurer, and secretary; the council is composed of these and other members—numbering eleven in all—elected by eligible voters of the tribe; women may, and do, hold office as well as men. All positions and operations are supported by the tribe. They have criminal and civil codes and police themselves, as well as administer their government.

The bulk of the Mescalero income is derived from timber sales and is deposited with the United States Treasury. Individual income is realized from cattle and wages, and a limited amount from small farm assignments which are made by the governing officers.

The Mescalero operate several profitable industries, including a store and Summit enterprise, a woodyard and Christmas tree market, and the Ruidoso recreation area with fishing and skiing developments. They also practice soil conservation and engage in cattle raising. They have an incorporated Cattle Growers Association with a manager under contract. A board of directors elected annually controls the operations. Not all members of the tribe are stockholders in the corporation, but all stockholders are tribal members. Over 4,500 head of cattle are run on more than seven hundred sections of the reservation. An annual tour-type sale attracts buyers to the Mescalero auction from far and near. A herd of good horses with numerous breeding mares is also maintained.

Of late, the Mescalero population has shown a steady increase. Reduced to 630 in 1915, they numbered 1,740 in 1970, and 2,384 in 1980. This figure includes the Mescalero, those of Chiricahua ancestry, and remnants of the Lipan and other bands.

The Jicarilla

During their days in the Southwest, two divisions of the Jicarilla Apache were recognized. The *Hoyero* (also spelled *Ollero*), or "mountain people," and the *Llanero,* or "plains people" (*see* Harrington 1940:511). At that time, they ranged from the Chama valley eastward across what is now central and eastern Colorado into western Oklahoma, and at least as far south as present day Estancia, New Mexico. In their easternmost contacts, the Jicarilla took over certain elements of Plains Indian culture, as did the Mescalero who roamed the eastern plains (*see* Gunnison, D. A. 1974; Gunnerson, J. H. 1979:167; Kessell 1979).

Among the features adopted was the style of moccasins and leggings worn by the Jicarilla; natural deerskin of the moccasins was whitened, rather than dyed yellow, and the toe was without the protective up-turned feature of some Apache groups. Soles were of rawhide or cowhide. The hip-length leggings, suspended from a belt, were distinct from those worn by other Apaches. They were made from a single piece of dressed deerskin, hair side out, with the addition of a cuff, fringe, and tabs—which may represent survival of the large cuff tabs in style on the northern plains one hundred to one hundred and fifty years ago. The bottom of the cuff was cut into four tabs, each with very short self-fringe, while the cuff top had fringe about two and a half inches long. The entire legging was colored with yellow ochre, and decorative stripes commonly were added in other colors; red and green were favored. Then, a band of beading was worked on the skin with simple design units, a row of beading across the cuff being characteristic.

The men parted their hair in the middle, plaited it into two braids, which were wound with strips of deerskin and worn in front over the shoulders. At one time, they wore bangs across the forehead on a line with the cheek bones and tied their hair in a knot at the back of the head, like the Navajo and most of the Pueblo men. The favored ornaments worn by the men were large earrings of the old Navajo type—a silver circlet with a loose silver bead dangling at its lower circumference. They also wore short bead pendants suspended from the pierced earlobe. A kerchief was commonly tied about the neck, with ends falling on the chest, "cowboy fashion."

Deerskin garments of Plains type were worn by the Jicarilla women; they never adopted the Mother Hubbard style of dress taken over by other Apache women.

The Jicarilla Apache were a problem to the white men during the mid-1850s (*see* Taylor 1970) and were among those pacified by Kit Carson in 1868. Following this event, they were first placed on the Mescalero reservation, and then in an area just to the east of the Navajo—putting them, it would seem, in or near the territory that had been occupied by their ancestors. In each instance, such hard fighting between the Jicarilla and other Indians resulted that they had to be moved again.

The north half of the present Jicarilla reservation was established in 1887; the south half was added in 1908; together, they include nearly three-quarters of a million acres of varied plain, semidesert, mountain and forest land dotted with small lakes. These holdings extend south from the Colorado border for approximately sixty-five miles to the vicinity of Cuba on N.M. Highway S-44. Altitude varies from 6,400 to 8,200 feet above sea level. The agency headquarters is at Dulce on Highway S-17, some twenty-seven miles west of Chama.

Within the last few years, the Jicarilla have improved their water and sewer systems; they have built many modern homes on the reservation and have remodeled old ones; a church has been erected. Several families live in new trailers. Many new miles of paved roads lead to and traverse the Jicarilla holdings. As of 1 January 1970, the census recognized 1,742 tribal members—a growth of 1,157 since an epidemic of influenza reduced them to 585 fifty years ago. The 1980 census counts about 2,000.

Apache men are good stockmen. The Jicarilla own thousands of head of sheep, fewer cattle, and many horses. Lamb and wool sales net significant income annually; cattle produce less revenue. Hundreds of gas wells have been drilled on the reservation, and more hundreds of producing oil wells. Royalties from these wells make up an important part of the Jicarilla income. New industries that will employ people dwelling there are being attracted to the reservation. Raw materials and products of agriculture, livestock, and forestry, all-year recreation activities, great power potential, and favorable market conditions are among the inducements at hand.

New Mexico has figured importantly in movie making the last few years, largely through undertakings of state agencies. Now, the Jicarilla have provided a good example of Apache acumen. On their own behalf, the initiative was taken to promote commercial motion pictures. Contacting Harvest Productions of Los Angeles, the Jicarilla agreed to finance the movie, *A Gunfight,* up to $2 million. Portions of the film were made near Santa Fe, interior scenes were shot in Hollywood, and other portions, including a bullfight, were made on location near Ocuña, Spain.

One of the Jicarilla men, who had been tribal accountant for nearly twenty years, resigned to become program affairs director for the BIA's Jicarilla agency. He and another of his tribesmen, the agency superintendent, went to Spain to help coordinate European sales of the film. They, incidentally, financed the trip from personal funds. European salesmen had already offered $1,750,000 for the movie. The first $2 million of profits was designated for the Jicarilla tribe; but by 1973 only a few thousand dollars had been received, and interest losses were mounting (Sandoval 1971). The picture, released in the spring of 1971, featured such stars as Kirk Douglas and Johnny Cash, and an Italian actor, Raf Vallone, for the bullfight scene.

Another Jicarilla accomplishment of note is the construction of an Olympic-size, heated indoor swimming pool and recreation area at Dulce. It was jointly funded by HUD and the tribe, the cost of $1.5 million being met on a fifty-fifty basis. With this underway, many of the Jicarilla—adults and children alike—began learning to swim. Arrangements were made with personnel of a camp on the Brazos River, near Chama, for two groups of twenty-one each to take four weeks of instruction. Tribal officials were included; some prepared themselves for lifesaving and instructor's certificates. The facility was dedicated on 7 January 1972.

The Jicarilla govern by means of an eight-member council of male and female members who stand for election every two years, in accordance with an adopted constitution and by-laws. A president, vice-president, secretary, business manager, director of the tribe's Game and Fish Department, and an executive committee are chosen by the council. According to the constitution, only business surplus can be distributed on a dividend basis, as with any other corporation. Funds of their corporation have been allocated for training of personnel and the construction of facilities to assist firms providing the greatest economic benefit to the Jicarilla.

More than two hundred Jicarilla derive individual income from tribal employment; over fifty have positions with the BIA and a few with the U.S. Public Health Service; others have miscellaneous sources of revenue. Education in general receives major attention in public school facilities provided by state funds. Years ago, the Jicarilla tribe placed one million dollars in an Albuquerque bank to finance education on the reservation for children and adults who want to learn new jobs, and to aid worthy students who do not have sufficient money of their own. Receipt of an NEH Youth Grant to assemble Jicarilla lore and history added stimulating teaching materials.

As a result of having shown such sound operation of their 742,303 acres of land, permitting balanced programs in range use, outdoor recreation, and game management, the Jicarilla were honored, in the spring of 1970, with a Department of the Interior Conservation Service Award—that department's top honor. In a letter to the president of the Jicarilla council, the Secretary of the Interior offered "recognition of the significant progress of the (tribe) not only in conservation and improvements of their natural resources, but also in the variety and intensity of the management of their own affairs, and their cooperation and involvement with other federal and state agencies" (Anonymous 1970c).

The Western Apaches

The major Western Apache divisions embrace the White Mountain, Cibecue, San Carlos, and northern and southern Tonto groups that now dwell in southeastern Arizona. Although each division has certain distinctions, such as linguistic dialects and religious and social practices, they share basic characteristics. Their terrain is cut by high mountain barriers which rise to well over 11,000 feet, from lowland areas of some 2,600 feet. These natural barriers tended to isolate one band from another, so that each came to have fairly well-defined territories. No political affiliations existed between the various groups, in the past or at present. They were relatively peaceful until forced to develop a raiding pattern by foreign peoples, Indian and non-Indian. As with other Indian peoples, treaties were made and broken.

The family constitutes the Apache economic unit. This includes the normal pattern of those adhering to a matrilineal system, where children are born into the clan of the mother: grandparents, married daughters and their husbands, unmarried sons, and children of the daughters. Each family is bound together by certain rights and duties. The clan system—which still operates to a degree—cuts across groups and bands. Marriage within one's clan is forbidden. In the Apache clans, cousins are called "brother" and "sister." Marriage between cousins is taboo. Families live in relatively large groups with the home of the mother being the family center. Mothers and daughters are very close and they carry on many tasks together. When a son marries, his obligations henceforth are to the family of his mother-in-law; he is to protect and work for the domestic circle into which he marries. If a man's wife dies, he may remarry. Frequently, he marries a sister of his deceased wife. Marriages now are in accordance with the white man's practices. *(Rel.* Basso 1973.)

In their chosen locale, livelihood did not come easily. Primary foodstuffs consisted of wild game and fruits, seeds and nuts of indigenous plants; some corn, beans, and squash were raised. Conflicts grew through the years, culminating in a terrific battle between the Anglo-Americans and the Apache in 1862. Mangas Coloradas, a Nednhi Apache, had come to the fore, and was then an elderly man; he was wounded in battle, but recovered. He was ready for peace. Tricked by a promising overture, he went to an army camp in New Mexico where he was murdered in January, 1863. His son, Mangus, became leader. An intensive and treacherous campaign against the Apache was waged by the army and by civilians. Scores of Apache were killed, but Victorio and other leaders retaliated. It is said that the U.S. government spent some $38 million from 1862 to 1871 in its effort to exterminate the Apache.

General Crook, who knew the Indians well, then was assigned the task of "taming" all of the Apache bands in Arizona. A few swift campaigns resulted in subduing the Western Apache and the Yavapai, with whom extensive intermarriage had taken place. They were placed on reservations at San Carlos and at Fort Apache. Crook hired Apache men as scouts, and programs in agriculture and livestock raising were initiated. Uneasy peace reigned for several years; no consistent Indian policy was followed. As related above, at one time the Chiricahua were forced to dwell among the Western Apache, as were the Tonto and some of the Yavapai. Of course, this was unsuccessful. In large part, Apache scouts led to the downfall of the Apaches—for they knew the haunts and practices of their people, and how to lead the soldiers to them.

Through all the tumultuous decades, the Chiricahua and associated bands were hardest hit by their foes. On the other hand, the Western Apache fared much better (see Goodwin 1942; Basso 1969, 1971; Kaut 1959). It is said that they had a population of about 4,000 in the 1860s and that in 1890 their census enumerated 4,138, and they still occupied their homeland, an area reaching from Flagstaff and Showlow to the Santa Catalina, Rincon, and Whetstone Mountains on the south, and from the Camp Verde-Superior alignment on the west almost to the New Mexico border on the east (see Baldwin 1965:52).

In November, 1871, the original White Mountain reservation was established; it included the present Fort Apache and San Carlos reservations. In 1897, the area was divided and separated into the Fort Apache and the San Carlos reservations respectively.

Over the years, their acreage was continually reduced by outsiders who hungered for the valuable resources of the Apaches—minerals and grazing lands especially. By 1920, leases held by whites amounted to approximately five-eighths of the San Carlos reservation, and the lands were being destroyed by illegal grazing of thousands of unregistered cattle. The San Carlos lands were not allotted, and it is said that "due to the peculiar topographical conditions of the reservation with its small patches of ground suitable for farming and its scattered watering places in the grazing areas, individual allotments would never be practical" (Arizona Writers' Project 1941:33).

Agents interested in the Apache welfare came on the scene by 1923, and the overgrazing situation began to change. Leases were gradually terminated and the lands returned to the Indians (the last outside grazing leases ran out in 1948) (Anonymous 1969d). Indian organization, or participation in Apache interests was started in 1924 with development of the resources of tribal and individual potentialities, "which consisted of cattle interests, small gardens, and a home security or social system" (Arizona Writers' Project 1941:33). Until 1932, these efforts were carried on by community meetings. Then, a Business Council was organized. Its plans were sound, and progress was constant. A self-supporting program was inaugurated and meetings held by various groups; grazing fees per head of all cattle sold were established, permitting the San Carlos to build up and maintain one of the largest cattle ownerships as a self-supporting economic venture, without required assistance from tribal or federal funds.

The Apache ability to understand the fundamentals of self-government by actual practice led to almost unanimous acceptance of the Reorganization Act of 1934 and a favorable vote on their constitution; the latter provides for the election by the Apache of a tribal council as the governing body. "This was followed by acceptance, with some amendments as applying particularly to this tribe (San Carlos, White Mountain), of the Law and Order Regulation as approved by the Secretary of the Interior November 27, 1935, and the immediate functioning of the reservation under these new regulations. The Indian Court, working with the Indian Council, claims they had been using practically these same regulations for several years, which resulted in little or no confusion in the change-over to an approved and regulated method of court procedure." And the San Carlos took over "the responsibility and duties of this splendid piece of legislation with little change in their economic or social standards and procedure" (Arizona Writers' Project 1941:34), with gratifying results. Law infractions were handled by native judges, with court order kept by native police. Court procedure is similar to that in a state district court.

Other programs administered include general administration, construction and maintenance of roads, employment assistance, forestry and range conservation, soil and moisture conservation, irrigation, plant management, education, and welfare. (See 1981 Tribal Directory for Arizona, pp. 36–39. These directories are issued annually; they provide population figures, acreage extent, names of officials, and other useful information.)

Agency headquarters of the 1,827,421-acre reservation located in Gila, Graham, and Pinal counties of Arizona is at San Carlos, southeast of Globe. Apache living on the reservation number about 6,050. Their sources of livelihood come primarily from livestock, mining, and timber activities. The tribe operates general stores at San Carlos and at Bylas, on U.S. Highway 70; and a few privately owned businesses are permitted on the reservation. A number of the San Carlos are employed at the copper mines in Globe, Miami, and Superior. Some work on a seasonal basis for highway contractors on road construction projects; others are employed by the BIA in various capacities on the reservation. Out-of-door recreation facilities have been developed, offering hunting, fishing, camping, horseback riding, and so on.

A combined BIA-public school for grades one through four is in operation at the agency headquarters. From the fifth grade up, San Carlos children attend the Globe Public Schools and the fully accredited Globe High School. A Catholic elementary school in San Carlos takes children through the second grade.

Unfortunately, the 1970s saw adverse changes among the San Carlos people. During 1973, Joel Nilsson, a general assignment reporter for the *Arizona Daily Star,* lived for a month on their reservation and looked at all facets of San Carlos life. He found unemployment—which fluctuated between 25 and 40 percent—responsible for many ills. Almost two thousand Indians were on one kind of welfare or another; over 900 of some 1,000-odd reservation homes were unfit to live in; about 20 percent of the population had alcohol problems, and the rate of suicide was rising. Although Apache law states that students must stay in school until the age of eighteen or until they have completed high school, about seventy youngsters between sixteen and eighteen were not attending school.

A struggle for leadership within the San Carlos group and questionable fiscal practices caused serious conflicts and added to the difficulties in the early 1970s (Anonymous 1973). The situation has improved now.

The White Mountain Apache live on the Fort Apache Indian reservation in the Navajo, Apache, and Gila counties of Arizona. This comprises 1,656,698 acres, or 2,601 square miles, adjoining the San Carlos reservation. Holbrook lies eighty-five miles north of the reservation headquarters at Whiteriver, about four miles north of Fort Apache (site of a former military post). From the semiarid southwest corner of the reservation, at about 2,700 feet, the terrain ranges upward to 11,459 feet at Mount Thomas in the northeast. Nearly half of the population lives in permanent cabins or modern homes. Wickiups, if used at all, are generally modified somewhat from the original structure pattern—a small entrance hall with door is common. Clan ties are maintained.

Like the San Carlos, the White Mountain Apache operate as a tribe under provisions of the Reorganization Act of 1934; they have a constitution. The council consists of a chairman and vice-chairman who are elected by popular vote for four-year terms; and nine members, two of whom are elected by popular vote of the Cibecue, Oak Creek, and Grasshopper districts, two similarly by the Carrizo, Forestdale, and Cedar Creek districts, and two by the East Fork, Turkey Creek, and Seven Mile districts, and three members by the Canyon Day and Whiteriver North Fork districts. Excepting the latter district, these are elected for terms of two and four years; those receiving the most votes serve for the longer period, and the others for the two-year term; the exception elects two members at alternating elections for four-year terms. The council has authority to appropriate tribal funds for the welfare and benefit of the tribe and for the development and protection of the reservation and its resources—with the approval of the Department of the Interior.

The White Mountain Apache entered into the cattle business to a limited extent in about 1900 with the introduction of cattle from Mexico. In 1917, some 800 head of grade Herefords were brought from Mexico to Fort Apache. From this beginning, the White Mountain Tribal Herd was increased by the purchase from time to time of cows and bulls, and the present herd of fine stock numbering in the thousands was developed. Issues were made to individual Indians. This enterprise operates a tribally owned ranch of nearly 138,000 acres on the southeast corner of the reservation.

Individual livestock owners were organized into eight livestock associations for management and sales, but all cattle are individually owned and branded. A stockman is chosen for each district to perform the duties of the old-time foreman; each district has a three-man board of directors. A manager is in charge of the tribally owned cattle, and a general livestock manager looks after the individual members' stock, which number 15,000 Herefords. This is one of the most competitive cattle spreads in the American West. The cattle industry alone puts approximately a half-million dollars back into the tribal coffers annually.

Various other enterprises are operated, each with a managing board of directors. One is the Fort Apache Timber Company, which employs over one hundred members of the tribe, and produces an annual income of several millions of dollars. Another undertaking, the White Mountain Apache Enterprises, consists of summer homesite leases, some stores and service stations, several boat dock concessions with boat rental, first class tourist facilities, a liquor store in McNary, and the Apache Flame. The White Mountain Recreation Enterprise, which includes the largest privately owned recreation area in the West (with several lakes and 300 miles of trout streams), controls game management, fishing and hunting licenses, campgrounds, and game wardens.

The White Mountain Apache, like the Jicarilla, were cited by the Secretary of the Interior in April, 1970. Their citation was in recognition of an "outstanding conservation program" for the "preservation of the Arizona (Apache) trout, which had faced extinction until the Apaches began their preservation work in 1952" (Anonymous 1970c). Efforts of the White Mountain Apache increased the number of trout and prevented further hybridization.

These Apache are also engaged in an intensive program to provide housing, training, education, and employment opportunities for their tribal members. Approximately 2,500 members are now attending school from preschool through university. School attendance of children between the ages of six and eighteen is enforced by the council. In 1956, a scholarship program was initiated for the aid of tribal members interested in continuing their education beyond high school. The majority of students are in public schools, nearly one-fourth attend BIA schools on the reservation, and about one-fourth are in mission schools. An outstanding summer youth program is carried on each year.

Health facilities are provided by the U.S. Public Health Service, with a hospital in Whiteriver and clinics in the various communities.

Law and order is maintained by a Special Officer and a force of ten policemen. All offenses are handled by the Tribal Court, with exception of the ten major crimes which, as among the other Southwestern Indian groups, go to the federal court (Young 1961:284). These offenses include murder, manslaughter, rape, assault with intent to kill, arson, burglary, larceny, robbery, incest, and assault with a deadly weapon. An eleventh crime is embezzlement of tribal funds. Tribal police have the same official status as officers in any other community, and they cooperate fully with county, state and federal law enforcement agencies. The tribal court was established in 1940; it consists of one chief judge and two associate judges. Cases coming within the jurisdiction of the court are heard daily and, where evidence is sufficient to convict, penalties are assessed according to the existing law and order code.

Religious Beliefs and Ceremonies

The Apache awareness of deity and their attitude toward a supreme being have been little understood, and less promulgated.

In general, the Apache recognize a supreme deity of impersonal character to whom no sex is attributed, but who is thought of as the creator—a deity that may be identified as *Yusn,* as *Ussen,* or Giver-of-life. This omnipotent one is the source of all supernatural power and is "the maker of world and man," but since the creation, little direct contact has prevailed between Giver-of-life and man.

However, supernatural power reaches mankind and exercises strong control over worldly affairs. In contrast to this, it is noted that the "Giver-of-life is remote and nebulous to the Apache mind. . . . The power of Giver-of-life becomes translated into specific ceremonies. It is these ceremonies which warmly and intimately impinge against Apache life . . . and dominate Apache religious thinking. Giver-of-life may be mentioned in the opening prayer of a rite. Thereafter, however, the attention shifts to the specific power whose aid the ceremony is attempting to win." (Opler 1935:66; 1941:281) says *Yusn* [Ussen] is from the Spanish *díos*—thus a Christian transfer of deific name.)

At every point in life, the Apache seeks supernatural aid in meeting his problems and conducting his affairs. These aids from the supernaturals are manifest as ceremonies that are markedly similar in pattern, though they differ widely in detail. Nearly all of them are initiated with ceremonial smoking, then throwing of pollen to the four directions, prayer, and singing.

The Apache, we are told, think of power

as a mighty force that pervades the universe. Some of it filters through to the hands of man. But to become manifest to man, power must approach him through the medium of certain agencies and channels, must "work through" something. The most conspicuous of these agencies are certain natural phenomena such as the lightning or sun, and a number of animals, principally the bear, snake, owl, and coyote . . . but there are scores of possibilities. (Opler 1935:66)

An Apache may accept or reject the power offered to him. Every Apache man or woman is a potential recipient of supernatural power. If the power is accepted, the recipient, it is said, ". . . is given directions for conducting a ceremony; he is instructed in the songs, the prayers, the four ceremonial gifts he must ask in return for his services, and the taboos, if any, which he must observe himself and impose on the one for whom he is working" (Opler

1935:67–68). One may be given as many as five different ceremonies. Thus, it is "that an Apache becomes 'loaded up with powers.' " A man's power is not public property (Opler 1935:68; cf. Ball 1970:11). Often, no one other than a person's own family may know of his ceremony. Ceremonies may be transmitted from one person to another, as from elder to younger people. When a ceremony is taught to someone outside the family circle, a fee is always charged by the teacher.

As do the Navajo, the Apache account for death, disease, and disaster as power manipulated by malevolent persons, or power itself seeking to do harm. Appropriate terms are applied to such agencies, as for beneficial supernatural powers.

The ceremonials of the Apache have not had the same publicity as have those of the Navajo. But ceremonies are performed as cures, to set things right, or to ward off possible evil. The majority of Apache ceremonies are curative rites which are carried out by shamans who have obtained supernatural power from a great number of sources, chiefly from the potent Mountain Spirits, supernatural beings called *Gáhan* or *Gáhe*. All Apaches consider the ceremonial circuit as clockwise; and few are the things not connected with the number four. *(Rel.* Farrer 1978.)

Once a shaman has been engaged to conduct a ceremony to cure an ill person, the procedure is to dress and paint the bodies of several men—usually four—to represent the Mountain Spirits. These dance into view, approaching the patient, or the camps from which the illness is to be exorcised; and by dancing, giving forth distinctive calls, and making gestures, the objective is attained. Songs are sung by the shaman while the dancers are being prepared and while they are performing. The songs function as messages to the supernaturals and acquaint them with an aid required by the shaman.

The Mountain Spirits are considered to be numerous and they inhabit many mountains. Like all supernaturals and ritual objects, they are associated with colors and directions. Therefore, the Mountain Spirits of each cardinal direction are represented by a leader, and a particular color is attributed to him. Although the associations vary somewhat, the most common color representations are said to be:

>Black Mountain Spirit is the leader of a single file
>from the east;
>
>Blue Mountain Spirit is the leader of a single file
>from the south;
>
>Yellow Mountain Spirit is the leader of a single file
>from the west; and
>
>White (or Grey) Mountain Spirit is the leader of a
>single file from the north.

The blue, or turquois, color and the cross are used extensively in ceremonial symbolism. Pollen represents growth and vitality (*see* Opler 1938a:154–155). Abalone is considered as pollen also, perhaps "water pollen."

Studies have revealed that not such a wide gulf exists between the Navajo and Apache basic cultures as was once thought. As might be expected, the major Jicarilla cycle of mythology closely parallels the Navajo. For instance, the Jicarilla puberty ceremony is similar to that of the Navajo. It is not tribal, but is held by a girl's family or clan when she is ready for marriage.

The Jicarilla observe a bear dance upon call of a curer, or shaman. The name is taken from a Ute Indian ceremony which has nothing to do with bears. In fact it is a Holiness rite (*see* Opler 1938b:27–44), performed within a brush corral, as is the Navajo Mountain Topway. Small fires are lit around the interior of the enclosure. A medicine tipi is erected at the west end. Where the Navajo would drum on a basket to set the rhythm, several Jicarilla men rub notched sticks together, resting the end of a rasp on a basket. This appears to be an element derived from the Ute. It produces a resonant, powerful sound which is very effective. While the main ceremony—the most sacred part, in which dry paintings (sandpaintings) are made—goes on in the lodge, women select partners and dance with them outside, somewhat after the manner of a Navajo squaw dance, except that no payment is made; one steps out when he tires of dancing. A dramatic entrance occurs when a group of masked dancers accompanied by sacred clowns comes onto the scene. Certain cautions have been advised by people who have attended the bear dance; it is suggested that visitors should not attempt to witness the ceremony unless they know the Jicarilla well, and unless they have found out they are welcome.

On 4 July, the Jicarilla hold a feast, without attendant ceremonies. Annually, a two-day celebration is held on 14 and 15 September, near Horse Lake. This reenacts the yearly reunion of the two divisions of the tribe—the mountain people and those of the plains. On the fifteenth, they perform an imitation of the ceremonial race that is run at Taos during the San Gerónimo fiesta. At night, a round dance is held. The friendship between the Jicarilla and Taos Indians is so close that each attends the other's feast, or *fiesta,* in large numbers; Taos people participate in the Jicarilla race, and a few of the Apache take some part in the ceremony at Taos.

Unlike other Southwestern Athabascan peoples, the Mescalero do not tell an emergence legend in the course of which reference is made to the creation and to the origins of the major ceremonials. Instead, they have utilized the *coyote cycle* to introduce these elements. This cycle is a connected series of episodes that describe the travels and adventures of a trickster, the attributes and characteristics of which are sometimes human, and again, those of an animal. Coyote is a type character that reveals a remarkable self-portrait of the Apache—a shrewd and powerful satire of his culture and of human foibles (Opler 1938a:214).

The Apache have a common custom of referring to something else than that which is mentioned, to something which resembles it, as for example, calling an owl's ears a "hat"—much to the merriment of all. In speech, direct reference is not made to a bear; to do so would "run the risk of seeing the bear shortly afterwards and of catching the sickness (a painful disease that might be contracted)" (Opler 1938a:217). To throw food about or to handle it carelessly is thought by the Apache to be very dangerous and unlucky. Bones are not thrown around; they are placed in a neat pile and disposed of at once. To do otherwise "is to invite the loss of hunting skill and shortage of food" (Opler 1938a:217).

With the Mescalero, the girls' puberty ceremony is their most important public observance; and this was also true of the Chiricahua (*see* Opler 1938a: 143–151). Two ceremonies are held for girls who go through the performance. Much symbolism is worked into the rites. At that time, Sun and Earth are important agencies. First, a large brush tipi is erected, representing the universe. It is said to be constructed of "old age staffs and gray hair"—to give long life to the girls for whom the ceremony is held. A girl being inducted to womanhood represents White Painted Woman, the Apache priestess who officiates with the Sun's representative; she is the model for all Apache womankind. The rites of induction, throughout, symbolize the recreation of White Painted Woman (comparable to Changing Woman of the Navajo). At the end of the rites, the tipi is taken down. All is in charge of the medicine man, or shaman. Second is the sun greeting ceremony. This takes place early in the morning of the first day of the observances, and again early in the morning of the final day.

MESCALERO APACHE SONG OF THE GOTAL CEREMONY

The black turkey gobbler, under the east, the middle
    of his trail; toward us it is about to dawn.
The black turkey gobbler, the tips of his beautiful tail;
    above us the dawn whitens.
The black turkey gobbler, the tips of his beautiful tail;
    above us the dawn becomes yellow.
The sunbeams stream forward, dawn boys, with
    shimmering shoes [sandals] of yellow.
On top of the sunbeams that stream toward us they
    are dancing.
At the east the rainbow moves forward, dawn maidens,
    with shimmering shoes and shirts of yellow
    dance over us.
Beautifully over us it is dawning.
Above us among the mountains the herbs are
    becoming green.
Above us on the top of the mountains the herbs are
    becoming yellow.

Above us among the mountains, with shoes of yellow
    I go around the fruits and the herbs that shimmer.
Above us among the mountains, the shimmering fruits
    with shoes and shirts of yellow are bent toward him.
On the beautiful mountains above it is daylight.

From *Gotal: A Mescalero Apache Ceremony,* by P. E. Goddard
(1909:216)—an adolescence rite for girls.

At night, the Gáhan—those supernatural beings who live in the mountain caves and beneath the horizon in the cardinal directions—appear as
masked dancers. For each four dancers, a shaman is present to dress and decorate them. He performs a ceremony while they are being painted and attired. The painting of the upper portions of the body is accompanied by a
song, and the mask and headdress are held toward the four cardinal directions before they are worn. The dancers must be painted differently for each
of the four nights of the ceremony. These dancers approach a large bonfire,
around which they dance. They come in single file from each of the four directions. They come four times, swaying and uttering a peculiar call. Each
carries painted wands which are brandished vigorously.

The headdresses are spectacular. They are made of thin strips of wood,
arranged in various patterns: crosses, fans, circles, and so on. They are colorfully decorated and further embellished with tin ornaments and downy plumes.
The upper, ornamented part of the headdress is supported on a length of small
sapling bent to fit around the head. This is covered with black cloth which
falls over the dancer's head and is gathered in to cover it closely. Tiny eye-
holes are cut in the front. Above these, shiny buttons or brass paper fasteners
or metal discs are attached, which give the mask a fantastic appearance in the
firelight. This striking headdress has led to incorrect designations of the dance.
It is spoken of as a "devil dance," or "crown dance," whereas it is actually the
mountain spirits dance. Since these mountain spirits, or Gáhan, are helpful
beings who introduced the dance to the Apache as a curing ceremony, one
sees how serious a misnomer is this. Portions of this dance are often presented
at public celebrations, such as pow-wows, the Nizhoni Dances in Albuquerque, programs at the Institute of American Indian Arts in Santa Fe, and the
like—where they are received with great enthusiasm.

Among the Gáhan personators is one called the Grey One, who may take
the place of White Mountain Spirit. He is a clown who caricatures the movements of the other dancers; he goes through all sorts of capers, amuses the
public in general, and serves as messenger. This character compares with Water
Sprinkler of the Navajo. While the Gáhan dance, rites are conducted in the
big tipi by the shaman, the girls participating, and the women attending
them. On the fourth night, the girls dance throughout the night. At first
daylight, they leave the tipi for a rest period, returning at sunrise.

Finally, the girls take part in a footrace, running to the east around a basket filled with ceremonial paraphernalia and back to where deerskins have been laid out on the ground in front of the tipi. The shaman and his assistants sing four chants and during each chant the girls run. Each time, the basket is moved nearer to the deerskins. During the last chant, the girls stop at the basket and each takes a feather from it. They then circle round the basket and run far to the east. When they return, they enter their own tipi. During these races, the ceremonial tipi is dismantled. Then, gifts are thrown to the spectators and the ceremony ends. The girls, however, must remain near their tipi for four days and nights. They must observe certain taboos. After this period, they return to everyday life (*see* Ball 1970:37–43, 207n2; *see also* Breuninger 1970).

After this ceremony, the girls, theoretically, are ready for marriage. Traditionally, the shaman will give instructions to the young men whenever they present themselves and request it. For instance, a youth may bring to the shaman a gift of pierced blue stone with an eagle feather through it. Then, night after night, until the young man has learned, the rhythmic beat of drums can be heard at the shaman's wickiup. Thus, the songs and dances are perpetuated and the unrecorded ceremonials preserved. A few of the minor ceremonies last a short time only. The major ones are given over a period of from one to four days. Some have their own set of songs, others have prayers with words similar to songs. The songs and prayers must be used in proper sequence. Many ceremonies have their own paraphernalia: charms, certain plants or animal parts. These contain power and are used for drawing out sickness from a patient. Pollen is the most important ceremonial offering; white shell, turquois, jet, and catlinite are sacred and potent, and each has directional significance; eagle feathers are important in religious rites.

Curing ceremonies are usually held for one person only, but a few rites can be given in time of epidemics to ward off the disease from all. Other ceremonies for the good of the community, holy rites, may be held in the spring and summer when lightning, snakes, and other harmful agents are present.

In olden times, after a young man had chosen a young women for a wife, it was required that he get the consent of his people; then he made his desire known to her parents. Generally, his father or uncle would do the honors for him, after which came the real proposal. Presents were offered to the young woman and to her family. Wealth was counted chiefly in horses and dressed deerskins; in the night, the suitor would tie one or more horses near her wickiup. (A single animal was considered a poor offering.) If she took the horses and fed and watered them, she was indicating that the proposal had been accepted. If the animals were not cared for, the proposal was rejected.

Wedding ceremonies were observed by a feast and celebration that lasted three days. During that time, the betrothed couple seldom saw or spoke to each other. Formerly, after a marriage, the young couple built a wickiup near that of the wife's mother; today they may live with whichever family group is more convenient.

The Mescalero hold the puberty ceremony at the beginning of July, the erection of the tipi taking place on the morning of 1 July. This is the only instance in which a Mescalero ceremony is conducted on a fixed calendar date, a fact that derives from an old government order which forbade the holding of ceremonies at any other time of the year.

Among the Western Apache, the puberty ceremony for girls was one of their major observances, when the mountain spirits appeared. In addition to its ritual importance, the occasion was an important social event. Wealthy families held the full four-day ceremonial, while poorer ones had a one-day event. Today, these ceremonials continue, but they have lost much of their significance and influence. They are usually conducted during the 4 July celebration and the reservation fair of the Fort Apache in August or September. The Gáhan attire and accoutrement are similar to those of the Mescalero, but the wands that are brandished and the headdresses are decorated in such manner as to make them distinctive, one group from the other.

The Western Apache still recognize and respect their shamans, but they have very limited influence, especially on the younger generations.

For further information on the Apache, readers are referred to the *National Geographic Magazine* (February 1980, pp. 260–290). There, well illustrated, factual articles on Apache history, economy, health, and ceremonies are presented by the Apache themselves and by a white man who married into the White Mountain group (about a third of some 8,000 Apache who dwell on the Fort Apache reservation).

A wireservice article reported on a San Carlos Apache woman who has become a doctor and is beginning a residency in orthopedic surgery. She respects the practitioners of Indian medicine and their methods, and says that their knowledge and that of modern medicine work well together (Phoenix AP, 16 November 1980).

NEW WAY, OLD WAY (NAVAJO)

Beauty in the old way of life—
The dwellings they decorated so lovingly;
A drum, a clear voice singing,
And the sound of laughter.

You must want to learn from your mother,
You must listen to old men not quite capable of becoming
     white men.
The white man is not our father.
While we last, we must not die of hunger.
We were a very Indian, strong, competent people,
But the grass had almost stopped its growing,
The horses of our pride were near their end.

Indian cowboys and foremen handled Indian herds.
A cowboy's life appealed to them until economics and tradition
     clashed.

No one Indian was equipped to engineer the water's flow onto a
   man's allotment.
Another was helpless to unlock the gate.
The union between a hydro-electric plant and
Respect for the wisdom of the long-haired chiefs
Had to blend to build new enterprises
By Indian labor.

Those mighty animals graze once more upon the hillside.
At the Fair appear again our ancient costumes.
A full-blood broadcasts through a microphone planned tribal action.
Hope stirs in the tribe,
Drums beat and dancers, old and young, step forward.

We shall learn all the devices of the white man.
We shall handle his tools for ourselves.
We shall master his machinery, his inventions, his skills, his medicine,
   his planning;
But we'll retain our beauty
And still be Indians!

By Dave MartinNez

From *Anthology of Poetry and Verse.*
Institute of American Indian Arts,
Santa Fe, N.M.

The Pueblo of Taos, north plaza, with Mount Wheeler (the highest peak in New Mexico) in the background. (Photograph by Bertha P. Dutton)

Summer dance in the Pueblo of San Juan's plaza. (Photograph by Sonni Cooper, Eight Northern Pueblos)

An eagle dance performed in the plaza at the Pueblo of Laguna. (Photograph by Bertha P. Dutton)

Tówa Yalanne, or Corn Mountain, as seen from the Pueblo of Zuñi. (Photograph courtesy of the Laboratory of Anthropology, Ben Wittick Collection)

Corn Mountain from the air. (Photograph by Fred Mang, Jr., National Park Service)

Hopi maidens in ceremonial attire. Their hair arrangement signifies they are of marriageable age. (Photograph by Elita Wilson)

Hopi woman making *piki* ("paper bread"). The batter is removed from a Hopi bowl and applied to a stone griddle with a whisk of the hand. She then places the baked piki in the yucca-ring basket on her left. (Photograph by Suzanne de Berg)

Navajo woman weaving a rug at Hubbell Trading Post, Ganado, Arizona.
(Photograph by Fred Mang, Jr., National Park Service)

Papago Indian cowboys cut out horses in one of their corrals built of mesquite poles. (Photograph courtesy the Bureau of Indian Affairs)

Ute Tribal Bear dance held in the spring. (Photograph courtesy the Uintah and Ouray Agency)

Lettuce harvest of the Mohavi-Chemehuevi on the Colorado River Indian Reservation (Photograph courtesy the Bureau of Indian Affairs)

A Mohave effigy jar. (Photograph by Leslie Buckland)

Baskets used for ceiling decoration in the old Lorenzo Hubbell home at Ganado Trading Post, Arizona. (Photograph by Fred Mang, Jr., National Park Service)

A Pueblo man from Hopiland weaving a woman's *manta* (dress) on a traditional upright loom. The loom is draped with textile belts and a small drum. The weaver's hair is cut at the sides only and worn chongo style. (Photograph courtesy the Santa Fe Railway, Elita Wilson Collection)

Western Apache arts and crafts: blue ribbons to a plaque woven by Ida Adams and a saddle bag made by Lydia Harney. (Photograph courtesy the Bureau of Indian Affairs)

Zuñi necklaces.

Sunset Crater near Flagstaff, Arizona, where the *katsinas* dwell. (Photograph by Fred Mang, Jr., National Park Service)

Fort Union National Monument as it now appears. (Photograph by Fred Mang, Jr., National Park Service)

4
The Ute Indians

Brief History

In the state of Colorado, only the Ute Indians dwell today as organized groups. They are descendants of a people who once claimed about half of the area of the present state, two-thirds of Utah, and bits of northern New Mexico as their domain. They required a large geographical area to sustain themselves.

The Ute, who called themselves *Nünt'z* ("The People") had a food gathering-hunting economy; they wandered on foot, collecting plant foods and hunting game. Their struggle to survive took much of their energy and precluded extensive social development. All social behavior was defined or controlled by the family, often through an older member. Defensive war and the social bear dance were the only activities requiring the cooperation of a tribal unit larger than the family.

No overall political organization was ever achieved by the Utes. They were divided into small bands, each with its own chief. Each band was an independent group. Among the larger bands whose names have come down through history were the *Uncompahgre,* or *Tabeguache,* whose central home was in the area around present day Gunnison and Montrose, Colorado; the White River and *Yampa* bands of northwestern Colorado; the *Mouache* who roamed along the front range of that state; the *Capote* who lived in the San Luis valley; and the *Weminuche* who occupied the San Juan basin of southwestern Colorado. The *Uintah* lived in eastern Utah.

After the Ute acquired horses from the Spanish immigrants, they were able to add greatly to their store of essentials. They became bison hunters and tipi dwellers. From 1630 to 1700, the seven bands consolidated into the Ute Confederation, and were able to transform from primary family units to warlike bands. (*Rel.* Schaafsma, C.F. 1978:61–64.)

The Ute bands often fought with other Indians and sometimes among themselves. Generally they were friendly with the non-Indians who invaded their mountain domain to trap, trade and prospect for minerals. But they were unprepared for the onslaught that was to follow. After the trappers, traders, and prospectors came the miners and settlers who crept ever westward, until they occupied various areas on Colorado's eastern slope. In 1863, the federal government called a council of all the Ute bands; it was held in the San Luis valley. Fearing trouble between the whites and the Indians, the government wished to persuade the Utes to move out of these areas and to remain west of the Continental Divide. The government negotiators found it difficult to deal with the numerous chiefs. Finally, at government insistence, an Uncompahgre leader named *Ouray* (meaning "arrow") was designated as spokesman for all the bands. At first, Ouray and other Ute leaders declined to move away from the San Luis valley and the other areas which the government wished them to leave.

Reduction of Ute Holdings

Gradually, however, the Ute ceded most of their lands to the federal government to be used by settlers for farming, ranching, mining, and the building of railroads and towns. Under a treaty made in 1868, the Utes promised to remain west of the Continental Divide. The treaty provided that virtually all of Colorado west of the Divide would be kept as a reservation for the Ute, with agencies established in the area of Gunnison and on the White River.

Before many years the treaty was broken by the settlers. Gold and silver were discovered in the San Juan Mountains, and miners invaded the Ute lands. A new treaty was negotiated in 1873, under which the Ute gave up the region in which minerals had been found.

The Mouache, Capote, and Weminuche bands were consolidated on a strip of land along the Colorado–New Mexico border, fifteen miles wide and 140 miles long. There the Southern Ute reservation, with an agency near present day Ignacio, Colorado, was established in 1877. Almost all of those Ute people came to live in or near the Pine River valley. Principal leaders were Buckskin Charley of the Mouache, Severo of the Capote, and Ignacio of the Weminuche.

The Weminuche considered that region as their own, and from the beginning of this arrangement they resented the location of the Mouache and Capote among them. It was impossible for them to get along with the other two bands. Heeding the counsel of their chiefs, the Weminuche declined to farm, which was the intent of the government agents.

In 1879, the Yampa and White River bands, whose agency was on the White River near modern Meeker, Colorado, became restive. Goods and payments that had been promised by the government had not been delivered; and the insistence of the agent, N. C. Meeker, that the Ute become farmers—even to the extent that he had their race track plowed up—led to an eruption. Before the trouble ended, twelve white employees at the agency, including Meeker, had been killed. Troops under Major T. T. Thornburgh that were enroute to the agency were attacked and thirteen soldiers were killed before the Ute withdrew. We read of these happenings as the "Meeker massacre" and the "Thornburgh ambush."

Ouray, who became the most prominent of all Ute leaders, died near Ignacio while visiting the southern bands in 1880. As a result of the Meeker incident, pressure mounted among the whites to have all the Utes removed from Colorado. In 1881, the White River and Uncompahgre bands were exiled into eastern Utah to a reservation that previously had been established for the Uintah. By 1882, two-thirds of the Colorado Utes had been removed from the state.

As part of their scheme to make farmers and cattle raisers of the Ute by settling them on reservations, the federal government offered to allot each family land in the Pine River valley area. Those who accepted allotments got 160 acres of land, apiece. The Mouache and Capote bands, merged as the *Southern Ute Tribe,* remained on these lands. When Chief Severo died, Buckskin Charley became chief of both these bands. They gradually accepted the change from a nomadic life to an agricultural one. After the allotments were made to individual Indians in the Pine River valley, other reservation lands were returned to the public domain and were opened to homesteading by non-Indians. For many years the Southern Ute have lived as close neighbors of Spanish-American and Anglo farmers and ranchers.

The Weminuche, however, in 1895 chose to move to the arid barren western end of the reservation, rather than accept allotted farm sites in the fertile river valleys to the east. With division of the original reservation, the Weminuche became today's *Ute Mountain Tribe,* with their own social organization and reservation. They have lived as stockmen, isolated to a great degree from non-Indians. On their western holdings, the "Ute Strip," the Weminuche eventually were furnished with an agency built at a point known as Navajo Springs, south of Sleeping Ute Mountain. About 1917 the agency was moved a few miles to the north, where a new community called *Tawaoc* (meaning "all right" or "just fine") was established.

The Modern Ute Peoples

In securing up-to-date data for inclusion in this book, an effort was made by the author to obtain modern illustrative material. In a very kind manner, an informant told me: "The Ute Mountain Tribe is isolationist by nature and prefers to be left alone if at all possible. I questioned tribal officials as to whether they would permit publication of pictures of themselves, their homes or their ceremonials. They responded that they would prefer not." (For general facts of the Utes of 1868, *see* Fowler and Fowler 1971: 38–76, 110.)

Although members of the Ute Mountain and Southern Ute groups speak the same Indian language, Shoshonean of the Uto-Aztecan family, and have the same physical characteristics, they are two distinct entities. Each has its own tribal government and conducts its business independently of the other. Both groups were impoverished until recent years.

In 1950, however, the Confederated Ute Tribes (the two Colorado groups and the Northern Ute—those who had been exiled to eastern Utah and live on what is known today as the Uintah and Ouray reservation) won a $31 million judgment from the U.S. government as a result of claims for lands wrongfully taken in the mid-1800s. *(Rel.* Smith, A.M. 1974.) The Ute Mountain Tribe received about $6,266,000 in judgment funds after attorneys' fees were paid. The Southern Ute received around $5,500,000. At about the same time the land claims were awarded, natural gas was discovered on Southern Ute lands. Since then oil and gas discoveries have enriched the Ute Mountain treasury also.

Following these events, both groups spent much time in studying ways in which their new wealth might best be spent for the benefit of their people. These studies resulted in rehabilitation programs which have brought about great improvements in living conditions. The people now live in modern homes. Health and sanitation standards have been raised. New roads have been built and old roads repaired. Tribal lands are being improved through good conservation practices. The children of the two groups have shared in the good fortune. They attend public schools, and scholarship programs of the tribes help young people who wish to attend colleges or vocational schools.

Traditional Observances

The old Indian way of life is fading on each of these reservations, but two annual events stemming from the ancient heritage of the Utes still are observed. These are the bear dance—the traditional welcome to spring—and the sun dance—a religious ritual that originated with the Plains Indians. The bear dances usually are held in April or May, and the sun dances in July or August. Since these are tribal festivals, rather than performances for tourists, the dates are not set far in advance. Each fall the Southern Ute hold a tribal fair to which visitors are welcome; and both they and the Ute Mountain Ute hold rodeos that are open to the public.

Reorganization

Upon petition of the tribal councils concerned, and approval of the Department of the Interior, the Consolidated Ute Agency at Ignacio was split into the Ute Mountain Agency at Towaoc and the Southern Ute Agency at

Ignacio. The change became effective on 29 December 1968. The agency staffs and other BIA personnel assist the tribal organizations in the fields of resources management (including soil and moisture conservation, land reclamation, irrigation, forest and range management, and realty problems), in community services (including welfare, education, and law and order), and in administration. The tribes receive certain assistance in health matters from the U.S. Public Health Service.

Joint objectives of the tribal organizations and the BIA are to give the Indian people greater economic security, to develop Indian resources to maximum productivity, and to help Indians take their place in American community life. It is said that both of these Ute tribes are making progress toward these objectives.

The Ute Mountain Ute

The Ute Mountain reservation is located in the extreme southwest corner of Colorado, with a small extension into New Mexico. Most of the reservation lies in Montezuma county, Colorado, with the remainder in La Plata county, Colorado, and San Juan county, New Mexico. The location in general is high, deeply dissected tableland; the climate is semiarid to arid. A small number of the Ute Mountain tribal members live in southeastern Utah on allotted trust land; although the allotments are not within the reservation itself they belong to the Ute and are considered as part of the reservation.

The reservation proper was established in 1895 by dividing the original Southern Ute Indian reservation. The established reservation is tribal trust land and has never been allotted to individual members. The total tribal holdings amount to 591,670 acres, which include tribal trust acreages of 448,030 in Colorado, 107,520 in New Mexico, and 2,328 in Utah, or 557,878 acres in all. Indian trust allotments add up to 9,459 acres in Utah, and 40 acres of government-owned trust, totaling 9,499. Tribal fee simple title lands totalled 24,293 acres. The tribe owns grazing permits on over 100,000 acres of U.S. Forest Service and Bureau of Land Management holdings. The majority of the land is used for livestock grazing. A number of oil and gas leases are on tribal lands.

An elected tribal council with seven members has governed the Ute Mountain group since 1940, when a tribal constitution was adopted. The hereditary chief of the tribe, Jack House, although no longer an elected member of the council, continued to have much influence on tribal affairs.

As a result of two conflicting surveys made by the federal government, disputes arose between the Ute and Navajo peoples. In 1972, ownership of the contested land was awarded to the Navajo. A bill requesting funds and land in compensation for the loss of oil and gas proceeds from the land given to the Navajo Tribe would have helped develop the Ute economy, but it was vetoed by President Carter in 1980. (*See Wassaja: The Indian Historian,* vol. 13, no. 2, 8 June 1980.)

The common tongue is Ute, although English is spoken and much non-Indian attire is worn.

The health of the population is good. Health care has been emphasized by the tribal government for a number of years, and is similar to health practices in general.

In the early 1950s, the average education of the Ute Mountain Ute was about fourth grade. Now the average is about sixth grade and is slowly rising. Younger children finish grade school, but the majority fail to complete high school. Concerted efforts by the tribal council, the tribal education committee, the BIA, and the public schools are helping, for more students reach the twelfth grade every year. Individuals are showing serious interest in vocational training, and several have taken advantage of programs offered by the BIA, OEO, and MDTA (Manpower Development and Training Act).

As of the 1980 census, the tribal rolls of the Ute Mountain people listed 1,402 members; a large number of these live in the community of Towaoc, the main reservation community. The average Ute family size is 4.7, and the average age in the tribe is sixteen. Other Indians, Spanish Americans, and Anglos also reside on the Ute Mountain reservation, or adjacent thereto.

Around a hundred Ute Mountain enrollees live on other reservations or off-reservation. Several hundred live in Utah. Descendants of small bands that always claimed the Blue Mountain region of Utah, and who refused to move to the Colorado reservation, reside on individual allotments of land at White Mesa in the vicinity of Blanding, Utah. The allotments were made in the 1920s and 1930s. There are some two hundred of these Blanding Ute, who are usually referred to as the Allen Canyon Ute.

The council members of this reservation recognize that jobs are greatly needed. They are seeking industrialists to locate labor-demanding enterprises on the reservation. Presently, only few industries exist. Major resources include oil and gas from the San Juan basin, and "a spectacular extension of major archaeological ruins of the Mesa Verde type." The reservation adjoins the Mesa Verde National Park. Some timber is owned by the Ute Mountain Ute, but its economic value is uncertain (Anonymous 1970b).

The Southern Ute

The Southern Ute Indian reservation also is in southwestern Colorado, occupying parts of La Plata and Archuleta counties. It has retained the fifteen-mile width of earlier times, but the length has been reduced to seventy-three miles. Within the boundaries of the reservation is some non-Indian land. The opening up of the reservation years ago to non-Indian homesteading resulted in an intermingling of Indian and non-Indian land holdings. In the 1930s the federal government returned to tribal ownership those acres contained in the Southern Ute reservation that had not been homesteaded. Of the present total of 818,000 acres within the exterior boundaries, some 307,000 acres are Indian land. Tribal trust land amounts to 299,443 acres; 4,967 acres are individually owned trust land.

The reservation lands vary from stream valleys to high mesas, with most of the area at an elevation of between 6,000 and 7,000 feet. The climate is temperate and semiarid.

Since the reservation's establishment the people have relied on an agricultural economy based on cattle and sheep production supplemented with some cash crops. Homes are built on irrigated farms in or near the Pine River valley. The land-base limitations and the general low economic level of agriculture in southwestern Colorado tend to prevent self-sustaining agriculture by a majority of the tribal members. For that reason, increasing tribal emphasis is being placed on development of employment opportunities in tourism and light manufacture.

In late 1971, a deluxe tourist center was opened at Ignacio. It includes

a 38-unit motel with meeting and banquet rooms, a pool, a lounge, a museum of Indian lore, an arts-and-crafts shop where guests may watch Indians at their native crafts, facilities for the display of motion pictures or slides, and a hall capable of accommodating four hundred.

In its auxiliary services, the tribe will supply fishing tackle and take its guests to the tribe's own Lake Capote for fishing. During big game season, guides will escort hunters on Southern Ute lands, and unexplored Indian ruins will be made accessible to guests.

Young members of the tribe were trained in tourist complex operations by restaurants, a motel, a hospital and the food service department at Fort Lewis College in Durango, 25 miles north of Ignacio. (Anonymous 1971b)

Aside from the dominant self-employment activities, wage employment is almost entirely of the service type, with the tribal organization and the BIA being the principal employers.

In 1936 a tribal constitution was adopted, and since then the Southern Ute have been governed by an elected tribal council of six members. Their last chief, Antonio Buck, Senior, son of famed Chief Buckskin Charley, died in February, 1961. His position had been largely honorary, and the tribe has not chosen a new chief.

Revenue for the tribal organization is from petroleum royalties and timber sales and interest from tribal funds on deposit with the U.S. Treasury.

Enrolled membership of the Southern Ute according to the 1980 census is approximately 990, of whom 600 or more are residents of the reservation; the remainder live in areas some distance from the reservation. Although Ute is the common language, most speak English. They dress as do their neighbors, for the most part, although a few of the women continue to wear shawls or blankets.

With the reorganization of agencies in 1968, the Southern Ute agency set up sixty-seven permanent positions, including about thirty people in school dormitory operations at Ignacio. This agency also provides some services to the Ute Mountain agency, such as plant maintenance when required. The latter agency has a staff of permanent employees.

The Northern Ute

The Northern Ute people live today on the Uintah and Ouray reservation, with agency headquarters at Fort Duchesne, west of Vernal, Utah, on U.S. Highway 40, approximately one hundred fifty miles east of Salt Lake City.

The reservation contains 1,008,192 acres of land situated in the Uintah basin of northeastern Utah. The elevation ranges from 4,655 to 9,200 feet above sea level, and the terrain varies from semidesert to forested mountains. In this environment, excellent hunting and fishing are provided,

On lands where the Uintah originally had been confined, the Uncompahgre and White River bands were moved by the federal government in 1881. Today about 1,200 full-blooded Ute of a total population of 1,880 reside on the reservation.

In 1952, the BIA closed the boarding school in Whiterocks. A few students attend off-reservation boarding schools. The elementary school children are in public schools in the Uintah and Duchesne school districts.

Public Health facilities are located in Roosevelt, Utah, seven miles from the tribal headquarters. A clinic with a full-time doctor, nurse, and dentist is operated for walk-in patients. If patients are to be hospitalized, they enter a new county hospital in the same building as the clinic.

The tribe has been very active in its economic development program. Its cattle enterprise is second to none in the state of Utah. During recent years, several hundred jobs have been opened on the reservation. The same period showed a decline of about 23 percent in the tribal welfare rate, and similar declines in the unemployment rate and arrest record.

The Ute Fabricating Company, a cabinet mill, initially employed a few full-time employees, with additional men in training. A housing program under HUD was set to build one-hundred-fifty three-bedroom houses, eighty-six of which were to be completed by October, 1970, and others later.

The Ute people here have no intention of waiting for things or opportunities to come to them. They have developed in the center of the reservation a multimillion dollar motel, restaurant, and recreational project called the "Bottle Hollow Complex." For this Bottle Hollow enterprise—so named because when federal troops were stationed at Fort Duchesne in the early 1900s, they hid their empty whiskey bottles in a gully near the site where the motel complex is being constructed—they have made sound and practical plans. Seventy members of the tribe were started in training for resort jobs, from desk clerk to lifeguard. Seventy more were to be trained as replacements.

The complex is in hexagonal form, employing a familiar symbol in Indian design. Fifty-two motel units form two large hexagons, one containing in its open center a six-sided swimming pool. Most of the furnishings of the motel—

from beds to restaurant tables—are hexagonal. Included in the plans are an arts and crafts shop, service station, a combined restaurant-convention center, and a hexagonal plaza. Fishing, boating, and water skiing are made possible at a nearby reservoir. At this impressive center, employees are given intensive courses in Ute history, English language skills, and the art of dealing with tourists.

The Northern Ute participate in tribal dances throughout the year. Most common are the bear dances held in springtime. A traditional celebration is held on 4 July, with war dances and social dancing at Fort Duchesne. In the summer, the sun dance is held. The public is invited to all dances, but no pictures may be taken at a sun dance.

A few years ago, a group of mixed-bloods voted to sever relations with the Northern Ute Indians and with the federal government. These are known as the Affiliated Ute Citizens of Utah.

As with the Navajo and other Indians, the best way to learn more about the Ute people is to visit their homelands. Ignacio and Towaoc, the principal towns on the Colorado reservations, and the Roosevelt-Fort Duchesne area of the Utah Utes, are easily reached by good highways. The people will be found to be friendly and courteous if visitors are. Books on the Ute Indians are listed in the bibliography.

Ute Beliefs and Ceremonies

The Ute bear dance, which is still performed by members of the Ute bands, has been mentioned. To gain information regarding this observance the reader is referred to an account given by a participant of the annual bear dance held in March, 1893, by the Southern Ute group. Mr. V. Z. Reed was an intimate friend of the then war chief and several other prominent members of the tribe, and was allowed to make a study of the dance. He could find no tradition antedating the dance itself on which the ceremonies were founded, but he believed the bear dance to be one of the oldest of all the Ute ceremonies (Reed, V. Z. 1896:237). Indians came from far and near to participate in the dance. All except the smallest children danced.

Veneration of the bear, in one form or another, tinges many of the Ute ceremonies. The bear is regarded as the wisest of animals and the bravest of all except the mountain lion; he is thought to possess wonderful magic power. Feeling that the bears are fully aware of the relationship existing between themselves and the Ute, their ceremony of the bear dance assists in strengthening this friendship.

The bear dance was formerly held in March—when bears recovered from hibernation—under the direction of some one person. In olden times this was usually a medicine man or chief, who had a number of assistants. Then, too, preparations lasted for two or three months.

A site was selected for the dance, and an enclosure, or *a-vik-wok-et,* "cave of sticks," erected. It was circular, from 100 to 150 feet in diameter, and represented a bear cave. Its one opening faced the south or southeast, toward the sun. The walls of timbers and pine boughs were built to a height of about seven feet; the enclosure was open to the sky.

Within this structure at one side, a location was selected for the stand of the musicians, and a hole was dug into the earth, simulating a cave. Over the hole a box or drum with an open bottom was arranged, and *moraches,* "singing sticks," were placed with one end on the lap of a rhythmist and the other end against the box. Up and down the notched sticks, bones or pieces of timber are rubbed, making a rasping sound which the boxdrum amplifies. Reed describes the sound as resembling muffled cymbals.

In his day, twenty or more musicians who had been specially prepared for the ceremonies sang and played their moraches. They were joined by others when old or familiar songs were sung; the singers were always men. The music, resounding in the little cave, is thought to be transformed into thunder, which arouses the sleeping bears in their mountain caves. The duration of the dance—four days and one night—was fixed by the time required by bears to recover from hibernation.

With the conclusion of the fourth day's feast, all ceremonies of the dance are over. The bears are believed to have fully regained use of their faculties, to have found mates, and to have been provided with food. It is felt that they will gratefully remember their Indian relatives and repay them by assisting in the practice of magic.

At the time of his participation in the bear dance, in 1893, Reed stated that in former times the dance was more exactly observed than at that date. As one witnesses a bear dance of the present time, he may compare the observances with those of many decades ago (*see* Emmitt 1954:34–40). The bear dances—traditional welcome to spring—continue on, although the time of celebrating has been altered somewhat, and the length of the ceremonies shortened so as to better meet the demands of modern life patterns.

The sun dance, a great summer ceremonial performed by Plains Indian groups, such as the Kiowa, Cheyenne, Sioux, Omaha, and others, was adopted by the Utes, adapted to their purposes, and continues to the present. The author had the privilege of attending the sun dance held near Ignacio, Colorado, July 1962, as a family member.

The fundamental object of the ceremony seems to be the over-coming of certain cosmic elements. All Indians performing it divide the ceremony into secret rites of one to four days' duration and a public performance. The secret rites include smoking, fasting, praying, and the preparation of objects that are to be used upon the altar or worn during the public performance.

On the last day of the secret rites a great lodge is built in the center of the camp circle, the selection of the site being the office of a special individual and attended with formal procedures. The ceremony of the sun dance abounds in symbolism, no rite being performed except in a prescribed manner. Of the sun dance in general, its ritual relates that once, in a period of famine an individual wandered forth with a female companion in behalf of his tribe, encountered a deity, fasted, learned the ceremony, returned to the tribe, caused the ceremony to be performed, and thus brought relief from famine through the appearance of the buffalo. The ceremony accordingly may be regarded as one of rebirth or reanimation.

It has been said that more than any other ceremony or occasion, the sun dance furnishes the Indians an opportunity for expressing emotion in rhythm, and for becoming more closely united.

Like the Navajo, the Ute people have taken on peyote ceremonialism.

SPEAK TO ME

O trees, say something.
One day you move back and forth,
Another day you are still.
How can I tell
What you are thinking, feeling?
Please speak to me.
Lovers carve names in you.
That must be painful.
I sit beneath your branches on sunny days,
When the wind blows and
Your leaves whisper and fly away,
Waiting for you to speak to me.
Are you angry at everybody?
Do you feel pain or delight?
Oh trees, please speak to me.

By Calvin O'John, Ute-Navajo

From *The Writers' Reader,* 1962–1966.
The Institute of American Indian Arts,
Santa Fe, N.M.

5

The Southern Paiute

The Paiute Indians

Linguistically the Southern Paiute belong to a Numic-speaking group of the Shoshonean branch of the Uto-Aztecan stock. It was said by J. W. Powell that the name Paiute properly belonged exclusively to the "Corn Creek tribe" [Pah-vants] of southwestern Utah, but that the term had been extended to include several other Shoshonean-speaking peoples (Hodge 1910). In general "Southwestern Paiute" has been applied to Ute-Chemehuevi groups. Since this section concerns the Southwestern Indians of the Four Corners states, attention is given only to those Paiute peoples of northwestern Arizona and southwestern Utah, although others of Paiute classification live in southwestern Nevada and parts of southeastern California.

Archaeological investigations and linguistic evidence have shown that "these Numic speakers spread across the Great Basin into the northern portion of the Southwest some time shortly after A.D. 1000, replacing prehistoric Pueblo or Pueblo-like peoples who had earlier lived in the region. In extreme southern Nevada and southwestern Utah, archaeologists have excavated the distinctive ceramic remains of the Southern Paiute in direct association with those of the Pueblos made around A.D. 1150. The Paiute pottery was brown or reddish-brown, conical with pointed bottoms, and often decorated with rows of "finger nail" incisions. This is easily distinguished from the highly decorated black-on-white, black-on-yellow, or polychrome pottery of the Pueblos" (Euler 1972a:2).

It is probable that Southern Paiute people learned to raise corn and certain other products from the Pueblo Indians, making it possible for them to initiate a semisedentary living pattern. Rude defensive features found at some of the mid-twelfth century pueblos suggest that strife may have arisen between the two groups, causing the Pueblos to leave the region and the Paiute to add to their holdings eastward. Primarily, the Paiute were wild plant gatherers and hunters of rabbits and mountain sheep—for which they used long bows and arrows and long nets. Their homes were probably temporary camps and, to some extent, along permanent streams where they could farm. Excavations have brought forth grinding implements with which seeds, piñones, corn, and meat were ground and pounded. These milling stones differ from those used by the Pueblos. Southern Paiute-Hopi relationships appear to have existed on a friendly basis from around A.D. 1300–1600; trade was a major factor in their contacts.

The Southern Paiute were little disturbed by the Spaniards, with whom they came in slight contact during the sixteenth and seventeenth centuries. Father Escalante, who traversed their territory in 1776, seems to have been the first European who attempted to describe them systematically. He went through southern Utah a few miles north of present day Cedar City, and met a seed-gathering party of Southern Paiute Indians (Bolton 1950; Euler 1972a). Later he encountered the Kaibab group.

In the same year, Father Garcés visited southern Paiute people known as the Chemehuevi, who dwelt near the Mohave on the lower Colorado River. It has been noted that Garcés "made it clear that the Chemehuevi, in the 18th century anyway, did not distinguish themselves from the Southern Paiute in the Las Vegas, Nevada, area immediately to the north" (Euler 1972a:18).

After the United States annexed New Mexico and California, the Paiute domain was encroached upon steadily, and some of the Indians were placed on reservations. The majority, however, remained scattered through their country. Friction between the Paiute and the settlers was minor until the 1840s, when it increased greatly (Euler 1966:44–74).

It has been said, only about 1,200 Southern Paiute still survive. A shabby settlement in Cedar City, Utah, reveals their cultural state, "too few to wield political power, too poor to pay for legal advice." The government cut them off from federal benefits in 1956, and it has been noted that:

Without birth certificates, Social Security numbers, or land deeds, they couldn't collect welfare or negotiate loans. For that matter, they didn't even know how to qualify for hunting and fishing licenses to seek food in the mountains and streams of their forefathers.

At the same time the federal government emancipated the Paiutes, it declared they were unable to manage their own affairs and directed [a bank] . . . to sell their reservations. (Anderson 1971)

The Indian Peaks band sold their 10,000-acre reservation for $40,000. (The 1980 census records a group population of 990.)

The few women here who made basketry—a craft already on slim grounds—
encountered further calamity. Due to extensive use of pesticides by farmers
or government agents who sprayed the vegetation, including the requisite
materials for basket making, several of the basket makers became ill from
drawing contaminated willow twigs through their teeth. As a result, they
were forced to go as far as central Nevada to find DDT-free materials. To
make the trip, the older women at least had to depend upon someone with a
car to take them. This and other factors have resulted in the decline of basket
production (Fowler, C. 1971).

The Kaibab Paiute

Just north of the Grand Canyon in Arizona, bordering on Utah, the small
Kaibab group is located. As late as 1869 this branch of the Southern Paiute
had scarcely been seen by non-Indians. They were seminomadic, with a hunting and food-gathering economy. They did some fishing, so their food consisted
of fish, jackrabbit and other small game, piñones, and seeds that were ground
into flour for bread. Their dwellings were brush shelters erected upon poles
planted in the ground, or upon an interlocking pole tripod conical in shape.
Shelters were very temporary and frequently in summer none were used.

The geographical location kept these a poor, unorganized people, unable
to resist outsiders' settlements pushing into their domain and usurping
their water. For years, they lingered in their original habitat near the new
villages being founded by Mormons in northern Arizona and southern Utah.
Anglo cattle, sheep, and farming caused the destruction of their native foods,
making life increasingly difficult. Gradually they attached themselves to the
Mormon communities. As they were peaceable, of high moral character, and
industrious, their willingness and efficiency made them necessary to the white
farmers. Apparently the Paiute had little or no religious organization, and as
a consequence the Mormon efforts toward conversion met with some success.

Mormons who settled in the 1860s at Moccasin Spring—the water of which
the Paiute had used exclusively for centuries—forced the Kaibab group to
move and become nomadic; they made their base in and near Kanab, Utah.
Some time later, but prior to establishment of the Kaibab Reservation in
1907, Mormon church officials negotiated a deal with the squatters at Moccasin Spring, whereby one-third of the flow of the spring was granted to the
Paiute and they were permitted to farm a small tract of land, watering it
from the spring (Euler 1972a:84,87). Thus the Indians came to practice a
little agriculture, with some irrigation. The BIA issued cattle to them at the
time the reservation was established. A good herd was built up, but soon
disseminated. Another herd, purchased in 1916, had become reasonably successful by 1930, but the depression that followed and the war of the 1940s
lowered the Kaibab Paiute to a state of mere existence.

Foremost of the Paiute arts was basketmaking, including conical baskets
for carrying burdens, parching trays for roasting seeds, water jars, hats and

semibasketry cradles for babies. As elsewhere in the Southwest, basket making is passing from the scene. Pottery production was always minor. Formerly, extensive use was made of animal skins for clothing and, to some degree,
shelters.

A social event—the round, or circle, dance—was held, and games were
played.

In time, the Paiute reluctance to accept a changing way of life was overcome. Progress has come rapidly. Numbering 224 in 1980, the Kaibab Paiute
continue to live in small groups on their 120,413 acres of reservation land
west of Fredonia, Arizona, on U.S. Highway 89. All commonly dress in western garb today.

The Kaibab Paiute operate under a tribal constitution adopted in 1951,
with a council of members of either sex elected annually. The officers are: a
chairman, vice-chairman, secretary-treasurer, tribal judge, and chief of police. The council meets each month in Fredonia. The chairman is the only
salaried employee of the tribe.

Their tribal headquarters is at Moccasin, in the west-central part of the
reservation.

Under provisions of the Indian Claims Act passed by Congress in 1946,
the Kaibab and several other Southern Paiute groups filed suit against the
government of the U.S.A., "claiming restitution payment for all their aboriginal lands that had been wrongfully taken from them by the Government
or agents thereof" (Euler 1972a:92). The case was not decided until 1970,
but the Indians won and a judgment was received. With a land claim settlement of slightly more than a million dollars, the Kaibab appeared to be destined for better times. It was then said:

Today, some fourteen families, comprising sixty-two people, live in the small settlement of Kaibab, two miles from Moccasin Spring. The remaining seventy-four
individuals live nearby. While a few still live in small, frame houses, ten other families reside in attractive and recently completed "self help" concrete block structures.
The main roads are paved, thus easing transportation problems especially in the snowy
winter months. A spacious tribal administrative building was officially dedicated on
June 2nd, 1970, providing adequate offices and meeting facilities for the tribal council
and other employees.

Reservation lands are not yet used to their full economic potential. Until recently,
approximately 10,000 acres of grazing land were leased to non-Indian ranchers but
the remainder was not in any type of production.

There are two private enclaves within the Kaibab Reservation boundaries. One of
these, 400 acres, comprises the Mormon settlement of Moccasin. The other tract, of
40 acres, is the National Park Service facility of Pipe Springs National Monument,
an early Mormon "fort" around a small spring.

The Kaibab Paiutes receive medical and dental care through contract services with
physicians and dentists in nearby communities, a program financed by the U.S. Public
Health Service. There is also a resident P.H.S. community health worker on the
reservation.

Paiute children—and of the total population of 136, forty-four are under the age
of 16—attend a one room public school in Moccasin. From the sixth grade through

high school, however, they are bussed to Fredonia, twelve miles to the east. Approximately 10 Paiute children are not in high school and four others are attending college. (Euler 1972a:92–94)

Opportunities for producing individual income on the reservation have increased. A few Indians are employed by federal or state agencies. For others, stock raising provides income, and some derive wages from work on nearby ranches owned by non-Indians. Tourism was initiated in the 1970s, providing many possibilities and promise.

Anticipating land claims funds, the Kaibab Tribal Council allocated 15 percent of the total claim payment to per capita distribution, at a rate slightly over $1,000 per individual. An additional 15 percent was budgeted for a "family plan." Those funds, distributed by the council, to enable families to pay off past debts, obtain household furnishings, and other immediate family needs. The remaining 70 percent of the land claim monies were budgeted as follows: education, 10 percent; tribal enterprises, 35 percent; community development, 15 percent; and administration, 10 percent.

The Shivwits Indian Reservation

In the very southwestern corner of Utah, on a desolate 27,000-acre reservation, a Paiute people called the Shivwits lived. They were only beginning to have contact with non-Indians by 1870. When their land was offered for sale some years ago through a Salt Lake City bank, no one who wanted to buy it could be found (Anderson 1971).

Theirs was plateau land, through which the Santa Clara River flows. U.S. Highway 91 led through the reservation from Saint George, Utah, to the Arizona and Nevada borders. Between 150 and 200 were on the census roll. They lived in broken-down shacks. It now appears that their separate identity is no longer noted.

The Chemehuevi Indians

Chemehuevi is the Yuman name for a group of Indians who were a part of the true Paiute, and were associated with them and the Ute in one linguistic subdivision of the Shoshonean tongue (see Fowler and Fowler, 1971:5,7). They called themselves Tantáwats, meaning "southern men."

Anciently, they lived in the eastern half of the Mohave Desert, and it has been estimated that there were between 500 and 800 of them. They lived in small huts of Paiute type, usually low shelters covered with dirt and of temporary nature. Their means of subsistence was seasonal plant-gathering and hunting, with a few attempts at growing meager crops near springs (Stewart 1967:14). They made excellent baskets. In 1776 no Chemehuevi lived on the Colorado River below Eldorado Canyon. Later, they settled on Cottonwood Island, about fifteen miles north of Davis Dam, in the Chemehuevi valley, and at other points on the Colorado River. Here they were under strong Mohave and Yuma influence, which are discussed in the following section.

It is reported that although the Chemehuevi continued to stress basketry, they began to imitate the Mohave in making a few pottery vessels, quite in the Mohave manner. The men started to wear their hair in Mohave fashion, rolling it into thin "ropes" that hung down the back. They took over the use of tule rafts and log rafts, and "the Yuman practice of ferrying goods and children across the river in large pots." The Chemehuevi had known the practices of interment and of cremation; they followed the Yumans in cremating bodies and possessions of the deceased in a special rite, and in a mourning ceremony wherein images of the dead were housed in a special structure (*see* Drucker 1937).

Another source states that, "Once on the river the Chemehuevi seem to have become a more definite political entity, with a chief called the *towintem*, who had more authority or at least more influence than Chemehuevi leaders had previously possessed." Their religion took on Mohave characteristics; they began to sing song cycles which told of mythological events, in the Mohave manner. And "like his Mohave counterpart, the Chemehuevi shaman dreamed his power to cure" (Stewart, K. M. 1967:16). The Chemehuevi also adopted certain Mohave modes of making war.

On 2 February 1907, the Chemehuevi Indian Reservation was created by the Secretary of the Interior, and became the home of the Chemehuevi. It was located roughly halfway between Parker, Arizona, and Needles in San Bernardino county, California. Then, in 1940, the river bottom lands totaling about 7,776 acres were sold to Los Angeles Metropolitan Water District and deeded back to the U.S. government for control. The Chemehuevi were paid $108,342 for the land. Eleven allotments—the only ones ever made on the Chemehuevi reservation—were assigned within the river bottom area. They were all sold and the land is now under water. The balance of the reservation—approximately 28,000 acres—was not productive without expensive irrigation facilities.

With the construction of Parker Dam on the Colorado River, which was completed in 1938, virtually all of the arable acres came to be inundated by the water of Lake Havasu. Insofar as was known in 1970, only one Chemehuevi was living on the reservation. The others were moved to the Colorado River Indian Reservation, and became enrolled members of the Colorado River Indian Tribes. It was estimated that the membership included 600 Chemehuevi.

The Chemehuevi observe no tribal or religious ceremonies. Indeed, it was found that only one old basket maker remained of the tribe.

AS ONCE, SO WERE WE

We are the native Americans;
This was our land from sea to sea.
Our thoughts were all thoughts,
As once, so were we.

But time seemed to change
When the white man came;
Came he, mighty in strength,
As once, so were we.

"Never mind," said my father,
"The world will go on."
And he chanted and prayed
and sang his death song:

The Earth is my Mother,
She will always be near.
The Sun, my Father,
I have nothing to fear.
The Moon is my Sister,
Standing with me at night.
The Stars are my Cousins
Who guide me in flight.
The Great Spirit is my God
Of life and of love.
We will soon be with Him
In His land up above.

By Raymond Hamilton, Mariposa-Paiute-Tuolumne

From *The Writers' Reader,* Fall, 1966.
The Institute of American Indian Arts,
Santa Fe, N.M.

6

The Ranchería Peoples

In contrast to the Pueblo peoples, the great majority of aboriginal dwellers of southern Arizona (and northwestern Mexico), although equally sedentary, did not live in compact, closely built settlements. Their houses might be scattered at some distance from each other, thus forming loose settlements here and there on the farmlands, or *rancherias*. A group occupying these locations might shift from one ranchería to another during the course of a year. They were all agriculturists, with farming their major activity. Among these peoples, as among the Pueblos, many similarities obtained. Especially in their economy were they alike; in community structure they were more disparate. Most of them spoke languages belonging to the Uto-Aztecan stock, such as the Pimans and Cahitans. But, other than these, the Yumans belonged to another linguistic family, the Hokan-Siouan. Their range was to the northwest of the other ranchería peoples.

The Colorado River Indian Tribes

The Colorado River Indian Reservation was established by Act of Congress, and approved by the President on 3 March 1865. The boundaries were subsequently fixed and determined by Executive Orders dated 22 November 1873, 16 November 1876, and 22 November 1915.

The reservation lies in a valley along the lower course of the Colorado River.

Although surrounded by mountains, the valley is definitely desert with an elevation of approximately 400 feet above sea level. Characteristic vegetation of the valley consists of cactus, mesquite, and *chaparral,* or dense thickets of thorny shrubs; arrowweed grows along the river. Average rainfall is about four inches per year. No snow falls in the valley, but the surrounding mountains are sometimes capped with light snow in the wintertime. The average humidity is generally 15 percent, but at times it runs between 55 and 60 percent. The mean temperature averages 71°F., ranging from an average minimum of 56°F. to an average maximum of 86°F., the average extreme maximum temperature being 97°F. In December and January the average low temperature is 39°F., and in June, July and August, the average high temperature is 110–113°F.

The first expenditure of federal funds for irrigation development in the U.S.A. was made for work on this reservation in 1867, with fifty thousand dollars being spent. All the work was done with shovels and baskets by about five hundred Indians. Because of faulty design and an unusually high water level in the river, the canal washed out as soon as the gates were opened. In 1874 another canal was completed; it too met with failure. Additional appropriations followed for canal construction, pumping facilities, engineering studies, and construction of Headgate Rock Dam, a diversion structure that was placed in operation on 4 July 1942.

In 1873 the first school on the reservation was opened.

During World War II, the War Relocation Authority built camps on the reservation and relocated approximately nineteen thousand Japanese there. These camps were closed and the Japanese removed in 1944. A year later, sixteen Hopi families were relocated on the Colorado River Indian Reservation. During subsequent years, one hundred and fourteen Navajo families and three Havasupai families were colonized on irrigated lands on the reservation. The program was ended in 1952.

The Colorado River Indian Reservation is approximately 264,250 acres in size, with 225,914 acres located in Yuma county, Arizona, and 38,366 acres situated in San Bernardino and Riverside counties, California. The reservation agency is headquarters for the Fort Yuma Subagency, Yuma, Arizona (located on the Fort Yuma Indian Reservation, California), and for the Indian reservations of Fort Mohave (Needles, California), Chemehuevi, and the Cocopah around the mouth of the Colorado River (Somerton, Arizona).

The Fort Mohave Reservation

This reservation is situated along both sides of the Colorado River, being partly within Mohave County, Arizona; San Bernardino County, California; and Clark County, Nevada. The land generally extends from a point across the river from Needles to a point about fifteen miles north of that city. The part west of the river begins some five miles north of Needles and is divided into two areas—one in California and one in Nevada. The northerly part of the lands is an integral area, while the southerly part, east of the river, is a checkerboard area, the sections alternating. The terrain is desertlike with brushy first bench land and river wash areas as well as portions of the river channel.

Agency headquarters is in Parker, Arizona, and the Mohave tribal offices are in Needles. The Fort Mohave Reservation was established by Executive Order, 19 September 1880. Another Order of 1 December 1910 enlarged the reservation, but one of 2 February 1911 revoked that order and added other lands to the reservation. Then an act of 8 July 1940 granted the right to take specific Mohave lands within the reservation that would be needed for construction of the Parker Dam and Reservoir, up to the 455-foot contour line. "At no time did they intend or authorize a taking for any other purpose. Nevertheless, when the trustee later issued an order designating the Mojave [see the Linguistic notes of p. xxvi] lands needed for the authorized purpose, no mention was made of the 455-foot contour limitation. Instead, the specific lands were erroneously described by metes and bounds, thereby resulting in an unauthorized seizure of several thousands of acres of Mojave land."

Then, we are informed:

. . . the Indian Claims Commission declared that title still resides in the Fort Mojave Tribe in regard to the several thousand acres of land to which reference has been made.

There are two categories of Mojave land included in the several thousand acres thus seized without authority: (1)Indian lands occupied and fenced by the Fish and Wildlife Bureau of [the] Department [of the Interior] far exceeding the area flooded by Parker Dam and in no manner required for that purpose; (2)Lands which have been flooded for which no compensation was paid. (Fort Mojave Tribal Council 1970. Letter of 27 October 1970.)

The present reservation of 22,820 acres is owned in undivided shares by tribal members, and is held in trust for them by the federal government. Slightly more than 500 people live on the reservation. That their claims to title have not had due recognition or protection from the federal government is observable through one injustice after another that the Indians have suffered for more than the past three decades.

In 1962, when a case arose between the Indians and the federal government, the U.S. Attorney, purportedly in behalf of the Indians, abandoned their cause and argued against them. Primary results were that the Indians lost possession of lands (which many think should be returned to them) and a legal barrier has been interposed, denying them redress in present claims—which have received no support, apparently, from the Justice Department. The Indians state that:

Seizure by the United States, trustee of Fort Mojave Indian Property, has transpired throughout the entire reach of the Colorado River as it traverses or borders upon the Fort Mojave Indian Reservation. That seizure stems in part from acquisitions by the Bureau of Reclamation in the name of the United States which have cut off entirely or gravely impeded the Mojaves' access to the Colorado River to which they are legally entitled. Loss of access is tantamount to imperiling for all time the full economic potential of the Mojave lands.

There are at least seve' ''bstantial areas in which the right to access of the Mojaves to the Colorado Rive. has been seized in its entirety or gravely impeded, all as stated above. In all, there are approximately 12 miles of land lying on both sides of the Colorado River where the irreparable damage to the Indians as described above has taken place. (Letter of 27 October 1970)

The Secretary of the Interior, as the principal agent for the government and trustee for the Indians, was beseeched to "take speedy and adequate steps fully to assert on behalf of the Mohave Indians their rights of access to the Colorado River which have been seized from them without authority." (Fort Mohave Tribal Council 1970. Letter of 27 October 1970, as follow up of an urgent telegram sent about six weeks before to the Secretary of the Interior.)

The Mohave People

The Mohave and Yuma peoples spoke a different language from that of the Chemehuevi, being of the Yuman linguistic group of the Hokan-Siouan family. It is said that the Mohave called themselves *Tzi-na-ma-a* before they came to live along the Colorado River. "Mohave" is taken from a native word, *hamakave,* referring to Needles, and signifying "three mountains" (Swanton 1952:356). These people came to dwell on both sides of the stream, mostly on the east side, between Needles and the entrance to Black Canyon. Theirs was a ranchería type of life. Early Spanish explorers mentioned their villages. Oñate met them in 1604–1605, and Garcés found their settlements in 1775–1776 (Galvin 1967:v, 12ff.). No Spanish towns or missions were established in the Mohave territory. The Mohave were said to number 3,000 in 1680 and 1770.

The earliest Anglos to enter Mohaveland were fur trappers and fur traders. They came from 1826–1834, but their visits had slight effect on Mohave culture. It was the coming of others, after the midcentury, that caused uneasiness among the Indians. In an encounter with soldiers in 1859, many of the Mohave were killed. From 1900 on, they apparently decreased steadily, and their enrollment shifted from one Indian agency to another.

The Mohave of Old

In their initial state the Mohave subsisted by small scale farming, gathering of wild plant foods, trapping, and hunting and fishing. A hunter gave away what he killed. Floodwater irrigation was utilized in the production of corn, melons, pumpkins, and several wild herbs. When floods did not occur and crops failed, the people ate mesquite beans; they ate beaver, but would not eat turtles, snakes or lizards as did the Chemehuevi and other desert dwellers.

The Mohave had hereditary chiefs in the male line—men of honor and dignity—but their functions are said to have been obscure. Much more influential were the brave men, war leaders, and shamans. Their enemies were the Cocopah, Pima, Papago, and Maricopa. Friendly peoples were the Yuma, Chemehuevi, Yavapai, and western Apache.

Homes of the Mohave were built of logs and wood, with roofs thatched with arrowweed and covered with sand. They were usually about twenty by twenty-five feet in size, and the door was always to the south because of the frequent cold north winds of the desert.

The Mohave attire generally was similar to that of other lower Colorado River peoples, but had its own characteristics. Both men and women commonly wore loincloths, covering the upper body only in inclement weather; they went barefoot and bareheaded. A woman's dress was made in two parts— separate back and front aprons of willow bark strips hung from waist cords. The front piece fell to the knees; it was donned first, with its cord tied in back. The calf-length back apron which was thicker was tied in front; it lapped over at the hips but left the outside of the thighs somewhat bare. A short underapron was worn at all times beneath the front apron; it was made of fine willow bark.

The breechclout of the men was held in place by a belt, the ends forming a short flip in front and a longer one in back—to the knees or below. These were made of willow bark strips in a checkerboard weave. When an upper garment was worn—a privilege of only a few—it was of rabbitskin strips held together with cords, obtained by trade from the Walapai Indians, or a wool poncho bartered from the Navajo. Sandals were worn by men and women only when traveling. No leggings were worn, nor hats. Sometimes men tied downy feathers or quills to the crown hair of their heads.

These people were long famous for the artistic painting of their bodies. Some tattooing was also done, though it is rare now.

Crafts and Implements

Pottery was made by the Mohave in at least three distinctive forms. A strong association was felt between their pottery and their agriculture. A harvest of food was not complete until bowls had been made for cooking and storing it. The men and women worked together. Clay had to be tempered with crushed standstone, and the pottery vessels were built up by the coiling process; they were decorated with a yellow ochre pigment, which turned to a dull red upon being fired—by means of an open wood fire.

Mohave basketry was very poor, both in quality and in its paucity of types; none is made today. The only true basketry receptacle made was a flat tray, slightly oval in outline, some eighteen inches broad at the wider end, and two feet long. These were made of slender willow twigs twined at intervals with split willow twigs, and a rim was fashioned of a thick willow branch

bound on with long split mesquite root strands. The trays were used for sift-
ing chaff from ground mesquite pods or corn, or for cooling parched seeds. A
netted structure supported by a framework of sticks served as a carrying frame.
A headring used for carrying was made of willow bark; women used these to
bear the forehead band of the carrying frame, or to support pottery or other
burdens carried on the head, including the baby cradles when carried lying
flat on the head. Otherwise cradles were held horizontally on the hip, never
on the back.

When imported glass beads became available, the Mohave accepted them
eagerly. To this day they do beautiful beadwork.

Gourds in a variety of shapes were used for carrying water and storing seeds.
Globular gourds were made into rattles, with a wooden handle inserted in
the stem end and fastened with gum of greasewood and arrowweed. Two parallel rows of tiny holes formed a decorative cross on the body of the rattle.

The Mohave used slim shinny sticks with moderate curve. Their bows were
shaped like a shallow *D*, nearly straight for most of the length and tips curved
toward the string. The bow staves were made of willow or screw bean (*tornil-
lo*), or mesquite. Length of a bow depended upon the height of the man who
carried it—the ideal length being from ground to the chin. Hunting bows
were shorter than war bows, averaging three and a half to four feet. The Mohave had great interest in warfare; they were brave and had notable leaders,
or war chiefs. Their fighting was primarily hand-to-hand, when they could
charge upon their enemies with war club and bare hands, or the bow and
arrow (Spier 1955).

Dream Life

In addition to their concrete day-to-day living, they set great importance
upon their dream life; and even today they passively drift away without ex-
ternal inducement, such as drink, drugs, dancing or costume garments. From
these dreams—which to the Mohave are regular visits with their ancestors—
come their decisions and their principal motivations. Religious interest re-
volves around funeral ceremonies, in which they cremate their dead with rites
and loud wailing; the meager supply of personal belongings is burned with
the owner.

Changes in Attire

After a time, the basic agricultural products were expanded to include beans,
cantaloupes, and wheat. With the improved economy, other changes took
place. The older women wear long, full dresses of bright print, with scarves
on their heads. When a death occurs in the family the women may cut their
hair which, otherwise, is worn long and straight. The older men dress as
most westerners, with denim pants, western shirts, boots, and large hats.

The younger men and women and the children dress as do their Anglo contemporaries.

The People and Their Ceremonies

The Mohave men are inclined to be tall, large-boned, and lean. The women are not so tall and are prone to be stout; they have good-natured faces. Skin color is of a noticeably yellow hue. The people are responsive, energetic, and smiling.

Most of the ancient Mohave ceremonies have become extinct. A bird dance has been preserved, and is colorfully performed by a small group, carefully costumed, at celebrations and public gatherings. Several times during the decade of the 1960s and thereafter, this group presented its dance at the Intertribal Indian Ceremonial at Gallup, New Mexico.

Altogether, the present cultural picture is in sharp contrast with that of the past.

Political and Economic Development

The Colorado River Reservation, 225,995 acres in extent, is on the Parker, Arizona, side of the river. There Mohave, Chemehuevi, Fort Yuma, and certain other Indians live together as the Colorado River Tribes. They number around 2,100, of whom perhaps 500 dwell off the reservation. They accepted the Indian Reorganization Act, have a constitution, and hold elections on the first Saturday of December every second year. The adult members vote by secret ballot. Their council, which governs the reservation, is made up of male and female members; it meets the second Saturday of each month at 9:00 A.M. in the council chambers in Parker.

They have several active committees, each with its chairman. Tribal operations relate to tribal government, enrollment, and claims; the improvement of social, economic, and political status; and the assuming of greater responsibility in the management of their own affairs. Programs under way include Community Action, Community Development, Headstart, and NYC (Neighborhood Youth Corps). They have their own code of law and order, tribal police and tribal court.

A new tribal administrative office building and a library have been built about a mile south of the agency. Across from these is a recreation center with a large building where fairs, socials, carnivals, and other events are held; there, too, is a baseball field and bleachers, an outdoor basketball court, and an outdoor stage for shows and contests. North of Parker the Indians are in the recreation business in a big way; they operate the Bluewater marina, with *cabañas,* trailer park, restaurant, gift shop, a boat launching pad, and judges' stand for boat racing. The Indians are attractive, gracious, and efficient hosts and hostesses. They are exceptionally progressive and farsighted, and are making great progress in their program to become entirely self-sufficient.

The winters there are so mild that fishing, boating, and picnicking continue throughout the year (*see* Brennan 1967). Several motorboat races are held during the spring, and a two-day rodeo in November. Hunting is good on the reservation (ducks, geese, quail and doves), as is fishing. Permits are issued for these sports.

It is the general mission of the Colorado River BIA to administer Indian affairs within its jurisdiction, in cooperation with the Indian people in planning, executing, and coordinating the BIA's extensive and varied programs. These cover education, welfare, law enforcement, soil and moisture conservation, range management, irrigation, extension, forest management, road construction and maintenance, realty, credit, plant management, development of local self-government and tribal undertakings, industrial development, employment assistance and vocational training.

Land and Water

The most important single program, probably, has to do with the maintenance of subjugated lands and the development of more such land. In this, the operation of an extensive irrigation system, carrying water diverted from the Colorado River on the Arizona side, and hydrographic investigation, surveying, construction of facilities, drainage and seeding activities are said to be of paramount importance. The Indians have shown marked ability to take advantage of the latest advances in farming, such as use of modern equipment, methods, fertilizers, and insecticides. Several packing sheds operate in Parker during various harvesting seasons.

The U.S. Supreme Court has ruled that the Indians have "perfected water rights from the Colorado River" and permission to grant long-term leases to non-Indians: twenty-five years for residential land, ninety-nine years for recreational and commercial land (Brennan 1967:18). Fifty thousand acres are now farmed by the Indians for themselves or lessees, and 107,000 acres are guaranteed a first-class irrigation system for the future. Market crops of alfalfa, barley, cantaloupes, carrots, cotton, corn silage double-cropped with maize, lettuce, and small grains are reported in truly fabulous yields and all the year round. Ten thousand sheep are wintered and cattle are fattened for market in feed lots. All prospects point to brilliant success, according to the most modern standards, if the Mojave can withstand the machinations and rapacity of financial dealings in the modern age.

Recently, like so many other of the Indian peoples, the Mohave and the Chemehuevi have developed a new awareness of their former cultural products. In 1970, upon learning of a collection of Mohave beadwork and pottery and Chemehuevi baskets which had been assembled by a pioneer storekeeper in Parker, Arizona, and was being auctioned off in Phoenix to settle an estate, members of the two Indian groups mortgaged their best land to raise fifty thousand dollars with which to purchase part of their heritage. They had to bid against dealers and collectors who were willing to pay as much as two hundred dollars each for the five hundred pieces which are irreplaceable today; nothing like them remained on the reservations. A Chemehuevi woman remarked that their basketry never had been made for sale, "but for use in this world and the next." She said, "It would never do to bury a Chemehuevi without a basket" (Anonymous 1970d). The items that they were successful in purchasing were for their tribal museum. The Indians' intent was to elicit as much information as possible regarding them from their old people, and to have the collection available for research purposes.

Employment, Housing, and Education

Many of the Indians on the Colorado River Reservation work for the BIA and the U.S. Public Health Service. The latter maintains a fully staffed hospital and field clinic at the agency for the people of the reservation; it can be used by the public in emergencies only. Positions for the Indians include clerks and office workers, carpenters, janitors, bus drivers, cooks, hospital aids, tractor and dragline operators, oilers, truck drivers, surveyors, stakemen, rodmen, engineering aids, ditchriders, mechanics, linemen and groundmen on the power crew, road grader operators, policemen, accountants, teachers, and nurses.

Quarters for the majority of the BIA employees have been furnished at or near the agency, at nominal rentals. They range from very good to poor, but all are equipped with coolers. Living accommodations in Parker are very scarce, and are generally more expensive. Electricity, natural gas, and bottled gas are all available in the area.

The public school system maintains a grammar school and a high school in Parker for both Indian and non-Indian children, and a grammar school at Poston, seventeen miles from Parker, for Indian and non-Indian children. The schools are considered very good; they are accredited, and they have good hot lunch programs. Transportation is provided for all pupils living out of town. Very active programs are provided for the youngsters in 4H, FFA, sports, and recreation.

An increasing number of Indian boys and girls from this reservation attend college. Several have won scholarships, and several others are assisted by grants from the tribes or the federal government. These students are said to encounter about the same problems as other college students, and they make about the same grades as average students.

Law Enforcement

Indians and non-Indians cooperate in law enforcement. Offenses committed by non-Indians on the Indian reservations of Arizona are handled by state or county officers exactly as if they had taken place in any non-Indian community. This applies also in most civil cases. Offenses committed by Indians on reservations within Arizona are handled through two courts: (1) if the offense committed is one of the eleven major crimes, it is handled through Federal District Court by the FBI and assistant U.S. Attorney General; (2) if the offense is of the misdemeanor type, the offender is arrested by the tribal policeman or BIA special officer and prosecuted by tribal court. All civil cases wherein the defendant is an Indian and the tort originated on the reservation are handled by tribal courts.

The Yuman (Quechan) People

Yuma is said to be an ancient Pima and Papago Indian term for the Indians that comprised one of the oldest groups of the old Yuman-speaking stock. Although commonly called "Yuman Indians," these people actually are *Quechan,* who speak a dialect of the Yuma language. "Quechan" derives from *xam kwatcan,* or "another going down" [on the legendary trail by which they came] (Johnston 1970:64). Their prehistoric domain "stretched from the Pacific coast in the region of the present international boundary eastward through the mountains, across the southern portion of the less arid south-central valley of California to the Colorado River and beyond into the western portion of the elevated area of Arizona north of the Gila River" (Ezell and Ezell 1970:170). In early historic times they occupied both sides of the Colorado, fifty or sixty miles from the mouth thereof, at and below its junction with the Gila. Fort Yuma was in the approximate center of that territory. *(Rel.* Cleland 1980.)

The first explorer to mention the Yuman people by name was Father Kino, in 1701–1702. Later Spanish travelers spoke of them increasingly. They numbered between 3,000 and 3,500. With the treaty of Guadalupe Hidalgo in 1848, most of the Yuma lands passed to the control of the United Sates; the Gadsden Purchase (1853) completed the transfer. Fort Yuma was established and relationships between the Yuma and the settlers in the territory became close.

The Fort Yuma Reservation

The Fort Yuma Reservation was established by Executive Order of 6 July 1883, amended 9 January 1884, and included approximately 48,608 acres in the reservation proper. Then, on 4 December 1893, through agreement between the Fort Yuma Indians and the United States all land not considered irrigable was returned to the public domain. Congress ratified that agreement, and a reservation of 8,661 acres was established. In 1912 the reservation was allotted to the Fort Yuma Indians. It now has 2,061 acres.

The elevation of the reservation land varies from one hundred and twenty-five feet along the river to one hundred and forty feet along the All American Canal. On the hill where the subagency headquarters is located, the elevation rises to two hundred and sixty seven feet above sea level. The land is very good for farming, and it produces high yields when proper practices are followed.

In the Yuma country the climate is very dry, and all farming is done by irrigation. Annual rainfall amounts to approximately three inches, sufficient to support desert flora only. The evaporation rate is very high. Mean annual temperature is 71.9°F. The summers are long and hot, with a maximum temperature of 125°F, and the winters are short and mild with a minimum of 22°F.

The Quechan have been battling federal authorities on the issues of land and water for many years. Irrigation canals bisect their reservation; they run full of water—into non-Indian hands. One of the Quechan men recently said: "We have a one-inch pipe that brings water into our reservation. At the end of the line, there just is no pressure. We have had to stand by helplessly while several houses there have burned." Despite the ample water in the canals, the Indians cannot get more for their own use (Mangel 1970:42–43).

Living on the Fort Yuma Reservation are some 1,500 enrolled Indians, several hundred of whom live off the reservation. As the Quechan Tribe they adopted a constitution and bylaws on 28 November 1936. A council of seven members governs the group; these men and women are elected to office by popular vote every four years.

The Cocopah People

The Cocopah represent the only remaining group of a series of important Yuman-speaking peoples that occupied the delta of the Colorado River in aboriginal times. All originally dwelt in Mexico, until the U.S. border extended into their territory. The name *Cocopah* is said to derive from Mohave *Kwi-ka-pah* (*see* Bahti 1968:63, 1980). They were first mentioned by Europeans about 1605 when they lived in nine rancherias near the river's mouth. These rancherias were inhabited by related people. In 1771 the Cocopah occupied all of the southern one-third of the delta, but four years later they had been pushed to the west side of the river. Garcés reached them in December of 1775. Later, they occupied scattered settlements on both sides of the stream; and in 1900 it was estimated that about six hundred resided on each side, in three major divisions.

Those most favorably located practiced small-scale farming, with corn, beans, black-eyed peas, pumpkins and melons, primarily. Cultivated foods were supplemented by wild ones: seeds, roots and fruits; fish, game and eggs. Nearly all vegetal foods and some fish—derived from the Colorado River and the Gulf of California—were dried and stored for winter. The Cocopah hunted singly on foot, but group hunting came about with the use of horses. Rats and dogs frequently were eaten.

The dwellings were of various types, ranging from thatched temporary structures to more permanent mud-and-wattle houses. Small granaries were constructed with floors elevated above the ground.

Formerly, shamanism was practiced extensively, primarily for curing the ill. Everything was dream-directed. Women were tattooed and men's features pierced for ornaments; this was believed to be necessary to prevent wandering of the soul after death. Religious activities revolved around death ceremonies, and the dead were cremated. The name of a deceased one was never spoken.

Socially, a loose division of labor was observed. Adult men and women with established families bore the main responsibilities. Men were responsible for the planting, hunting and fishing; women did most of the gathering; and everyone participated in the harvesting. Children had only occasional chores.

Some pottery was made for domestic use, but this industry died out a number of years ago. Loom weaving was practiced and crudely woven cylinders of basketry were made. These were without bottom or top and were set upright on the ground and filled with beans and other items. Shell beads were made to some extent, and several kinds of nets for catching fish.

The Cocopah engaged to a considerable degree in warfare, mostly of the club and bow and arrow variety. War activities were carried on for hundreds of years, with formalized war patterns and leadership, yet the concept of leadership was not expanded to their political and social systems. It has been said that:

> Disintegration of Cocopa culture and economy probably began with the disruption of war in the 'fifties, which removed a major field of interest for which, apparently, no substitute was found. Then came the river boats, and an appetite was created for American goods and foods. Finally, after 1900, when the irrigation companies began harnessing the Colorado, the Cocopa served as a source of cheap labor, and a wage economy was inaugurated. During the years between 1905 and 1907, when the Colorado was flowing into the Salton Sea, the Cocopa were left high and dry in their delta habitat. Not only was there no water for their farms, but the same lack prevented the growth of wild plants, and reduced the fish and game supply. It was a question of move or starve. (Kelly, D. S. 1950:167)

Lacking leadership of political, religious, or social nature, their economy and culture declined rapidly. As a people, the Cocopah became impoverished to an almost unbelievable degree. They lived under substandard conditions. It was estimated that probably no more than three hundred of them lived on each side of the International border (Johnston 1970:64).

An article written by the senior editor of *Look* (2 June 1970), and factually illustrated, revealed the Cocopah's plight.

Driving along the dirt bank of an irrigation canal, the author noted that

> The canal itself, conduit for the valuable water flowing to farmers inland, is neatly cemented and fenced, sharp contrast to the shanties lining its side. The desert grit cuts your eyes and seeps into your mouth and nose even after the car windows roll shut. The kids wipe uselessly at running noses with their sleeves. (Without adequate shelter, clothing, diet or medicine, Indian children remain the number one victims of the respiratory infections that other Americans no longer consider dangerous.) (Mangel 1970:39)

This article was not exaggerated; anthropologists found conditions to be as revealed here.

The writer described one of the houses as a nine by twelve foot shelter made of flattened cardboard cartons; the six-foot high roof, made of the same materials, was held down by two old automobile tires. Income of the person who lived in it was $67 a month from welfare. Other residents were found to be living under similar conditions. Cocopah unemployment was cited as "an incredible nine out of ten men."

It was further reported that:

Welfare keeps them alive, with a family income of about $1,000. Among the adolescents, virtually everyone I met had quit school. They desperately seek release from boredom and poverty. Indians have the highest suicide rate in the nation. Two young Cocopah killed themselves the month before I arrived. One was 16, the other, 18. Both had left school years before.

Timidity clouds the Cocopah future. Penniless, disorganized, they are uncertain of their own direction or of where to turn for aid. The BIA, under new and tougher local leadership, is beginning to stir, but slowly. (Ten houses—abandoned when a Marine air base was closed—have been trucked in to one of the three different sites that comprise the Cocopah reservation.) The bedrock problems of schools and job training and employment remain untouched. Cocopah men and women, like Indians elsewhere, are slow to leave the reservations for jobs even if they have the skills and the perseverance to withstand employer prejudice (33 Indian men went to Yuma two years ago to enroll with the Federal employment office; not one has yet been offered a job). The public schools to which most Indian children today are assigned clearly are failing them (eight Indians from one local school attempted junior college in the past few years; none could handle it). (Mangel 1970:41–42)

Now, two decades later, it may be reported that outside assistance came to the Cocopah who lived on about 1,772 acres of reserved land (*Tribal Directory,* Arizona Commission on Indian Affairs, 1981:6). The U.S. Public Health Service helped the Cocopah to improve their houses to some extent, to better the sanitary conditions, and to bring electricity and running water to the community.

Other governmental agencies also rendered aid. The OEO stimulated revolutionary happenings among the Cocopah people, and within the BIA which had ignored them much of the time since 1917. Private foundations and individuals moved to assist the Cocopah to achieve a satisfying life. Under competent Cocopah leadership, they are now on the move. (*See* Alvarez de Williams 1974.)

The Cocopah Reservation

An Executive Order of 27 September 1917 established the Cocopah Reservation, setting apart 528 acres for use of the Cocopah Indians; and Public Law 87-150 of 17 August 1961 granted 81 acres of public domain to them. Of the 609 acres, about one hundred are used for small subsistence plots and some for growing cotton. All reservation lands are held by the tribe. Individual plots are assigned for family farms and homesteads. A few of the Cocopah and the Quechan farm for a living, but most of them work for other ranchers or are employed as wage earners in and around the city of Yuma. Water is currently plentiful, and irrigation water is supplied at a reasonable cost.

Approximately 835 Cocopah Indians are enrolled on the Cocopah roster. A number of Cocopah are not eligible for enrollment because of their Mexican birth. Those born in the United States are citizens and eligible for enrollment. Membership in the tribe and residence on the reservation is open to all Cocopah, whether enrolled or not. Enrollment originally was a matter of individual family choice.

Cocopah government is under the control of a five-member council, elected to office by popular vote. Elections are held in even numbered years on the second Friday in July. The council meets monthly, every second Friday at 1:00 P.M., at Somerton, Arizona.

YUMA CURING SONG

Your heart is good.
[The Spirit] Shining Darkness will be here.
You think only of sad unpleasant things,
You are to think of goodness.
Lie down and sleep here.
Shining Darkness will join us.
You think of this goodness in your dream.
Goodness will be given to you,
I will speak for it, and it will come to pass.
It will happen here,
I will ask for your good,
It will happen as I sit by you,
It will be done as I sit here in this place.

From *Ethnography of the Yuma Indians*
by C. Daryll Forde.

The Pai

"The People": One Ethnic Group

It is said that the native northeasternmost Pai Indians considered themselves as one ethnic group—"the only true human beings on earth," or, in the prevailing notion, "The People." These Pai occupied an area in northwest-central Arizona, "between the Colorado River on the west and north, its Little Colorado tributary on the east, and on the south a line through the San Francisco Peaks, Bill Williams Mountain, Picacho, and down Chino Creek, the Santa Maria River, and Bill Williams Fork." We are told:

These Indians not only spoke a common language but shared a common culture at the time they were first seen by Europeans. During the long period of Spanish and Mexican sovereignty in the Southwest, this group always was designated in Spanish as *Cosninas,* a hispanicized form of the Hopi term for these people, *Ko'ho'-nin* [Cohonina]. The Spaniards, few of whom beside Fray Francisco Garces achieved direct contact with the Pai, preserved the native Indian concept for the "tribal" or cultural unity of this group.

When Anglo-Americans invaded the Southwest and conquered its native peoples, accidents of geographic patterning of their contacts with the Pai led them to conceive of this ethnic group as two "tribes." For a century, therefore, Anglo-Americans have written and thought about "Walapais" and "Havasupais" while the Indians in question continue still to think of themselves as simply Pai. (Dobyns and Euler 1960:49)

"Walapai," or "Hualapai," is said to come from the native Yuman word, *Xawálapáiya,* meaning "pine tree folk" (Swanton 1952:365). It appears that the first mention of them was made in 1776 by Father Garcés, but it is possible that other Spanish explorers encountered them earlier. At any rate, they were never directly affected by the Spaniards. It has been stated that the major effects that Spanish colonization had on the Pai were:

1. an intensification of Pai trade and social intercourse with the Western Pueblos, with a corresponding shift in Pai reference group orientation toward the east, and 2. the beginning of deterioration in some native Pai handicrafts caused by the importation of Spanish goods, which led eventually to substitution of European-made artifacts for native products on a very large scale. In 1776 Garces found the westernmost band of Pai already using Spanish belts, awls, and other implements they had acquired from New Mexico indirectly via Hopi middlemen.(Coues 1900, II:320)

Beginning in 1826, hostilities arose between the Pai and non-Indians; first with French-Canadian and Anglo-American trappers, and then with slave raiders from the Territory of New Mexico. About 1842, the Pai, who for some years avoided all possible contacts with outsiders, bridled their fear of non-Indian expeditions and began to engage in military actions to preserve their independence and integrity.

After the Southwest was acquired by the U.S.A., a new era of exploration and colonization opened. Captain Lorenzo Sitgreaves, in 1851, encountered eastern Pai bands northeast of Flagstaff, Arizona, and in the upper Truxton Canyon area; and one of his guides (Leroux) was attacked by the Cerbat Mountain Pai band (Dobyns and Euler 1960:50). Six and seven years later, Lt. E. F. Beale traversed the country of the Pai, and mention was made of a Pai band at Peach Springs, Arizona.

The western bands became known to the federal troops as "Walapai," from the *Hawhala pa'a* band—the one Garcés had noted in 1776. By the close of the War of the Rebellion, "a number of small prospectors' camps were scattered along the western slopes of the Cerbat and Hualapai Mountains where two mining districts had been organized" (Dobyns and Euler 1960:53, 1961:8–22).

Mining developments, establishment of military posts, and freighting roads wrought increasing changes during the nineteenth century. In 1866, "a typical race-prejudiced frontier type" killed the principal chief of the southern Pai bands. Those bands and the western Pai responded in accord with their time-hallowed traditions and exacted vengeance on the settlers, precipitating "the Walapai War" (Dobyns et al. 1957:61).

Unfortunately for the Pai, the western bands went over to the offensive just after the end of the civil conflict in the United States, when men who had found a taste for military life during the war years sought to justify their continued employment in a reduced but still oversized military establishment with far too many senior officers. In the summer of 1867 the river steamers deposited at Fort Mojave contingents of veteran regulars under Lieut. Colonel William Redwood Price to undertake the subjugation of the western Pai bands, labeled "Walapai" and thought of as a tribe.

Lieut. Colonel Price pursued a policy of harrying the elusive western and southern Pai bands as often as possible with the aid of detachments from the post at Fort Whipple, seeking to precipitate a decisive battle. Actually, the Pai won all the pitched battles fought, choosing their ground carefully, and accepting battle commitment only when they enjoyed equal or superior firepower and superior tactical position behind good rock cover. Price's scorched earth tactics eventually brought the "Walapai" to admit defeat and sue for peace. Effective peace was re-established in 1869, the western and southern Pai admitting Anglo-American military superiority. (U.S. Senate 1936, *in* Dobyns and Euler 1960:53–54)

The social relationship between the conquerers and conquered peoples was yet to be fully clarified, however, for the Pai had still to experience the full range of Anglo-American culture and society. . . .

In 1871 the Pai began to learn that the U.S. Bureau of Indian Affairs considered itself the government agency in charge of administering their transition from native life to subordinate cultural and social status in the United States. A one mile square reservation for the western Pai was set aside in that year.

Committed to the general policy of removing conquered Indians from their ancestral lands to a distinct Indian Territory, the Bureau sought army aid in moving the western Pai to the Colorado River Indian Reservation. The Pai had been placed under the charge of the agent of that reserve in 1873, and in the spring of 1874 the army forcibly moved the western Pai under its direct control to La Paz in the Colorado River Jurisdiction, in the Pai version of the "Long Walk" or "Trail of Tears." The eastern Pai bands, already differentiated from the western groups by pre-contact experiences, safety during the Walapai War, and continued isolation from mines and military posts, were further distinguished from the relocated Pai by their escape from removal. The one or possibly two bands now called Havasupai, the Pine Springs Band, and some of the Peach Springs Canyon Band Pai waited out deportation in the isolated fastnesses of the Grand Canyon and its southern tributaries such as Cataract, National, and Prospect Canyons. (Dobyns and Euler 1960:54–55)

On the low-altitude river flood plain location, the Pai suffered extensively. The government rations on which they were forced to depend were often scarce. Farming had to be attempted under conditions foreign to the experiences of the Pai. Old and young encountered new diseases and died in large numbers.

By the spring of 1875, we are told, the decimated bands could take no more; they fled back to their ancestral homeland.

Once safely back in their former territory, the escaped western Pai suffered no illusions as to their fate. They clearly realized that they could not hope to return to their former way of life, because Anglo-American ranchers had thrown great cattle herds onto their grasslands and settled at their best springs. The old harvesting-hunting activities would—and, to the extent they were practiced, did—bring demands by the ranchers for final and irrevocable removal. The western Pai realized that to exist in their homeland they must adopt the white man's expedient of working for wages, and their wholehearted plunge into daily work at the mines gained them the mine operators' support against the antagonistic ranchers, and sealed their differentiation from the still-isolated eastern Pai.

Reservations of lands for the Pai were set aside on the plateau in the prehistoric range of the northeastern bands. The western bands known to Americans as "Walapai" received a 997,045 acre reservation in 1883 . . . and the eastern "Havasupai" group a much smaller plot of 518 acres of its once extensive range in 1882 . . . For nearly half a century neither reservation had much meaning to its theoretical occupants.

Under provisions of the Indian Reorganization Act of June 18, 1934 (48 Stat. 984), separate "tribal" governments were organized on these two jurisdictions, the "Havasupai Tribe" in 1938 and the "Havasupai Tribe" in 1939. (Kelly, Wm. H. 1953:49,53) By such historic processes and United States administrative actions, arising from a view of the Pai which does not correspond to the native concept, have two formal, self-governing "tribes" been created where only one ethnic group existed in pre-contact times. This process of alienation of Pai bands continues to the present in administrative actions which, for example, send "Havasupai" children to be educated at Indian Bureau boarding schools on the White River Apache reservation while "Walapai" children attend public schools in their homeland. (Dobyns and Euler 1960:55–56)

And thus is explained briefly the circumstances whereby the Yuman-speaking Pai people were divided into the groups which follow.

[It should be noted that while the author generally favors the results of field investigations and thinking of certain scholars (Dobyns and Euler 1960) (Euler 1972b) who feel that both the Hualapai and the Havasupai are directly descendent from the Cerbat branch of the Pai, at least one researcher holds that the Havasupai alone derive from the Cohonina, (Schwartz 1956) and other views are held. (*See* Whiting 1958; McGregor 1951,1967; Schwartz 1959:1062.)]

The Havasupai (Eastern Pai)

Location and Early History

The eastern Pai, the Havasupai (HAH-vah-soo-pie), or "people of the blue-green water," inhabit a tiny patch of ground at the bottom of Cataract Canyon, a side branch of the Grand Canyon of Arizona. This is within the area occupied by their ancestors since the 1100s at least. During the spring and summer corn, beans, and squash were irrigated with the ever-flowing clear, blue-green water. The crops were supplemented by hunting and gathering over a wide range of altitude. Food stuffs were stored in crevices or small caves above the reach of often occurring flood waters.

Social Organization

When the Spanish entered the Southwest, the Havasupai were a peaceful, industrious, intelligent, and hospitable people. The family was the social unit, with small groups loosely bound into larger ones by blood relationships. No clan existed. Inheritance was in the male line, but wives enjoyed greater privileges and prerogatives than did most women of Arizona Indian peoples. (*See* Robinson 1954:125.) No marriage or divorce laws were observed. When young people wished to marry, the man took up residence with the girl's family. They lived with her parents for a year or two, by which time they had a child or two. Then a home was built near that of the man's parents, from whence his inheritance would come. Family association was free of taboos. Women had no share in the house, land, or other property; they owned the pottery, baskets, and their personal effects.

Havasupai homes were rock shelters or houses of two types: One was circular and constructed on a framework of poles. The sidewalls and the domed roof were thatched with bundles of willow branches held in place by small, flexible poles lashed through the thatching to the framework. The other was rectangular and was constructed "by setting four posts in the ground with forks at the top in which poles were laid lengthwise and other poles crosswise, with brush on top . . . and the sides thatched with reeds and willow" (Robinson 1954: 127). In both instances the roof was covered with earth. No provision was made for the escape of smoke.

Six men of equal status were recognized as "chiefs," and one of them usually served as spokesman and discussion leader. They had little power, their principal duty being to give advice and to lead discussions. Chieftainship was theoretically inherited, but prestige had much to do with the selection. No office of war chief existed; rather the most competent available leader took charge of the rare defensive fighting of the Havasupai.

Religion was little developed. Prayers, in which prayer sticks were utilized, were addressed to the sun, earth, water, rocks and other natural features. The Havasupai believed in a future life and in ghosts. Shamans, or "medicine men," by means of their possession of familiar spirits, dreams, and knowledge of various magical practices, cured diseases and bone fractures, snake bites, and the like, and engaged in weather control.

At some past time the Havasupai are known to have had three dances, but the number decreased. Approximately sixty years ago, a dance of masked and painted men was performed, to bring good fortune and prosperity to the people. The largest celebration came to be a general reunion with dancing which was held annually in the early autumn. Men and women danced in a circle, to the rhythm of drum and voice. Formerly, special attire was worn, but this practice was discarded some time ago. In a measure, the dance was a prayer for rain, but social aspects predominated. Addresses by the chiefs and visitors were given at intervals.

Leisure time was spent in bathing in sweat lodges (small, domed structures about six feet in diameter and four feet high), playing games, and playing with dolls. Games included shinny, hoop-and-pole, cup-and-pin, and gambling. Wrestling, foot- and horse-racing, and other pursuits were common.

Economy

The Havasupai were successful farmers, and became famous for their crops. In Cataract Canyon, where there was considerable irrigation, corn became the principal crop. Beans, squash, melons, sunflowers, and tobacco also were raised. The men did the irrigating, and the women did most of the harvesting. Plants that were gathered included mescal, cactus and yucca fruits, peaches and figs, mesquite pods, juniper berries, piñones, and the seeds and leaves of several edible vegetal items. Crops were stored in stone granaries which were sealed for protection. Wild honey was collected, and salt was obtained from the Grand Canyon.

Meat was an important part of the diet, as deer, antelope, mountain sheep, wildcat, mountain lion, raccoon, rabbit, and squirrel were hunted. Dogs were used in hunting, but were not eaten. Fish, lizards and other reptiles were not eaten. Men and boys participated in drives to kill rabbits. Other meat came from various rodents. Turkeys, quail, and doves were favorite fowls. Meat was commonly dried. Roasting and boiling were the general methods of cooking. Most of the cooking and eating took place out of doors. Three meals a day were the early practice as well as the modern.

Attire

Clothing of the Havasupai was made from animal skins until recent times—when manufactured garments came into use. The working of skins and the making of women's clothes was done by the men.

The female attire consisted of a two-part dress—an apron hung from the neck and reaching from breast to ankles in front—and a shorter piece that hung from the waist in back. Under this dress, a short apron was sometimes worn from the waist to the knees. As with the Mohave, the two parts of the dress were overlapped and held in place by tie strings. Around the waist a yucca fiber belt or a textile belt—usually obtained from the Hopi—was worn. Women's clothes had long fringes and were trimmed with metal or hoof tinklers. Later, ornamental shawls made of several colored kerchiefs sewn together also were worn. The moccasins had hard soles and a high upper which was wrapped around the calf. Sometimes the women went barefooted.

Men wore shirts, loincloths, moccasins and leggings. The shirts were similar to those worn by the Plains Indians, but influence of non-Indians crept in, altering the cut and sewing. The ankle-high moccasins had hard soles. Both men and women wore rabbitskin or cotton blankets for warmth; later they adopted wool blankets.

Face painting and tattooing were practiced to some extent. Adornments consisted of necklaces and ear pendants of Pueblo and Navajo shell and silver (*see* Douglas 1931:2–3).

Native Crafts

The Havasupai women made pottery which traditionally was fired in an oxidizing atmosphere, like that of the Hopi and other Pueblo pottery makers. The vessels were brown, predominantly globular pots of coarse texture, unslipped and unpainted. They were built up by coiling and then finished by a paddle and anvil process. After being dried in the sun for some twenty-four hours, they were baked, one by one, in hot coals.

Basketry was made by the women following two techniques, coiling and twining. Training in the craft began when a girl was seven or eight years old. Shallow trays or bowls were coiled, using twigs of cottonwood or of a plant said to be known only by its Havasupai name. The sewing of the coils was on a three-rod foundation. Simple geometric and banded designs were worked in martynia black. Conical burden baskets, globular water jugs, and shallow trays or bowls were made by twining. For these, twigs of acacia were preferred, although cottonwood and willow also were used. Some of the baskets were used as cooking containers.

The burden baskets and water jugs had loops for carrying; these baskets were decorated with simple designs achieved by varieties of twining and the use of martynia, or devil's claw. The water vessels and some parching trays were coated with a yucca, or soapweed, paste colored red with hematite, over which a coating of piñon gum was applied for waterproofing. This resulted in almost completely obscuring the designs.

In weave, the old Havasupai baskets displayed some similarity to those of the Yavapai, but not those of the Walapai. Today, Havasupai baskets are extremely rare. Those made in recent times are of coil technique, and made primarily for the tourist trade.

Havasupai babies were placed on basketry cradleboards, and kept there until they were nearly old enough to walk. Care of the children was shared by both parents.

Trade

The Havasupai and their kinsmen, the Hualapai, both of whom were great traders, widely traded seashells from the Pacific and red hematite (for paint) to the Pueblo peoples.

Significantly, the historic trade routes had similar or identical prehistoric counterparts; these are indicated by a wide distribution of trade items (*see* Colton 1941). We are told that lima beans, for which the Hopi have become well known, apparently were obtained originally from the Havasupai; and the latter received peaches from the Hopi. "Some Havasupai lived with the Hopi regularly, during the winter months, for a period of years" (Whiting 1958:58). For grinding purposes the Havasupai used a flat pounding-grinding rock and rotary mortars.

Impacts of Foreign Culture

The period of peaceful stability of the Havasupai ended near A.D. 1600, with the first impacts of foreign culture. As non-Indians moved onto the up-lands for cattle ranching, the territory of the Indians was gradually usurped. Most of the aboriginal articles were still being made: pottery in paddle and anvil technique, clay pipes for smoking, stone knives (which among other uses, were utilized for cutting up squash), bone tools, fire drills and hearths, bows and arrows, basketry, skin clothing, and related items. Three main architectural forms persisted: a brush structure (wickiup), the rock shelter, and a talus top granary. Many old customs, such as cremation, persisted (*see* Schwartz 1956:83; *see also* Whiting 1958:58).

The historic Havasupai were individualists in their economic pursuits, their house types, and in their lack of well organized social or religious groups. It has been stated that:

While at times they borrowed extensively from the Hopi in economic and religious matters they remained reluctant farmers (especially after there were horses to ride or, better still, to race), indifferent craftsmen, inartistic, nonreligious and magnificently self-sustaining people. The dead, who were greatly feared, were socially ostracized and physically buried at a considerable distance from the living areas. The mode of burial varied. (Whiting 1958:56)

Upon death, the home and personal possessions were burned, and one or more horses killed on the grave. A man's saddle might be burned, or left on one of the horses (*see* Dobyns and Euler 1971:44). His bow and arrows, war club, and personal effects were buried with him.

Modernization

Havasupai acculturation really began with the establishment of a reservation for them in 1880. Toward the end of the following decade, the federal government sent a farmer into the canyon, and then a schoolteacher. New and improved tools, modern methods, and the English language were introduced. The school forced the children to remain in the canyon. Clothing rapidly changed to the white man's garb, western style. The typical burial practice of cremation was altered to burial directly in the ground (Whiting 1958:56) in extended position, although for another generation "there continued to be cremations, often of the medicine men. There is some hint that these men, ultra-individualistic in life, demanded to be different in death, no matter what the current pattern. Even in their treatment of new ideas this group behaved as an almost accidental amalgamation of individuals." Mourning rites of the Yuman type prevailed in the Havasupai culture.

Despite the fact that the Havasupai borrowed extensively from the Hopi at times, the rituals in imitation of the Hopi katsina dances "were strictly individually sponsored affairs. When the sponsoring individual died or when his proposed reform failed, as when prayers for rain were answered with a disastrous flood, the movement evaporated" (Whiting 1958:56).

A big flood in the Havasu canyon in 1910 washed out most of the farms and homes there and the talus top granaries, after which small wooden frame houses were erected, along with rebuilding of the brush shelters. For a time the Havasupai, like many other Indian peoples when initially confronted with non-traditional types of dwellings, used the frame houses for storage purposes while preferring to live in the old style homes.

The National Park Service established a village near the Grand Canyon Park settlement on the plateau, which came to be a center of Havasupai life. Most of the Indians work for the Park Service or for some non-Indian concerns engaged in servicing the park and visitors. Some eke out a meager living by growing garden crops and raising a few cattle.

The Havasupai Reservation

Certain lands in Arizona were reserved by an Executive Order of 8 June 1880 for the "Suppai" Indians. That order was revoked by another of 23 November 1880, which set aside other lands; that in turn was revoked on 31 March 1882, at which time still other lands were reserved for the "Yavai Suppai" Indians. The reservation itself consists of 518 acres, which are owned in undivided shares by the enrolled members.

The Havasupai lost their eastern fields and hunting and grazing lands on the plateau above the canyons. (*See* Dobyns and Euler 1971:21–24, 30–33). The reservation acreage is reported to be 188,077 (Arizona *Tribal Directory,* 1981:6). The U.S. Forest Service and the NPS issue a year-to-year permit for the Havasupai to graze their stock on land adjacent to the reservation in the Kaibab National Forest and the park.

The beauty and isolation of Cataract Canyon—now commonly called the Havasu—long have been the root resource of the Havasupai. Homes, school and other facilities could be reached only by trails on either side of the canyon, which cuts through the reservation. These are accessible by roads from the Grand Canyon and from Highway 66, just east of Peach Springs, Arizona. Horse and mule transportation and guide service are provided by the Indians, and overnight accommodations at Supai Village, a little oasis. Airlift by helicopter is available for visitors, but the Indians in need of supplies must travel to Kingman, one hundred miles from their homes. From there, it is said that merchants will ship goods back to the canyon at a 40 to 60 percent premium. (Anonymous 1969c:21.)

The Havasupai Tribe

The Havasupai organized under a constitution and bylaws which were approved on 27 March 1939. A tribal corporate charter was ratified on 5 October 1946.

All individuals listed on tribal rolls as of 1938 are members. New members are added as follows: (1) all children born to any member after January 1, 1938, who are three-fourths or more Indian blood, and (2) by action of the Tribal Council through the passage of ordinances covering future membership and adoption of new members, subject to the approval of the Secretary of the Interior. No person is eligible for adoption into the Hualapai (*sic.*) [Havasupai?] Tribe who has not resided upon the reservation for a probationary period of five years. (Kelly, Wm. H. 1953:55)

The Havasupai in 1980 numbered 475. The population is predominantly young, with rising birth rate (*see* Dobyns and Euler 1971:1, 61–62). As a people, the Havasupai have moved from traditional practices toward modern government in a practical manner. It was recorded that: "The governing body is a tribal council consisting of four regular councilmen, and three recognized hereditary chiefs of the tribe who are selected by the remaining subchiefs. Each of the chiefs, as a regular member of the Council, continues his duties as councilman until death or resignation, at which time a new chief is selected by the subchiefs. Any member of the Council, not a chief, may be subject to recall if he fails to fulfill his duties as a councilman . . ." (Kelly, Wm. H. 1953:55). Today all members of the council are elected.

The Havasupai Tribal Council meets the second Saturday of each month at 9:00 A.M. at the Havasupai Community Center in Supai. All members of the council must be qualified voters of the reservation and thirty-five years of age or older. Elections are held every year on 25 December. Tribal officers and tribal employees are selected by the council. The chairman and vice-chairman must be members of the council; the secretary and treasurer need not be council members. Officers also include a tribal judge and police chief. Men or women may serve on the 8-member council. Special meetings are at the call of the chairman. The Havasupai have several operating committees, each under an official designated as a manager or director. Each is assigned to a specific category.

Education is provided by the BIA in Supai, for those in the pre-primary through fourth or fifth grades—depending upon the need. Thereafter, students are sent to school in Fort Apache or in Phoenix. The nearest professional medical care available is at the Grand Canyon.

The Havasupai Today

By national standards, a decade ago the Havasupai were considered to be one of the most impoverished groups in the nation. They were almost totally dependent on the BIA.

It was then said that:

> Young Havasupai who attend Government boarding schools return to the reservation confused about their place in the world. They feel inferior both to the white man [*haigu*] and to fellow Indians from larger, more advanced tribes.
>
> Of the 142 Havasupai men able to work, only eight hold permanent jobs. While the tourist season lasts, the tribe's 300 horses are used to pack visitors to the canyon (at $16 a round trip). Some 6,000 came by foot or horseback last year, but the tribe has almost nothing in the way of handcrafted goods, restaurants or inns that might encourage visitors to leave their money behind. Moreover, the horses help to keep the tribe isolated. Efforts to put a cable car line or jeep trail into Supai have been resisted by the Indians, who fear that their only reliable source of income will be destroyed.
>
> Havasupai are forbidden to bring alcohol onto the reservation, but it is bootlegged into the canyon and sold at exorbitant prices. Increasingly, the younger tribe members have been the best customers. . . .

The Havasupai family structure may appear to be almost nonexistent. But this is not the case. Actually, the family is extremely important; "it is the most important institution (after the BIA) in the community" (Martin 1972).

It has been noted that:

> Without privacy, children imitate their elders and begin sexual activity early. Illegitimacy is rampant, birth control ignored. Havasupai men . . . practice "sequential marriages," (Martin, 1972) taking one wife after another. Matches between first cousins are routine; mental retardation is common [evidence to support this statement is questioned]. (Euler 1972b) Disease, poor diet and high infant mortality combine to give the Havasupai a life expectancy of only 44 years (U.S. average 70). They also have a suicide rate 15% above the national average. (Anonymous 1969c:21.)

Since then, predictably, governmental agencies and humanitarians have carried forth an improvement of the Havasupai condition.

During the summer of 1969, a government-financed airlift set about to bring modern housing to the isolated Havasupai Indians in Havasu canyon. Helicopters, in some eighty flights, lowered five prefabricated, three-bedroom houses, section by section, to the canyon floor 5,300 feet below the rim for the Indians to erect. These structures cost about $12,000 each. They were provided at random for some of the most needy families. Later, ten more houses were put up in Supai, and thirty-five were scheduled for installation.

As in prior times, the Indians had to be talked into accepting the new houses. They knew their neighbors would be antagonistic and jealous; and the dwellings, although wired for electricity, had no source of power. The wood stoves that were supplied would be sources of trouble in an area where a firewood shortage prevails . . . and so the houses would be impossible to heat.

An official of the BIA said that the Agency planned to provide each Havasupai family with a modern house eventually, thus replacing the sub-standard shacks, many without floors (Anonymous 1969a).

The writer of the article quoted above remarked:

Until now, the Bureau of Indian Affairs has invested only limited funds and manpower to ease the tribe's plight. Little in the way of imaginative social work has been attempted. Putting shingled rooftops over each Havasupai's head is a questionable response to his needs, and even this will be done only gradually (Anonymous 1969c:21.)

Construction of houses, a community building and federal facilities, with supplemental work, and employment at the power plant provided an unusual "bonanza" for the workers. However, this will end "and the Havasupai will then be thrown back on tourism and welfare" (Martin 1972).

HAVASUPAI PRAYER

Sun, my relative
Be good coming out
Do something good for us.

Make me work,
So I can do anything in the garden
I hoe, I plant corn, I irrigate.

You, sun, be good going down at sunset
We lay down to sleep I want to feel good.

While I sleep you come up.
Go on your course many times.
Make good things for us men.

Make me always the same as I am now.

From *Havasupai Ethnography*
by Leslie Spier (1928:286).

The Hualapai or Walapai (Western Pai)

Anciently, the western Pai, or Hualapai, appear to have occupied territory between present day Kingman, Arizona, and the Colorado River. Around A.D. 1150, the Cerbat group moved onto the plateau east of the Grand Wash Cliffs, where they displaced the Cohonina people. Their closest contacts were the Yuman-speaking Halchidhoma, and the Southern Pai and Hopi peoples (Euler 1972b). They had hostile encounters with the Yavapai. Before 1880 the Hualapai probably numbered more than 1,100, but they declined steadily to the present.

A major occupation was food gathering and hunting; vegetal products were primary, for game was limited. The main food supply consisted of fruits, berries, and nuts gathered by the women, and deer, antelope, mountain sheep, rabbits, and other game hunted by the men. Farming was practiced where moisture was sufficient to raise crops, as in many canyons tributary to the Colorado. In western Grand Canyon the Hualapai practiced agriculture as extensively as did the Havasupai in Cataract Canyon.

Dwellings commonly were small, not very substantial structures of dome-shape, made of small poles and branches covered with juniper bark or thatched and without earth covering. Sturdier winter houses were sometimes built. Rock shelters were often used to live in. Sweat houses were in common use, and a rectangular, flat-roofed shelter was built occasionally for summer shade.

Few ceremonies or dances were held, although the Pai traditionally had great faith in shamanism—usually in the hands of a medical practitioner. Some are said to believe that the spirit of the dead goes to the west for judgment and, if condemned, goes to the underworld; others have no concept of future life. In times past, the dead were cremated and their possessions burned. An annual community burning of food and clothing commemorated the dead. Cremation was replaced by the practice of burial—preferably at the place of birth.

Basketry was made exclusively by the Hualapai women. They fashioned undecorated plaques and household baskets, often covered with pitch on the interior; more or less cylindrical baskets with geometric designs in martynia, rarely painted bluish, red or white on the outside, and similarly shaped with bail-like handles; large conical carrying baskets with limited decoration; finely worked small plaques, the splints of which were dyed; baby cradles and items of fanciful shapes. The weaving technique is that of coil on three rods and splint foundation; and the products resemble those of the Apache. In time, the basketry art almost died out, but tourist demands caused its continuance to the present. The modern baskets are made of sumac twigs and in brighter colors; predominantly of bowl shape. Some beadwork is also produced for the tourist trade. Formerly, some pottery and pottery pipes were made. Tobacco grew wild in the Hualapai country; it was not cultivated (Robinson 1954:117).

The Hualapai Indian Reservation

Rugged and varied terrain lies between Peach Springs, Arizona, on U.S. Highway 66, and the Colorado River west of Grand Canyon National Park. This relatively large reservation has only a few tillable spots near streams and springs. Small crops such as corn and beans may be raised, but the chief means of livelihood is by stockraising, while the most profitable source of income is from the sale of timber, which is treated as a capital asset with the return invested in range improvement.

The reservation in its entirety is owned in undivided shares by the enrolled Indians, and is held in trust for them by the federal government. Consolidation of the reservation was accomplished in 1947, when title to more than 500,000 acres in odd numbered sections previously held by the Santa Fe Railroad Company was quieted in the government in trust for the Hualapai (*see* Kelly, Wm. H. 1953:50). The land is used for individual homes and farms, for grazing by their cattle association, and by the Indians acting as a corporation. Size of the reservation is now 992,463 acres.

The Hualapai Trading Company at Peach Springs was established in 1944 by the "tribe," for the purpose of providing a local source of groceries and other merchandise, with credit privileges. All cattle on the reservation are owned by members of the Hualapai Livestock Association, with exception of the tribal herd.

The Hualapai Tribe

This group of Indians was organized as the Hualapai tribe, with a constitution and bylaws approved 17 December 1938; and a corporate charter was ratified on 5 June 1943. All individuals listed on the rolls as of 1938 are members, and children born to any member after 1 January 1938, who are of one-half degree or more Indian blood, are also members. Others admitted by action of the tribal council "through the passage of ordinances, subject to the approval of the Secretary of the Interior, governing future membership and adoption of new members" may be added to the rolls. The local population is approaching 1,000.

The tribal council consists of nine members, in addition to "one hereditary chief of the tribe selected by the subchiefs of the various recognized bands and who holds office for life." Councilmen must be qualified voters of twenty-five years or more of age, members of the Hualapai tribe, and residents of the reservation. All tribal officers, committees and tribal employees are selected by the council. Council officers consist of a chairman and vice-chairman, secretary, treasurer, judge, and police chief; the first two named must be members of the council, but others may be chosen from the tribe as a whole. They have added a Tribal Assistant Administrator.

As to their responsibilities:

> The Hualapai Tribal Council has jurisdiction over all matters pertaining to the management of tribal property, conduct of Indians and non-Indians on the reservation, tribal business enterprises, and the welfare of tribal members. The only limits to its power are in some specific instances where the Secretary of the Interior must give approval for action, and in other instances where action must be referred to a vote of the people. (*See* Kelly, Wm. H. 1953:49.)

The group has many committees—each with a chairman or director— which give attention to enrollment, housing, personnel selection, overall economic development, investments, tribal associations, and law and order, as well as utilities and emergency energy, health, education, recreation, and other matters.

The Hualapai received $2.9 million compensation for lands taken from them in northwestern Arizona in 1883. They decided to use 25 percent of this fund for a program to better their standard of living, and 75 percent for resources development and investment programs (Anonymous 1970e).

The council meets the first Saturday of each month at 9:00 A.M. in the tribal office in Peach Springs. Terms of office are for three years, with elections held annually on the first Saturday in June.

There is no BIA school for children who live on the Hualapai reservation; they are all being educated in public schools, as in Kingman, Truxton Canyon, and Seligman; or they go to other off-reservation boarding schools. Almost without exception, the people speak English; many retain their native tongue. The Hualapai have a PHS clinic in Peach Springs, where a medical doctor, several nurses, and other personnel are assigned. Ambulance service is provided where necessary for those requiring hospitalization, as in the Kingman Hospital.

The Hualapai at Big Sandy

Some years past, a few members of the Hualapai tribe lived at Big Sandy, southeast of Kingman. But, by 1963–1964 all that remained was "one shack, some fields, fences and the irrigation ditches. . . . the 'owners,' who were many, lived in Kingman. Several commuted to plant, irrigate, weed and harvest some small kitchen gardens" (Martin 1972). No tribal land exists in the Big Sandy; all tracts are held in trust allotments. Mohave county assumes responsibility for law and order.

The Salt River Indian Agency

The Salt River Agency was given full status as of 1 July 1962. Prior to that time it functioned as a sub-agency of the Pima Indian Agency located at Sacaton, fifty miles distant. The administration headquarters for Indians living in the Salt River Pima-Maricopa community and the Fort McDowell Yavapai-Apache community is located where the two reservations meet each other, about seven miles east of Phoenix. Its purpose is to provide facilities for the education, assistance, and guidance of the Indian residents of these lands, "so that they may become more self-sufficient, may improve their social and economic status, and develop and protect their natural resources" (King 1967).

The Salt River Reservation

This reservation was established by Act of Congress on 28 February 1859, and by subsequent executive orders. It begins approximately two miles northeast of Tempe and extends up the Salt River past the granite reef diversion

dam and beyond the junction with the Verde River. On the west the reservation approaches Scottsdale. The reservation contains 45,627 acres of which
25,229 acres are trust allotted to individual Indians in tracts of five to 30
acres; and 21,398 acres are community land. Forage on range lands is undependable. Carrying capacity is rated at 145 head of cattle. Vegetation includes
sahuaro, mesquite, palo verde, cat-claw, cacti, creosote bush, salt cedar, and
arrowweed. Animal life consists primarily of jackrabbit and cottontail, mourning and whitewing dove, gopher, muskrat, desert beaver, and quail.

Virtually all of 15,000 acres of irrigated land is leased to non-Indian farmers who have developed a successful agricultural project. Valuable water rights
go with the lands in this project.

The irrigated area on the west side of the reservation is the center of the
Indian community, with the remainder of the reservation practically vacant
of human habitation.

Flat desert land to the north and east could be used for agriculture if sufficient water were available. To the east, the reservation is made up of rolling
deserts, some of spectacular beauty, rising into rocky prominences.

The average elevation of the cultivated lands is approximately 1,300 feet;
the highest point in the reservation is Mount McDowell, which rises to 2,828
feet. The winters are mild but killing frosts may occur from November to
March. Moderate rains fall from December to April and thunderstorms may
appear in July, August, and September; the average annual rainfall is 7.96
inches. The summers are hot, the temperature ranging from 115° to 131°F,
and averaging about 70.2°F. Relative humidity is generally low.

The Pima-Maricopa Community

About 3,300 Pima-Maricopa people live in the Salt River community, pri-
marily in the western area of some 51,730 acres. They organized under the
Wheeler-Howard Act, with a constitution and bylaws approved 11 June 1940.
These people are descendants of Pima and Maricopa bands that migrated to the
area beginning in the 1860s when the waters in the Gila River failed. A minor-
ity of Papago and Indians of other tribes have married into the community.
Several hundred tribal members live immediately adjacent to the reservation.
The clothing worn is that of the regional inhabitants.

A tribal council of nine members is active, with a president and vice-
president appointed from within the popularly elected council membership;
other officers are tribal judges and a secretary, treasurer, and police chief.
Elections are held every even year, the first Tuesday in September. The community has its own law and order code. Real leadership is being developed
within the community, several committees operate effectively, and governmental pursuits are expanding. The council meets each Wednesday at 4:30
P.M. in Scottsdale at the tribal council chambers.

Compared with some of the other Arizona Indians, the Pima-Maricopa are
relatively well educated; almost all persons under the age of fifty years have at

least a sixth grade education. Many have completed high school, some, college. Virtually everyone speaks English. Despite these facts, the economic conditions on the reservation have not been good. A significant percentage of the work force is unemployed or works intermittently. Urbanization has robbed the Indians of the traditional agricultural activities in which they were experienced. Some basketry is woven; in fact a revival of the craft is noticeable, with younger Indian women and some non-Indians learning to weave in the traditional manner.

Because the community is in an area which is one of the largest winter tourist resort centers in the nation, future development is a certainty. Industry is getting a foothold in the area, increasing the population and economy throughout the Salt River valley. The Indians will relate to future developments. A program to upgrade the reservation's work force through vocational training is under way, and a program of social development of the Indian community is being pushed. Several colleges are available.

Among the projects being advanced are those of self-help housing, improved domestic water under the U.S. Public Health Service, establishment of a large Community Center—where an annual Indian Trade Fair has been held since the spring of 1962—and various youth programs. To aid in achieving these objectives, the agency staff has been expanded to include a resources development officer, a juvenile officer, a graduate social worker, and others.

During the 1970s a gradual transfer of students from BIA to public schools took place. Most of the Pima-Maricopa community is in the Mesa School district. A contract with the state of Arizona provides for education of Indian children in both elementary and high school. Educational grants are sought for higher education. Interest in native tongues has been rekindled.

The Yavapai Indians

The Yavapai (YAH-vah-pie) are a Yuman-speaking group which the Mohave called the "People of the Sun" (*Enyaéva*—"sun"; *pai*—"The People"). They were first mentioned by Espejo in 1582. They wandered in small independent bands or family groups over the semi-desert reaches bounded by the mountains generally north of the Gila River. Their number is said not to have exceeded 1,500 (Robinson 1954:84). These groups occupied three geographical districts, comprising the western, northeastern, and southeastern Yavapai respectively. They intermingled and intermarried. Leadership was achieved through personal merit based on wisdom, personality and ability as a warrior (Robinson 1954:85).

Until the late 1800s, Yavapai subsistence was derived from hunting small animals, rabbits and deer (they used a recurved bow), and the gathering of native plants; occasionally corn was obtained from the Pima and Papago Indians. They were active traders and participated in expeditions to the west coast, south into Mexico, north to the Paiute country, and to the Hopi and

Zuñi pueblos. They were important factors in the exchange of handiworks and in the mingling of the cultures of the diverse Indians they visited.

The Yavapai made use of caves for shelter, or built temporary pole, brush, and mud houses. Small quantities of corn were planted along stream bottomlands, but the yield was not sufficient to be counted as a staple food. A variety of fine baskets was woven for utilitarian purposes (*see* Robinson 1954: 79–84), and a few stone tools were used. Food appears to have been cooked in pottery vessels. The clothing, if worn, was made from hides; personal adornments were few. Small crosses were sometimes tied to the hair.

Their religion was like that of most other Yuman peoples. Prominent features were veneration of the sun, shamanism, and belief in dream omens. Social dances were held on occasion.

The Yavapai were long associated with the Apache, and writers have often confused them. Both being warlike, the Yavapai found it to their advantage to be associated with the Apache. They intermingled and intermarried to some extent, and were similar in attire and even physical appearance. Here the similarities ended. The Apache, of Athabascan stock, assumed an attitude of warfare against all those regarded as outsiders, while the Yavapai philosophy permitted more flexibility. They demonstrated a greater willingness to change and, in time, made the effort to learn the ways of their neighbors and to coexist with them.

General Crook was one who did not recognize the Yavapai as a people apart from the Apache—to him they were one and the same, all Apache (*see* Robinson 1954:91). In 1872 some 750 Indians—mostly Yavapai—were living on a reservation at Camp Date Creek, southwest of present day Prescott. The surgeon there, Dr. Corbusier, was one of those more discerning than Crook and recognized the difference between the Yavapai and the Apache. However, the next year, in May, they were all transferred to the Camp Verde Reservation which had been established in 1871. Many Indians escaped from there, some of them to resume raiding the settlers of Arizona and Mexico. After an extensive campaign in April, 1873, the Yavapai, Hualapai (eastern Pai), and Tonto submitted to armed forces, or were brought in the following year. At that time the San Carlos Reservation was established, and the Yavapai, being identified as Apache, were forced to go there. It has been recorded that:

> The Indians walked all the way while the soldiers rode ponies. They followed only trails, for there were no roads. Moccasins and clothes wore out, torn by rocks, cactus, and brush, and many, sick at heart, wanted to die—and did. With no time for burial, these were left lying along the way. Many streams and a large river running high were crossed. These were negotiated the best way they could, one way or another. Some of the weaker were lost at the river crossing.
>
> Rations were meager, and were augmented by edible weeds, roots, and seeds, when they could be found. To the Yavapai Indians, this move is known as the "March of Tears" . . .

During the next several years, many of the Yavapai drifted away from the San Carlos Reservation and went to live in the area north and west of Fort Whipple and the Verde. The four branches of the Yavapai Indians and their area headquarters may be said to be divided as follows: "Weepukapa" (Camp Verde); "Tolkepaya" (Arlington); "Kewevkopaya" (Fort McDowell); and "Yavepe" (Prescott) [in the spelling "Yawape," this term is said to mean "crooked mouth people," or "sulky"]. (Bahti 1980:68) The Arlington branch has practically disappeared, the remaining members having been absorbed into the Prescott and Fort McDowell branches. (Barnett 1968:3–4)

It has been said that the older Yavapai women taught the Apache to make bowls and dishes, and also improved coiled basket making techniques while they were together at San Carlos from 1875–1900. The two peoples spent many hours working together, thus accounting for the materials, techniques, and many decorative designs that are found in the baskets of both. However, the Apache lacked legend or background for their craft (Robinson 1954: 78–84).

It is pointed out that:

> Many design elements, such as the diamond for example, are claimed by the Yavapai weavers as originating with their tribe. The star (starflower) design is common in Yavapai baskets, and is a sacred symbol with the weavers. Some, but not all, of the best baskets begin with the design of the story of creation. The swastika is a mystic symbol of good luck to the Indian, and brings good fortune when used on baskets, pottery and blankets. It is believed by the Indians that this symbol was given to them by the Great Spirit.
>
> No dye or artificial color is used in a Yavapai basket. Young shoots of cottonwood and mulberry trees, and sometimes the fine roots of the yucca or soapweed are used for the natural color. The black color is made from stripped ears of the devil's claw seed pods. Generally the first coil of a Yavapai basket is black, though some weavers do not always hold to this. (Barnett 1968:33)

To finish a basket, the last row of weaving—the rim as it were—is always done in black. Yavapai baskets are now extremely rare; only a few women can make them.

The Yavapai-Apache and Mohave-Apache

The Fort McDowell Reservation

Originally established as Camp McDowell Military Reserve on 1 January 1873, this reservation was released to the Department of the Interior on 1 February 1891 for disposal under government procedures (Acts of 5 July 1884 and 23 August 1894), reserving legal subdivisions occupied by government improvements. Some of the land subsequently was taken up by non-Indian settlers.

In November, 1901, the Federal Land Office was directed to reserve the land for Indian purposes; and an Executive Order of 15 September 1903 set aside the land of Camp McDowell that was not legally settled. Purchases and the Act of 2 April 1904 compensated the settlers for their improvements and claims, thus changing all of Camp McDowell to an Indian reservation.

Most of the present inhabitants of Fort McDowell are descendants of those Yavapai who were taken as prisoners to San Carlos in 1874–1875. They are related to and acquainted with Yavapai living in the Camp Verde vicinity and at Prescott. At the time of imprisonment the Yavapai numbered approximately 1,500; twenty-five years later only 200 remained (Barnett 1968:4).

A limited number of Apache have intermarried with the Fort McDowell Yavapai, or "Mohave-Apache"—as they were called erroneously by the early settlers—and live on the Fort McDowell Reservation, which is located twenty-eight miles northeast of Phoenix and adjoins the Salt River Reservation on the northeast side. It contains 24,680 acres, none of which is allotted. Total length of the reservation is ten miles, and its four-mile width is bisected lengthwise by the Verde River, beginning one and a half miles above the junction with the Salt River. The elevation of the bottomland varies from 1,350 to 1,900 feet. Some 1,300 acres of irrigable lands of the Fort McDowell Reservation were provided water by rights granted by the Kent Decree in 1910.

The climate in which the Indians reside, that of the Southwest arid region in general, is somewhat modified by proximity to the mountains. Winters although mild do experience some moderate frosts, a little snow, and limited rains from December to April. The summers are long, hot and dry, with thunderstorms in July, August, and September. Temperature during the year varies from a recorded high of 115°F to a low of 13°F and averages about 70°F. The annual rainfall is ten inches. Heavy clothing is seldom needed.

On 3 March 1965, the Indian Claims Commission ruled that the Fort McDowell Reservation was part of 9,238,600 acres of Yavapai tribal land confiscated by the U.S. government on 1 May 1873. This meant that the Indians owned the land all the time, and in 1904 were getting only what had been theirs all along. Following this ruling, the federal government paid the Indians $5,100,000 for the Yavapai tribal lands that had been taken—the settlement amounting to about fifty-three cents an acre!

This reservation became important to the Central Arizona Project, or CAP, because of the need for storage reservoirs. The project is supposed to help the state of Arizona, but it will put about half of the Fort McDowell Reservation lands in flood danger, and will force the Indians living there either to relocate their homes or live within the shadow of possible disaster, because practically all of the residences are located in the flood plain (see Winchell 1980:45).

According to a report in *The Arizona Republic:*

When the CAP bill was passed, it included the construction of Orme Dam, either at the confluence of the Salt and Verde Rivers or at Granite Reef Dam a short distance to the south.

In either case, the dam will create a flood plain of 12,823 acres along the always-flowing Verde River, which runs through the middle of the reservation.

The flood plain boundary is based on the biggest flood of the last 100 years, and much of the land might not be inundated for several generations. But there will always loom the possibility that the 100 year flood might strike again tomorrow.

Land in the flood plain can be used for farming and grazing and other purposes, but construction of the permanent structures will be restricted.

Within the flood plain will be . . . 5,347 acres near the river designated as the "conservation pool," or the mud flats. Water will be backed into this area when the reservoirs are fullest during a normal year's runoff.

The federal government, meanwhile, is willing to help the Indians relocate their small village, Ft. McDowell, and to reimburse the tribe for the land in the flood plain. Also, the CAP bill provided for the gift of 2,500 acres in federal lands to the tribe. This land will probably come from nearby Forest Service lands.

But the tribe is sometimes suspicious of the way the federal government operates. For example, the tribe thought the government would set aside comparable land east of the reservation to trade for the property in the flood plain.

However, the government recently traded that land to the Page Land and Cattle Co. for land elsewhere. Now, according to a former tribal chairman the Indians have no place to get the kind of terrain they are giving up.

The chairman said that the Indians are reasonable people and that they recognize the importance of the CAP. In speaking of the federal government, however, he remarked: "They took away 9 million acres from us; then they said we'll give you this 24,000 acres and let you alone. Now they want to take half of that. My people are starting to think that they won't stand by their word" (Murray 1969).

The Yavapai here number well over a hundred families, totaling about 380 persons. Most of the people have adequate housing; a few have cinder block dwellings chiefly built under a self-help program. They have their own government with elected council members and working committees. Both men and women hold office. The Fort McDowell Council meets in the community building in Fort McDowell at 7:00 P.M. on the first Tuesday of each month. Elections are held every year for president, vice-president, secretary, treasurer, police chief, and tribal judge. Law enforcement is subject to Title 25 of the U.S. Code. Tribal policemen have jurisdiction over misdemeanors committed on the reservation by Indians.

Little farming is underway today, and the principal source of income is from wages paid to tribal members as employees in pumping stations of the city water system of Phoenix. A notable number commute to off-reservation employment. The sale of permits for duck hunting, fishing, and picnicking provides a small income for the tribe.

Educational and recreational needs are met in surrounding towns, such as Phoenix, Mesa, Tempe, and Scottsdale. There, too, shopping is done, and medical and dental services secured. Churches of most denominations are available. Arizona State University at Tempe is about ten miles from the agency headquarters. A few of the younger Yavapai are college graduates.

The pressures inherent in the accelerated growth of the surrounding cities continue to mount as those communities enlarge on the periphery of the Salt

River Reservation and the Fort McDowell Reservation. Both tribal groups are engaged in such studies and community redevelopment activities as may best assure them of a meaningful place in the future of the valley. Maximum coordination with the surrounding communities in developmental planning is believed to have assured a mutually advantageous future.

Viable tribal housing and sanitation programs are in operation. Modern building codes and ordinances have been adopted and all educational and developmental opportunities offered through the OEO and other federal sources are being utilized to the fullest by the tribal councils.

Annual income from leases, licenses, fees and recreation receipts approximate $76,000 for the Fort McDowell group, and $300,000 for the Salt River community.

Both of these groups have coordinated their athletic and entertainment programs with those of the surrounding communities. No special Indian-type tourist shows are held.

One criminal investigator is employed at the agency. He is charged with maintaining law and order on these two reservations; he drives a police car equipped with a two-way radio. Radio contact is maintained with the Pinal and Maricopa county sheriffs' offices, and messages can be relayed to police in all surrounding towns through their networks.

The Camp Verde Yavapai-Apache

An Act of 1 August 1914 appropriated $20,000 for purchase of lands for Indians under jurisdiction of the Camp Verde Indian School, said lands to be held in trust and subject to the General Allotment Act (38 Stat. 588, c 222).

The Yavapai-Apache Band was organized under a constitution and bylaws approved 12 February 1937. A tribal corporate charter was ratified on 11 March 1948. All individuals listed on tribal rolls as of 1934 and the 1936 supplement are enrolled as members; new members are added according to certain stipulations.

The governing body is an organization known as the Yavapai-Apache Tribal Council consisting of eight members elected by the qualified voters. The council

elects from its own membership by secret ballot a chairman and vice-chairman, and from within or without its membership a secretary, treasurer and such other officers and committees as may be deemed necessary. Council officers elected from without the council membership have no vote in the council. Members hold office for two years and elections are held annually on the second Saturday of July with four councilmen being elected each year. Regular meetings are held on the second Saturday of January, April, July, October, and December. (Kelly, Wm. H. 1953:57)

These meetings are held at the Middle Verde Indian Community. They are now annual, on the second Saturday in July.

The Camp Verde Reservation

Actually this reservation is comprised of two parts: one located on the outskirts of the town of Camp Verde, which consists of some forty acres of farmland, mostly undeveloped; and a second area about six miles to the northwest known as Middle Verde. The latter holding was established about 1916, when the U.S. government purchased 460 acres of land for use of the Indians. The paid price of $22,500 included water rights and interest in the irrigation canals which supply water to Indian and non-Indian farmers. This system is operated under a cooperative ditch association, and operation and maintenance costs are met by assessments against those using the water. A few acres are used for nonirrigated farming, 70-odd for irrigated farming, and more than 400 acres for grazing cattle.

Around two hundred of the Yavapai here share the reservation with perhaps two hundred and fifty Tonto—with whom it is said cooperation has always been difficult. The term "Tonto" has been applied to a number of distinct peoples of Apache and Yuman affiliation. "It is said to have been given to a mixture of Yavapai, Yuma, and Maricopa, with some Pinaleño Apache, placed on the Verde River Reservation, Arizona, in 1873, and transferred to the San Carlos Reservation in 1875; also to a body of Indians, descended mostly from Yavapai men and Pinaleño women" (Swanton 1952: 365; see Morris 1972:105–110).

Because of the limited resources of this reservation, only a few families could derive a living from farming. Most must earn their livelihood from off-reservation employment in and around Clarkdale and Cottonwood. They do various wagework, some engage in small scale mining, and a few lease lands for farming and grazing from the Yavapai-Apache Indian Council. More than one hundred families account for a population around 520, with many new homes.

Medical facilities are not provided locally for the Camp Verde Yavapai, but patients are cared for at the hospital in Cottonwood, under contract with the government.

The Yavapai Indians at Prescott

An Act of 5 June 1935 transferred seventy-five acres of land in Arizona from the Veterans' Administration to the Department of Interior, title to remain with the agency in trust for the Yavapai Indians (49 Stat. 332, c. 202). Agency headquarters is in Valentine.

This group, numbering over seventy, lives on the north edge of the city of Prescott, in an area of rolling hills on which juniper, piñon and live oak grow. Land within the reservation accommodates homesites and necessary community developments, including a cemetery. The soil is rocky and water is in short supply, so agriculture is not practiced. Adjoining acreages amounting to 500 acres are used for a small stockraising enterprise. Most of the Indians' income is derived from wagework in Prescott. This group holds 1,409 acres. It has a tribal council of six members, who meet in their community building monthly on the second Friday at 10:00 a.m. Elections are held the second Saturday in July every even year. Law and order is handled by Yavapai county and has been very effective; the expenses are met by the county and the state of Arizona.

Education for the young people of this group and for those on the Camp Verde Reservation is through the public schools. Medical facilities are provided for the Prescott Indians, under contract with the government and local physicians.

The "Payson Apache" (Tonto Apache)

Recently a group of people designated as Payson, or Tonto, Apache, numbering eighty-five and dwelling in a small community within the confines of the Tonto National Forest in Arizona, sent two of their kinsmen as representatives to Washington, D.C., to seek trust title to 85.9 acres of land upon which they live. Above all, they sought legal recognition of the Payson Apache Indian community as a tribe—a status the federal government had long denied. (*See* Brandon 1970a:35: " 'Indian Community' means a tribal community with a quasi-sovereignty of its own and a sense of relatedness among its people akin to that of a religious community"; 1970b:27: "The people of an Indian community generally will not sell out for individual opportunities no matter how alluring; will undergo any privations to remain part of their living community. The community superlife, calling for inter-personal harmony rather than inter-personal striving, is in absolute opposition to the orthodox American gods of work-as-a-virtue and amassing personal wealth as a measure of success.")

Troubles stemmed from gold-discovery days in the 1860s. "The Rio Verde Reserve was established in 1871 for the Tonto and Yavapai Indians. But it was dissolved four years later, and the Payson Apaches claim their Tonto ancestors were forcibly removed to the San Carlos Reservation." Then, "about the turn of the century, some of the Tontos returned to Payson and took up residence in the forest just south of town. Now, about 70 years later, these Payson Apaches are considered squatters in the eyes of the law."

As the Apache representatives in Washington pointed out, because they were not considered a tribe but lived on National Forest land, they were not able to bring in electricity, running water, or sewage facilities. Most of their houses were made of scrap lumber from nearby mills, or of old lumber. All of the adult males were employed in the saw and planer mills; and none of the Payson Apache families were on welfare, as far as this writer knows.

Certain Arizona legislators introduced legislation and gave other support in behalf of these Indians, but their success to date has been nil. A speaker for the Department of the Interior remarked that title could be given to the land requested by the Payson Apache, but he said they should not recognize them tribally. In the attitude of so many bureaucrats, an assistant secretary for Public Land Management is quoted as saying: "We do not now recognize this group and believe we should not now recognize them. If this group wishes to avail itself of Indian services, they need only remove themselves to the San Carlos Indian Reservation, which they have refused to do for a number of reasons" (Anonymous 1971a). The San Carlos reservation is some one hundred miles from Payson.

Recognition came in 1972 when President Nixon signed a bill giving the Tonto trust title to the 85 acres they were seeking. The bill provided for receiving federal aid and a vast array of services—education, health, and economic development—privileges that other Indians were extended. Consequently, the little band eagerly began the task of building a secure and self-reliant community. However, their number had decreased to 67 by 1981.

SMALL AND WARM

She was small and warm
her hands like cotton
her face like ropes
her hair like a waterfall
her smile like a stone
her mind like the sky
her life like a river
her death like a fever of sorrow
her memory small and warm

By Courtney Moyah, Pima-Apache

From *Art and Indian Children*,
Curriculum Bulletin No. 7, 1970.
Institute of American Indian Arts,
Santa Fe, N.M.

The Pimans

Brief History

The Piman peoples have a long history which reaches back into the prehistoric past. First reporting of the Pima began in 1539 by Fray Marcos de Niza, the Franciscan who introduced Christianity. Jesuit missionaries encountered Piman-speaking Indians in the state of Sonora, in northwestern Mexico, and these came to be designated as the Lower Pima when, some seventy-five years later, missions were extended into present day Arizona, *Pimería Alta*, or the territory of the Upper Pima. The Upper Pima were "a single tribe" only in that they spoke a single language. Marked cultural differences existed. Those Pima dwelling in the San Pedro valley (the Sobaipuri) and on the Gila plain, for instance, "lived in fairly concentrated rancherias sustained by agriculture," while those farther west were nomadic food-gatherers. "Moreover, there was no permanent political organization linking more than a few rancherias in any part of the Pimería. Political coordination of rancherias for any purpose but warfare seems to have been unknown, although there were games and customs of ceremonial cooperation between the rancherias. The widest political organization probably did not link more than fifteen hundred people" (Spicer 1970:119).

It has been recorded that when the early Spaniards encountered the valley dwellers of the Gila and Salt rivers, they asked many questions of them. The usual Indian reply was *pi-nyi-match,* or "I don't know." From this, the Spaniards took to calling them "Pima." The name by which they indicate themselves is *ah-kee-mult-o-o-tom,* meaning "River People." Thus the term *Pima,* like the word *Apache,* has no linguistic significance.

Father Eusebio Francisco Kino, an energetic Italian, who was as much an explorer as a missionary, came among the Pima in 1687, intent upon reducing the ranchería people to pueblo dwellers. His campaign lasted for twenty-five years, keeping, it is said, "at a high intensity conflicts of interest between the Indians and the Spanish settlers." The Pima were considered wild and difficult, extremely savage, inasmuch as they resisted impressment by the Spaniards for work in the developing Mexican mines and on the ranches.

Kino soon demonstrated that the majority of the Pima were friendly, industrious, and peaceful, ready to ally themselves with the Spaniards, or to live quietly under the mission system. Kino introduced livestock, wheat and other crops which the Indians readily accepted, along with metal tools. He found them carrying on some trade with other indigenous peoples, but this did not comprise an important part of their economy. By standards of the day, the Pima were better off than neighboring groups. Lacking a highly developed social organization, they did not persist in their native religious ceremonies after contact with the Spaniards and Christianity (insofar as Kino knew).

In the regions where the Pimans dwelt, little attire was necessary. Children ran about naked most of the time. Women wore a one-piece, wraparound skirt that reached from waist to the knees. These were made of a piece of deerskin or from home-woven cotton cloth. Men wore a loincloth of the same materials, and sometimes sandals, fashioned from mountain sheep skin or of twisted fibers. The hair of all individuals was allowed to flow freely—a chief sign of beauty. Ornaments of turquois and other stones were made into ear pendants; these sometimes hung to the shoulders; they were worn by men and women alike.

Women, in particular, painted designs on their bodies for special occasions.

They were tattooed with lines that extended from the mouth to the chin. Although a painful practice, all girls over sixteen years old had these decorations.

Kino died in 1711, after which the missions soon became a thing of the past. The Pima revolted against the Spaniards in 1751, and this "constituted a shock from which the Jesuit missions had not recovered by the time of the expulsion in 1767" (Spicer 1970:132). The Franciscans who followed in missionary efforts were relatively weak, although certain individuals, such as Father Garcés, were successful in their undertakings.

On the whole, reports indicated that the upper Pima "had returned to their 'ancient barbarism.' " And it has been said that: "An important factor in the increasing isolation was the intensification of the Apache raids after about 1810. During the late 1700s Piman-speaking people had steadily retired westward from their border position on the San Pedro River. By 1800 there were no Pimans east of a line between San Ignacio near Magdalena and San Xavier. Many had been killed, and a few had been absorbed into the central Sonoran communities of Opatas and Spaniards. The remaining Pimans, who were not at the mission sites along the Santa Cruz and Magdalena, were living in desert villages in the present area of the Papagos or the river villages along the Gila" (Spicer 1970:132–133).

In the early 1800s the Franciscans exerted themselves to bring the Pima into the Santa Cruz River missions (San Xavier and Tumacacori), and apparently were successful in getting numerous converts.

The Apache raids were intensified during the 1830s and 1840s, and the following decade saw the raiding extended throughout the southern Upper Pima domain, past the Altar valley to the coast of the Gulf of California.

Through the Gadsden Purchase in 1853, the Piman land holdings became a part of the United States. This transaction brought about immediate and important changes in the lives of the Upper Pima. Foremost was the different political condition.

The new international boundary surveyed in 1858, traversed the region of the headwaters of the San Pedro and Santa Cruz rivers and ran through the middle of the desert lands to the west. This automatically placed at least three-quarters of the remaining Upper Pima as residents of the United States. As much as sixty years later there were still Pima in the desert rancherías, under the leadership of a headman named Pia Muchita, who seemed unaware of the change and still professed allegiance to Mexico. Nevertheless, the invading Anglo-Americans regarded the Upper Pima territory north of the new line as part of the United States and proceeded to act accordingly. (Spicer 1970:133–134)

The Calendar

The Piman year begins with the rainy season, when characteristic plants and animals appear. The year is based on the moon periods, thus a lunar calendar of twelve "moons" is followed (or was into the present day). The sahuaro, or giant cactus, which ripens at the beginning of the rainy season is highly significant in the life of the Piman peoples. It was customary for a family to establish a permanent camp in the nearest sahuaro area. The figlike fruits and seeds were gathered for food in late June and July, before the rains began. The fruit, brought down by a long, pointed staff, was fermented to yield an alcoholic beverage which was drunk ceremonially—to bring rain (Underhill 1940:48). Sahuaro harvesting, then, marked the beginning of the new year in the native calendar.

Sahuaro ribs were used on occasion in making house walls, and calendar sticks were made from them also. Some of the recent history, dating from just before the time of the Gadsden Purchase, is recorded on notched sticks—a device like computer records to remind one of events that occurred in successive years. Perhaps six feet long, a smooth, slightly flattened inner support of the giant cactus, about an inch and a half in diameter, had mnemonic symbols representing happenings recorded on the smooth side.

In some instances, dots and circles bespeak major ceremonies for the most part, although other events may be recorded. One stick has been described as follows:

At the beginning of each year . . . a notch is cut across the stick and, at the beginning of the next year, another, an inch or two further on. Between them is placed some crude geometrical sign, such as a triangle, cross or parallel lines to indicate the outstanding event of the year. Occasionally, two events are represented. The symbols are painted with red clay, such as was used for face paint, and blue soot collected from embers of greasewood, *Covillea glutinosa,* used for tatooing [*sic.*]. (Underhill 1938a:7)

The calendar keeper invented his own symbols. The sticks appear to have been kept in various villages. They are considered as private possessions, and it was customary to break one's stick and bury it with the owner upon his death.

The Anglos, knowing little and caring less about the Piman relationships, made distinctions between the Indians who dwelt on the Gila River (whom they often called "Pimos") and those who lived in the vicinity of Tucson and westward therefrom. The Spaniards had called the desert dwellers "Papagos," and the term became general with the Anglos for all Piman-speaking peoples who lived south of the Gila residents, whom they called the "Pima."

The Pima (The River People)

Living at the very northern edge of the Spanish frontier, the Pima of the Gila River valley—where they had dwelt since prehistoric times—had the least contact with the Spaniards. With permanent water from the Gila, the Pima had irrigated their agricultural lands by means of an elaborate canal system. Kino had come among them in 1694, and other missionaries followed.

Spanish officials had presented canes to the Pima, as they did to the Pueblo peoples. Accepting these, or at least official designations, the Pima "had acquiesced in a nominal obedience to the King of Spain."

Friendly relations existed between the Indians and the Anglos. During the 1820s fur trappers passed through the Pima territory, following the Gila trail. On these occasions the trappers were furnished food by the Pima. Reports of these contacts and those of General Kearny and the Mormon Battalion stated that the Gila Pima were the "most civilized Indians in the United States." Thousands of Anglos traversed the Pima holdings during the gold rush to California, beginning in 1849. They, too, found the Indians friendly, peaceful, and the source of plentiful food. The Pima were anxious to trade for metal and other goods.

It was not until 1855 that Pima leaders learned that their territory had come under the control of the United States as result of the Mexican War and the Gadsden Purchase. One of them consulted with the U.S. Boundary Commission, and was "assured that the United States had friendly intentions, that the land right under the Spaniards would be fully recognized, and also that the United States government had in mind giving the Pimas agricultural implements to assist them in the valuable service they were rendering providing food for parties of travelers" (Spicer 1970:147).

In characteristically tardy manner, it took the government four years to get the implements delivered, but the promise was fulfilled and this consolidated friendly relations between the Pima and the whites. At that time, however, the federal policy began to be applied to the Pima.

The Pima Reservation

An act of 28 February 1859 "required the President to have the boundaries of the lands then occupied by the confederated bands of Pima and Maricopa Indians near Gila River, Arizona, surveyed and to have it set apart as a reservation, not exceeding 100 square miles and $10,000 was to be presented to said Indians (11 Stat. 401, c. 66 sec. 305)" (Kelly, Wm. H. 1953:61). The reservation was established south of Phoenix, on the Gila and Santa Cruz rivers; and the Pima agency was located in Sacaton about forty-two miles southeast of Phoenix, in 1871 (Robinson 1954:15). The appropriation of ten thousand dollars was used in part to buy tools for the Indians' use, but the remainder had to cover "the expense of a survey of the land on the Gila River for the purpose of setting aside not more than sixty-four thousand acres as a reservation" (Spicer 1970:149). The Pima who had lived on the Gila for centuries, having descended, it is believed, from Hohokam ancestors, claimed a much larger area and the issue remained in dispute for a decade. In 1869, the survey was increased by 81,000 acres, giving a total of 145,000 acres—still far less than the Pima claimed.

Drought and the encroachment of settlers from the east caused the Pima to appeal to the federal government for consideration of their mounting problems. Leaders went to Washington in 1873 to present their case—and learned of the power of the white officials. "It was proposed that the Pima problems could be solved by removal to Indian territory." One of the leaders, Antonio Azul, went to Oklahoma and looked over the land to which they might be assigned. He was favorably impressed, but all the other Pima were opposed to any removal from their homeland. As a result of the failing water supply some twelve hundred, or more than a quarter of the Pima group, moved north on the Salt River, where they farmed among the white settlers; the remaining Pima spread along the Gila in three major areas of water seepage, where marginal farming was carried on.

As one authority has stated:

> The period . . . from about 1870 to about 1900 was one of increasingly intensive contact with Anglos and of numerous changes in Pima life. The surrounding of their land by Anglo settlers became an established fact. The Southern Pacific Railroad traversed their territory in 1878. Florence on their eastern margin became an important territorial town with an increasing population. By 1887 the irrigation canal constructed to take water out of the Gila River for the white settlers utilized the whole flow. No water reached any of the Pima fields downstream. Settlers were pressing to the edge of the reservation from the south in the Casa Grande area. Protests and representations had no effect except to increase by small parcels the size of the reservation. The real need, however, was for water, not land, as most government reports recognized; yet no effort whatever was made to protect the Indian water rights. The government ignored the problem, although agents in rapid succession continued to push for the Indian rights. (Spicer 1970:149)

During all this period from 1876 to 1915 no less than a dozen U.S. executive orders increased or reduced their land or modified the boundaries (*see* Kelly, Wm. H. 1953:61). The procedure continues to this day.

New Ways for the Pima

In 1881, the BIA established a boarding school in Sacaton—long after the Presbyterian Church, which was active among the Pima, had started a day school there (in 1868). A force of Indian police was initiated, and a Court of Indian Offenses set up. "An Indian Bureau farmer was brought to the reservation to give agricultural advice. At the same time that the Indian Bureau made these efforts to give some services to the Indians, activities of the Presbyterian Church were intensified" (Spicer 1970:149).

This authority tells of the work of a particular missionary-schoolteacher (Charles H. Cook) who, following a pitched battle between two Pima villages, began a vigorous missionary campaign, not only to baptize Pima people, but in an effort to reorganize their deteriorating communities. "Poverty through lack of water with which to farm and replacement of functions formerly performed by village headmen through the government agency had resulted in some degree of demoralization of the Indians." Three distinct factions had developed from water problems.

Before 1899, the missionary had baptized half of the Pima and established churches throughout the reservation.

In each community he appointed an elder, assisted by deacons, whom he held responsible for law and order and general moral standards. The elders were usually former village headmen. Gradually a transformation in village life took place, centering around the new religious organization. Annual revival meetings took the place of old ceremonies. Christian mythology and theology replaced older beliefs and the strict morality of the Presbyterians tended to reintegrate the disintegrating villages. The church affairs were almost entirely in the hands of the local Pimas, and ministers were trained to do the preaching. The Presbyterian missionary, Cook, became the most influential force from Anglo society among the Pimas, although at the same time the Sacaton Boarding School and other boarding schools set up elsewhere by the Indian bureau were well attended by Pimas and worked together with the missionary in the transformation of Pima society.(Spicer 1970:149–150)

Inasmuch as the influence of one particular man on the Pima people was so great, surely he should have more than passing mention. Mr. Cook, living in Chicago in 1870, heard of the spiritual need of the Pima and recognized this as his call. No church or denomination was back of him, but he left for the Southwest, taking a small organ which cost him thirty dollars. The train, then, went only to Dodge City, Kansas. From that point Cook continued on by coach and by walking; his funds were reduced to twenty-five cents by the time he reached Cow Springs, New Mexico.

Preaching along the way resulted in an unexpected but gratifying small sum of money. Cook continued on his weary route, reaching his destination, the Sacaton agency, on 23 December. In January 1871 he was hired as a teacher to the Pima Indians, at six hundred dollars per annum. On 15 January he started a little school with thirty-five youngsters whom he found well behaved and apt for learning.

During his years of service, Cook was awarded a medal by President U. S. Grant. In his old age he retired to Iowa where he died and was buried. To the last, he loved the Pima people.

The Cook Christian Training School, at Tempe, Arizona, was established in Dr. Cook's honor, and a centennial celebration was observed on 6 February 1971—with Indian dances and singing, art exhibit and a drama of Cook's life, and an open pit barbecue. In March a formal banquet was held (*see* Walker, G. 1970).

Worsening Economy

Economically, conditions on the reservation continued to worsen. In 1895 food rations had to be issued by the government. Individual Pima efforts did little toward solving the overall problem. And, "the Indian Bureau attempted nothing that would involve it in the matter of water rights on the Gila. It did however begin a program for solution of the water problem—the digging of wells to be served by electric pumps—in the eastern and central part of the reservation. Some fifteen wells were put into operation between 1903 and 1910" (Spicer 1970:150).

In 1914 the BIA put an allotment plan into effect, with the result that some of the Pima began coming back to the reservation to take up ten-acre plots. The consequence was wide scattering of the Indians over the reservation, "again disrupting community life."

Climatic Influences

Although the Gila River Indian Reservation of today encompasses 371,933 acres—good farming land, if irrigated, and nonirrigable stretches—the physical conditions influence the lives of the approximately 9,400 souls who are enrolled there. Pima comprise the majority, with a few Maricopa and Papago included in the census. At Sacaton, which may be reached by Arizona Highways 87 and 93, the highest rainfall occurs in July and August, and summer temperatures have been as high as 117°F. The lowest rainfall is in April, May and June. The temperature rarely goes below 20°F. Mean daily range of temperature between day and night is 35°F. The frost-free period is about 263 days.

Largely through efforts of representatives of the Presbyterian Church, the San Carlos Project Bill was passed in 1924, and construction of a dam near the old San Carlos Apache agency was initiated. This promising action was welcomed by the Pima and many began returning to their reservation to make land ready for the water. Two years later, an advisory council of Pima men was formed by the BIA, primarily to have some tribal body with which to deal on legal matters pertaining to the entire Pima group.

In 1930, after completion of Coolidge Dam and the San Carlos reservoir, preparation for the new supply of irrigation water began. "At the same time extensive road-building programs were instituted, there was a shift to day schools from boarding school, and agricultural extension service was put into operation. In 1934 under the Indian Reorganization Act the Pima prepared a constitution and formed a tribal council. In 1937 District Farmers Associations were formed over the reservation, and in 1938 a high school was established at Sacaton" (Spicer 1970:151).

The farm program resulted in misunderstandings and disputes, and loss of prestige of the tribal council. Family income declined and the Pima farmers lost interest. In 1951 the council initiated a tribal farm which became a paying venture; but individual farming declined in importance.

Assimilation

At the time, 94 percent of all the Pima were literate, and 98 percent spoke English. It has been said that, "The Gila Pimas probably were the most nearly culturally assimilated of all Indians in New Mexico or Arizona. The Pima

Tribal Council continued in operation but it did not function as a political institution for Pimas as a whole. The tribe as a unit of social organization or culture had ceased to exist in the Arizona milieu. The tribal organization existed as a rather specialized mechanism for managing some economic matters for Pima settlements nearest the agency" (Spicer 1970:151).

Modern Government

The Gila River Pima-Maricopa Community was organized under a constitution and bylaws approved 14 May 1936, and a tribal corporate charter was ratified on 28 February 1938.

In establishing tribal status:

All individuals listed on the official allotment roll of the Gila River Reservation are members. New members are added as follows: (1) all descendants are entitled to membership if they are of at least one-quarter degree of Indian blood—those having a lesser degree may be admitted to membership by a majority vote of the council of the community; (2) members who have remained away from the reservation continuously for a period of 20 years and automatically forfeited their membership may be reinstated by a majority vote of the council with the consent of the district in which he or she proposes to take up residence; and (3) persons of Indian blood marrying members of the Gila River Pima-Maricopa Indian Community may be adopted into the community by a three-fourths vote of the council. (Kelly, Wm. H. 1953:61)

A community council made up of seventeen members is the governing body; these must be twenty-five years of age or over, and a resident for at least one year immediately preceding the election of the district from which he or she is elected. Councilmen hold office for three years, with one-third of the membership being elected each year. The council meets on the first and third Wednesday of each month at 9:00 A.M., in Sacaton, Arizona. Meetings on the third Wednesday of each month are held in the districts. The usual officers, committees, and extra law enforcement officers are selected by the council. Tribal officers are selected from within or without council membership; if selected from without the membership they do not have a vote in the council. The presiding officer, however, has the right to vote in case of a tie (Kelly, Wm. H. 1953:62).

Affairs of the community are in the hands of numerous committees, each with its manager or director. The committees are concerned with: economic development, education, government and management, resource development, legislation, health, agriculture, home sites, planning and zoning, enrollment, water conservation, financing, arts and crafts—all these with many ramifications.

For a century, the Pima and other central Arizona Indians have been fighting for their water rights, struggling against Interior Department decisions and court opinions. To date, the water table of their homelands has been lowered some 300 feet at an average rate of 10 to 15 feet annually—due to exploitation, primarily, by non-Indian developments and excessive draining of water flow from the Gila-Salt and Verde rivers. In 1968, Congress authorized the Central Arizona Project (CAP) to divert huge quantities of water from the Colorado River to the Phoenix-Tucson area by a 200 mile viaduct—a project costing billions, and threatening unfair distribution of water—even flooding of fertile farmlands of the Indians, submerging significant cultural evidence, and causing extensive relocation. Vital problems here continue into the political readjustments of 1981.

Present-Day Economy

Principal income for years has come from leases of lands to Anglo farmers. Other revenue is derived from traders' licenses, apiary rents, and sand and gravel sales. Since 1 July 1966 the Gila River Indian Community has been in the midst of what is almost "a non-native revival movement, a home-grown and BIA and OEO supported economic, social, and political development program they call *Vh-thaw-hup-ea-ju,* 'It Must Happen' " (Fontana 1967). This was set up as an eighteen-month accelerated program with some fifty-one projects. By the end of the first year significant progress had been made, and has continued under the direction of the Indians but utilizing resources and assistance available from the BIA, federal and state agencies, and those of neighboring communities.

The Gila River Indian Community attacked the problem of unemployment by luring industry to the reservation and preparing the available work force for jobs in industry. The industrial development was centered primarily in three industrial parks, the site improvement of which was funded by the Economic Development Administration. This development was geared to be supplemented by service facilities, commercial enterprises and residential construction. Systematic development of the interchange areas on Interstate Highway 10 was also part of the program. It was anticipated that a significant number of new jobs would be created on the reservation. Other aspects of economic development centered around increasing income from agriculture and development of the reservation mineral potential (Cumming 1967).

Social Development

The Economic Opportunity Act of 1964 provided stimulus to social development on the reservation. The Community Action Program had a number of components: Headstart, Day Care Center for children, guidance, adult education, alcoholism prevention and treatment, health aides, and community improvement. Other OEO activities included a NYC program, a state-administered Title 5 work experience program, VISTA program, and agricultural loans under Title 3.

The BIA branch of Social Service, HEW (division of Indian health) social workers personnel of Title 5, and the Gila River Indian Community Action Program cooperated in social service programs aimed at helping those families with social problems to make satisfactory adjustments.

During 1967 the public school was consolidated with the BIA school at Sacaton. The facilities are used jointly, and the first grade was transferred from the BIA to the public school. Thenceforth, each year, a successively higher grade has been transferred, with the end that the BIA school was phased out.

Since 1966 an increasing number of new, mutual self-help houses have been built. In the Casa Blanca area, many new bathrooms were added to existing structures. Several modern homes have been constructed through FHA insured loans, and a number have been renovated. Water and sanitation systems have been improved at Casa Blanca and Upper SanTan.

One of the major objectives of the Vh-thaw-hup-ea-ju plan was to improve management and government by the Gila River Indian Community. Projects included a review of the Community constitution, development of a tribal roll, codification of tribal ordinances, development of a law and order code, and a management review of the community organization structure.

As in many of the other Indian communities, the primary function of the BIA is coming to be one of providing services to the Gila River Indian Community and individual Indians, so that they may better attain their goals.

Pima Arts

Pima women have long been noted for their beautifully woven and artistically decorated basketry. They harvest, prepare, and weave the following plants: willow, devil's claw (*Martynia*), and cattail, or tule (*Typha angustifolia*).

It has been estimated that in the old days six out of ten Pima women were basket weavers. Today the number who practice this time-consuming art has dwindled to a few.

The Pima use three types of design: geometric, symbolic, and original. The fret design is the most common. The squash blossom is next in popularity, and is executed in numerous styles. Other favored designs are butterfly wings and the whirlwind—or "dust devil"—a common phenomenon of Southwestern desert areas. In some instances, design motifs may be used in combination with other features, such as swastikas and coyote tracks. Basket weavers, like potters, usually do not draw their designs beforehand, but bear them in mind through the creative process.

The most universal form of Pima basketry is that of shallow bowls. Formerly made in quantity, storage baskets of wheat straw and the bark of young mesquite trees have become increasingly rare. Basketry jars are made in various sizes, including miniature, and almost exclusively for the tourist trade. A few of the Pima weavers continue to make horsehair baskets—also for tourists. The old style burden basket, or *giho (kiaho),* has not been made for many years. (*See* Robinson 1954.)

Much of their traditional ceremonialism has been lost to the Pima, yet social events go on: annual fairs, for example, are favorite celebrations. On a Saturday and Sunday in March, one may witness the *Mul-chu-tha*, or fair, at Sacaton, south of Phoenix. They have a rodeo, parade, and exhibits. Indians from several of the Pima villages, such as Bapchule, assemble to present rain and basket dances, and to engage in a *taka* game and various contests. It is now customary to select a Miss Mul-chu-tha Queen annually.

The Papago (The Desert People)

The native name for these Piman-speaking people, *Tóno* (TOH-ono) *oótam*, signifies "people of the desert." They have, among other designations, been called *papáh óotam*, or "bean people" (Swanton 1952:357). They occupy the southwest portion of the Southwest—the foothills and valley floors of northern Sonora (Mexico) and southern Arizona.

It appears that Father Kino was the first non-Indian to visit their territory, in 1694. He found them living essentially as they did until very recent times. Other than not having so much contact with the whites as did the Pima, the history of the two groups has been similar. Cultural differences are minor. They recognize themselves as one people. The location of the Papago has made them less agricultural than the Pima; in early times some of the former completely lacked farming opportunities.

CELEBRATION

I shall dance tonight.
When the dusk comes crawling.
There will be dancing and feasting.
I shall dance with the others
    in circles
      in leaps,
        in stomps.

Laughter and talk
    will weave into the night,
Among the fires of my people.
Games will be played
and I shall be
    a part of it.

By Alonzo Lopez, Papago

From *The Writer's Reader*, 1962–1966.
The Institute of American Indian Arts,
Santa Fe, N.M.

The Papaguería

The lands of the Papago—*Papaguería*—are hot and arid. Elevation runs from 1,400 to 3,000 feet, encompassing extensive flat plains from which short mountain ranges or peaks rise rather abruptly. Rainfall varies in different parts of the area, amounting to from four to twelve inches during the year. Typically desert vegetation grows there: "creosote predominates the low dry plains, mesquite and paloverde line the usually dry stream beds, and the hill slopes are variably covered with cacti" (Gabel 1949:12).

Two periods of rain occur, one in winter and one in summer; the latter permits limited, undependable farming. Understandably, the Papago long engaged in hunting—chiefly of rabbits, some deer, antelope, and other animals—and gathering wild foods; and they traveled considerable distances to get drinking water. Largely for these reasons, they were somewhat less sedentary than the Pima. During the summer they moved from their more permanent villages in the foothills, where the water supply was constant, to lower areas where they could take advantage of increased opportunities for farming and food gathering afforded by the rains. They were good farmers who worked their small plots intensively. Their aboriginal crops were maize, beans, pumpkins, gourds and cotton. The wild foods consisted of yucca and cactus buds and fruits, mesquite beans, seeds of ironwood and paloverde, certain greens (such as amaranth, lamb's quarter, saltbush, and *cañaigre*), and sand root—sometimes called wild potato.

No permanent streams or lakes are in the Papago territory, and springs are widely scattered. The usually dry, sandy washes, or arroyos, carry flood waters for short distances and then spread out on the flood plains. Such a place is known as *Ak Chin,* "mouth of the arroyo." Several locations were so called by the Papago. This confused the government people, with result that the designation was conferred on a single village south of the Maricopa station on the Southern Pacific Railroad, on Vecol Wash.

The generally inhospitable nature of the Papago habitat helped spare the Indians from white aggression to a degree. Yet, following the Gadsden Purchase, when the land of Papaguería was considered available for non-Indian settlement, "many springs, wells and grazing areas were soon claimed by ranchers moving into the area. Little was done to secure land for the exclusive use of the Papagos . . . " (Papago Indian Agency 1970:12). The nature of the region, to some extent, "made the Americanization of the Papago a relatively peaceful and unhurried process. It was not until the twentieth century that miners and cattlemen began encroaching in sufficient numbers to create the need for a reservation" (Gabel 1949:15).

Reservations Anglo Style

On 1 July 1874 an executive order established a reservation adjoining the city of Tucson, San Xavier del Bac. Next, an executive order of 12 December 1882 set apart lands just north of Gila Bend for the Papago living there; and an executive order of 16 June 1911 established small reserves of 80 acres each at Indian Oasis (now Sells) and San Miguel. Four executive orders of 28 May 1912 set up the Maricopa, Cockleburr, *Chui Chuisch,* and *Tat-murl-ma-kutt* reservations.

Then it followed that:

An Executive Order of December 5, 1912, added another reservation at the foot of Boboquivari Peak—Santiergos. An Executive Order of January 14, 1916, established the "Sells," Nomadic Papago, or Papago Villages, Reservation which included the area formerly within the Cockleburr, Chui Chuische, Tat-Murl-Ma-Kutt, land (the Maricopa Reservation became a part of the Piman Indian Reservation). Congressional Acts in 1926, 1931, 1937 and 1940 authorized the purchase of patented land to be added to the Papago Reservations in addition to inclusion of public domain land." (Papago Indian Agency 1970:12)

All of the orders and acts brought about a total of 2,855,894 acres of reserved lands for use of the Papago Indians. Within the present Sells reservation are 2,774,370 acres; 71,201 acres within the San Xavier reservation; and 10,409 within the Gila Bend reservation. The main reservation stretches ninety miles across Pima county, and from the Mexican border north to within about ten miles of the town of Casa Grande, Arizona. Of the Papago holdings only some 7,000 acres are irrigated; about 1200 acres are at San Xavier. It is said that "little change of any importance in Papago land holdings has been made since 1940, but a very important change in the nature of Indian title came about in 1955 when, by Act of Congress, the Papagos were given all mineral, as well as surface rights to the reservations" (Papago Indian Agency 1970:12).

Early in 1971 a grant of $82,398 was made by the BIA for a pilot project on the Papago reservation at San Xavier. Given to the environmental research laboratory of the University of Arizona, the money was to be used for "designing and studying the feasibility of establishing controlled greenhouses on Indian reservations (using a technique which utilizes a farming-under-plastic idea—the plants being grown under huge sheets of plastic)" (Anonymous 1971g). If feasibility were proven for the raising and marketing of small vegetables, it was expected that construction could begin and actual marketing of products could start within the following year.

Late in the same year, an 800-acre farm, to be known as the San Xavier Indian Cooperative, was established through federal grants and loans of $115,000 to more than 175 landowners on the Papago Indian Reservation. For more than ninety years the Papago land has been divided among descendants from generation to generation "until no one landowner can make a living from the small, desert plots" (Anonymous 1971c). Products grown on the cooperative farm are to be "channeled into the commercial market, with emphasis on selling the products to other Papago Indians."

Currently, seventy-four settlements on the main reservation are inhabited, forty-three of them permanently. Nine of the communities are considered as

major villages. Of these, Sells on Arizona Highway 86 is the largest, and it is
the Papago headquarters; its population was 11,307 in 1981. The other major
villages include *Ali Chukson, Topawa, Quijotoa, Gu Achi, Gu Vo, Pisinimo, Gu
Oidak,* and *Chuichu.* The total Papago population was 16,307.

Administration

For purposes of administration the main reservation is divided into nine
districts: Baboquivari, Chukut kuk, Gu Achi, Gu Vo, Hickiwan, Pisinimo,
Schuk Toak, Sif Oidak, and Sells. The Gila Bend and San Xavier reservations
make up two more districts, bringing the total to eleven. Each district has its
own elected council and also elects two delegates to the Tribal Council. The
latter meets on the first full week of each month at 9:00 A.M., in Sells. Elections are held in the tribal complex every other year in May for district and
general council members whose terms expire. Elections for chairman and
vice-chairman are held in May every four years.

The basic political document of the Papago is the constitution and bylaws
ratified by the tribal members on 12 December 1936, and approved by the
Secretary of the Interior on 6 January 1937. The council has twenty-three
members, men and women who are elected for two-year periods. Each district is self-governing in local matters under its elected District Council, made
up of not less than five members. Should vacancies occur in the Tribal Council they are filled by the district councils. All individuals listed on the official
census roll of 1936 are tribal members. Additional members include all children of resident members; and children born off the reservation may be adopted
by the council if they are offspring of members and have at least one-half
Indian parentage.

All tribal officers, committees, and tribal employees are selected by the
council and serve for one year. The officers are: chairman, vice-chairman, secretary, treasurer, four judges, and chief of police. Committees include: education, health, housing, legal services, mining, overall economic planning,
elections, a rodeo board, and others.

Law enforcement is a combined tribal-federal activity. Personnel includes
a non-Indian investigator, a Papago captain of police, and seven tribal policemen. A radio system keeps the police department in touch with county
and state police, with whom close cooperation is maintained. The first woman
to hold an elective office among the Papago was selected as tribal judge. Office of the police department, jail, tribal court, and living quarters for the
police captain are in the municipal center.

Economy

Although the Papago number over 16,000, most of these do not live in
their reservation homes all of the time; ties, however, take them back. Approximately 7,000 reside on the main reservation. Gila Bend residents number

about 335, and San Xavier has a population of 4,665. Income of the Papago has long been one of the smallest of any Indians in Arizona, but is now improving. For years, cattle raising and some subsistence farming yielded most of the livelihood. The land is overstocked and crop failures occur about one out of five years. Because of the very limited economic resources many have been forced to leave the reservation yearly to seek work of various types. A number engage in agricultural labor.

The total of Papago people employed in 1970 was 3,107. Federal employment brought in 62 percent of all wage income. Per capita income for the Papago was then estimated to average about $700 annually. It has since increased.

Permanent colonies of Papago have grown up in Tucson, Casa Grande, and Ajo—south of Gila Bend on Arizona Highway 85—and in a number of other southern Arizona communities. An entirely new village has been built at Gila Bend. About forty Papago families live in the Sonoran Desert of Mexico; although they are Mexican citizens they maintain close ties with the Arizona Papago.

Dwellings

Among the changes to be observed today in Papaguería are the types of dwellings. The old Papago homes were constructed with strong, tough ocotillo (*Fouquieria splendens*) stalks or sahuaro ribs placed upright and with occasional horizontal stalks laced together and covered with adobe plaster, or wattled; sometimes, if available, rocks were used in the walls. Roofs were of ocotillo withes covered with brush.

A decade ago, almost 65 percent of 980 houses enumerated on the reservation were considered to be below minimum standards. The Papago Tribal Housing Authority and the BIA worked in close cooperation with HUD to obtain modern, durable housing for the Papago people. Construction planning called for five hundred new housing units by 1975. Since then, many more homes have been built.

Family Rights

In commenting on the family responsibilities of the Papago in maintenance of the household, the late Mr. Robinson said:

If a woman needs a new dress or some article for the house, it is her responsibility to provide the money for its purchase. Likewise, the man must purchase his overalls or his harness or farm implements with *his* earnings. This attitude toward a division of communal earnings and property extends even down through inheritance rights. The parents or the brother of the husband feel that, upon his death, their right to his farm implements or livestock supersedes that of his wife, and it is only through the application of the white man's inheritance laws that justice is achieved in such cases. In the case of death of the wife, her mother or sister may make claim to personal or household articles which she had made or purchased. (Robinson 1954:42–43)

Papago Arts

Encouragement is given to the traditional art of basketry. It has been said that, despite the attention given to the making of baskets, no records have been found to indicate that they have had a part in the religious ceremonies and rituals of the Papago. They have long been highly prized, and may be kept in a family for generations. They have had extensive use as gifts; often such gifts have been buried with a recipient upon death.

No dyes are used in Papago basketry. The materials are much like those of the Pima; they are prepared and woven in natural colors. On a white (natural) background, designs are worked in green or black, or both, and occasionally in red. Thin, flexible leaves of narrowleafed yucca (*Yucca elata*) are used for white, yellow and green, and devil's claw for the black; the red is derived from yucca root or root of the desert willow (*Salix nigra*). Yucca grows only on a small portion of the Papago country. The leaves, therefore, constitute an economic item, being used by the gatherer, traded, or sold.

Papago baskets are made by the coil method with foundation bundles of beargrass (*Nolina erumpems*) or yucca, sometimes of cattail, sewn with willow splints or *sotol*—usually the latter if the baskets are made to be sold. Two types of stitching are used. Designs are chiefly geometric, though life forms are produced also. More devil's claw appears in the decoration of Papago baskets than in those made by the Pima. Forms include bowls—some with high curving walls, others shallow trays—jars with or without lids, tall containers with straight or outward sloping walls, miniatures, and figurines in the likeness of animals, reptiles, birds, cacti, humans, and composites of these.

The Papago produce more basketry today than any of the other Indian peoples. Nearly three thousand baskets are marketed annually through the Papago Self-help Program alone. Outstanding items are sold at many state and county fairs and rodeos, as well as in museum shops and various stores and trading posts. Outlets for basket sales have been opened in Los Angeles and Toronto, Canada; and annual sales are held in Massachusetts and New Jersey.

The use of pottery has been found to reflect "the daily life of the members of the cultures which produce it," according to a recent anthropological study. The writers of that work say:

> In the case of the Papagos, canteen water jars, vessels with a small mouth and a long, constricted neck, ceased to be made when wells were drilled and when aluminum canteens were introduced. A reduction in the number of saguaro-wine vessels suggests a similar reduction in the frequency of certain Papago ceremonies. Items such as pottery ashtrays, toothpick holders, and piggy banks being made today tell us that Papago life has changed sharply in the last sixty or seventy years; these items even offer some suggestion as to the nature of this change. (Fontana et al. 1962)

The work mentions that pottery is the keystone of much archaeological analysis, and it points out that the study of pottery of a living culture has a great deal to offer the archaeologist, "suggesting to him the culturally significant limits of pottery analysis. There is a point in the study of pottery remains which arrives at technological sherd-splitting, going beyond limits that have any meaning for the understanding of a culture. The study of Papago pottery shows at what point this is true and why it is so."

It was found in the study conducted that numerous problems relate specifically to the Papago Indians, their culture and their history, which could be clarified by examination of their pottery, modern and archaeological. "One of the most intriguing of these problems," the writers found, "is the relation between the Papago Indians and the prehistoric Hohokam culture of the same area." (Both made their ceramics by the paddle and anvil technique.)

Pottery forms and decorations, when considered as a whole, have meaning. "Both are tradition-bound, just as is the technique of making pottery. The clay body, inasmuch as the component clay and temper derive from the same environment, has meaning. So does slip. But the difficulty in always being able to distinguish Pima from Papago pottery, even at this contemporary date, should tell the student of prehistory to beware" (Fontana et al. 1962:136).

Today, the only vessels made for Indian use are bean pots, water-cooling jars, and an occasional small syrup jar. The others are made for the tourist trade—but that market is collapsing; the Papago black-on-red pottery is in little demand. It is predicted that within another generation no more Papago pottery will be manufactured (Fontana et al. 1962:137).

Industries

The Papago tribe maintains a small herd of registered cattle under professional management; and it sustains an all-Indian Credit Union.

Because of an unusually severe drought which began in 1969 and continued for several years, wells ran dry and the water holes (charcos), upon which the Papago cattlemen depended for water for their stock, dried up completely. Hundreds of their cattle died, reducing the already destitute people almost to total devastation. Entirely on their own, a Livestock Relief Operation was formed by the Papago. It was headed by the late Tom Segundo, a Papago graduated from the University of Chicago Law School. (Most unfortunately, Mr. Segundo, then tribal chairman, was killed at the age of fifty-one years in an air crash at Casa Grande on 6 May 1971.) The Operation determined the specific needs of the stockmen, itemized them carefully and applied to the BIA for a grant of $500,000. Reporting on this a syndicated writer stated:

A bureaucratic powwow in Washington decided to grant the Papago $200,000 of which $40,000 was to be used for overtime payments to Indian Affairs Bureaucrats. Not a single Indian was invited to the meeting.

The Washington sages also solemnly forbade the Papago to use the money for cattle feed, despite the fact this was the most urgent need. Cattle feed, it was decided in Washington, was the responsibility of tribal families. (Anderson 1969)

The same writer commented that the Papago are a proud and intelligent people; and he mentioned their domestic water supply:

Most villages have one well for a water supply. The residents have to haul water to their homes in large metal oil drums. In some cases, it has to be carried over long distances, which requires a truck. For this, the family has to pay $1 a barrel. The Indian Affairs Bureau long ago decided that plumbing was too expensive to install. (Anderson 1969)

With $145,000 of the BIA grant, the salaries were paid, and the Papago were enabled to buy hay and pay for water hauling, and other items. Disaster was averted. Domestic water is being supplied by the PHS.

In 1971 the Papago received more emergency funds, which provided for technical advice, mechanical equipment, and about $92,000 for buying hay and getting water relief—including cleaning of the charcos. Some of the wells are still pumping; water is hauled in critical areas. As a result, death losses have been lessened, though hot weather heightens the risk. The relations between the Papago and the BIA have been greatly improved (Whitfield 1971).

The Past versus the Present

Taxes on cattle sales, income from land and mineral leases, license fees paid by traders and hunters, and court fines have been the chief sources of tribal income. At the present, the Tribal Council is actively working to bring about the optimum economic development of the reservations. As a result, a new day is dawning in Papaguería, as shown by the following developments. Three large mining companies, Hecla, Newmont, and American Smelting & Refinery, each discovered significant deposits of highgrade copper ore in the northern part of the reservation and initiated full mining operations there. Training of Papago for this kind of employment prepared several hundred individuals, who eventually became regular, full-time workers receiving full-scale wages. More jobs and land lease income were generated by the opening of the San Xavier Industrial Park. Funded by a loan from the Economic Development Administration, the 40-acre park attracted several light industries to the San Xavier district. Additional industrial acreage lay ready to match demand (*see* Papago Indian Agency 1970 and later), but the demand has lessened.

In 1972 settlement between the San Xavier district and the American Smelting & Refinery pertaining to the claim that the copper mining firm had "continued to mine reservation lands [and use of reservation water] past the expiration dates of the leases," was reached. From the original $20 million suit, the settlement figure was $2.1 million. It included a 25-year renewable mining and water lease for the company—which guaranteed the tribe "minimum royalties of $610,000 per year" (News releases).

The Papago derive sums amounting to many thousands of dollars per year from fire-fighting engagements. This provides employment for several hundred of the Papago.

Educational Facilities

Elementary and secondary school facilities are provided on the Papago reservation at the Sells Public School (Indian Oasis School District Number 40). Elementary schooling is provided by the federal government for those students who live an excessive distance from Sells; adult education classes are conducted through tribal and governmental cooperation. Four reservation parochial schools are maintained by the Franciscan Order.

The Papago tribal youth have a great interest in higher education. Several score of them attend college, or go to special schools. A few students go for training at the Institute of American Indian Arts in Santa Fe, New Mexico. The Papago are diligently working toward providing adequate scholarship funds for their youth. The officials are planning, and achieving, new schools as needed.

Public lodging facilities are not located on the reservation proper. A post office, a few shops, and a youth club are in Sells. Some fifteen miles west of the reservation is the community of Ajo, and the town of Casa Grande is about ten miles north of the reservation. Lodging is available there, as are photographic shops, sport shops, restaurants, and so on.

Other Community Facilities

The BIA and PHS offices are in Sells. For the latter, a 50-bed hospital, costing $2,260,000 was opened in 1961; it is entirely modern, well equipped and well staffed. It provides medical and dental care for both inpatient and outpatient.

Religious Groups

Religious activities are available through Catholic and Protestant groups. More than three-fourths of the Papago are of Catholic faith and have churches in every sizable village. Among the Protestants, the Presbyterian, Baptist, Assembly of God, and Nazarene denominations likewise have churches.

Festive Occasions

Today, the Papago sponsor a rodeo and fair at Sells, which is one of the most exciting shows of its kind in Arizona; it is held on the last Saturday and Sunday in October. Hard-riding Indian cowboys display their skills in daring events. Also featured are dances and ceremonials. The Papago have erected comfortable and adequate grandstands for spectators, and they treat their guests to a barbecue. There are exhibits and sales of Papago arts and crafts. Attendance runs in the thousands.

YONDER STANDS A YOUTH

Yonder stands a youth beyond
   the fires of the sunset.
In his eyes a misty cloud floats,
   telling that he weeps.
His crystal-white tears add to
   the sea of negligence
Which stretches endlessly before him,
Barring his crossing into the
   land of happiness.
Within the palms of his hands,
He cradles the jewel of his life,
Waiting hopefully for one to
   cast it to.
But, walking the sands
   of their own contentment,
Those who have reached the shore
   refuse to look toward him.

Look yonder!
There stands a helpless youth,
   crying as a child;
Toward you,
   outstretched, his hand.

By Alonzo Lopez, Papago

From *The Writers' Reader,* Fall, 1966.
Institute of American Indian Arts,
Santa Fe, N.M.

The Maricopa, Movers by Choice

From prehistoric times, various Yuma-speaking Indians moved up the Gila River and settled.

About the beginning of the nineteenth century a group of Yuma-speaking Indians who called themselves *Pipatsje,* or "The People," occupied an area along the Colorado River, south of present-day Parker, Arizona. The Anglos called these people "Maricopas." Apparently these disagreed with the other Yuma Indians with regard to selection of their leaders. As a consequence, they withdrew from the Colorado and moved eastward up the Gila River, where they made friends with the Pima Indians. There they were given land and protection from their hostile kinsmen. The Pima and Maricopa fought as allies in the battle of 1857 against Yuma and Mohave forces, whom they defeated severely. Although the Pima and Maricopa could not understand each other's mother tongue, this proved no barrier to a lasting relationship.

The retreat of the Maricopa from the Colorado left a large area of river bottom land vacant, and it was into this territory that the Mohave expanded from the north, and the Ute-related Chemehuevi also, to become residents of what would be the Colorado River Reservation (*see* page 165–166).

Descendants of the Maricopa are found today among the Pima on the Gila River Reservation and on the Salt River Reservation, as previously discussed. Today, two Maricopa Indian settlements are recognized: one on the northwest corner of the Gila River Reservation and the other in the Lehi district of the Salt River Reservation. From their long association with the Pima, the Maricopa seem to have lost all knowledge of their ancestors having lived elsewhere. However, until recently they followed certain practices of the past, and it was said:

> Their lives are dream directed as are the Mohaves; they cremate their dead; they have a clan-name system; and they speak the Yuman tongue. . . . In 1858, the U.S. Army census listed 518 Maricopas. Today, through intermarriage with Pimas they have lost most of their Yuman identity. They have adopted much of the Piman culture and are now almost one with them. (Johnston 1970:58.)

Maricopa Arts

The Maricopa women produced pottery of utilitarian type, with vessels for many uses, and chiefly without design—made much like that of the Pima and Papago Indians. An outstanding ceramist of the Maricopa was Ida Redbird, whose mother, *Kwehadk,* taught her the art. Like so many of the Indian people, Mrs. Redbird had a wide command of the English language as well as her mother tongue. She served as informant and interpreter for several well-known scientists. Although her eyes dimmed with advancing age, she continued to make fine pottery and contributed to the advancement of her people until the time of her tragic death. During a thunderstorm on 10 August 1971, a tree fell on her while she was resting, and she was crushed to death. Her age was said to be seventy-nine (Anonymous 1971e:21; Anonymous 1971f:1).

Several other Maricopa women produce good vessels. Their effigy pottery is traditional and is still made. But the majority of pieces decorated with black-on-red or black-on-buff are largely of non-Indian concept; they are made for the tourist trade, and are highly popular. A variety of jars and bowls of glossy red or buff, or a combination of the two, with simple designs are attractive. The long-necked jars are adapted from an old form used for syrup, or for the safe-keeping of enemy scalps. The Maricopa have not been producers of basketry.

Old ceremonies, the great emphasis on dreams, and distinctive native social customs now are nonexistent.

Farming

The economy today rests mainly on subsistence farming, cotton raising, and wage work. Most of the individual Maricopa land allotments are too small to be farmed profitably; for this reason most lands are leased to non-Indians for agricultural development.

It has been noted that the Maricopa dwell on the Gila and the Salt reservations. They do not, as one might expect, live on the Maricopa Indian Reservation (Ak Chin) just south of Maricopa, Arizona. This is another good example of the confusion concerning Indian groups that has come to obtain— particularly in Arizona—since the coming of non-Indians. It is the Papago Indians, over two hundred of them, who occupy 21,800 acres of Maricopa Indian Reservation lands.

The Cahitans

The Yaqui Indians

Of the Indians speaking Cahitan, those known as the Yaqui (YAH-key) are the southernmost of the Indians discussed, south of the Papago. The Cahitan-speaking people of the Uto-Aztecan stock lived in southern Sonora, Mexico (*see* Kurath and Spicer 1947:11; McGuire 1977). They dwelt at the mouths of large rivers, and along the entire length of the Río Yaqui. With abundant water, they tended to have somewhat concentrated settlements, or rancherias, and practiced dry farming. The density of their population led to development of genuine tribal organization with permanent ceremonial groups. In addition to shamanism, at least rudimentary forms of priesthood came into being. Emphasis on warfare led to integration of all the Yaqui rancherias.

Brief History

The armed intrusion of the Spaniards into the Yaqui territory was resisted from the beginning. The first contact occurred in 1533, and the Yaqui were eminently successful in the encounters. They were strong enough to set their own terms for the entrance of the Jesuit missionaries. In time, the relationship became both hostile and friendly. After a major affray in 1609, in which the Yaqui were victorious, it is said that:

Suddenly, to the surprise of the Spaniards, the Yaquis asked for peace. This was an event which the Spanish in their chronicles spoke of as unprecedented in military history. The reasons for the Yaqui action remain uncertain; there were two versions current. One held that Hurdaide [Spanish captain headquartered on the site of modern Sinaloa] circulated stories about the arrival of the reinforcements by sea. Another version was that the Yaquis were so impressed by the Spanish military ability and

Hurdaide's miraculous escape [from the conflict] that they thought it would be safest to ally themselves with the Spaniards rather than keep on fighting. (Spicer 1970:47)

Yaqui acceptance of the Jesuit missions was rapid. For several score years unusual tranquility prevailed, with economic and religious development. Government of the towns, except for the Spanish captain-general, was in the hands of the Indians.

With the discovery of rich silver mines at Alamos in 1684, things began to change, but the Yaqui initially were not much affected. In less than a half-century, however, the antagonism of one of the Spanish governors against the missionary program led to increasing discontent. In 1740, the Yaqui and their kindred, the Mayo, revolted. Just what precipitated the revolt and what actually occurred is not known, but it was costly to the Indians and Spaniards alike. Over one thousand Spaniards were killed and more than five thousand Indians.

Practically all of the mines were abandoned; all missionaries were forced to leave; livestock was killed or driven away; and an atmosphere of suspicion and distrust had been created (*see* Spicer 1970:52). A new governor was named and he began to rule "with an iron hand."

The Jesuits returned to the missions when things quieted down, and the governor instituted "a series of restrictive measures, requiring that no Indian be permitted to leave any pueblo without the permission of missionaries, impressing Indians for forced labor on mines and haciendas, and requiring that there be daily recitation of prayers by all Indians in the mission communities. . . . After 120 years the typical Spanish frontier situation had finally developed in the Yaqui-Mayo country. . . ." (Spicer 1970:52–53)

With the return of the missionaries to their missions—which had not been destroyed—an attempt was made to reestablish things as they had been before. But the attitude of the Indians was changed, and their old level of prosperity was not regained. The Yaqui population, like that of the Mayo, declined; it was estimated that some 23,000 Yaqui remained. This was partly due to the migrations that were taking place. It was reported in 1760 that thousands of Yaqui were living away from the lower Yaqui River settlements; the people were widely dispersed. "This emigration dismayed the missionaries and gave the civil authorities the feeling that an era of decline had set in in the formerly thriving Sonoran missions" (Spicer 1970:53). They intensified their efforts among the Indians who remained, and the civil authorities concerned themselves with ways and means of increasing economic activity.

By the early 1800s, it is said, "The blending of Spanish-Catholic theocracy and Indian democracy resulted in very stable and tightly organized communities. These communities were not, however, conceived by the Indians as units in a European nation. Rather the Yaquis and Mayos, for example, still conceived themselves as independent tribal units holding their land from immemorial times and not by fiat of the Spaniards. It was growing clear that the Spaniards were fearful of challenging that view" (Spicer 1970:59–60). It was not until the Mexican government attempted to integrate the Mayo and the Yaqui into the dominant cultural pattern that hostilities really came to a head.

After the War of Independence (1821), the Mexicans considered the Indians to be citizens of Mexico and therefore taxable. The Yaqui, who had never been taxed, consistently resisted efforts to divide their land for individual ownership; they endeavored to maintain their own local government as distinct as possible from provincial or state governments, and refused to pay taxes. Conflicts ensued. Laws were enacted to integrate the Indians. These the Yaqui could not comprehend.

Through the years administrations changed; sometimes the Indians were deeply involved, again they were left practically alone for years. Perhaps one Yaqui group would take a certain action, while another had no part in the transactions or encounters. Military conflicts were many; sometimes the Yaqui winning, and at other times their opponents. Many of the defeated Yaqui were in desperate circumstances, without food and clothing, and decimated by smallpox and other illnesses. Prisoners were sent out of the Yaqui country to work, or sold as slaves.

Beginning in the 1880s, some of the Yaqui left their homeland and moved northward into southern Arizona and settled in rancherias. They were accepted there as refugees. Of the stronger groups, some Yaqui retaliated by raiding the ever encroaching farms and ranches of the Mexicans and settlers from the United States. By 1900 their numbers equaled those of the Yaqui in the old Yaqui territory. In 1919 only three of the original Yaqui towns remained. After 1900 a conspicuously large influx of Yaqui into Arizona occurred.

A visit of President Obregón to the Yaqui country in 1926 precipitated a battle between the Mexican troops and the Yaqui. As a result, more of the Indians fled to the United States to live in a half-dozen communities that had grown up in southern Arizona.

The history of the main Yaqui groups in their encounters with and reactions to the foreigners who invaded their country makes fascinating reading. The publications of Spicer, who has studied the Yaqui in great detail, and the references to other authorities which he has cited, are recommended (*see* bibliography).

The Arizona Yaqui (Pascua Yaqui)

Our interest lies with those Yaqui who have come to dwell in Arizona. Their migrations, incidentally, continued slowly to the present time. Here, in several recognized settlements and lesser clusters, Yaqui ceremonial organizations have persisted, minus the accompanying political organizations that affect the Sonoran Yaqui. Cultural ties are maintained between the Arizona and the Mexican groups.

Probably the best known of the Yaqui villages was Pascua, once on the outskirts of Tucson, then engulfed by the spreading metropolis, and finally demolished by an Urban Renewal project. Dwellings in Pascua were fashioned of adobe bricks and corrugated sheet iron. Each house had a yard enclosed by a wire fence, with a few trees, small plots of green and colorful flowers. Almost every family had an open ramada in which much of the living took place and which served as a gathering center at fiestatime. At one end of the village plaza was a small church, brillantly white; at the opposite end, the fiesta ramada which was under the direction of the ceremonial societies. A wooden cross stood in front of each of these structures. At the side was a community kitchen in which the Yaqui women prepared foods over open fires—tortillas, stew, and coffee, primarily—during the fiestas. Many ceremonies took place in the plaza. Similar scenes may be witnessed in other Yaqui villages.

Just north of the San Xavier Indian Reservation of the Papago, the Yaqui have built a whole new village on a section of land provided by the government. At first, as they became able to do so, those who wished to leave the old village and build homes in the new community might do so. Then, with the razing of Pascua, those who had remained there moved to the new village or elsewhere. Another Yaqui settlement, Barrio Libre, has been established in South Tucson.

Other Yaqui villages are Guadalupe near Tempe (see Anonymous 1980:C–6), and another in the Phoenix area—Water Users Village at Scottsdale. About 1,800 Yaqui dwell in the two communities. Marana and Eloy each have Yaqui villages. All together, the Yaqui in Arizona now number in excess of 5,000. The village organization is entirely in terms of the ceremonial groups in each instance. In each of their locations the Yaqui merge with the neighboring populations, Indian and Anglo.

The men have made a place for themselves in the cotton fields, on ranches and farms, in the construction trades, and in other jobs. Because the Yaqui speak a tongue foreign to the other Indians living in Arizona and the Anglos alike, and since many of them have lacked educational opportunities, the Yaqui have found these factors something of a barrier to significant economic advancement.

Yaqui Ceremonials

Being of Old Mexican origin and long influenced by the Catholic religion, the ceremonial pattern of the Yaqui is a rich blend of aboriginal and introduced traditions. The ceremonies—based on Miracle Plays of the Jesuits, in which the life of Jesus was dramatized, and to which the Yaqui added their own beliefs and rituals—are enacted with a devoted consecration. The Yaqui remember no native supernatural beings, "but legend and memory remind them of the belief, similar to that of other Indians in the Southwest, that special power was obtainable from the natural world of forests, mountains, caves, and from dreams" (Painter and Sayles 1962:5).

The symbolism that the blood of Jesus "as it fell from the cross was by a miracle of heaven transformed into flowers," is found throughout the Yaqui ceremonies. Flowers are offered as tribute to the holy ones. Especially during Holy Week and climaxing with Easter, crowds gather in the Yaqui villages, particularly in the Tucson locations and at Guadalupe, where religious rituals, processions, dancing and pantomime continue through the night—deer dances, *matachines, pascolas, fariscos,* and related activities. At dawn special prayers greet the morning. Members of the ceremonial societies serve in "fulfillment of vows made to Jesus or to Mary in return for help in time of crisis. The work of carrying out these sacred duties is known as 'flower.' It must be done faithfully and 'with good heart' to merit heavenly reward of 'flower.' Some of the regalia is also called 'flower' " (Painter and Sayles 1962:5; *see* Spicer et al. 1971).

One who has viewed many of the colorful Yaqui ceremonies and written of them, tells us that:

Melodious bells and the rustle of cocoon ankle rattles herald the arrival of the Pascolas. When a Pascola dances to the high notes of the flute and the pervasive rhythm of a drum played by one man he wears his painted wooden mask over his face and beats on his palm with a small instrument [*matraca*] that jangles like a tambourine. For the alternate music of violin and harp he pushes his mask to one side. The string that ties his hair in a top knot is called 'flower.' In addition to dancing, the Pascolas delight the people with nonsense, double talk, jokes, and stories, some of age-old tradition. (Painter and Sayles 1962)

As to a deer dance, it is said that:

With a brisk shake of his gourds and his belt of deer-hoof rattles, the Deer dancer makes his entrance. His headdress is a stuffed deer head tipped with red ribbons which symbolize flowers. A red ribbon between the antlers is tied in the form of a cross. The deer songs to which he dances are treasured poetry from the past, reminiscent of the forest home of the deer, of flowers, clouds, rain, and wild creatures. The three Deer singers play native instruments of water drum and swift-moving raspers. The songs and dances were originally hunting rituals. (Painter and Sayles 1962:6; *see* Spicer et al. 1971)

Visitors to the Yaqui ceremonies will better understand what they are observing if the work cited, or other sources, are read in advance. Painter and Sayles include a calendar of annual events.

It should be remarked that not only do the Yaqui of Arizona attend the ceremonies given there, but they go by the hundreds to Magdalena, Sonora, which is fifty-five miles south of Nogales, to attend the fiesta of Saint Francis of Assisi on 4 October of each year. There they mingle with the Sonoran Yaqui and Mayo, as well as with Papago and Pima peoples.

STAR, STAR, MY LITTLE ONE

Star, Star, my little one
Star, I love you.
The name Star was taken
Out of the sky
And given to you, my little one.
Let me water you with
Shining praise, listen to
Your grandmother. She shall
Give you part of her knowledge
And me, I only have love
For you.
        You will learn lots.
You will be of beauty
With the knowledge, love, courage
Following you, taking every
Step with you.
Star shine bright for
Everyone to respect
You and your name.

By Sharlene Enos, Pima

From *Art and Indian Children,*
Curriculum Bulletin No. 7, 1970.
Institute of American Indian Arts,
Santa Fe, N.M.

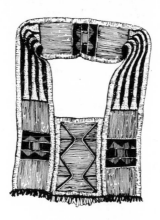

7
Arts and Crafts

Indian crafts had their practical and esthetic origins in needs of the Indian peoples. In the days of easy access to manufactured goods, the crafts might have disappeared completely had it not been for sales to non-Indian connoisseurs. The Indians are practical as well as artistic and imaginative, and through the years they have modified traditional forms to suit the tastes and purposes of others. For example, the burden basket became a waste basket, the water bottle served as a container for flowers, and the bowl-shaped baskets made fine bread or fruit bowls. Indian potters fashioned lamps, table settings, ash trays, cigarette boxes, and candlesticks. Weavers made beautiful floor coverings or wall hangings, and ties for draperies, or bell calls. Metalsmiths worked in silver, brass, and copper to create handsomely designed belts, bracelets, rings, earrings, pins, money clips, and boxes. Many articles were set with turquois or coral, and occasionally jet and other semiprecious stones.

Basketry and Weaving

Basketry and weaving were among the earliest of handicrafts in the Southwest. (It is probable that they developed simultaneously at a time when the Pueblos lived in pit houses, or much earlier.) The distinction between the two crafts is often an arbitrary one, based upon form and use rather than upon method of construction. One authority has said that basketry has two fundamental classes: coiled, which leads to the needle, and woven, which leads to the loom.

Coiled basketry was preceded by twined types and wickerwork, which date back to about 7000 B.C. Sandals woven of fibers were made in ancient times. Coiled baskets have been made in the Southwest for more than two thousand years.

Relatively little basketry is produced today by the Indians in New Mexico and Colorado. A few of the Pueblo Indians still weave wickerwork baskets of willow and basket bowls of beargrass or yucca. Jémez produces the latter in some quantity; and the Hopi make attractive ones in contrasting colors. So extensive are the taboos pertaining to the making of Navajo basketry that the Navajo make but a small number of the baskets which they use. They find it much simpler to purchase those made by the Ute or Paiute, who accommodate them by weaving baskets with typical Navajo designs (see Stewart, O. C. 1938a, b).

When the program of Navajo Community College was being arranged, it was found that of all the residents on the reservation only two Navajo women still were weaving ceremonial wedding baskets. They were taken to the college to teach this skill to others; the tour of duty was one year at a time for each. As students developed proficiency under this intense tutelage, they took over the teaching of basketry making. Women and a few Navajo men now make baskets.

Similarly, other artisans skilled in weaving textiles, producing leather work, pottery making, and silversmithing had to be located and brought to the college. The late Kenneth Begay, for instance, famous the world over for his silver working, left a lucrative practice in Scottsdale, Arizona, to return to the reservation and teach his people this art (see Barry 1971; Rosnek and Stacey 1976:64, 113–117, 141). Begay died in 1978.

The beautiful coiled bowls of split yucca, characteristic of the Mescalero Apache, are now rarely, if ever, produced. Attempts to stimulate basketry weaving among the Mescalero women have been made, but these were short-lived. The Jicarilla Apache continue to make a few of their coiled baskets, some of fine workmanship, others of inferior quality. The western Apache continue the art to a certain degree (see Robinson 1954:57–84).

Among the Hopi, fine wicker plaques are made on Third Mesa, and beautiful coiled baskets on Second Mesa (see Tanner and Tanner 1979:69–75). The Papago and some of the Pima-Maricopa still make fine basketry (see Cain 1962; Dedera 1972; Robinson 1954:1–53; Shreve 1943). Some women make as many as 100 baskets in a year. A very few women know how to fashion the watertight baskets used in Papago ceremonies. Yavapai and Havasupai baskets are now very rare; the Hualapai make some bright colored baskets for the tourist trade (see Dedera ibid.). Good modern baskets are expensive and old ones are still higher—running to hundreds of dollars, even thousands.

The weaving of cotton textiles has existed among the Pueblos since about A.D. 750. The oldest known piece of cotton fabric is thought to have been made in A.D. 858. During the fourteenth century, the Pueblos reached their highest development in this art. Fine openwork, delicate gauzes, and elaborately patterned damask fabrics were all produced, along with the simpler techniques still practiced.

Weaving in wool began some time around 1600, after the introduction of sheep into the Southwest by the Spaniards. The Pueblo and Navajo looms are practically identical, and they show no European influence to this day. *(Rel.* Kent, K. P. 1976.)

By 1706, Navajo weaving was well enough established to attract the attention of a Spanish chronicler. In the following years rapid progress was made in beauty and quality. The oldest known examples of Navajo weaving have come from Massacre Cave, Canyon del Muerto, in Arizona, where a group of Navajo women and children were killed in 1805. The golden age of Navajo weaving came after that date, and by 1850 Navajo women had brought their weaving to its peak of perfection. From 1863–1868, the Navajo were confined at Fort Sumner. After their return to their home country, changes in weaving took place (1875–1890), with the introduction of commercial dyes, commercial yarns, and new ideas of design. *(See* Amsden 1934—a classic.)

After 1890, rugs began to take the place of blankets. Until about 1910 there was a "dark age" in Navajo weaving; quality fell off, and the native designs almost ceased; bordered specimens predominated. Then came a change for the better, due largely to efforts of the traders to raise the standard of Navajo weaving. Art lovers and scientists did their part, too. Again, relatively thin blankets began to appear, with stripes, terraces, and colors of an earlier day. With government help, new soft colors were developed from native plants. Fineness of weaving and quality increased. *(Rel.* Dedera 1975; Rodee 1977; Rodee 1981.)

All of the family helps with shearing the sheep, but the woman washes, cards, dyes, and spins the wool. She still uses the primitive spindle—a smooth, slender hardwood stick about two feet in length, which is pushed through a thin wooden disc from four to five inches in diameter. The loom consists of two upright poles and two cross bars supporting the warp frame. The weaver works from the bottom up, and manipulates her batten, comb, and yarns with dextrous fingers.

At the present some outstandingly fine weaving is being produced by a few Navajo, but in general the work seems to bespeak an approaching demise of the weaving art. Fewer looms operate. The situation may be compared to "fancy work."

Practically no textile weaving is done now by the Pueblo Indians, with exception of belts, head bands, and garters, which are made by men or women, and by girls in the schools. It was the ancient custom for men to weave the shoulder robes and black dresses (*mantas*), sashes, and belts. In most of the pueblos the ordinary clothing worn by the women is purchased from a store or trading post. Ceremonial weaving is largely obtained from the Hopi Indians who still produce traditional garments and accessories. Embroidery, formerly a man's craft, may now be taught to girls in school. *(Rel.* Rodee 1977: 115 ff.; Rodee 1981.)

The Navajo women weave some of the red belts that they wear, and these are almost indistinguishable from those woven by the Hopi. The Apache do no weaving other than what the girls may do in school.

Pottery

Pottery making was introduced into the Southwest from Mexico. The earliest evidences, found in southern New Mexico and Arizona, date from a few centuries before the Christian era—that is, 350 B.C. at Snaketown. *(See* Dittert 1972; Gummerman and Haury 1979:78–79.) After considerable time this art spread to the Pueblo Indians.

Traditionally, only women made the pottery. Throughout the centuries household vessels were created, broken, and thrown out on the refuse heaps. With this simple procedure, history was written—history which the archaeologists can read almost as easily as a book. To reveal the records of the past, the archaeologist cuts a trench through one of the abandoned middens, thus exposing layer upon layer of accumulated debris. In these strata, fragments of pottery withstand the passing of time and tell their story. Thanks to the fact that the pot makers were conformists, they have provided (and are still supplying) an invaluable archive of their activities. In the various regions, certain forms, types, manufacturing techniques, and styles of decoration, were developed; and from time to time changes in color, shape, quality of paste (clay mixed with water), occurred. Thus these bits of broken pottery show sequences and modification, and trade from one area to another. *(See* Lambert 1966; Dittert and Plog 1980:16–26; *rel.* Stanislawski 1978:17, 21.) They contribute much toward reconstruction of the ancient cultures. If the visitor in the Southwest can learn only a little of what these potsherds mean, if he can place but a few of them in their proper historical position, it will add much to the enjoyment of his travels through the land.

With astonishingly little effort, one can learn to distinguish the pottery styles of the modern pueblos. Design patterns are traditional and, in the main, each pueblo holds to its own. A market day spent under the portal of the Palace of the Governors or a few hours at the Museum of New Mexico in Santa Fe, the Arizona State Museum in Tucson, the Museum of Northern Arizona at Flagstaff, the Heard Museum and Pueblo Grande in Phoenix, or museums in other Southwestern cities, will send the observant traveler away rich in new lore. The sky band, bird, and cloud motifs of Zía; the floral designs and realistic fauna of Cóchiti; the strong geometric arrangements of Santo Domingo (Chapman 1936); the precision and beauty of Acoma workmanship; and the mask and conventionalized bird symbols of the Hopi, are but a few of the characteristics that will cling in his memory. *(Rel.* Brody 1979b:603 ff.)

By the early part of this century, pottery making in the Río Grande pueblos had in some instances died out entirely, while other villages were producing mainly utility wares. A few pueblos were making polished red and/or polished black, black-on-cream, or polychrome wares. It is known that polychrome ware was being made at San Ildefonso by 1875; it was the dominant type in the 1890s, and continued until about 1920. The plain black ware, similar to that long produced at Santa Clara, also may have been made at San Ildefonso as early as 1875. (See Hill 1982:83–90.)

In 1908, while excavating in a cave in the Rito de los Frijoles, archaeologists of the School of American Research uncovered some prepared pottery clay which had never been fashioned into vessels by the prehistoric artisans. The material was given to Marie, or María, and Julian Martínez of San Ildefonso, who made several pieces of pottery from it, decorating the specimens and firing them according to the procedure of that period. The results were very satisfactory. This, and encouragement given María (Po-ve-ka) by members of the School of American Research staff, appears to have stimulated her and other Tewa artisans to produce wares of increasing quality and quantity. (Julian died in 1943, María in July, 1980, at the age of 94; see Peterson 1977.)

During the early 1900s the black-on-red style of the San Ildefonso potters, which appears to have been made as early as the first half of the nineteenth century, gained some popularity and improved in quality, but the public never responded to it very well. About 1919, experiments were begun at San Ildefonso which resulted in the now popular black burnished and matte ware. Santa Clara began to produce a similar ware about 1930. The first pieces made at both pueblos had the mass dull and the design burnished. Then, with exception of the *awanyu,* or serpent, element of San Ildefonso—which is always polished—this combination was sometimes reversed. Today the standardized ware has the mass burnished and the design in matte (see Chapman and Harlow 1970; Harlow 1973).

The incised pottery of San Juan represents a revival of an old form of decoration. About 1931, the late Mrs. Regina Cata began copying the technique employed on an archaeologic ware known as *Potsuwi'i Incised,* which occurs commonly at ruins on the Pajarito plateau. The deeply carved wares in red and black are of recent origin in the Tewa pueblos. Tesuque did not adopt this form of embellishment until 1942. (Frank and Harlow 1974; *rel.* Edelman and Ortiz 1979:334, Fig. 8; Toulouse, B. 1977:20 ff.)

In 1954, the French government presented the much coveted *Palmes Académiques* to two Pueblo pottery-makers, María Martinez of San Ildefonso, and Severa Tafoya of Santa Clara, both now deceased. (See LeFree 1975; Toulouse, B. 1977:17–19.)

It is to be hoped that the visitor in the Southwest, as well as those who dwell here, will be selective in making their purchases of Indian products. In the markets, trading posts, and pueblo homes, both good works and bad will be found. If one selects good pieces, he himself will be the gainer. And he will also assist the Southwestern Association on Indian Affairs, and others, in their efforts to maintain high standards for Indian-made goods. It will add interest if he informs himself about the classic designs. The conventionalized serpent, the triangular rain bird, the different water symbols—rain at a distance, rain nearby, and so on; when he can recognize some of these he will have taken a step back into a time when myth was reality.

Commercialization has brought about changes in some of the pueblos. It has resulted in new and smaller forms, often lowered quality and careless execution, and flamboyant use of color in decoration. At Tesuque, for instance, several good potters can produce fine pottery (and they will do so if good ware is appreciated), but most of the present output consists of the gaudily painted (with show card colors), novelty items that are made expressly for the tourist trade. They cannot even be classed as true Indian ceramics, inasmuch as the decoration is applied *after* the pottery is fired. Jémez, Isleta, and Santo Domingo, lamentably, are also producing similar pseudo-Indian ceramics. In defense of the Indian, however, it should be explained that the idea for this type of product seems to have originated with a non-Indian. The designs are often well done, however. Finely wrought pieces in new styles have appeared gradually.

A variation in decoration of Maricopa pottery may be noted, and that of some other Indians of southern Arizona, who sometimes repaint their designs and fire vessels a second time. The firing must be in the tradition of the makers, utilizing a simple outdoor kiln and fuels of immemorial usage. Manufacturing techniques, shapes, designs and colors must be representative of the pueblo or cultural group in which the pottery originates (*rel.* Dutton 1966:5). The Papago still make a few bean pots, water cooling jars, and syrup jars.

Visitors who wish to know more than can be suggested here, will find exhibits on display at most of the Southwestern museums.

In examining the collections of Southwestern pottery, it may be of interest to remember that the method of manufacture is as traditional as the form and design. The smoothing stone used by the potter may be centuries old, handed down from mother to daughter, or picked up from an ancient ruin. An Indian woman does not sit down to make a vessel at random. Much preparation is necessary. Clays must be brought in from the hills and prepared. For strengthening the clay, tempering materials must be at hand. Paints are to be collected, such as the mineral earths to be obtained for the colored washes and designs, and perhaps *guaco,* or Rocky Mountain bee plant, or Tansy mustard, to be gathered and boiled to produce a black pigment. Paint brushes are the leaves of the spiked yucca or soap weed, chewed until only the stiff fibers remain.

No potter's wheel is used. All aboriginal American pottery is strictly handmade. A pancake of paste is patted into shape for the base of the bowl, and the walls are built up by successive coils of rolled clay, which are afterward smoothed to uniformity. After a vessel is made it is dried for a while in the air, then the slip is applied and after further drying it is decorated. Finally the pottery is fired. A convenient dry spot is selected near the home of the potter, and a fire is made on the ground. When a bed of coals is formed, a rude grate is constructed from items at hand—bits of iron, stones, old bricks, tin cans. Then the pottery is arranged over the grate, usually upside down. Cakes of dried dung are placed around and over the vessels. The fire is renewed with shredded juniper bark or other suitable material. Small pieces of dung are tucked into the crevices, but space is left for air to circulate.

The black pottery is a highly polished red before it goes into the fire. If it is to remain red, it is fired with an oxidizing flame. If black is desired, the fire is smothered with fine, loose manure, permitting the smudge or carbon to penetrate the porous clay.

Hopi pottery has shown much degeneration, but good pieces are still produced on First Mesa. In southern Arizona, as among the Papago and Maricopa, a paddle-and-anvil method was used, rather than coiling and scraping of the Pueblo and other Indians. (See Dittert and Plog 1980:30–37 ff.)

The Apache Indians have not made pottery for a number of years. The Navajo continue to make their cylindrical vessels in some quantity, pots with pointed or flat bottoms, which may be arranged easily in the coals of a campfire. From the Pueblos they have learned to make certain Pueblolike pieces, which are primarily decorated with red on a buff colored background. Tin cans and commercially manufactured utensils are too readily available to make pottery production worth the effort to most of the Navajo of today (see Brugge 1963). Recently Navajo pieces based on the styles of Casas Grandes of Mexico have been produced.

Jewelry

Often we speak of turquois and silver in the same breath. But turquois has been cherished by the Southwestern Indians for centuries, while the use of silver came to them through white men. The cult of the turquois is legendary. The stone was said to have benign powers; even a bead of it tied in the hair would ward off calamity, and the wearer would be immune to many of life's hazards. The Indians have traveled great distances to obtain turquois. The hard, deep blue stones have always been the most prized.

Metal work among the Navajo dates from about the middle of the nineteenth century. The first work was done in iron. A few learned metal working from the Spanish-Americans, but it was mainly while detained at Fort Sumner that some of the Navajo men learned the craft. There they were given coils of brass and copper which they fashioned into bracelets and ornaments for ring bits. No silver work was done until after the Navajo returned home from Fort Sumner. From then on the production of silver increased gradually. Their equipment was incredibly crude. One of the early metal workers used a discarded shovel as a melting pot, and his tools were scissors, a hammer, and a file. Bells were hammered from quarters, and American dollars were melted and made into tobacco canteens, bridles, bow guards, etc. Then the American coins were discarded for the Mexican *peso*, which was richer in silver content and more malleable. The Indians now use slug, sheet, and wire silver.

A wide range of silver articles, in many patterns and for many uses, is now made by the Navajo, but the objects they make primarily for their own gratification as well as that of the tourist are largely items of personal adornment: conchas for belts, buttons, bracelets, finger rings, earrings, necklaces, hat bands, and so on. The common type of Navajo necklace is made of large, hollow, silver beads separated by flower-shaped pendants, with a crescent-shaped ornament in front. These are generally called "squash blossom" necklaces, from the pendant features. Actually, this is a misnomer, for the blossom element is derived from the Mexican trouser and jacket ornaments fashioned to represent the young fruit of the pomegranate. The pomegranate pattern has been a favorite Spanish design for centuries. The terminal crescent, or *najah,* which may also be used as a bridle decoration, is likewise traceable to a Moorish origin; on the other hand, a similar form was known to the ancient Pueblos, for shell ornaments of this shape are found in ruin sites.

Silver bow guards were formerly made for use by the Navajo, and they may still be worn as ornaments. The practical need for the *ketoh* was to protect the wrist when using the bow and arrow. They may well serve in that capacity today, with the archery enthusiast, or as an unusual wrist ornament for dress occasions—particularly with evening wear—or with sport attire. As to the conchas (*concha* is the Spanish word for shell), the silver discs secured on leather belts, some authorities feel that it has been conclusively demonstrated that the Navajo derived them from the Plains Indians, their traditional enemies, such as the Kiowa and Comanche. On the contrary, since conchas identical with those found on old Navajo belts are made as bridle ornaments throughout Mexico, and by the Arabs on the southern edge of the Sahara desert, others think that their Old World derivation is certain. (*See* Jernigan 1978.)

Until about 1880, no settings of any kind were made. Then bits of glass, beads, buttons, and native garnets and jet began to be used. Turquois was not set in quantity much before 1900. No symbols are represented by the designs stamped and engraved on Navajo jewelry; most of them are the same as those used for centuries by the Spanish and Mexican leather workers. Of course, innovations occur.

The French *Palmes Académiques* was awarded to Ambrose Roanhorse, in 1954, for outstanding production of Navajo silverwork.

The Pueblo Indians, as well as the Navajo, are masters in jewelry making. They have known the art of carving turquois, shell and other substances, for centuries. Of the Pueblos, the people of Zuñi rank foremost in the production of jewelry. Their work in metals also started with the use of iron. They hold that they learned metal craft from the Spaniards, but this is questionable. About 1830–1840, they began to fashion jewelry from brass and copper. Old pots and pans, melted and hammered into shape, became buttons, rings, bracelets, and bow guard mountings. Later, copper and brass wire were used. Around 1870, the Zuñi learned from the Navajo how to work silver and make dies. When silver was introduced, working in brass and copper gradually died out for the most part. (Silver substitutes are appearing now that the price of silver has increased.)

During the 1870s and 1880s, Zuñi silver was simple and massive, like that of the Navajo. After the Zuñi learned to set turquois, about 1890, their craft became increasingly complex in design. Until about 1920, the silver output of the Zuñi smiths was sold or traded entirely to Indians of that or other pueblos or to the Navajo. Then the traders began buying their jewelry for the tourist trade. At that time not over eight silversmiths were practicing at Zuñi. Today there are hundreds; practically every man, woman, and child learned the art during the days of World War II, and the amount of production was astounding. Popular modern designs found in Zuñi jewelry include Knife Wing and Dragon Fly figures; men and women dressed in Zuñi attire; deer, butterflies, and other realistic figures in flat relief work. Some carving in the round, as of fetishes, occurs. (*See* Rosnek and Stacey 1976.)

Originally it was easy to distinguish Zuñi style from that of Navajo silversmiths—though it might be impossible to correctly identify individual pieces. With Zuñi jewelry, emphasis is on the *turquois;* almost every piece shows many small, individually set stones, or channel or mosaic work in larger stones. Zuñi silver pieces are of lighter weight than those of the Navajo. With the Navajo, it is the *silver* that counts most, and the turquois settings are secondary. Almost every piece of Navajo workmanship shows stamped designs, but the Zuñi smith uses dies most sparingly, if at all. There are other minor differences which may aid one in telling Zuñi jewelry from the Navajo. Now, many Navajo wear jewelry made by the Zuñi Indians. Distinctions have blurred.

It was long a practice of many traders who engaged Indian jewelry makers to have Navajo craftsmen fashion the basic pieces in silver, and then have Zuñi artisans set the stones, shell, jet, or other decorative elements. More recently, other dealers have taught Pueblo peoples to make silver pieces ornamented with the traditional materials. From Mexico, the use of tortoise shell, or *carey*, was introduced, especially to the Zuñi smiths. This is easily worked and harmonizes well with the traditional substances, but the Mexican source has been stopped. It is now illegal.

Some Hopi silverwork has been done since the latter part of the nineteenth century, having received its inspiration from Zuñi and Navajo smiths. In 1938 the Museum of Northern Arizona made silver manufacture among the Hopi one of its major projects. Hopi designs were utilized and distinctive pieces produced. Today, Hopi silverwork stands on its own merits; overlay is especially popular. *(See* Wright, M. N. 1972; Rosnek and Stacey 1976: 64–67; Loloma 1980:8–10; and Jacka and Hammack 1975.)

Several of the other pueblos have a history of silverworking which dates back roughly to 1890. Acoma and Isleta had a few silversmiths in the early days. Some of the younger people have learned this craft in school or in shops in the cities. The Laguna Indians have known silversmithing since 1870 or earlier. Among the Río Grande villages, the Santo Domingo people make more jewelry than the other Indians. The silver craft has been known there since 1893. Santo Domingo silver jewelry was essentially an imitation of the Navajo. But the traditional jewelry of this pueblo consisted of necklaces made of small disc beads of shell or turquois; of shell beads and chunk turquois; of jet—plain or inlaid with turquois—and turquois; and jet, shell, and turquois mosaic. These necklaces often had a crescent pendant of jet or shell inlaid with turquois. In later years, though the necklace form had changed little, jet gave way to the similar appearing materials afforded by old phonograph records or battery cases; shell largely was superseded by cylindrical beads made of gypsum; and shell and turquois mosaic work was frequently replaced by red-dyed gypsum and teeth from colored plastic combs.

Modern necklaces, together with rings, bracelets, and various types of Indian jewelry, may often be purchased from itinerant Pueblo traders on the streets of Santa Fe and Albuquerque, and often in more distant cities.

Santa Ana and Jémez took up silversmithing about 1890, when they learned the craft from the Navajo. Santa Clara had taken up this style of jewelry making a few years earlier (cf. Bedinger 1973:174–175). Several Pueblo silversmiths work in Santa Fe, Albuquerque, and Taos. Probably a few silversmiths reside in each of the pueblos.

The Apache and Ute Indians engage in the making of beadwork to some degree. Their clothing of yore was beautifully beaded, as were their moccasins and other accoutrement. Currently, most of the beadwork is in the form of necklaces, small bags, and miscellaneous items attractive to the tourist trade.

The Mohave Indians made beadwork in the form of yokes, necklaces, and other craft items. Other Yuman peoples, such as the Hualapai, produce a few beaded specimens.

The Genuine versus the Imitation

The buyer of native Indian arts and crafts items needs to exercise caution, and particularly with regard to jewelry. Unfortunately, things are not always what they seem. Most dealers are honest and conscientious, but a large quantity of so-called Indian arts and crafts is commercially manufactured and sold as of genuine Indian make in many parts of the country, particularly in the Southwest. Even some Indians may include commercially manufactured silverwork or treated or imitation turquois or coral settings with their native handicrafts. Frequently they are duped by some disreputable trader.

If you want a truly *handmade* Indian article, be sure to inquire about its authenticity. Some Indians are employed by commercial establishments in the manufacture of jewelry, and some do make such items in part, but the term *genuine Indian handmade* means jewelry that an Indian silversmith fashions with his own hands with tools of his own, and using real silver—not stainless steel or nickel-plated copper.

In order to distinguish the genuine from the imitation, it is suggested that you take some simple precautionary measures. Find out about the reliability of the firm or the individual with whom you are dealing. In buying a piece of jewelry, be especially wary of perfection! In a handmade piece, the silver work or the setting is rarely perfect. Examine the materials carefully; even an untrained eye can usually tell the difference between a semiprecious turquois and a reconstructed or imitation stone.

To be classified as authentic, an article must have a high sterling silver content (today, not all handmade silver pieces are sterling), and the stone, if turquois, must be genuine and unaltered. In most imitation pieces, the mounting is copper plated with nickel, and the stone is plastic or altered turquois.

In a genuine Zuñi channel inlay piece, the materials (turquois, shell, coral, jet, etc.) are cut and laid into silver partitions, leaving a slight metal break between the setting and the partition. In imitation articles, materials resembling settings are poured in, leaving no break. And in the imitation pieces, the blue is too blue for turquois, the red is too red for coral or shell, and the white is too white.

The sawtooth bezel (housing for a setting) on an imitation piece does not really grasp the setting, as it does in a Zuñi piece of cluster work. The spurious article is cast in a mold, after which the setting or stone is glued in.

A Navajo imitation setting has a vinyl tile effect, and the metal in a fake Navajo bracelet has no ring to it when struck with a hard object. Moreover, the design around the stone is obviously pressed out, rather than soldered to horizontal bands as it would be on a genuine Indian-made bracelet. A machine-made bracelet never has the design stamped as deep as a handmade article.

A sure test for determining the validity of the silver in a piece of jewelry is with a drop of nitric acid. Sterling silver turns white when the acid is applied; coin silver will be a little darker than sterling; Mexican silver may vary from a high silver content to very low, and the coloring from the acid reaction will vary from white for high silver content to dark for lower content. Nickel-plated copper in imitation jewelry will turn green.

New Mexico and Colorado laws require imitation Indian jewelry to be so labeled, but enforcement varies. Thus, you have to rely on reputable traders and merchants, or your own good judgment. *Get a signed receipt describing your purchases!*

An Indian craftsman turns out a piece of authentic jewelry slowly and laboriously. Assembly-line jewelry can be manufactured and turned out by the hundreds in the time it takes an Indian craftsman to make one piece. The Indians cannot begin to compete with the manufacturer of Indian jewelry, but the uninformed buyer often pays as much for the imitation as for the genuine. Silversmithing and other Indian crafts provide a livelihood for many Indians; they are important sources of income for the Indians.

With a little care you can know what you are buying, and demand the genuine. It is essential to the preservation of the traditional in Indian arts and crafts. You are justified in feeling proud of genuine Indian jewelry. It is truly beautiful, and many honest Indians, through many years, have been proud to make it so you may wear it.

Paintings

Countless artistic records of the Indians of the Southwest are pecked, incised, or painted on the rocks—petroglyphs and pictographs (see Schaafsma, P. 1980a, b; Wellman 1979). Pottery, from prehistoric times to the present, shows an extensive array of art forms. Occasionally, kiva paintings from ruin sites are uncovered. Fine examples of these wall paintings were found at Kuaua, an ancient pueblo near Bernalillo, New Mexico, now the Coronado State Monument. The kiva walls were found to have been covered with at least eighty-five layers of thin plaster, seventeen of which were decorated in true fresco painting (see Dutton 1963b). The kiva was restored, and the walls painted with replicas of the original frescoes. Other examples of these ancient works of art are shown in the Kuaua museum.

Archaeologists of the University of New Mexico unearthed beautiful kiva paintings at Pottery Mound, a prehistoric pueblo on the Río Puerco, southwest of Los Lunas (see Hibben 1975; Jernigan 1978). Some of these are similar to the Kuaua murals, others are very much like those excavated by Peabody Museum of Harvard University at Awatovi, in northeastern Arizona (see Smith, W. 1952, 1980:29–37). The Museum of Northern Arizona at Flagstaff has built a replica of a Hopi kiva and has reproduced kiva paintings on its walls. At the Tiwa pueblo of Picurís in the northern Río Grande drainage, ancient ceremonial rooms were excavated and found to display paintings on the walls (see Brown 1979:270). A chamber of this nature has been built in cross section in a new multiple purpose building, which contains a museum, and some of the paintings are reproduced on the walls. Other archaeological sites have revealed paintings (see Schaafsma, P. 1965).

In a canyon east of Bloomfield, New Mexico (in the Denétah, or old Navajoland) a fallen slab of sandstone with Navajo figures painted on it was discovered. Following a cooperative salvage project, this rare and culturally priceless record of the Navajo past was installed at the former Museum of Navajo Ceremonial Art, Inc., in Santa Fe (see Olin and Hadlock 1980:26–31). When that institution was reorganized in 1975, as the Wheelwright

Museum, this early eighteenth-century survival was sold to the Navajo Tribe in Window Rock. Payment was made with monies provided by patrons concerned with its safe deposition and exhibition on the Navajo Reservation.

When the Indians decorate their pottery or weave rugs of intricate patterns, they do not first draw the design and measure the space as other artists might do, yet the pattern of a good artist never fails to come out even and well balanced. Another example of sure eye and steady hand is illustrated by the Navajo sandpaintings. The "painters," depending upon the size and complexity of a painting, usually start near the center and work outward. The only marking of space is made by a string snapped on the background sand for the tall ye'ii figures; the rest is freehand. According to most authorities, the Navajo learned the art of sandpainting from the Pueblos, who still make drypaintings during certain ceremonies. The Jicarilla Apache, Pima, and Papago use drypaintings in some rituals (see Johnson, B. 1960:28–31).

The former Museum of Navajo Ceremonial Art had a collection of more than six hundred copies in color of sandpainting designs. From these, many 8 by 8 feet reproductions had been made and used as exhibitions. These were given by the Wheelwright to the Ned A. Hatathli Culture Center Museum, Navajo Community College at Tsaile, Arizona, together with medicine bundles pertaining to them. They now have been installed in that museum in an outstandingly significant manner (see Walters 1980). The exhibit is worth going hundreds or thousands of miles to see and appreciate.

Early in this century, a few Indian School teachers and other individuals began to take an interest in the drawings that certain young Indians produced when given colored crayons or water colors and paper. Pupils in the San Ildefonso day school were encouraged to draw the dance figures and to make cut-out patterns in colored papers, using Indian designs. Among these young artists showing promise were *Wen Tsireh* and *Awa Tsireh* (Alfredo Montoya and Alfonso Roybal respectively). In 1910 the paintings of Alfredo were furthered by providing him with suitable materials. Soon he was painting pictures which his white friends were glad to purchase. Unfortunately the young artist died in 1913. But he had influenced others at San Ildefonso.

A cousin of Alfredo's, Cresencio Martínez, according to the custom of that pueblo, was painting designs on the pottery made by the womenfolk of his family. Then he began making water color paintings. In 1917, he announced that he could paint all of the costumed figures in their ceremonial dances. He was given supplies, and promptly made good his claim. His work attracted the favorable attention of eminent artists. But he, too, was destined for an early death, in 1918.

Within a short time after Cresencio began painting ceremonial figures, other Indian boys made it known that they also could paint pictures. One of these was Awa Tsireh (see Dunn 1968:204–207). Another was a Hopi boy, Fred Kabotie (see Belknap and Kabotie 1977), and Otis Polelonema (see Brody 1980:91, Fig. 69), also a Hopi; and the late *Ma-pe-wi,* or Velino Shije Herrera *(see* Dunn 1968:207–208), of Zía. These young men, inspired by Cresencio's example and by the appreciation accorded his work, showed the same singular talent which he possessed. Never were any experiments made with their colors or patterns. Each picture was mentally completed, then with elaborate precision in drawing and color it was skillfully executed.

In 1919, an exhibit of Indian water colors was held in the Arts Club of Chicago. Three years later, the School of American Research in Santa Fe employed Awa Tsireh, Velino, and Kabotie to paint a few hours each day; no one instructed or influenced them, but their work during the period has never been excelled for color and composition. Velino appears to have been the first to introduce the element of pure design into Pueblo water color painting. At the same time, he was painting beautiful, action-filled horses in a masterly way. He continued to produce excellent works throughout the years, until an auto wreck on Christmas eve, 1956, incapacitated him extensively. Kabotie has painted less, but has written and has taught arts and crafts among his people. Polelonema was inactive for many years, while raising and educating a family, but resumed his art. Awa Tsireh painted hundreds of pictures until his death, in March, 1955. The day before he died, he was in Santa Fe to get paper for more paintings. One of the first young women to attract attention by her artistic production was the late Tonita Peña *(see* Dunn 1968:202–203, 210–211, 217 ff.), a San Ildefonso girl married to a Cóchiti man. Some dealers have the works of these artists for sale, and museums all over the country exhibit their pictures.

Indian art is as distinct from European or American art as is Chinese or Japanese, to which Indian art is more nearly related. It is decorative and imaginative, usually two-dimensional, although the Hopi and other individuals have painted in the round. Seldom is a background shown, but a few more recent painters have indicated backgrounds in a simple, thoroughly original, but satisfying manner. Sacred subjects such as rain, the rainbow, and clouds are represented symbolically. Indians do not paint from models; because of their powers of observation and memory they have no need for them. Traditionally, more important objects may be made larger or more prominent. In some ways, it may be said that Indian art is four-dimensional; they actually paint the rhythm and steps of the dance, the action of the horse, the speed of the antelope, the heat of the desert.

As late as 1928, it was the general practice to forbid the painting of Indian subjects in the government Indian schools. But, in 1932, the Bureau of Indian Affairs established a painting department in the Santa Fe Indian School, and placed it under the direction of Miss Dorothy Dunn (now Mrs. Max Kramer) *(see* Dunn 1968). Some good paintings were also produced in the Albuquerque Indian School at that time. One of the outstanding artists to come from that institution was José Rey Toledo of Jémez *(see* Tanner 1957, 1973:164–168).

Each year, exhibitions of Indian paintings from the Santa Fe Indian School were held in museums all over the United States and in many foreign countries, including galleries in London and Paris. The department was not only self-supporting through the sales of student work (paying 50 percent to the artists), but it also contributed to other school activities. In 1940, one of the students, Ben Quintana of Cóchiti pueblo, won the Youth Administration prize of $1,000, over more than fifty thousand contestants from all parts of the United States. In 1951, Vidal Casiquito, Jr., Jémez, was one of twelve winners in a poster contest sponsored by the National Cartoonist Society and the U.S. Treasury. Indian artists have won many honors and awards.

After about a decade of outstanding artistic productions by students in the art department, the war's demands on the young people, changes in policy at the Santa Fe School, and a variety of factors resulted in an appalling degeneracy of Indian art. Fortunately, a few of the prewar artists continued to produce fine works. The Apache artist Allan Houser *(see* Dunn 1968:282, 311, 321, 330, 352), and Fred Kabotie were both honored by the Guggenheim Foundation with fellowships to continue their art work. When the *Palmes Académiques* were presented to Indian artists in 1954, those recognized for their paintings were: Fred Kabotie, Joe H. Herrera, Pablita Velarde, Harrison Begay, Allan Houser, Awa Tsireh, Velino Herrera, and Andrew Tsihnahjinnie, a Navajo painter from Arizona *(see* Dutton and Olin 1979aI: mid-book and ff.).

The initial days of promoting painting and allied arts at the Santa Fe and Albuquerque Indian schools were followed by similar programs at the Phoenix Indian School and other schools which Southwestern Indian students attended. At the same time, some of the reservation schools gave attention to Indian art, as at Zuñi, the Hopi villages, and elsewhere *(see* Dutton and Olin 1979bII). A number of artists came to the fore and their works found buyers from the world over. Some have continued painting while others have given up their art, at least for the most part *(see* Dunn 1968; Tanner 1957, 1973).

New ideas of education for the Indians were developed, and as a result the Santa Fe Indian School was discontinued. In its stead a new establishment came into being and, as the Institute of American Indian Arts, was opened in October, 1962, with a two-year AFA degree-granting program. A stated purpose of the Institute was to "open new doors of opportunity for self-expression [of young Indians from Federally recognized groups, with at least one-quarter Indian blood] in the whole rainbow of the arts." A comprehensive liberal arts program for selected students is offered for college enrollees of the Institute. The college program is intended for art students preparing for fine arts work, or preparing for technical schools, or completing their academic degree in other art schools or colleges. As of 1981, 70 percent of the Institute students granted AFA degrees are continuing their training. The Institute started with a small student body. The second year saw enrollment increased to 140, and in 1970–71 it was 288. Then in 1978 the high school program was dropped upon recommendation of the government. Accordingly, the attendance fell back—just ten years after the school's opening, to 150.

In 1981, a division of programs was arranged. The studio classes (three-dimensional courses) and the museum remain where they have been; the administrative functions, liberal arts, creative writing, and the two-dimensional art classes were transferred to the College of Santa Fe campus. Courses related to the arts are offered including business training and mathematics. The curriculum also includes English, literature, folklore, history, applied science, Indian history and identification, ethnic studies, and other subjects.

Many of the administrative officers and staff members are Indians. They are sensitive, creative, and attuned to the youth of today. Students come from throughout the United States. A former director of IAIA said:

Thus far in our job, we have found that by stressing cultural roots as a basis for creative expression and by offering a wide range of media in which to work, Indian students can be inspired to new personal strengths in dimensions heretofore unrealized. As a result of the Institute's heritage-centered approach, a gratifying number of its students do discover who they are and what it is thay have to say to the world; and they develop the self-respect and confidence to express themselves accordingly. They are helped to function constructively, in tune with the demands of their contemporary environment but without having to sacrifice their cultural being on the altar of either withdrawal or assimilation. (*See* New 1968:12.)

Despite vicissitudes, the IAIA still prevails.

The "old school" became an Indian high school under the management of the Pueblo Indian Council. Students from the Albuquerque high school were transferred there beginning in the fall of 1981.

Katsina Figures

We have already mentioned the importance of the katsina cult in Pueblo social organization. The small wooden representations of katsinas are commonly called "dolls." They are not dolls or toys as non-Indians think of them however. They are likenesses of a whole array of supernaturals who, through various manifestations, interact between man and his deity; thus they are messengers. As such, they may appear in numerous forms, with specific identifying characteristics. This class of katsina representations has a separate designation within the Indian groups. For instance, the Hopi call them *tihü* or *katsintihü*. While they are not play things, it is not considered wrong if an Indian child carries one of them about, as a non-Indian youngster might carry a doll.

Primarily, the katsinas are benevolent beings who reside in the mountains, clouds, springs and lakes, and who are purveyors of many blessings, especially rain, good crops, and general well-being. However, as all good has its contrary agency, some katsinas are ogres or demons with disciplinary functions. Ogres have a reputation for eating children who are not good, and if the katsinas are not obeyed. Indian lore and social mores are transmitted from generation to generation by means of the katsinas. In many ways the supernatural ones and the katsina organizations reflect the ordinary life of the Pueblo peoples; the family relationship is the same: father, mother, children, grandparents, uncles, and so on (*see* Washburn 1980a, b).

In further explanation of the little wooden figures, it has been noted that, faithfully portrayed they provide a means of education; they also serve as gifts at ceremonials, and as decorative articles in the home; but, transcendently, they act as a constant reminder to the Indians of the "real" katsinas.

Not all of the figurines represent katsinas. How, then, does one distinguish them? Although it is sometimes difficult to determine, the essential feature is the mask. Unmasked figures are *not* katsinas. Examples of these are buffalo, deer, eagle, and snake dancers, and the like.

Another expression of Indian art, consequently, is to be seen in the carved wooden figures of katsinas or ceremonial personages. Here, the Hopi Indians lead, for religious restrictions in the Río Grande valley do not allow production of ceremonial figures in the manner that is permitted the Hopi. The late James Kewanwytewa, a Hopi well known at the Museum of Northern Arizona, in Flagstaff, won the *Palmes Académiques* in 1954 for his katsina productions. Although many katsinas, or dolls, are offered for sale, one has to be careful that he is securing authentic specimens, for non-Indians are making many imitations.

If made in traditional Hopi manner, katsina figures are carved from a solid piece of root wood from a dead cottonwood tree; for this reason, they are of a very light weight. They should be so well balanced as to stand alone. Protruding eyes, ears, and nose, horns, and headdress ornaments may be attached with tiny pegs. Clothing and costume articles are indicated by painting. First, a coat of very fine white clay, called kaolin, is applied over all of the figure. Then colored pigments are laid on. Formerly these were native earth or mineral colors. Today, opaque water color paints are used commonly as well as other more modern types.

The Zuñi style, and that of some of the Río Grande Pueblos, calls for the use of pine wood for katsina figures. These are then painted, and are dressed in costumes of deerskin, fur, feathers, and cloth—miniature replicas of the human size beings. Zuñi "dolls" are generally taller, more slender, and heavier in weight than the Hopi figures, and they usually have movable arms. They do not stand without support, as a rule. The Zuñi also make some bead dolls.

Indian Markets and Exhibits

There are so many fine Indian artisans that it would be impossible to discuss them all in this limited space. We recommend that readers avail themselves of the privileges of seeing exhibits of Indian works in museum and art departments, and at the numerous Indian arts and crafts fairs. Some of these opportunities are considered below.

Visitors who are fortunate enough to be in Santa Fe during the summer months will find the Indians and their products under the *portales* surrounding the plaza. Purchases may be made there directly from the Indians.

In 1983, the Southwestern Association on Indian Affairs observes the sixty-second Indian market that it has sponsored. In front of the Palace of the Governors and streets around the plaza, rows of colorful, canvas-covered booths are erected for the two-day event. The Market is held annually two weeks *before* the Labor Day weekend. *(Rel.* Bennett, C. 1982:1–5.)

Early in the morning on market days, the Indians, carrying their wares wrapped in pieces of cloth or packed into paper cartons, come into town and arrange themselves for the day. They sit on rugs or on low stools; some have counters or show cases.

Each exhibitor has an assigned space for which a fee has been paid. This fee helps defray the expenses of holding the Market. Here, the Indians spread their pottery, drums, dressed dolls, jewelry, baskets, moccasins, tanned goat skins, paintings, beaded trinkets, textiles, and unpredictable articles. Indians are imaginative and inventive, and each year they come forth with new examples of their productive minds.

Usually the price is fixed for items sold in the Indian markets, though sometimes the Indians enjoy a little bargaining. But be assured that the Indians are quite as shrewd as you are. They will not sell for less than an article is worth.

Association judges view the exhibited items and displays, and award prizes for outstanding achievements. The exhibitors include artisans from the Río Grande pueblos and from Hopiland, Navajo, Apache, Ute, and some of the Plains Indians. Together with their displays they afford an unforgettable sight.

Twice daily on Saturday and Sunday, complementing the Market, the association arranges Indian dances in the patio back of the Palace of the Governors.

Annually, the Museum of Northern Arizona centers a Hopi Arts and Crafts show around July 4, when thousands of the Hopi and western Navajo, as well as their Indian neighbors, gather at Flagstaff. Another set event is their annual *Navajo Craftsman Exhibit;* these are interspersed with other special showings of Indian arts and crafts. On these occasions fine productions may be purchased. *(Rel.* Brody 1979a:86–95.)

After more than a half-century, an Intertribal Indian Ceremonial was held in Gallup, New Mexico. Due to highway changes, the old Ceremonial site had to be abandoned. A beautiful location in the red rock "hay stacks" was selected for a new home a few miles east of Gallup, off I-40. As a consequence the Red Rocks Park became the site of the annual Ceremonial, from the first Thursday through Sunday of August. For information contact: Intertribal Indian Ceremonial Association, P.O. Box One, Church Rock, New Mexico 87311.

Colorful fairs are held in the Navajo country during the autumn season at Shiprock, New Mexico, and Window Rock, Arizona. Visitors will do well to attend either or both of these events. The New Mexico State Fair at Albuquerque in late September, and the Arizona State Fair in Phoenix in early November, have exhibits of fine Indian arts and crafts which are for sale.

On the Salt River reservation, near Scottsdale, Arizona, an annual Indian Trade Fair was initiated in 1967. Not only do the local Pima-Maricopa and Yavapai-Apache peoples display their productions, but they are joined by the Navajo, some of the Apaches, Havasupai, Mohave, several from the Plains Indian groups, and many others. As at the celebrations on the Navajo reservation, at the Museum of Northern Arizona, and elsewhere, artisans demonstrate their skills: weaving baskets or rugs, making jewelry, perhaps carving and painting katsinas, doing beadwork; and on occasion making certain of their native foodstuffs.

In 1971, the Zuñi initiated a mid-May Arts and Crafts Fair with the local artists showing their paintings, jewelry, pottery, katsinas, and other wares— these for display and sale. A panel of judges awards prizes.

Since 1959, the Santa Clara Indians have brought their ancient homesite, Puyé, an important ruin with mesatop and cliff dwellings, to life again with a spectacular festival during a weekend late in July. The Santa Clara Indians and those from other pueblos assemble there, displaying and selling artistic products and performing dances. [Note: this event was cancelled in 1982.]

On or off of the highways are trading posts which handle Indian products. Throughout the Hopi-Navajo country, certain trading posts, or booths, exhibit Navajo rugs and other items to attract the traveler. With the Navajo goods one may also find Chimayó textiles for sale. These are fine in their own way, but they definitely are *not* Indian. They are made by Spanish-American weavers in their small villages in the upper Río Grande drainage. Trading posts in Arizona and Colorado handle more Hopi and Papago items, and wares of other groups. Traveling through the various Indian lands, especially in Papaguería or among the Pueblos, one may find places where wares may be purchased directly from the maker. And among the set events that afford opportunities is the Annual Indian Fair at the Heard Museum in Phoenix.

For the traveler who has limited knowledge of Indian arts and crafts, it is recommended that he do his buying from established dealers or exhibitors throughout the Four Corners region. Their trained buyers make frequent trips to the reservations or pueblos and select the best. They often have arrangements with craftsmen of particular skill to take their entire output, or they have expert Indian workmen in their own shops.

In the past decade imitation Navajo rugs suddenly appeared for sale in many places. Most of them were of Mexican origin. Many are beautiful and well woven, but they are *not* Navajo. Beware of deceptions! (*See* Bennett, N. 1973.)

Inspired by the popularity and current value of carved katsina figures, some Navajo have taken up the carving of yé'ii and dance personators. Also other expressions of Navajo life, such as craftsmen at work and nativity assemblages, have been carved. Looms in miniature are made, sometimes with weavers dressed in typical Navajo clothes. Similar portrayals of corn grinders are produced. The demand for such items far exceeds the supply.

In late years certain Santo Domingo jewelry makers have used turquois, coral, and silver, as well as shell, for beads of exceedingly small diameter in stunning necklaces. When bead chokers were popular, their makers enjoyed vast sales (see Bedinger 1973). Many non-Indian artisans have copied the works of the Indians so well that their products may be indistinguishable. Improved techniques for creating imitation or altered turquois have made it increasingly difficult to differentiate the true from the false. Do be sure of your dealer's reliability.

The Indian Arts & Crafts Association was created to provide an organization capable of coping with the problems and situations confronting American Indian arts and crafts today, including the ever-increasing thefts of Indian jewelry, rugs, and other valuable articles. It is structured to benefit all concerned: craftsmen, traders, jobbers, dealers, collectors, museums, and other interested parties; the chief concerns are security, ethics, and public image.

As interest and needs for such an organization widened, the IACA has grown into a national nonprofit association. It seeks to enhance and maintain the image and marketing of handmade American Indian arts and crafts. Under the leadership of a well chosen group of working directors and officers— Indian and non-Indian—representatives of businesses and related professions, a membership is built up. For information, write to the Indian Arts & Crafts Association, Darrow Building, 4301 Lead, S.E., Albuquerque, New Mexico 87108.

For several years, Pueblo Indian leaders of New Mexico foresaw the desirability of developing an enterprise that would provide cultural and economic benefit to a whole community. As they point out, unlike many of America's population groups, "whose cultural blending accounts for the 'melting pot' designation of our nation," the Pueblo people have preserved their identity. Through vicissitudes mentioned in the Note to this edition (p. xix), they have continued to persevere. Dwelling in relatively small clusters, within close-knit social organizations that emphasize family ties and respect for their heritage, they have withstood many of the ravages of civilization.

As a result of the efforts of Pueblo leaders, one of the great attractions in Albuquerque is the beautifully designed Indian Pueblo Cultural Center, 2401 12 St. N.W., dedicated to "advancing understanding and insuring perpetuation of Pueblo culture."

The three-level structure opened in August, 1976. It accommodates a museum highlighting details of the state's pueblos, an arts and crafts market wherein authentic, hand-crafted Indian objects are sold. There is a restaurant offering typical Pueblo meals; and living arts and educational programs. In addition, many special events are scheduled.

Like the Indian Arts & Crafts Association, this is a nonprofit organization without government funding. Both are well worth your visits and support.

Calendar of Annual
Indian Events

The pueblos have their plazas; the ranchería peoples and other Indian groups have their dance places where ceremonial events are presented. Many observances occur over a period of several days, but of these the major portions are held in the kivas or in places where only the initiated ones may witness them. Parts that may be seen by the public are customarily attended by adults and children, Indian and non-Indian.

Ceremonies are held in Hopiland throughout the year. The dates of these are determined according to Hopi customs and traditions, without reference to the BIA personnel. Exact dates are made known—even to the Hopi—only a few days in advance. During the summer, one or more ceremonies or dances are held usually each weekend.

Indian dances and ceremonies are based on Indian needs and Indian time. To translate these to the Gregorian calendar is not always practicable. It is advisable to check locally whenever possible.

NOTE: Do *not* take photographs, make sketches or recordings, or take notes without obtaining permission. *Remember that these are sacred and commemorative rituals.* It is expected that visitors will be *quiet* and *respectful*.

Jan 1	TAOS: turtle dance, usually *(see* Dutton 1972:3–12). Dances in many of the pueblos on New Year's and/or three succeeding days, for example, the cloud dance at SAN JUAN.
Jan 3	ISLETA: corn, turtle, and other dances
Jan 6	King's Day: installation of secular officers. TAOS: buffalo or deer dance. SAN ILDEFONSO: eagle dance. KERES pueblos: dancing. Dancers go to the houses of people named *Reyes* (kings), where dwellers are waiting on the roofs. After the dancers perform for a while, the house owner and family members throw gifts to them and the crowd gathered below. Everybody scrambles for presents. The gifts include bread, canned and boxed foods, fruit, tobacco, soft drinks, and household items. Many pueblos have dances on the three succeeding days.
Jan 23	SAN ILDEFONSO: feast day—animal dances in one plaza, Comanche dance in the other
Late Jan	ACOMA and LAGUNA: governor's fiesta
Feb	(Usually) HOPI: Powamû (bean dance)—first rites of the katsina cult
Feb 4–5	TAOS: *Llano* dances, *Los Comanches* (Spanish-American interpretation of Plains Indian dances)

251

Feb 15   SAN JUAN: dances. TAOS: perhaps turtle dance. SANTO DOMIN-
            GO: eagle dance.
Late Feb   ISLETA: evergreen dance

Mar   Phoenix Plains Indian Club sponsors Scottsdale All-Indian Day
Mar   GILA RIVER PIMA: *Mul-chu-tha* at Sacaton, Arizona
Mar 27   KERES PUEBLOS and JEMEZ: dances
Late Mar   PIMA-MARICOPA and YAVAPAI-APACHE communities (near Scotts-
            dale, Arizona): Indian Trade Fair
Mar-Apr   Palm Sunday. MOST PUEBLOS: green corn dances, ceremonial
            foot races
Mar-Apr   Easter Sunday and following two or three days. MOST PUEBLOS:
            dances and ceremonial foot races. Several pueblos observe the
            opening of the ditches, or *acequias,* with dances; some play cer-
            emonial shinny.
Mar-Apr   During Holy Week, with the high point on Easter Day. YAQUI:
            elaborate celebrations at Barrio Libra (south Tucson) and at
            Guadalupe near Phoenix. Deer dancers, *matachines, pascolas,
            fariseos,* et al., take part. *(See* Painter and Sayles 1962:24.) On
            the first Friday after Easter, the Tucson Festival Society sponsors
            an annual pageant that commemorates the founding of Mission
            San Xavier del Bac. Papago and Yaqui dancers participate.
            (Rel. Evers 1980.)

Spring   COLORADO RIVER TRIBES: motor boat races and Northern Yuma
            County Fair at Parker, Arizona

Apr   Last Saturday in April. *Nizhoni* dances at Johnson Gymnasium,
            University of New Mexico, Albuquerque, N.M. Numerous
            Indian groups in beautiful costumes (benefit)
Apr or May UTE MOUNTAIN UTE: bear dances

May 1   SAN FELIPE: feast day—green corn dance (two large groups)
May 3   TAOS: ceremonial races (about 8:00–10:00 A.M.). COCHITI:
            corn dance (Coming of the Rivermen)
May 14   TAOS: San Ysidro fiesta (blessing of the fields)
Late May   About 29 May through June 4. TESUQUE: corn or flag dance
            (blessing of the fields)
Late May   SALT RIVER PIMA: Industrial Fair
May or June Last week of May or first week of June. SOUTHERN UTE: bear
            dance

June 6   ZUNI: rain dance
June 13   SANDIA: feast day, corn dance. TAOS (corn dance), SAN JUAN,
            SANTA CLARA, SAN ILDEFONSO, COCHITI, and PAGUATE: dances
            in observance of San Antonio Day
June 20   ISLETA: governor's dance
June 24   SAN JUAN: feast day—dances. TAOS (afternoon), ISLETA, COCHITI,
            SANTA ANA, LAGUNA: dances in observance of San Juan's Day.
            ACOMA and JEMEZ: rooster pulls. NOTE: Since Isleta adopted
            its constitution, the ceremonial calendar has undergone chang-
            es. One may see dances performed by either the Laguna group
            that dwells in the pueblo, or by the Isleta group. Dates should
            be checked annually.

June 29	San Pedro's Day. LAGUNA, ACOMA, SANTA ANA, SAN FELIPE, SANTO DOMINGO, COCHITI, and ISLETA: rooster pulls
Late June or During July	HOPI: *Nimán* ("going home")—last rites of the katsina cult; katsinas are believed to go to their traditional home on San Francisco Peak. One of the ceremonial officers from Shungopavi announced that the Nimán and snake dances are closed because "rules against recording, picture taking and hand-drawing have been disregarded again by both Hopis and non-Indians . . . and sacred prayer feathers have been taken away" *Albuquerque Journal,* 15 August 1972).
July 1–4	MESCALERO APACHE: *Gáhan* ceremonial at Mescalero, N.M.
July 4	JICARILLA APACHE: feast (no ceremonies). NAMBÉ: celebration at Nambé Falls—special events and dances
July 4	Flagstaff Pow-Wow (check annually)
July 14	COCHITI: San Buenaventura Day—corn dance
Mid July or August	UTE: sun dance, Ignacio, Colorado
July 24	ACOMA: rooster pull
July 25	ACOMA, LAGUNA, COCHITI, and TAOS: Santiago Day—dances, rabbit hunt
July 26	SANTA ANA: feast day—corn dances. TAOS: corn dances
Late July	SANTA CLARA: festival at Puyé cliff ruins, including arts and crafts exhibits and dances. The entrance fee entitles one to take photographs. (Check annually.)
Aug 2	JEMEZ: old Pecos bull dance
Aug 4	SANTO DOMINGO: feast day—corn dance—large and fine, two groups
Aug 10	San Lorenzo's Day. PICURIS, LAGUNA, and ACOMITA: corn dances
Aug 12	SANTA CLARA: feast day—corn dances
Aug 15	ZIA: feast day of Nuestra Señora de la Ascensión—dances
Mid to Late Aug	Two weeks before Labor Day. Dances in the patio of the Palace of the Governors, Santa Fe, N.M., in conjunction with the annual Indian Market sponsored by the Southwestern Association on Indian Affairs
Aug 28	ISLETA: San Agustín fiesta
Late Aug	HOPI: snake dance—a solar observance. (Usually takes place about 4:00 P.M.) Held in even years at Shipaulovi Shungopavi, and Hotevila, and in odd years at Mishongnovi and Walpi. Alternately, when snake dances are not held in a village, flute ceremonials are given. The dances are announced sixteen days before they are due to happen. *See* the note under "Late June"
Sept	(Usually) HOPI: *Maraüm,* women's social function
Sept 1	SOUTHERN UTE: fair
Sept 2	San Estéban Day. ACOMA: corn dance atop mesa
Sept 4	ISLETA: feast day—harvest dance
Sept 8	ENCINAL (LAGUNA): harvest and social dances
Sept 8	SAN ILDEFONSO: harvest dance
Sept 14–15	JICARILLA APACHE: celebration at Horse or Stone Lake
Mid-Sept	Mid-September or earlier. Navajo Tribal Fair, Window Rock, Arizona, including exhibits, horse races, rodeo, and dances

Sept 19	San José Day. LAGUNA: harvest and other dances, and trading
Sept 29	The eve of San Gerónimo Day. TAOS: sundown dance, begins at sunset
Sept 30	San Gerónimo Day. TAOS: relay races (early A.M.) and pole climbing and dances (P.M.)
Fall	Sometime in the fall. SOUTHERN UTE: fair. NORTHERN UTE: sundance
Oct	(Usually) HOPI: *Oáqol,* women's social function
Oct 4	San Francisco Day. NAMBÉ: dances. At Magdalena, Sonora, Mexico, hundreds of Papago, Pima, Yaqui, and Mayo Indians (who are affiliated with the Yaqui) converge for the Fiesta of Saint Francis of Assisi.
Late Oct	Last weekend in October. PAPAGO: rodeo and fair, Sells, Arizona
Oct 31–Nov 2	On one of these days, ceremonies in MOST OF THE PUEBLOS— gifts to the padres, and gifts to the dead placed on graves
Nov	(Usually) HOPI Wüwüchim—tribal initiation ritual for all boys about ten to twelve years of age
Nov	COLORADO RIVER TRIBES two-day rodeo at Parker, Arizona
Nov 1–2	In the SAN XAVIER cemetery, near Tucson, hundreds of candles are lighted around the graves at night, as is true in all PAPAGO cemeteries
Nov 12	JEMEZ and TESUQUE: feast day of San Diego, dances
Nov–Dec	(In November or December) ZUNI: Shalako, dancing in new houses and in house of the Koyemshi
	NAVAJO reservation: Nightway and Mountain Topway ceremonies
Dec	HOPI: *Soyala*—winter solstice rites, opening of the katsina season, to induce the sun to start on the first half of its journey. After this ceremony, the katsinas may appear at any time during the next six months.
Dec 3	SAN XAVIER: ceremony in honor of Saint Francis Xavier
Dec 10–12	Fiesta of TORTUGA INDIANS in honor of Our Lady of Guadalupe, near Las Cruces, New Mexico: processions and dancing
Dec 12	Guadalupe day at ISLETA and SANTO DOMINGO—gift throwing
Dec 12	JEMEZ: *matachines;* TESUQUE: flag, deer, or buffalo dances
Dec 25	TAOS: deer or *matachines* dance (afternoon)
	Christmas Day and two or three days following, dances at MOST OF THE PUEBLOS
Dec 31	LAGUNA, SANDIA, SAN FELIPE, SANTO DOMINGO, and OTHER PUEBLOS: celebration and dances

New Mexico Indian Population

1980 Census

Classification	Population	Classification	Population
ATHAPASCANS		*Tanoan-speaking (continued)*	
Jicarilla Apache	2,289	San Ildefonso	520
Mescalero Apache	2,349	San Juan	1,806
Navajo Nation	59,826	Santa Clara	1,374
PUEBLO PEOPLES		Tesuque	312
Keresan-speaking (Eastern)			4,574
Cochiti	918	*Tiwa* (Northern)	
San Felipe	2,145	Picurís	245
Santa Ana	517	Taos	1,951
Santo Domingo	2,857		2,196
Zía	645	*Tiwa* (Southern)	
	7,082	Isleta	3,262
Keresan-speaking (Western)		Sandia	312
Acoma	3,592		3,574
Laguna	6,233	Guadalupe Indian Village	Unknown
	9,825	*Towa*	
Tanoan-speaking		Jemez	2,181
Tewa		*Zuñian-speaking*	
Nambé	438	Zuñi	7,388
Pojoaque	124		

NOTE: The Ute Indians are estimated to number about 6,200. About twelve hundred of the Southern Paiute live in the Southwest.

Because several Indian groups have challenged the 1980 federal census, the New Mexico figures are based on estimates. Since data have been made available by several Indian reservation groups, it has been possible to determine that the estimates are running close to the actual total, varying possibly by 5 percent. The total New Mexico Indian population may result in showing 5,000 more Indians than the official census.

Arizona Indian
Reservation Population

April 1981 Census

Reservation	Classification	Population
AK-CHIN	Papago-Pima	389
CAMP VERDE	Yavapai-Apache	521
COCOPAH	Cocopah	835
COLORADO RIVER	Mohave-Chemehuevi	2,070*
FORT APACHE	Apache	8,100
FORT McDOWELL	Yavapai	348
FORT MOJAVE	Mojave	700*
FORT YUMA	Quechan	1,500*
GILA RIVER	Pima-Maricopa	9,404
HAVASUPAI	Havasupai	475
HOPI	Hopi	8,253
HUALAPAI	Hualapai	1,133
KAIBAB-PAIUTE	Paiute	224
NAVAJO	Navajo	83,000†
PAPAGO	Papago	16,307§
PASCUA YAQUI	Pascua Yaqui	4,772
SALT RIVER	Pima-Maricopa	3,313
SAN CARLOS	Apache	6,090
TONTO APACHE	Tonto Apache	67
YAVAPAI-PRESCOTT	Yavapai	73

NOTE: The 1980 figures were supplied through the courtesy of the Bureau of Indian Affairs and do not include the thousands of off-reservation members of tribes. The Navajo population figure was supplied by the Navajo tribe, and is for Arizona only.

*The population figures include California for Colorado River, Fort Mojave, and Fort Yuma.

†In addition to the Navajo people living in Arizona and New Mexico, sufficient numbers living off the reservations swell the total account to approximately 160,000.

§The Papago figure includes population for Sells (11,307), Gila Bend (703), and San Xavier (4,665). (Arizona Commission on Indian Affairs 1981:6)

Bibliography

Aberle, David F. (1967) "The Navaho Singer's 'Fee': Payment or Prestation," in *Studies in Southwestern Ethnolinguistics*, ed. Dell H. Hymes with William E. Bittle. The Hague: Mouton.

Adams, E. Charles, and Deborah Hull (1980). "The Prehistoric and Historic Occupation of the Hopi Mesas," in *Hopi Kachina—Spirit of Life*, ed. Dorothy K. Washburn. Seattle: University of Washington Press; California Academy of Sciences.

Agogino, George A., and Michael L. Kunz (1971). "The Paleo Indian: Fact and Theory of Early Migrations to the New World," *The Indian Historian* 4(1):21–26. San Francisco: Indian Historical Society.

Alvarez de Williams, Anita (1974). *The Cocopah People*. Phoenix: Indian Tribal Series.

American Association on Indian Affairs (1979). "Alamo Community Seeks Local School," *Indian Affairs* 99:1–2, 8.

Amsden, Charles Avery (1934). *Navaho Weaving: Its Technic and History*. Reprinted; Santa Ana, Calif.: Fine Arts Press.

Anderson, Jack (1969). "Papagos Living in Severe Poverty," *Albuquerque Journal*, 15 November.

——— (1971). "Paiutes Nation's Most Deprived Tribe," *Albuquerque Journal*, 11 August.

Anonymous (1967). "Archeologists Find Apache 'Pueblos' Near Las Vegas," *The New Mexican*, 23 April

——— (1969a). "On Grand Canyon Floor. Havasupai Tribe to Get Houses," *Albuquerque Journal*, 15 June.

——— (1969b). Article on Navajo industries, *Arizona Republic*, 12 December.

——— (1969c). "Indians: Squalor Amid Splendor," *Time*, 11 July.

———— (1969d). "White Mountain Apache Cattlemen," *New Mexico Stockman*, March, p. 49.

———— (1970a). "The Peyote Story," *Diné Baa Hane* 1(11):12–13.

———— (1970b). "Ute Mountain Utes Ask Industrial Visits," *Albuquerque Journal*, 16 April.

———— (1970c). "U.S. Government Honors Apache Tribes," *Albuquerque Journal*, 26 April.

———— (1970d). "Indian Tribes Buy Part of Heritage," *The New Mexican*, 1 May.

———— (1970e). Article on Hualapai Indians, *Albuquerque Journal*, 10 July.

———— (1970f). "Zuni War Chief Dies," *The New Mexican*, 30 January.

———— (1970g). "Action Line" column, *Albuquerque Journal*, 15 February.

———— (1971a). "Arizona's 85 Payson Apaches Stump for Title to Tonto Land," *Albuquerque Journal*, 22 August.

———— (1971b). "Luxury Complex Planned. Southern Ute Tribe Will Enter Tourist Business." *Albuquerque Journal*, 26 November.

———— (1971c). "Papago Indians Get Farm Grant," *Albuquerque Journal*, 25 December.

———— (1971d). "Indians Build $2 Million Resort," *The New Mexican*, 16 May.

———— (1971e). "Master Potter of Maricopas Crushed to Death under Tree," *Arizona Republic*, 11 August.

———— (1971f). "Ida Redbird Dies," The Heard Museum *Newsletter*, September-October.

———— (1971g). "Fannin Asks Indian Aid," *The New Mexican*, 14 February.

———— (1972a). News release from Window Rock, Arizona, 18 February.

———— (1972b). "Action Line" column, *Albuquerque Journal*, 15 August.

———— (1972c). "Alamo Reservation Building Pre-School," *Albuquerque Journal*, 10 September.

———— (1973). Article(s) in *The New Mexican*, 5 August.

———— (1980a). "Yaquis Keep Pride Amid Poverty," *Albuquerque Journal*, 20 October.

———— (1980b). "Pueblo Says Religious Customs in Jeopardy," *Albuquerque Journal*, 9 November.

———— (1981a). "King to Hail Governors of Pueblos," *Albuquerque Journal*, 14 March.

———— (1981b). "Spiritual Chief Granillo of Tigua Indians Dies," *Albuquerque Journal*, 26 June.

———— (1982a). "Watt Given Arizona Water Plan," *Albuquerque Journal*, 15 August.

———— (1982b). "Study Starts on Why Many Pimas Diabetics," [*Central Phoenix Sun*], 7 September.

Arizona Commission for Indian Affairs (1981). *Tribal Directory*. Phoenix.

Arizona Writers' Project, WPA (1941). "The Apache," *Arizona Highways* 17(11): 32–35, 42.

Arnon, Nancy S., and W. W. Hill (1979). "Santa Clara Pueblo," in *Handbook of North American Indians*, vol. 9, ed. Alfonso Ortiz. Washington, D.C.: Smithsonian Institution.

Bahti, Mark (1980). "Kachina," *Pacific Discovery* 33(3):2–7.

Bahti, Tom (1980). *Southwestern Indian Tribes*. Las Vegas, Nev.: KC Publications.

Baldwin, Gordon C. (1965). *The Warrior Apaches*. Tucson: Dale Stuart King.

Ball, Eve (1970). *In the Days of Victorio*. Tucson: University of Arizona Press.

Barnett, Franklin (1968). *Viola Jimulla: The Indian Chieftess*. Yuma, Ariz.: Southwest Printers.

Barry, Norm (1971). "Light in the Desert," *Mountain Bell* 2(2).

Bartel, John (1970). "First Indian High School Starts Classes at Ramah," *Gallup Independent*, 12 August.

Barton, Robert S. (1953). "The Lincoln Canes of the Pueblo Governors," *Lincoln Herald*, winter, pp. 24–29.

Basehart, Harry W. (1967). "The Resource Holding Corp. Among the Mescalero Apache," *Southwestern Journal of Anthropology* 23:277–91.

——— (1970). "Mescalero Apache Band Organization and Leadership," *Southwestern Journal of Anthropology* 26(1):87–104.

Basso, Keith H. (1969). *Western Apache Witchcraft*, Anthropological Papers of the University of Arizona, no. 15. Tucson: University of Arizona Press.

———, ed. (1971). *Western Apache Raiding and Warfare: From the Notes of Grenville Goodwin*. Tucson: University of Arizona Press.

——— (1973). "Southwestern Ethnology: A Critical Review," *Annual Review of Anthropology* 2:221–52.

Bedinger, Margery (1973). *Indian Silver: Navajo and Pueblo Jewelers*. Albuquerque: University of New Mexico Press.

Belknap, Bill, recorder (1977). *Fred Kabotie, Hopi Indian Artist*. Flagstaff: Northland Press; Museum of Arizona.

Bennett, Charles (1982). "Indian Market: The Judging Process," *Quarterly of the Southwestern Association on Indian Affairs* 17(2):2–5.

Bennett, Noël (1973). *Genuine Navajo Rug—Are You Sure???* Window Rock, Ariz.: Navajo Times. Santa Fe: Museum of Navajo Ceremonial Art.

Berman, Mary Jane (1979). "Cultural Resources Overview, Socorro, New Mexico," *Archaic Notes*, pp. 17–27.

Blanchard, Kendall (1971). *The Ramah Navajos: A Growing Sense of Community in Historical Perspective*, Navajo Publications, Historical Series, no. 1. Window Rock, Ariz.: Navajo Tribal Museum.

Bloom, Lansing B. (1940). "Who Discovered New Mexico?" *New Mexico Historical Review* 15(2):101–32.

Bodine, John J. (1967). "Attitudes and Institutions of Taos, New Mexico: Variables for Value System Expression." Ph. D. diss., Tulane University.

——— (1972). "Acculturation Processes and Population Dynamics," in *New Perspectives on the Pueblos*, ed. Alfonso Ortiz. Albuquerque: University of New Mexico Press, School of American Research Advanced Seminar Series.

——— (1979). "Taos Pueblo," in *Handbook of North American Indians*, vol. 9, ed. Alfonso Ortiz. Washington, D.C.: Smithsonian Institution.

Bolton, Herbert E. (1950). "Pageant in the Wilderness," *Utah Historical Quarterly* 18(1–4):1–250.

Brandon, William (1969). "American Indians: the Alien Americans," *The Progressive* 33(12):13–17.

——— (1970a). "The American Indians: the Un-Americans," *The Progressive* 34(1): 35–39.

——— (1970b). "American Indians: The Real American Revolution," *The Progressive* 34(2):26–30.

Brandt, Elizabeth A. (1979). "Sandia Pueblo," in *Handbook of North American Indians*, vol. 9, ed. Alfonso Ortiz. Washington, D.C.: Smithsonian Institution.

Brennan, Bill (1966). "This is River Country" (article in two parts: "The Colorado River Indian Reservation" and "Parker, Arizona—the Heart of the River Country"), *Arizona Highways* 42(2):9–39.

——— (1967). "Parker—Power Boat Racing Capital of the Southwest," in *The Parker-Lake Havasu Story*. Phoenix.

Breuninger, Evelyn P. (1970). "Debut of Mescalero Maidens," *Apache Scout* 16(5):1–5.

Brew, John Otis (1979). "Hopi Prehistory and History to 1850," in *Handbook of North American Indians*, vol. 9, ed. Alfonso Ortiz. Washington, D.C.: Smithsonian Institution.

Brewer, Steve (1981). "Tribe Thought to Be Extinct Now Fighting for El Paso Land," *Albuquerque Journal*, 5 April.

Brody, J. J. (1979). "Pueblo Fine Arts," in *Handbook of North American Indians,* vol. 9, ed. Alfonso Ortiz. Washington, D.C.: Smithsonian Institution.

———— (1980). "Modern Hopi Painting," in *Hopi Kachina—Spirit of Life,* ed. Dorothy K. Washburn. Seattle: University of Washington Press; California Academy of Sciences.

Brown, Donald N. (1979). "Picuris Pueblo," in *Handbook of North American Indians,* vol. 9, ed. Alfonso Ortiz. Washington, D.C.: Smithsonian Institution.

Brugge, David M. (1963). *Navajo Pottery and Ethnohistory.* Window Rock, Ariz.: Navajo Tribal Museum.

———— (1969). "A Navajo History." Manuscript.

Brugge, David M., and J. Lee Correll (1971). *The Story of the Navajo Treaties.* Navajo Historical Publications, Documentary Series, no. 1. Window Rock, Ariz.: Navajo Tribal Museum.

Brugge, David M., and Charlotte J. Frisbie, eds. (1982). *Navajo Religion and Culture: Selected Views.* Santa Fe: Museum of New Mexico Press.

Buge, David (1980). "Big Kivas and Tewa Prehistory," *Masterkey* 54(1):24–29.

Bulow, Ernest L. (1972). *Navajo Taboos.* Navajo Historical Publications, Cultural Series, no. 1. Window Rock, Ariz.: Navajo Tribal Museum.

Bunzel, Ruth L. (1932a). "Introduction to Zuni Ceremonialism," in *Bureau of American Ethnology Annual Report* 47:471–544. Washington, D.C.: Government Printing Office.

———— (1932b). "Zuni Katcinas [sic]: An Analytical Study," in *Bureau of American Ethnology Annual Report* 47:843–903. Washington, D.C.: Government Printing Office.

Cain, H. Thomas (1962). *Pima Indian Basketry.* Phoenix: The Heard Museum.

Carlson, Roy L. (1982). "The Polychrome Complexes," *Arizona Archaeologist* 15: 201–229.

Carta Contenante le Royanne du Mexique et al Floride (n.d.). Old French map of early 1700s. Santa Fe: New Mexico State Record Center.

Chapman, Kenneth M. (1936). *The Pottery of Santo Domingo Pueblo: A Detailed Study of Its Decoration.* Santa Fe: W. F. Roberts. Rev. ed. 1953, Santa Fe: Laboratory of Anthropology. Reissued 1977, Albuquerque: University of New Mexico Press; School of American Research.

———— (1970). *The Pottery of San Ildefonso Pueblo.* Albuquerque: University of New Mexico Press; School of American Research.

Cleland, Charles F. (1980). "Yuma Dolls," *American Indian Arts Magazine* 5(3):36–39.

Clemmer, Richard O. (1980). "Hopi History, 1940–1974," in *Handbook of North American Indians,* vol. 9, ed. Alfonso Ortiz. Washington, D.C.: Smithsonian Institution.

Cole, Fay Cooper (1955). "Tesuque Rain Gods," *The Living Magazine* 16(9):550–51.

Colee, Philips (1969). "Ethnohistoric Research on the Southern Tiwa," paper presented at the Third Summer Colloquium, Eastern New Mexico University, Armijo Lake.

College of Ganado (1980). *Profile and Update,* February. Ganado, Ariz.: College of Ganado.

Collins, John J. (1968). "A Descriptive Introduction to the Taos Peyote Ceremony," *Ethnology* 7(4):427–49.

Colton, Harold S. (1941). "Prehistoric Trade in the Southwest," *Scientific Monthly* 52(4):309–19.

Connelly, Carlotta (1980). "Piki," *Pacific Discovery* 33(3):28–32.

Connelly, John C. (1979a). "Hopi Social Organization," in *Hopi Kachina—Spirit of Life,* ed. Dorothy K. Washburn. Seattle: University of Washington Press; California Academy of Sciences.

——— (1979b). "Hopi Social Organization," in *Handbook of North American Indians*, vol. 9, ed. Alfonso Ortiz. Washington, D.C.: Smithsonian Institution.

Coues, Elliot (1900). *On the Trail of a Spanish Pioneer: The Diary and Itinerary of Francisco Garcés in his Travels Through Sonora, Arizona, and California*. 2 vols. New York: Francis P. Harper.

Coze, Paul (1952). "Of Clowns and Mudheads," *Arizona Highways* 28(8):18–29.

——— (1971). "Living Spirits of Kachinam," *Arizona Highways* 47(6):2.

Cumming, Kendall (1967). Personal communication, 21 April.

Davis, Irvine (1959). "Linguistic Clues to Northern Rio Grande Prehistory," *El Palacio* 66:(3):73–83.

Dedera, Don (1972). "Bringing Back the Basketmakers," *The Humble Way* 11(3):2–9.

——— (1975). *Navajo Rugs: How to Find, Evaluate, Buy and Care for Them*. Flagstaff: Northland Press.

DiPeso, Charles C., Arthur Woodward, Rex E. Gerald and M. V. Gerald (1953). *The Sobaipuri Indians of the Upper San Pedro Valley, Southwestern Arizona*. Publication no. 6. Dragoon, Ariz.: Amerind Foundation.

Dittert, Alfred E., Jr. (1958). "Preliminary Archaeological Investigations in the Navajo Project Area of Northwestern New Mexico," *Papers in Anthropology*, no. 1. Santa Fe: Museum of New Mexico Press.

——— (1959). "Culture Change in the Cebolleta Mesa Region, Central Western New Mexico." Ph.D. diss., University of Arizona.

——— (1967). Personal communication.

——— (1972). "They Came from the South," *Arizona Highways* 48(1):34–39.

Dittert, Alfred E., Jr., and Fred Plog (1980). *Generations in Clay: Pueblo Pottery of the American Southwest*. Flagstaff: Northland Press; American Federation of Arts.

Dobyns, Henry F., and Robert C. Euler (1960). "A Brief History of the Northeastern Pai," *Plateau* 32(3):49–56.

——— (1961). "The Origin of the Pai Tribes," *The Kiva* 26(3):8–22.

——— (1971). *The Havasupai People*. Phoenix: Indian Tribal Series.

Dobyns, Henry F., Paul H. Ezell, Alden W. Jones, and Greta Ezell (1957). "Thematic Changes in Yuman Warfare: Cultural Stability and Cultural Change," *Proceedings of the American Ethnological Society*, annual spring meeting. Seattle.

Dockstader, Frederick J. (1954). *The Kachina and the White Man: A Study of the Influences of the White Culture on the Hopi Kachina Cult*. Bulletin no. 35. Bloomfield Hills, Mich.: Cranbrook Institute of Science.

——— (1979a). "The Hopi World," in *The Year of the Hopi*. Washington, D.C.: Smithsonian Institution.

——— (1979b). "Hopi History, 1850–1940," in *Handbook of North American Indians*, vol. 9, ed. Alfonso Ortiz. Washington, D.C.: Smithsonian Institution.

Dooling, Anna (1981). "The Craft of Patience," *The Santa Fe Reporter*, 23 April.

Douglas, F. H. (1931). *The Havasupai Indians*. Leaflet no. 33. Denver: Denver Art Museum.

Dozier, Edward P. (1954). *The Hopi-Tewa of Arizona*. University of California Publications in American Archaeology and Ethnology, vol. 44, no. 3. Berkeley and Los Angeles: University of California Press.

——— (1957). "Rio Grande Pueblo Ceremonial Patterns," *New Mexico Quarterly* 27(1–2):27–34.

——— (1966a). *Hano: A Tewa Indian Community in Arizona*. New York: Holt, Rinehart, and Winston.

——— (1966b). "Factionalism at Santa Clara Pueblo," *Ethnology* 5:171–85.

——— (1970a). "Making Inferences from the Present to the Past," in *Reconstructing Prehistoric Pueblo Societies*, ed. William A. Longacre. Albuquerque: University of New Mexico Press, School of American Research Advanced Seminar Series.

———— (1970b). *The Pueblo Indians of North America*. New York: Holt, Rinehart, and Winston.

Drucker, Philip (1937). *Cultural Element Distributions: V. Southern California Archaeological Records* 1(1). Berkeley and Los Angeles: University of California Press.

Dunn, Dorothy (1968). *American Indian Painting of the Southwest and Plains Areas*. Albuquerque: University of New Mexico Press.

Dutton, Bertha P. (1963a). *Friendly People—The Zuñi Indians*. Santa Fe: Museum of New Mexico Press.

———— (1963b). *Sun Father's Way: The Kiva Murals of Kuaua*. Albuquerque: University of New Mexico Press.

———— (1966). "Pots Pose Problems," *El Palacio* 73(1):5–15.

———— (1972a). "The New Year of the Pueblo Indians of New Mexico," *El Palacio* 78(1):3–13.

———— (1972b). *Let's Explore: Indian Villages Past and Present*. Santa Fe: Museum of New Mexico Press.

———— (1977). "A Primer of Navajo Textiles," in *Navajo Weaving Handbook*. Guidebook Series. Santa Fe: Museum of New Mexico Press.

———— (1980). "Cultural Gaps and a Construct," in *Papers of the Archaeological Society of New Mexico* 5:211–218. Albuquerque: Albuquerque Archaeology Society Press.

———— (1983). *Indian Villages and Ancient Ruins: Tour Guide for Albuquerque-Santa Fe Areas*. Santa Fe: Museum of New Mexico Press.

Dutton, Bertha P., and Caroline B. Olin (1979a). *Myths and Legends of the Indians of the Southwest: Navajo, Pima, Apache*. Santa Barbara: Bellerophon Books.

———— (1979b). *Myths and Legends of the Indians of the Southwest: Hopi, Acoma, Tewa, Zuñi*. Santa Barbara: Bellerophon Books.

———— (1982). "Sandpaintings of Sam Tilden, Navajo Medicine Man," in *Navajo Religion and Culture: Selected Views*, ed. David M. Brugge and Charlotte J. Frisbie. Santa Fe: Museum of New Mexico Press.

Eddy, Frank W. (1965). "The Desert Culture of the Southwestern United States." Lecture at St. Michael's College (College of Santa Fe), 9 February.

———— (1966). *Prehistory in the Navajo Reservoir District, Northwestern New Mexico*. Papers in Anthropology, no. 15, pt. 1. Santa Fe: Museum of New Mexico Press.

———— (1974). "Population Dislocation in the Navajo Reservoir District, New Mexico and Colorado," *American Antiquity* 39(1):75–84.

Edelman, Sandra A., and Alfonso Ortiz (1979). "Tesuque Pueblo," in *Handbook of North American Indians*, vol. 9, ed. Alfonso Ortiz. Washington, D.C.: Smithsonian Institution.

Eggan, Fred (1950). *Social Organization of the Western Pueblos*. Chicago: University of Chicago Press.

———— (1979). "Pueblos: Introduction," in *Handbook of North American Indians*, vol. 9, ed. Alfonso Ortiz. Washington, D.C.: Smithsonian Institution.

Eggan, Fred, and T. N. Pandey (1979). "Zuni History 1850–1970," in *Handbook of North American Indians*, vol. 9, ed. Alfonso Ortiz. Washington, D.C.: Smithsonian Institution.

Eklund, D. E. (1969). "Pendleton Blankets," *Arizona Highways* 45(8):40.

Ellis, Florence Hawley (1964). "Archaeological History of Nambé Pueblo, 14th Century to Present," *American Antiquity* 30(1):34–42.

———— (1979a). "Isleta Pueblo," in *Handbook of North American Indians*, vol. 9, ed. Alfonso Ortiz. Washington, D.C.: Smithsonian Institution.

———— (1979b). "Laguna Pueblo," in *Handbook of North American Indians*, vol. 9, ed. Alfonso Ortiz. Washington, D.C.: Smithsonian Institution.

Emmitt, Robert (1954). *The Last War Trail—The Utes and the Settlement of Colorado.* Norman: University of Oklahoma Press.

Euler, Robert C. (1961). "Aspects of Political Organization Among the Puertocito Navajo," *El Palacio* 68(2):118–20.

——— (1966). *Southern Paiute Ethnohistory,* Anthropological Papers, no. 78. Salt Lake City: University of Utah Press.

——— (1972a). *The Paiute People.* Phoenix: Indian Tribal Series.

——— (1972b). Personal communication, 7 July.

Evers, Larry, ed. (1980). *The South Corner of Time: Hopi, Navajo, Papago, Yaqui Tribal Literature.* Tucson: University of Arizona Press.

Ezell, Greta S., and Paul H. Ezell (1970). "Background to Battle: Circumstances Relating to Death on the Gila, 1857," in *Troopers West: Military and Indian Affairs on the American Frontier,* ed. Raymond Brandes. San Diego: Frontier Heritage Press.

Faris, Chester E. (n.d.). "Pueblo Governors' Canes." Mimeographed manuscript.

Farrer, Claire R. (1978). "Mescalero Ritual Dance: A Four-Part Fugue," *Discovery* 5:1–13.

Fewkes, Jesse Walter (1902). "The Pueblo Settlements near El Paso, Texas," *American Anthropologist* n.s. 4(1):57–75.

Fontana, B. L. (1967). Personal communication, 6 January.

Fontana, B. L., William J. Robinson, C. W. Cormack, and E. E. Leavitt, Jr. (1962). *Papago Indian Pottery.* Seattle: University of Washington Press.

Ford, Richard I. (1972). "An Ecological Perspective," in *New Perspectives on the Pueblos,* ed. Alfonso Ortiz. Albuquerque: University of New Mexico Press, School of American Research Advanced Seminar Series.

Ford, Richard I., A. H. Schroeder, and S. L. Peckham (1972). "Three Perspectives on Puebloan Prehistory," in *New Perspectives on the Pueblos,* ed. Alfonso Ortiz. Albuquerque: University of New Mexico Press, School of American Research Advanced Seminar Series.

Forde, C. Dary II (1930). "A Creation Myth from Acoma," *Folk Lore* 41:359–87.

Forrest, Earle R. (1961). *The Snake Dance of the Hopi Indians.* Los Angeles: Westernlore Press.

Forrestal, Peter P., trans., and Cyprian J. Lynch, introd. and notes (1954). *Benavides Memorial of 1630.* Washington, D.C.: Academy of American Franciscan History.

Fort Mohave Tribal Council (California-Arizona-Nevada) (1970). *Letter and Resolution,* 27 October, Needles, California.

Fowler, Catherine S. (1971). Personal communication, 14 June.

Fowler, Don D., and Catherine S. Fowler, eds. (1971). *Anthropology of the Numa: John Wesley Powells' Manuscripts on the Numic Peoples of Western North America, 1868–1880.* Contributions to Anthropology, no. 14. Washington, D.C.: Smithsonian Institution.

Fox, J. Robin (1967). *The Keresan Bridge.* London School of Economics Monograph in Social Anthropology, no. 35. London: The Athlone Press.

——— (1972). "Some Unsolved Problems of Pueblo Social Organization," in *New Perspectives on the Pueblos,* ed. Alfonso Ortiz. Albuquerque: University of New Mexico Press, School of American Research Advanced Seminar Series.

Fox, Nancy (1975). *Pueblo Weaving and Textile Arts.* Guidebook Series. Santa Fe: Museum of New Mexico Press.

Frank, Larry, and Francis H. Harlow (1974). *Historic Pottery of the Pueblo Indians, 1600–1880.* Boston: New York Graphic Society.

Frigout, Arlette (1979). "Hopi Ceremonial Organization," in *Handbook of North American Indians,* vol. 9, ed. Alfonso Ortiz. Washington, D.C.: Smithsonian Institution.

Gabel, Norman E. (1949). *A Comparative Racial Study of the Papago.* Publications in Anthropology, no. 4. Albuquerque: University of New Mexico Press.

Galinat, Walton C., Theodore R. Rinehart, and Theodore R. Frisbie (1970). *Early Eight-Rowed Maize from the Middle Rio Grande Valley, New Mexico* Botanical Museum Leaflets, vol. 22, no. 9. Cambridge, Mass.: Harvard University.

Galvin, John, trans. and ed. (1967). *A Record of Travels in Arizona and California, 1775–1776, Father Francisco Garcés.* San Francisco: John Howell Books.

Garcia-Mason, Velma (1979). "Acoma Pueblo," in *Handbook of North American Indians,* vol. 9, ed. Alfonso Ortiz. Washington, D.C.: Smithsonian Institution.

Gerald, Rex E. (1958). "Two Wickiups on the San Carlos Indian Reservation, Arizona," *The Kiva* 23(3):5–11.

Gilliland, H. M. (1972). Personal communication and data sheets, 16 March. Keams Canyon, Ariz.: Hopi Indian Agency.

Goddard, Pliny E. (1909). "*Gotal*—a Mescalero Apache Ceremony," in *Putnam Anniversary Volume: Anthropological Essays Presented to Frederic Ward Putnam,* pp. 385–94. New York: G. E. Stechert.

Gonzales, Clara (1969). *The Shalakos Are Coming.* Santa Fe: Museum of New Mexico Press.

Goodman, James M. (1982). *The Navajo Atlas: Environment, Resources, People, and History of the Diné Bikeyah.* Norman: University of Oklahoma Press.

Goodwin, Grenville (1942). *The Social Organization of the Western Apache.* Chicago: University of Chicago Press.

Graves, Howard (1970). "Jobs, Tradition, Urbanization Key Navajo Race Factors," *Albuquerque Journal,* 24 August.

Gummerman, George J., and Emil W. Haury (1979). "Prehistory: Hohokam," in *Handbook of North American Indians,* vol. 9., ed. Alfonso Ortiz. Washington, D.C.: Smithsonian Institution.

Gunnerson, Dolores A. (1974). *The Jicarilla Apaches.* DeKalb: Northern Illinois University Press.

Gunnerson, James H. (1960). "An Introduction to Plains Apache Archaeology—the Dismal River Aspect," Bureau of American Ethnology Paper no. 58. Washington, D.C.

——— (1969a). "Apache Archaeology in Northeastern New Mexico," *American Antiquity* 34:23–39.

——— (1969b). "Archaeological Survey on and near Pecos National Monument— Preliminary Report." Mimeographed report.

——— (1979). "Southern Athapaskan Archaeology," in *Handbook of North American Indians,* vol. 9, ed. Alfonso Ortiz. Washington, D.C.: Smithsonian Institution.

Gunnerson, James H., and Dolores A. (1970). "Evidence of Apaches at Pecos," *El Palacio* 76(3)1–6.

——— (1971a). "Apachean Culture: A Study in Unity and Diversity," reprinted from *Apachean Culture History and Ethnology.* Anthropological Papers, no. 21. Tucson: University of Arizona.

——— (1971b). *Apachean Culture History and Ethnology.* Anthropological Papers, no. 21. Tucson: University of Arizona.

Hackett, Charles Wilson (1937). *Historical Documents Relating to New Mexico, Nueva Vizcaya, and Approaches thereto, to 1773.* 3 vols. Washington, D.C.: Carnegie Institution.

Hale, Kenneth (1972). "A New Perspective on American Indian Linguistics," in *New Perspectives on the Pueblos,* ed. Alfonso Ortiz. Albuquerque: University of New Mexico Press, School of American Research Advanced Seminar Series.

Hale, Kenneth, and David Harris (1979). "Historical Linguistics and Archaeology," in *Handbook of North American Indians,* vol. 9, ed. Alfonso Ortiz. Washington, D.C.: Smithsonian Institution.

Hanlon, C. J. (O.F.M.) (1972). "Papago Funeral Customs," *The Kiva* 37(2):104–12.

Harlow, Francis H. (1973). *Matte-Paint Pottery of the Tewa, Keres, and Zuni Pueblos.* Santa Fe: Museum of New Mexico Press.

Harrington, John P. (1940). "Southern Peripheral Athapaskawan Origins, Divisions, and Migrations," in *Essays in Historical Anthropology of North America.* Smithsonian Miscellaneous Collections. Washington, D.C.: Smithsonian Institution.

Hartmann, Horst (1978). *Kachina-Figuren der Hopi-Indianer.* Berlin: Museum für Völkerkunde.

Hawley, Florence (1950). "Big Kivas, Little Kivas, and Moiety Houses in Historical Reconstruction," *Southwestern Journal of Anthropology* 6(3):286–300.

Hawley, Florence, and Donovan Senter (1946). "Group-designed Behavior Patterns in Two Acculturating Groups," *Southwestern Journal of Anthropology* 2(2):133–51.

Hayes, George (1971). Personal communication, 18 November.

Hester, James J. (1962). *Early Navajo Migrations and Acculturation in the Southwest.* Papers in Anthropology, no. 6. Santa Fe: Museum of New Mexico Press.

Hewett, E. L., and Bertha P. Dutton (1945). *The Pueblo Indian World.* Albuquerque: University of New Mexico Press.

Hibben, Frank C. (1975). *Kiva Art of the Anasazi: at Pottery Mound.* Las Vegas, Nev.: KC Publications.

Hieb, Louis A. (1972). "Meaning and Mismeaning: Toward an Understanding of the Ritual Clown," in *New Perspectives on the Pueblos,* ed. Alfonso Ortiz. Albuquerque: University of New Mexico Press, School of American Research Advanced Seminar Series.

——— (1979). "Hopi World View," in *Handbook of North American Indians,* vol. 9, ed. Alfonso Ortiz. Washington, D.C.: Smithsonian Institution.

Hill, W. W. (1940). "Some Aspects of Navajo Political Structure," *Plateau* 13(2): 23–28.

——— (1982). *An Ethnography of Santa Clara Pueblo,* ed. Charles H. Lange. Albuquerque: University of New Mexico Press.

Hodge, Frederick W., ed. (1910). "Handbook of American Indians North of Mexico." Bureau of American Ethnology Bulletin no. 30, pt. 2.

Hoebel, E. Adamson (1958). *Man in the Primitive World.* New York: McGraw-Hill.

——— (1979). "Zia Pueblo," in *Handbook of North American Indians,* vol. 9, ed. Alfonso Ortiz. Washington, D.C.: Smithsonian Institution.

Hoijer, Harry (1938). *Chiricahua and Mescalero Apache Texts.* Chicago: University of Chicago Press.

——— (1956). "The Chronology of the Athapaskan Languages," *International Journal of American Linguistics* 22(4):219–32.

Hoijer, Harry, et al. (1963). *Studies in Athapaskan Languages.* Publications in Linguistics. University of California.

Hopi Reservation. 13 page leaflet. Keams, Ariz.: Hopi Tribe.

Houser, Nicholas P. (1972). "The Camp—An Apache Community of Payson, Arizona," *The Kiva* 37(2):65–71.

——— (1979). "Tigua Pueblo," in *Handbook of North American Indians,* vol. 9, ed. Alfonso Ortiz. Washington, D.C.: Smithsonian Institution.

Hume, Bill (1970a). "Sandia Pueblo Adopts Best of Two Cultures," *Albuquerque Journal,* 9 August.

——— (1970b). "Prehistoric Site, Scenic Canyon Boost Santa Clara's Finances," *Albuquerque Journal,* 4 October.

——— (1974). "The Havasupai Prisoners of Grand Canyon," *Indian Affairs* 86:1–2,7.

Huscher, B. H., and H. A. Huscher (1942). "Athapascan Migration via the Inter—montane Region," *American Antiquity* 8(1):80–88.

——— (1943). *The Hogan Builders of Colorado.* Gunnison, Colo.: Colorado Archaeological Society.

Irwin-Williams, Cynthia (1973). "The Oshara Tradition: Origins of Anasazi Culture," in *Eastern New Mexico University Contributions in Anthropology*, no. 5. Portales: E.N.M.U. Paleo-Indian Institute.

———— (1979). "Post-Pleistocene Archaeology, 7000–2000 B.C.," in *Handbook of North American Indians*, vol. 9, ed. Alfonso Ortiz. Washington, D.C.: Smithsonian Institution.

Jacka, Jerry D., and Nancy S. Hammack (1975). *Indian Jewelry of the Prehistoric Southwest*. Tucson: University of Arizona Press.

James, Harry C. (1956). *The Hopi Indians*. Caldwell, Id.: Caxton Press.

Jelinek, Arthur J. (1967). "A Prehistoric Sequence in the Middle Pecos Valley, New Mexico," in *Archaeological Papers of the Museum of Anthropology*, no. 31. Ann Arbor: University of Michigan.

Jenkins, Myra Ellen (1972). "Spanish Land Grants in the Tewa Area," *New Mexico Historical Review* 47(2):113–34.

Jernigan, E. Wesley (1978). *Jewelry of the Prehistoric Southwest*. Albuquerque: University of New Mexico Press; School of American Research.

Johnson, Barbara (1960). "The Wind Ceremony: A Papago Sand-Painting," *El Palacio* 67(1):28–31.

Johnson, Virginia (1980). Article in the *Albuquerque Journal*, 6 January.

Johnston, Bernice (1970). *Speaking of Indians*. Tucson: University of Arizona Press.

Kammer, Jerry (1980). *The Second Long Walk: The Navajo-Hopi Land Dispute*. Albuquerque: University of New Mexico Press.

Kaut, Charles R. (1957). *The Western Apache Clan System: Its Origins and Development*. Bulletins in Anthropology, no. 9. Albuquerque: University of New Mexico Press.

———— (1959). "Notes on Western Apache Religious and Social Organization," *American Anthropologist* 61(1):99–102.

Kealiinohomoku, Joann W. (1978). "Hopi Social Dance Events and How They Function," *Discovery* 27–40.

Kelly, Dorothea S. (1950). "A Brief History of the Cocopa Indians of the Colorado River Delta," in *For the Dean*, eds. Erik K. Reed and Dale S. King. Tucson and Santa Fe: Hohokam Museums Association and the Southwestern Monuments Association.

Kelly, Isabel (1964). *Southern Paiute Ethnography*. Anthropological Papers, no. 69. Salt Lake City: University of Utah Press.

Kelly, William H. (1953). *Indians of the Southwest: A Survey of Indian Tribes and Indian Administration in Arizona*. Bureau of Ethnic Research, Annual Report, no. 1. Tucson: University of Arizona.

Kennard, Edward A. (1979). "Hopi Economy and Subsistence," in *Handbook of North American Indians*, vol. 9, ed. Alfonso Ortiz. Washington, D.C.: Smithsonian Institution.

Kent, Kate Peck (1976). "Pueblo and Navajo Weaving Traditions and the Western World," in *Ethnic and Tourist Arts: Cultural Expression from the Fourth World*, ed. N. H. H. Graburn. Berkeley and Los Angeles: University of California Press.

Kent, Susan (1981). "A Recent Navajo Pottery Manufacturing Site, Navajo Indian Irrigation Project, New Mexico," *The Kiva* 46(3):189–95.

Kessell, John L. (1979). *Kiva, Cross, and Crown: The Pecos Indians and New Mexico 1540–1840*. Washington, D.C.: National Park Service.

King, William S. (1967). Information from Salt River Indian Agency, Scottsdale, Ariz., 11 April.

Kluckhohn, Clyde, W. W. Hill, and L. W. Kluckhohn (1971). *Navaho Material Culture*. Cambridge, Mass.: Harvard University Belknap Press.

Kluckhohn, Clyde, and Dorothea Leighton (1962). *The Navajo*. Garden City, N.Y.: Doubleday.

Kluckhohn, Clyde, and Leland C. Wyman (1940). "An Introduction to Navaho Chant Practice," *Memoirs of the American Anthropological Association* 53. Menasha, Wisc.

Koenig, Seymour H. (1982). "Drawings of Nightway Sandpaintings in the Bush Collection," in *Navajo Religion and Culture: Selected Views*, eds. David M. Brugge and Charlotte J. Fisbie. Santa Fe: Museum of New Mexico Press.

Kubicek, Earl C. (1968). "The Cane That Lincoln Gave," *Mankind* 1(10):61–64.

Kunitz, Stephen J., and Jerrold E. Levy (1981). "Navajos," in *Ethnicity and Medical Care*, ed. Alan Harwood. Cambridge: Harvard University Press.

Kurath, Gertrude P., and Antonio Garcia (1970). *Music and Dance of the Tewa Pueblos*. Santa Fe: Museum of New Mexico.

Kurath, William, and Edward H. Spicer (1947). *A Brief Introduction to Yaqui, a Native Language of Sonora*. Tucson: University of Arizona Press.

Ladd, Edmund J. (1979a). "Zuni Social and Political Organization," in *Handbook of North American Indians*, vol. 9, ed. Alfonso Ortiz. Washington, D.C.: Smithsonian Institution.

———— (1979b). "Zuni Economy," in *Handbook of North American Indians*, vol. 9, ed. Alfonso Ortiz. Washington, D.C.: Smithsonian Institution.

Lambert, Marjorie F. (1966). *Pueblo Indian Pottery: Materials, Tools, and Techniques*. Popular Series Pamphlet no. 5. Santa Fe: Museum of New Mexico Press.

Lange, Charles Henry (1959). *Cochiti: A New Mexico Pueblo: Past and Present*. Austin: University of Texas Press. Rpt. Carbondale: Southern Illinois University Press; Arcturus Books.

———— (1979a). "Cochiti Pueblo," in *Handbook of North American Indians*, vol. 9, ed. Alfonso Ortiz. Washington, D.C.: Smithsonian Institution.

———— (1979b). "Santo Domingo Pueblo," in *Handbook of North American Indians*, vol. 9, ed. Alfonso Ortiz. Washington, D.C.: Smithsonian Institution.

Largo, Jim (1957). Article in the *Albuquerque Journal*, 15 May.

———— (1973). "Cañoncito: 'Where One Dips Water from a Well'," *Albuquerque Journal*, 16 July.

LeFree, Betty (1975). *Santa Clara Pottery Today*. Albuquerque: University of New Mexico Press; School of American Research.

Levy, Jerrold E. (1965). "Navajo Suicide," *Human Organization* 24(4):308–18.

Levy, Jerrold E., Stephen J. Kunitz, and Michael Everett (1969). "Navajo Criminal Homicide," *Southwestern Journal of Anthropology* 25(2):124–49.

Lewis, Catherine (1982). "The Story of the Wedding Vase," *Pueblo Horizons* 6(7):2.

Link, Martin A. (1968). Introduction to *Treaty Between the United States of America and the Navajo Tribe of Indians*. Flagstaff, Ariz.: KC Publications.

Lister, Robert H. (1958). *Archaeological Excavations in the Northern Sierra Madre Occidental, Chihuahua and Sonora, Mexico*. Series in Anthropology, no. 7. Boulder: University of Colorado.

Loloma, Charles (1980). "Artist in Two Worlds," *Pacific Discovery* 33(3):8–10.

Lumholtz, Carl (1902). *Unknown Mexico*. 2 vols. New York: Charles Scribner's Sons.

McAllester, David P., and Susan W. (1980). *Hogans: Navajo Houses and House Songs*. Middletown, Conn.: Wesleyan University Press.

McCrossen, Eric (1973). Article in the *Albuquerque Journal*, 8 February.

McGimsey, Charles R. (1980). *Mariana Mesa: Seven Prehistoric Settlements in West-Central New Mexico*. Papers of the Peabody Museum of Archaeology and Ethnology, vol. 72. Cambridge, Mass.: Harvard University.

McGregor, John C. (1951). *The Cohonina Culture of Northwestern Arizona*. Urbana: University of Illinois Press.

———— (1967). *The Cohonina Culture of Mount Floyd, Arizona*. Lexington: University of Kentucky Press.

McGuire, Thomas R. (1979). "Yaqui Farmers, Yaqui Fishermen: Towards a Political Economy of Ethnicity," *Discovery* 1–23.

McNitt, Frank (1970). "Fort Sumner: a Study in Origins," *New Mexico Historical Review* 45(2):101–15.

Mangel, Charles (1970). "Sometimes We Feel We're Already Dead," *Look* 34(11): 38–43.

Martin, John (1972). Personal communication, 3 April.

Martin, Paul S. (1959). *Digging into History—a Brief Account of Fifteen Years of Archaeological Work in New Mexico.* Popular Series in Anthropology. Chicago: Natural History Museum.

——— (1979). "Prehistory: Mogollon," in *Handbook of North American Indians*, vol. 9, ed. Alfonso Ortiz. Washington, D.C.: Smithsonian Institution.

Matthews, Washington (1887). "The Mountain Chant: A Navajo Ceremony," in *Bureau of American Ethnology Annual Report* 5:385–467. Washington, D.C.

——— (1897). *Navaho Legends.* New York: American Folklore Society.

——— (1902). *The Night Chant: A Navajo Ceremony.* Memoirs of the American Museum of Natural History, vol. 6. New York: Knickerbocker Press.

Mauldin, Barbara (1982). "The Laboratory of Anthropology Celebrating Its 50th Anniversary," *The Quarterly of the Southwestern Association on Indian Affairs* 17(2):13–17.

Mickey, Barbara (1956). "Acoma Kinship Terms," *Southwestern Journal of Anthropology* 12:249–56.

Miller, Wick R., and Curtis G. Booth (1972). "Introduction: The Place of Shoshoni Among American Languages," in *Shoshoni Language Course Materials*, by Wick R. Miller and Curtis G. Booth. Owyhee, Nev.: Duckwater Tribal Council.

Miller, Wick R., and Irvine Davis (1963). "Proto-Keresan Phonology," *International Journal of American Linguistics* 29(4):310–30.

Mindeleff, Cosmos (1898). "Origin of the Cliff Dwellings," *Bulletin of the American Geological Society* 30(2):111–23.

Montgomery, Ross Gordon, Watson Smith, and J. O. Brew (1949). *Franciscan Awatovi, the Excavation and Conjectural Reconstruction of a 17th Century Spanish Mission Establishment at a Hopi Indian Town in Northeastern Arizona.* Papers of the Peabody Museum of Archaeology and Ethnology, vol. 36. Cambridge, Mass.: Harvard University.

Montgomery, William (1970a). "Fruitland Mine, Plant Liked," *Albuquerque Journal*, 18 August.

——— (1970b). "Black Mesa Coal Provides Indians Jobs," *Albuquerque Journal*, 19 August.

——— (1970c). "Navajo Generating Plant Now Building," *Albuquerque Journal*, 22 August.

——— (1970d). "Water Key to Southwest's Growth," *Albuquerque Journal*, 26 August.

Moon, Sheila (1970). *A Magic Dwells.* Middletown, Conn.: Wesleyan University Press.

Morris, Clyde P. (1972). "Yavapai-Apache Family Organization in a Reservation Context," *Plateau* 44(3):105–10.

Murray, Clyde A. (1969). "Homes in Flood Plain: CAP to Displace Indians," *Arizona Republic*, 9 November.

Nabokov, Peter (1969). "The Peyote Road," *New York Times Magazine*, 9 March.

National Geographic (1980). Articles on White Mountain Apache Indians, *National Geographic Magazine* 157(2):260–90.

Navajo Census Office (1970). *Report.* Window Rock, Ariz.

Navajo Community College (n.d.). *Introducing the Navajo Community College.* Brochure, 25 pp. Tsaile, Ariz.: Navajo Community College.

Navajo Nation (1980). *Annual Progress Report* (April). Window Rock, Ariz.

Navajo Times (1980). Miscellaneous articles from the *Navajo Times.*

Navajo Tribal Museum (1968). *Historical Calendar of the Navajo People.* Window Rock, Ariz.

New, Lloyd (1968). "Cultural Difference as the Basis for Creative Education," *Native American Arts* 1:4–12.

Niklaus, Phil (1974). Article in the *Albuquerque Journal*, 21 July.

Noble, David Grant, ed. (1981). *Pecos Ruins*. School of American Research Annual Bulletin *(Exploration)*. Santa Fe: School of American Research.

Olin, Caroline B. (1982). "Four Mountainway Sandpaintings of Sam Tilden," in *Navajo Religion and Culture: Selected Views*, ed. David M. Brugge and Charlotte J. Frisbie. Santa Fe: Museum of New Mexico Press.

Olin, Caroline B., and Sally Hadlock (1980). "Recording the Roots of Navajo Culture," *Exxon USA* 19(2):26–31.

Opler, Morris E. (1935). "The Concept of Supernatural Power Among the Chiricahua and Mescalero Apaches," *American Anthropologist* 37:65–70.

———— (1938a). Ethnological notes in *Chiricahua and Mescalero Apache Texts* by Harry Hoijer. Chicago: University of Chicago Press.

———— (1938b). *Myths and Tales of the Jicarilla Apache Indians*. Memoirs of the American Folklore Society, vol 31. New York.

———— (1941). *An Apache Life-Way: The Economic, Social, and Religious Institutions of the Chiricahua Indians*. Chicago: University of Chicago Press.

———— (1942). *Myths and Tales of the Chiricahua Apache Indians*. Memoirs of the American Folklore Society, vol. 37. New York.

———— (1943). "Navaho Shamanistic Practice Among the Jicarilla Apache," *New Mexico Anthropologist* 6 and 7(1):13–18.

Oppenheimer, Alan James (1957). *An Ethnological Study of the Tortugas*. M.A. thesis, University of New Mexico.

Ortiz, Alfonso (1969). *The Tewa World*. Chicago and London: University of Chicago Press.

———— (1972a). "Ritual Drama and the Pueblo World View," in *New Perspectives on the Pueblos*, ed. Alfonso Ortiz. Albuquerque: University of New Mexico Press, School of American Research Advanced Seminar Series.

————, ed. (1972b). *New Perspectives on the Pueblos*. Albuquerque: University of New Mexico Press, School of American Research Advanced Seminar Series.

———— (1979). "San Juan Pueblo," in *Handbook of North American Indians*, vol. 9, ed. Alfonso Ortiz. Washington, D.C.: Smithsonian Institution.

Owings, Nathaniel A. (1980). "The Hopi Way," *Pacific Discovery* 33(3):1.

Painter, Muriel Thayer, and E. B. Sayles (1962). *Faith, Flowers, and Fiestas*. Tucson: University of Arizona Press.

Papago Indian Agency (1970). *Facts about the Papago Indian Reservation and the Papago People*. Mimeographed report. Sells, Ariz.

Parsons, Elsie Clews (1925). *The Pueblo of Jemez*. Andover, Mass.: Phillips Academy.

———— (1939). *Pueblo Indian Religion*. 2 vols. Chicago: University of Chicago Press.

Peterson, Susan Harnly (1977). *The Living Tradition of Maria Martinez*. Tokyo, New York, and San Francisco: Kodansha International.

Phoenix (Arizona) Associated Press (1980). Press release, 16 November.

Powell, John W. (1891). *Indian Linguistic Families of America North of Mexico*. Bureau of American Ethnology Annual Report 7. Washington, D.C.: Government Printing Office.

Reagan, Alfred B. (1920). "Who Made the Kayenta National Monument Ruins?" *American Anthropologist* 22(4):387–88.

Reed, Erik K. (1943). "The Southern Tewa Pueblos in the Historic Period," *El Palacio* 50(11):254–264.

———— (1956). "Types of Village Plan Layouts in the Southwest," in *Prehistoric Settlement Patterns in the New World*, ed. G. R. Willey. Viking Fund Publications in Anthropology. New York: Wenner-Gren Foundation.

Reed, Verner Z. (1896). "The Ute Bear Dance," *American Anthropologist* 9:237–244.

Reichard, Gladys A. (1963). *Navaho Religion*. New York: Pantheon Books, Bollingen Series.

Reno, Philip (1981). *Mother Earth, Father Sky, and Economic Development: Navajo Resources and Their Use*. (Rpt. 1982 as *Navajo Resources and Economic Development.*) Albuquerque: University of New Mexico Press.

Richards, David (1970). "America's Silent Minority," *TWA Ambassador* 3(5):7–12.

Riley, Carroll L. (1982). *The Frontier People—The Greater Southwest in the Protohistoric Period*. Occasional Papers of the Center for Archaeological Investigations, no. 1. Carbondale: Southern Illinois University.

Robinson, A. E. (Bert) (1954). *The Basket Weavers of Arizona*. Albuquerque: University of New Mexico Press.

Rodee, Marian E. (1977). *Southwestern Weaving*. Rev. ed. 1981. Albuquerque: University of New Mexico Press.

———— (1982). "Navajo Ceremonial Pattern Weaving and Its Relationship to Drypainting," in *Navajo Religion and Culture: Selected Views*, eds. David M. Brugge and Charlotte J. Frisbie. Santa Fe: Museum of New Mexico Press.

Rosnek, Carl, and Joseph Stacey (1976). *Skystone and Silver: The Collector's Book of Southwest Indian Jewelry*. Englewood Cliffs, N.J.: Prentice-Hall.

Ruffing, Lorraine Turner (1979). "A Mineral Development Policy for the Navajo Nation," [*Economic Development of American Indian Reservations*].

Sando, Joe S. (1979). "Jemez Pueblo," in *Handbook of North American Indians*, vol. 9, ed. Alfonso Ortiz. Washington, D.C.: Smithsonian Institution.

Sandoval, H. (1971). "Views on 'A Gunfight'," *Jicarilla Chieftain*, Dulce, N.M., 1 November.

Sapir, Edward (1929). "Central and North American Languages," in *The Encyclopedia Britannica*, 14th ed., vol. 5.

Sayles, E. B., and Ernst Antevs (1941). *The Cochise Culture*. Medallion Papers, no. 29. Globe, Ariz.: Gila Pueblo.

Schaafsma, Curtis F. (1975). *An Archaeological Clearance Survey: Report on Abiquiu Reservoir—the Cerrito Recreation Site*. Santa Fe: School of American Research.

———— (1978). "Archaeological Studies in the Abiquiu Reservoir District," *Discovery* 40–67.

Schaafsma, Polly (1965). "Kiva Murals from Pueblo del Encierro (LA-70)," *El Palacio* 72(3):7–16.

———— (1966). *Early Navaho Rock Paintings and Carvings*. Santa Fe: Museum of Navaho Ceremonial Art.

———— (1980a). "Kachinas in Rock Art," *Pacific Discovery* 33(3):20–27.

———— (1980b). *Indian Rock Art of the Southwest*. Albuquerque: University of New Mexico Press; School of American Research.

Schevill, Margaret Erwin (1947). *Beautiful on the Earth*. Santa Fe: Hazel Dreis Editions.

Schoenwetter, James, and Alfred E. Dittert, Jr. (1968). "An Ecological Interpretation of Anasazi Settlement Patterns," in *Anthropological Archaeology in the Americas*, ed. Betty J. Meggers. Washington, D.C.: Anthropological Society of Washington.

Schroeder, Albert H. (1963). "Navajo and Apache Relationships West of the Rio Grande," *El Palacio* 70(3):5–20.

———— (1975). *The Hohokam, Sinagua and the Hakataya*. Occasional Papers of the Imperial Valley College Museum, no. 3. Imperial, Calif.

———— (1979a). "Prehistory: Hakataya," in *Handbook of North American Indians*, vol. 9, ed. Alfonso Ortiz. Washington, D.C.: Smithsonian Institution.

———— (1979b). See (1979a).

———— (1979c). "Pueblos Abandoned in Historic Times," in *Handbook of North American Indians*, vol. 9, ed. Alfonso Ortiz. Washington, D.C.: Smithsonian Institution.

Schwartz, Douglas W. (1956). "The Havasupai 600 A.D.—1955 A.D.: A Short Culture History," *Plateau* 28(4):77–84.

———— (1959). "Culture Area and Time Depth: the Four Worlds of the Havasupai," *American Anthropologist* 61(6): 1060–69.

———— (1970). "The Postmigration Culture: A Base for Archaeological Inference," in *Reconstructing Prehistoric Pueblo Societies*, ed. William A. Longacre. Albuquerque: University of New Mexico Press, School of American Research Advanced Seminar Series.

Seagrave, Jane (1980a). "Geothermal Plant Opponents Want Two Issues Aired," *Albuquerque Journal*, 30 August.

———— (1980b). "$134 Million Jemez Geothermal Project Faces Final Hurdle," *Albuquerque Journal*, 30 November.

Sekaquaptewa, Emory (1980). "Prologue," in *Hopi Kachina: Spirit of Life*, ed. Dorothy K. Washburn. Seattle: University of Washington Press; California Academy of Sciences.

Shepardson, Mary (1963). "Navajo Ways in Government: A Study in Political Process," pt. 2 of *Memoirs of the American Anthropological Association* 65(3). Menasha, Wisc.

Shreve, Margaret (1943). "Modern Papago Basketry," *The Kiva* 8(2).

Simmons, Marc (1979). "History of the Pueblos Since 1821," in *Handbook of North American Indians*, vol. 9, ed. Alfonso Ortiz. Washington, D.C.: Smithsonian Institution.

Smith, Anne Milne (Nan). (1966). *New Mexico Indians: Economic, Educational, and Social Problems*. 2d ed. 1969. Research Records. Santa Fe: Museum of New Mexico Press.

———— (1968). *Indian Education in New Mexico*. Division of Government Research, Institute for Social Research and Development. Albuquerque: University of New Mexico.

———— (1974). "Ethnography of the Northern Ute," in *Navajo Religion and Culture: Selected Views*, ed. David M. Brugge and Charlotte J. Frisbie. Santa Fe: Museum of New Mexico Press.

Smith, Watson (1952a). "Kiva Mural Decorations at Awatovi and Kawaika-a, with a Survey of Other Wall Paintings in the Pueblo Southwest," in *Reports of the Awatovi Expedition*. Papers of the Peabody Museum of Archaeology and Ethnology, vol. 37, no. 5. Cambridge: Harvard University.

———— (1952b). *Excavations in Big Hawk Valley, Wupatki National Monument, Arizona*. Flagstaff: Museum of Northern Arizona.

———— (1971). *Painted Ceramics of the Western Mound at Awatovi*. Reports of the Awatovi Expedition, no. 8. Papers of the Peabody Museum of Archaeology and Ethnology, vol. 38. Cambridge: Harvard University.

———— (1980). "Mural Decorations from Ancient Hopi Kivas," in *Hopi Kachina—Spirit of Life*, ed. Dorothy K. Washburn. Seattle: University of Washington Press; California Academy of Sciences.

Smith, Watson, Richard B. Woodbury, and Nathalie F. S. Woodbury (1966). *The Excavation of Hawikuh by Frederick Webb Hodge: Report of the Hendricks-Hodge Expedition, 1917*. New York: Museum of the American Indian; Heye Foundation.

Sonnichsen, C. L. (1958). *The Mescalero Apaches*. Norman: University of Oklahoma Press.

Southwestern Monuments Association (1937). Monthly Report, Supplement for November. Coolidge, Ariz.: U.S. Department of the Interior, National Park Service.

Speirs, Randall H. (1979). "Nambe Pueblo," in *Handbook of North American Indians*, vol. 9, ed. Alfonso Ortiz. Washington, D.C.: Smithsonian Institution.

Spencer, Katherine (1947). *Reflection of Social Life in the Navaho Origin Myth*. Anthropology Publications, no. 3. Albuquerque: University of New Mexico Press.

Spencer, Robert (1940). *A Preliminary Sketch of Keresan Grammar*. M.A. thesis, University of New Mexico.

Spicer, Edward H. (1970). *Cycles of Conquest: The Impact of Spain, Mexico, and the United States on the Indians of the Southwest, 1533–1960.* Tucson: University of Arizona Press.

Spicer, Edward H., Phyllis Balastrero, and Ted DeGrazia (1971). "Yaqui Easter Ceremonial," *Arizona Highways* 47(3):2f.

Spier, Leslie (1928). "Havasupai Ethnography," in *Anthropological Papers of the American Museum of Natural History*, vol. 29, pt. 3, pp. 286f. New York.

———— (1955). *Mohave Culture Terms.* Museum of Northern Arizona Bulletin no. 28. Flagstaff: Northern Arizona Society of Science and Art.

Spinden, Herbert J., trans. (1933). *Songs of the Tewa.* Published in New York, N.Y., under the auspices of the Exposition of Indian Tribal Arts, Inc.

Stanislawski, Michael B. (1978). "Pots, Potters, and Potsherds: Ethnoarchaeology of Hopi and Hopi-Tewa Pottery Making and Settlement," *Discovery* 14–25.

———— (1979). "Hopi-Tewa," in *Handbook of North American Indians*, vol. 9, ed. Alfonso Ortiz. Washington, D.C.: Smithsonian Institution.

Stephen, Alexander M. (1936). *Hopi Journal*, 2 vols., ed. E. C. Parsons. Contributions to Anthropology, vol. 23. New York: Columbia University.

Steward, Julian H. (1955). *Theory of Culture Change.* Urbana: University of Illinois Press.

Stewart, Kenneth M. (1967). "Chemehuevi Culture Changes," *Plateau* 40(1):14–20.

Stewart, Omer Call (1938a). "The Navajo Wedding Basket," *Plateau* 10(9):25–28.

———— (1938b). "Navaho Basketry as Made by Ute and Paiute," *American Anthropologist* 40(4):758–59.

Strong, Patricia Turner (1979a). "San Felipe Pueblo," in *Handbook of North American Indians*, vol. 9, ed. Alfonso Ortiz. Washington, D.C.: Smithsonian Institution.

———— (1979b). "Santa Ana Pueblo," in *Handbook of North American Indians*, vol. 9, ed. Alfonso Ortiz. Washington, D.C.: Smithsonian Institution.

Strong, William Duncan (1927). "An Analysis of Southwestern Society," *American Anthropologist* 29(1):1–61.

———— (1929). "Aboriginal Society in Southern California," in *University of California Publications in Archaeology and Ethnology* 1(1). Berkeley, Calif.

Sturtevant, William C., ed. (1979). *Handbook of North American Indians.* 20 vols. Washington, D.C.: Smithsonian Institution.

Swadesh, Morris (1967). "Linguistic Classification in the Southwest," in *Studies in Southwestern Ethnolinguistics*, ed. Dell H. Hymes with William E. Bittle. The Hague: Mouton.

Swanton, John R. (1952). *The Indian Tribes of North America.* Bulletin of the Bureau of American Ethnology. Washington, D.C.: Smithsonian Institution.

Tanner, Clara Lee (1957). *Southwest Indian Painting: A Changing Art.* 2d ed. 1973. Tucson: University of Arizona Press.

Tanner, Clara Lee, and John F. Tanner (1980). "Contemporary Hopi Crafts: Basketry, Textiles, Pottery, Kachinas," in *Hopi Kachina—Spirit of Life*, ed. Dorothy K. Washburn. Seattle: University of Washington Press; California Academy of Sciences.

Taylor, Morris F. (1970). "Campaigns Against the Jicarilla Apache, 1855," *New Mexico Historical Review* 45(2):119–33.

Tedlock, Dennis (1979). "Zuni Religion and World View," in *Handbook of North American Indians*, vol. 9, ed. Alfonso Ortiz. Washington, D.C.: Smithsonian Institution.

Thrapp, Dan L. (1967). "Christian Missions Bested: 45% of Navajos Accept Peyote-Oriented Church," *Los Angeles Times*, 17 August.

Titiev, Mischa (1944). *Old Oraibi: A Study of the Hopi Indians of Third Mesa.* Papers of the Peabody Museum of Archaeology and Ethnology, vol. 22, no. 1. Cambridge: Harvard University.

Toulouse, Betty (1977). *Pueblo Pottery of the New Mexico Indians*. Santa Fe: Museum of New Mexico Press.

Trager, George L. (1969). "Navajo Mountain—Navajo Molehill?" *Newsletter of the American Anthropological Association* 10(10):2.

Turner, Virginia (1978). "Canes Symbolize Tigua Offices," *El Paso Herald-Post*, 12 August.

Uintah and Ouray Agency (Ute) (1970). Personal communication, Fort Duchesne, Utah, 3 September.

Underhill, Ruth M. (1938a). *A Papago Calendar Record*. Anthropology Series, vol. 2, no. 5. Albuquerque: University of New Mexico Press.

——— (1938b). *Singing for Power*. Berkeley: University of California Press.

——— (1940). *The Papago Indians of Arizona*. Sherman Pamphlets, no. 3. U.S. Office of Indian Affairs.

——— (1969?). *A Brief History of the Colorado Utes*. Mimeographed report.

——— (1970). Personal communication, 18 August.

Van Valkenburgh, Richard (1945). "The Government of the Navajos," *Arizona Quarterly* 1:63–73.

Vestal, Paul A. (1952). *Ethnobotany of the Rimrock Navajo*. Papers of the Peabody Museum of Archaeology and Ethnology, vol. 40, no. 4. Cambridge, Mass.: Harvard University.

Vogt, Evon Z. (1951). *Navajo Veterans—A Study of Changing Values*. Papers of the Peabody Museum of Archaeology and Ethnology, vol. 41, no. 1. Cambridge, Mass.: Harvard University.

Wade, Edwin L. (1980). "Hopi Pottery: A New Typology—The Thomas Keam Collection," *American Indian Arts Magazine* 5(3):55–61.

Wade, Edwin L., and Lea S. McChesney (1980). *America's Great Lost Expedition—The Thomas Keam Collection of Hopi Pottery from the Second Hemenway Expedition, 1890–1894*. Phoenix, Ariz.: Heard Museum.

——— (1981). *Historic Hopi Ceramics—The Thomas V. Keam Collection of the Peabody Museum of Archaeology and Ethnology*. Cambridge, Mass.: Harvard University; Peabody Museum Press.

Waliczed, John (1970). "Navajo High School Opens Door at Home," *The (Santa Fe) New Mexican*, 6 September.

Walker, George W. (1970). "Celebrating the Arrival of Dr. Charles H. Cook, after Whom Cook Training School is Named, at Sacaton, Arizona," *Indian Highways*, no. 134.

Walker, Willard (1979). "Zuni Semantic Categories," in *Handbook of North American Indians*, vol. 9, ed. Alfonso Ortiz. Washington, D.C.: Smithsonian Institution.

Walters, Harry (1980). *Plains Indians and Navajo: Contact and Influences*. Tsaile, Ariz.: Navajo Community College.

Washburn, Dorothy K. (1980a). "Hopi Kachina: Spirit of Life," *American Indian Arts Magazine* 5(3):48–53.

———, ed. (1980b). *Hopi Kachina—Spirit of Life*. Seattle: University of Washington Press; California Academy of Sciences.

——— (1980c). "Kachina: Window to the Hopi World," in *Hopi Kachina—Spirit of Life*, ed. Dorothy K. Washburn. Seattle: University of Washington Press; California Academy of Sciences.

Wassaja: The Indian Historian (1980). Vol. 13, no. 2.

Wellman, Klaus F. (1979). *A Survey of North American Indian Rock Art*, Graz, Austria: Akademische Druckund Verlagsanstalt.

Wetherington, Ronald K. (1968). *Excavations at Pot Creek Pueblo*. Publication no. 6. Taos, N.M.: Fort Burgwin Research Center.

Wheat, Joe Ben (1955). "Mogollon Culture Prior to A.D. 1000," *American Anthro-*

pologist 57(2); rpt. Memoirs of the American Anthropological Association, vol. 57, no. 2, pt. 3.

Wheelwright, Mary C., recorder (1940). "The Song of the Two Who Went About Together," in *The Myth of Sontso*. Navajo Religion Series vol. 1, pp. 29–30. Santa Fe: Museum of Navajo Ceremonial Art.

White, Elizabeth Q. (Polingaysi Qoyawayma) (1964). *No Turning Back: A Hopi Indian Woman's Struggle to Live in Two Worlds*. Albuquerque: University of New Mexico Press.

White, Leslie A. (1935). "The Pueblo of Santo Domingo, New Mexico," in *Memoirs of the American Anthropological Association* 43:1–210.

——— (1960). "The World of the Keresan Pueblo Indians," in *Culture in History: Essays in Honor of Paul Radin*, ed. Stanley Diamond. New York: Columbia University Press, for Brandeis University.

Whitfield, Charles (1971). Personal communication, 11 May.

Whiting, Alfred F. (1958). "Havasupai Characteristics in the Cohonina," *Plateau* 30(30):55–60.

Whitman, William III (1947). *The Pueblo Indians of San Ildefonso*. Contributions to Anthropology, no. 34. New York: Columbia University.

Willey, Gordon R. (1966). *An Introduction to American Archaeology*, vol. 1. Englewood Cliffs, N.J.: Prentice-Hall.

Winchell, Dick (1980). "The Treachery of Orme Dam," *Wassaja: The Indian Historian* 13(4):45–47.

Woodbury, Richard B. (1979a). "Prehistory—Introduction," in *Handbook of North American Indians*, vol. 9, ed. Alfonso Ortiz. Washington, D.C.: Smithsonian Institution.

——— (1979b). "Zuni Prehistory and History to 1850," in *Handbook of North American Indians*, vol. 9, ed. Alfonso Ortiz. Washington, D.C.: Smithsonian Institution.

Wright, Barton (1973). *Kachinas: A Hopi Artist's Documentary*. Flagstaff: Northland Press.

——— (1977). *Hopi Kachinas: The Complete Guide to Collecting Kachina Dolls*. Flagstaff: Northland Press.

——— (1979). "Hopi Ritual," in *The Year of the Hopi: Paintings and Photographs by Joseph Mora, 1904–06*. Traveling Exhibitions Service. Washington, D.C.: Smithsonian Institution.

Wright, Margaret Nickelson (1972). *Hopi Silver: The History and Hallmarks of Hopi Silversmithing*. Flagstaff: Northland Press.

Yazzie, Ethelou, ed. (1971). *Navajo History*, vol. 1. Many Farms, Ariz.: Navajo Community College Press.

Young, Irene (1982). "A Visit with Helen Hardin," *Pueblo Horizons* 6(7):1.

Young, Robert W. (1961). "The Origin and Development of Navajo Tribal Government," in *The Navajo Yearbook*. Window Rock, Ariz.: Navajo Agency.

——— (1968). *The Role of the Navajo in the Southwestern Drama*. Gallup, N.M.: The Gallup Independent.

Young, Robert W., and William Morgan (1943). *The Navaho Language*. Phoenix: U.S. Indian Service Education Divison.

——— (1980). *The Navajo Language: A Grammar and Colloquial Dictionary*. Albuquerque: University of New Mexico Press.

Index

275